D0793519

The
BERLIN
RAIDS

The Bomber Battle
Winter 1943-1944

MARTIN MIDDLEBROOK

Pen & Sword
AVIATION

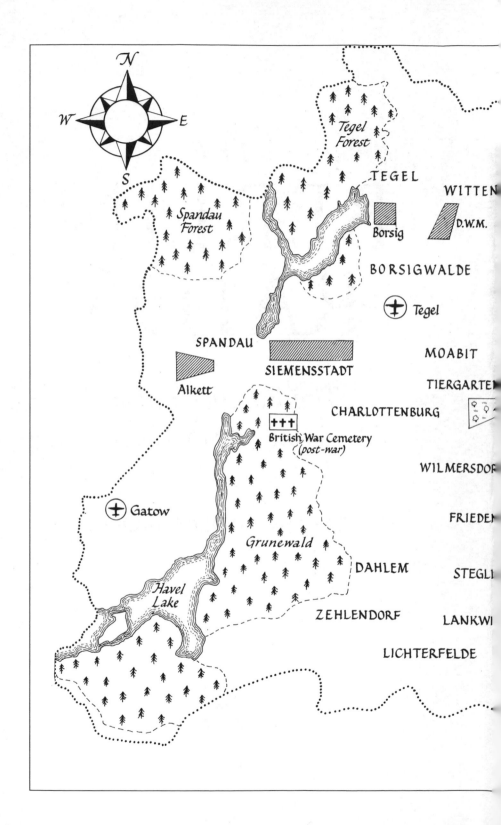

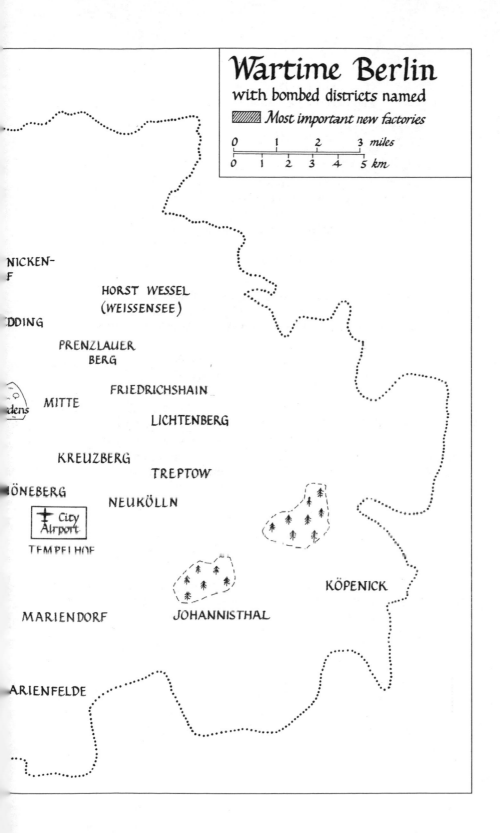

Wartime Berlin
with bombed districts named
////// Most important new factories

0   1   2   3 miles
0   1   2   3   4   5 km

NICKEN-
F

HORST WESSEL
(WEISSENSEE)

DDING

PRENZLAUER
BERG

FRIEDRICHSHAIN

dens   MITTE

LICHTENBERG

KREUZBERG

TREPTOW

ÖNEBERG

NEUKÖLLN

City
Airport

TEMPELHOF

JOHANNISTHAL

KÖPENICK

MARIENDORF

ARIENFELDE

First published by Viking in 1988
Reprinted in this format in 2010 by
Pen & Sword Aviation
an imprint of
Pen & Sword Books Ltd
47 Church Street
Barnsley
South Yorkshire S70 2AS

ISBN 978 1 84884 224 3

A CIP catalogue record for this book is
available from the British Library

Printed and bound in England
by CPI

Pen & Sword Books Ltd incorporates the imprints of
Pen & Sword Aviation, Pen & Sword Maritime, Pen & Sword Military,
Wharncliffe Local History, Pen & Sword Select,
Pen & Sword Military Classics and Leo Cooper,
Remember When, Seaforth Publishing and Frontline Publishing

For a complete list of Pen & Sword titles please contact
PEN & SWORD BOOKS LIMITED
47 Church Street, Barnsley, South Yorkshire, S70 2AS, England
E-mail: enquiries@pen-and-sword.co.uk
Website: www.pen-and-sword.co.uk

Contents

List of Photographs   vi

List of Maps and Diagrams   vii

Introduction   1

1   'Berlin Next'   6
2   The Adversaries   10
3   Berlin: the City Target   21
4   The Battle Opens, 23 August 1943   29
5   31 August to 3 September 1943   77
6   A New Start   98
7   Under the Bombs   140
8   The New Year   173
9   January – Pressing on   220
10   February – Turning Away   262
11   One More Try   275
12   The Reckoning   306
13   The Aftermath   326
     Experiences   334

     Appendix 1   R.A.F. Bomber Command Order of Battle
     and Operational Performances in the Battle of
     Berlin   353
     Appendix 2   Luftwaffe Night-Fighter Order of Battle in
     the Battle of Berlin   371
     Appendix 3   Bomber Command Statistics   376
     Appendix 4   156 Squadron Lancaster   387

Acknowledgements   390
Bibliography   397
Index   399

Photographs

1   Stirling (Flight International)

2   Halifax II (Public Archives of Canada)

3   Lancaster

4   Stirlings and aircrew, 90 Squadron (Imperial War Museum)

5   Aircrews, 101 Squadron (A. McCartney via K. Maun)

6   Debriefing (K. Forester)

7   Crashed Halifax, 77 Squadron (Imperial War Museum)

8, 9   The women of Berlin (I. Paetzke)

10   Messerschmitt 109 (H. Schliephake)

11   Messerschmitt 110 (Swiss Air Force)

12, 13   Night-fighter crews

14, 15   Flak towers (H. Möller)

16 to 19   Berlin bombing scenes (Imperial War Museum)

20   Damaged flats (Landesbildstelle Berlin)

21   Dead Berliner (Imperial War Museum)

22   Dead R.A.F. man (Imperial War Museum)

23 to 25   Berlin bombing scenes (Imperial War Museum)

26, 27   Flak tower demolition (Landesbildstelle Berlin)

28   Bomb rubble (Landesbildstelle Berlin)

29   Berlin War Cemetery (Commonwealth War Graves Commission)

Maps and Diagrams

Maps

Berlin   ii, iii
1   23/24 August 1943   31
2   Berlin, 23/24 August 1943   63
3   31 August/1 September 1943   79
4   3/4 September 1943   85
5   18/19 November 1943   105
6   Routes for 22/23 and 23/24 November
        1943   113
7   26/27 November 1943   124
8   2/3 December 1943   133
9   16/17 December 1943   177
10   23/24 December 1943   190
11   29/30 December 1943   197
12   1/2 January 1944   203
13   2/3 January 1944   211
14   20/21 January 1944, the introduction of
        Tame Boar   226
15   27/28 January 1944   233
16   28/29 January 1944   240
17   30/31 January 1944   249
18   15/16 February 1944   264
19   24/25 March 1944   280

Diagram

Night-fighter attack methods   181

Maps drawn by Reginald Piggott

Other books by Martin Middlebrook

*The First Day on the Somme**
*The Nuremberg Raid**
Convoy
The Sinking of the Prince of Wales *and* Repulse*
(with Patrick Mahoney)
*The Kaiser's Battle**
The Battle of Hamburg
*The Peenemünde Raid**
The Schweinfurt-Regensburg Mission
The Falklands War
*The Argentine Fight for the Falklands**
*Your Country Needs You**
*The North Midland Territorials Go To War**
*The Middlebrook Guide to the Somme Battlefields**
(with Mary Middlebrook)
The Bruckshaw Diaries (ed.)
Everlasting Arms (ed.)
*Arnhem 1944**

* denotes titles in print with Pen & Sword Books Ltd

Introduction

At twenty-four minutes to eight in the evening of 23 August 1943, a Lancaster bomber took off from an airfield near Lincoln. A further 718 aircraft followed from other air-fields, carrying 1,800 tons of bombs. Their target was Berlin. Seven months later, in the early hours of 25 March 1944, 739 bombers returned from another raid to Berlin, on this night leaving 72 aircraft lost over German-occupied territory or having crashed into the sea. Between these two events, a further seventeen heavy attacks were made on Berlin. More than ten thousand bomber sorties were dis-patched against the German capital during this period; more than thirty thousand tons of bombs were dropped in or near the city. Even before it started, the R.A.F. was call-ing this campaign 'the Battle of Berlin', a title accepted by history after the war.

The period of the bombing war in which the Battle of Berlin fell was in what Sir Arthur Harris, in his post war dispatches, would call 'the Main Offensive'. Emerging from a mostly experimental preliminary phase of Harris's oper-ations at the end of 1942 and uncommitted to helping with the Normandy invasion until April 1944, Bomber Com-mand could devote its entire effort to attacks on Germany's main cities. What may be called 'the bomber dream' was now put to the test. This was the hope that strategic bomb-ing on a large enough scale and relentlessly pressed home would cause the collapse both of German industrial pro-duction and of the spirit of the German people. If this was successful the war would end. There would be no need for a prolonged land campaign after the invasion, with all its fears of a repeat of a 1914–18 Western-Front-type slaugh-ter. Most of Germany's industrial cities were attacked dur-ing this period, but Harris's Main Offensive was further divided into three campaigns against selected areas. From March to July 1943, the main weight of attack fell on the industrial areas of the Ruhr. Severe damage was caused, and, although the strong German defences in this area took their toll of the bombers, Bomber Command's natural growth at this time left it in stronger form at the end of what became known as the Battle of the Ruhr. There followed in July and early August 1943 the short campaign against Hamburg when Germany's second city suffered devastating damage, mostly as a result of a firestorm which occurred on one night, and the city temporarily ceased to contribute to the German war effort. That was the Battle of Hamburg.

With these undoubted successes achieved and with the longer nights of autumn, Bomber Command was ready for what Harris intended to be the final battle, the offensive against Berlin to which the whole of the coming winter could be devoted. Weather conditions and tactical considerations would demand that other targets besides Berlin be attacked, but nineteen major raids would be carried out against that main target. It had required only four attacks to put Hamburg out of action! If the hopes of the R.A.F. commanders could not be achieved by the following spring, they would never have another chance to defeat Germany by bombing alone. If the 1943–44 period was Harris's 'Main Offensive', then the Battle of Berlin was the climax of that main offensive and Bomber Command's greatest test during the war.

Let there be no misunderstanding of Sir Arthur Harris's expectations. I make no apology for reproducing yet again his famous letters to Churchill and to his superior, Air Chief Marshal Sir Charles Portal, Chief of the Air Staff. To Churchill in November 1943:

We can wreck Berlin from end to end if the U.S.A.A.F. will come in on it. It will cost between us 400 and 500 aircraft. It will cost Germany the war.

And to Portal in December:

It appears that the Lancaster force alone should be sufficient, but only just sufficient, to produce in Germany by April 1st 1944, a state of devastation in which surrender is inevitable.[1]

The attempt to bring in the Americans was not successful, partly because they were following a jointly agreed selective policy and partly because it would have been prohibitively expensive in casualties for their daylight bomber force to raid Berlin before its long-range fighter escort became available, and that would not happen until the Battle of Berlin was almost over. The second of Harris's claims, made after it was clear that the Americans would not join in the battle, was dependent upon Bomber Command receiving priority in the production of Lancaster bombers. Bomber Command did receive that priority.

Who believed in these claims by Harris? Certainly not the Army and the Navy, nor the Americans. Even Harris's superiors at the Air Ministry were in two minds over the concentration on Berlin – more about this later. What of Harris's aircrews, his shock troops who had to 'go over the top' thirty times before gaining a rest from operations? They may have been briefly impressed and inspired with talk of destroying Berlin from end to end and finishing off the war, but these young men were more concerned with such matters as surviving the next raid, getting in some drinking with the crew, their position on the leave roster, making progress with the current girlfriend and scrounging some more coke for the stoves of their chilly Nissen huts.

Could it have been achieved, that aerial victory at Berlin and the German surrender? The prospect may seem a fantasy, in view of the effort required by the Allied armies to finish off Germany between June 1944 and May 1945. And, yet, it might have been if one condition had been satisfied. *If only the Bomber Command Pathfinders had possessed the technical*

1 The quotations are from Sir Charles Webster and Noble Frankland, *The Strategic Air Offensive against Germany 1939–1945*, 1961, Vol. II, pp. 190 and 56. This work will be referred to as the British Official History.

ability to place their Target Indicators accurately over the selected Aiming Points in Berlin, the existing 'Main Force' of bombers had showed over the Ruhr and Hamburg that it was capable of producing the concentrated bombing and the resulting conflagrations which might have knocked out the city. If such a scale of destruction had been achieved in Berlin and in the other targets attacked that winter in inland Germany, the German powers of resistance might have collapsed by the spring of 1944 – after, it should be mentioned, the additional effect of a Russian winter offensive.

I have looked forward with great interest to writing this book. Among my earlier works are *The Battle of Hamburg, The Peenemünde Raid* and *The Nuremberg Raid.* Those subjects come neatly just before the opening of and at the close of the period about to be covered in this book. I have always regarded the Battle of Berlin as being the ultimate challenge in describing Bomber Command's unique war. May I make a few comments on the technique to be used in covering this subject?

First, there are different interpretations about just when the Battle of Berlin started. A group of three raids at the end of August and early September 1943 are regarded by some people as the start of the battle, but then there was a gap when Berlin was not attacked, and others say that the battle's true start was not until November. I choose to regard the earlier raids as being the opening of the battle and hope to show that it is valid to do so.

Secondly, it will be impossible to describe all nineteen raids in detail. Much of the battle will be split up into monthly periods (lunar months not calendar ones), but three nights will be selected for more detailed treatment. The first of these will be 23/34 August 1943, the opening of the battle, a suitable night for describing the Bomber Command tactics employed at that time and also the major encounter with the Luftwaffe which took place on that night. The second raid will be that of 22/23 November, when the city of Berlin came closest to being overwhelmed. The third raid which has been chosen for special treatment is that of 24/25 March 1944, the last raid on Berlin during the period.

Next, I must apologize for devoting little space to the raids on targets other than Berlin. Slightly over half of Bomber Command's effort during the period was directed to other German cities. These operations were sometimes as dangerous for the bomber crews as those to Berlin, but there will not be space for more than passing reference to them.

Finally, although I happen to be an Englishman, I have attempted to write my story impartially. There will be no 'us' and no 'them'.

I 'BERLIN NEXT'

It was no secret. Everyone knew, even the Germans. British newspapers, encouraged by official briefings, had been proclaiming it for weeks: 'BERLIN NEXT'.

Looking back at the official documents of the period, however, the authority for a winter-long campaign by the R.A.F. against Berlin was a divided one. This period of the war was still being covered by the famous Casablanca Directive, produced after the conference of Allied leaders and staffs held at that place in January 1943. This referred to

the progressive destruction and dislocation of the German military, industrial and economic system, and the undermining of the morale of the German people to a point where their capacity for armed resistance is fatally weakened.

Berlin was specifically mentioned as a target suitable for attack by Bomber Command and the city was raided several times before the longer nights of spring called a halt for that winter. But the Casablanca Directive was updated on 3 June 1943[1] when, because of the serious threat now posed by a growing Luftwaffe fighter force to the prospects of the coming invasion of Europe, the American 8th Air Force

1 The Casablanca Directive is quoted in full in the British Official History, Vol. IV, pp. 153–4, and the 3 June 1943 Directive on pp. 155–7.

and R.A.F. Bomber Command were urgently ordered to concentrate on targets associated with German aircraft and ball-bearing industries. Harris did not comply with this latest directive but continued with his area bombing offensive against large cities, taking advantage of some vague terminology in the latest directive and a very loose rein being held by his superiors, who were showing an ambivalent attitude to Bomber Command's operations all through this period.

Harris had the direct ear and the strong sympathy of Churchill, whom he often visited at Churchill's weekend home at Chequers, which was near Bomber Command Headquarters. Portal, although being a party to the joint Allied decisions and issuing the necessary directives, was still leaving Harris with the freedom to interpret the directives in the way Harris chose. This attitude caused much frustration to those staff officers at the Air Ministry whose duty it was to implement the joint Allied decisions. Sidney Bufton, at that time Air Commodore, Director of Bomber Operations, says, in a discussion on the Battle of Berlin period:

Portal showed extraordinary patience, hoping that Harris would conform. There was much correspondence over a long period. Harris replied with his tactical reasons why he could not conform with the directives, and all the time was doing his own thing. We suspected that we were being put off but we had nothing cast-iron and, as a background, Harris had this access to Chequers where he went at least once a week. In a way, it was subversive, going behind Portal's back, and in my opinion he was thoroughly disloyal to Portal in pursuing his own idea of how to win the war.[1]

In fact, when the Battle of Berlin opened on 23 August 1943, Bufton and the views of the joint planners had no chance of gaining Harris's compliance. Churchill was

1 All personal quotations are from conversations or correspondence with participants unless other sources are indicated. Ranks are those held in August 1943.

behind it all. The Public Record Office has a file of correspondence[1] between Churchill and the Air Ministry, urging
attacks on Berlin, first in 1942 and early 1943 to help and
impress the Russians, and more recently to follow up the
Hamburg success as quickly as possible. (In April 1943,
Churchill had pressed the quaint plan that 300 heavy bombers should drop entire bomb loads of 250-pound delayed-
action bombs on the administrative section of Berlin. Portal
tactfully replied that a Lancaster could only carry a 3,500-
pound load if restricted to such bombs, half of its normal
load.)

A more relevant letter is that of 19 August 1943, in which
Churchill stated his satisfaction with the recent raids on
Hamburg and the American raid on the Messerschmitt factory at Regensburg and pressed for further attacks on
Berlin. That same day, Portal passed on the request to the
Vice Chief of the Air Staff, Air Marshal Sir Douglas Evill,
and received the welcome news that Harris intended to go
for Berlin 'as soon as the moon wanes', but with Harris
warning that '40,000 tons of bombs' would be needed in 'a
prolonged attack' on Berlin. This startling figure of bomb
tonnage would represent between twenty and twenty-five
raids using the full strength of Bomber Command, while
Hamburg had required only just over 8,000 tons of bombs
in four raids! On 21 August, Portal informed Churchill
that the attacks on Berlin were about to commence, and
the first raid took place three nights later. Harris often
overstated his case but here he was making sure that his
superiors knew exactly what his plans for the coming
period were and what scale of attack he estimated would be
needed to destroy the German capital.

It would be interesting to know what Portal thought
about that '40,000 tons of bombs' figure. Everyone was hoping for a swift, Hamburg-style stroke on Berlin. Even Sidney Bufton, struggling to implement the joint, selective
approach, says, 'Hamburg had come like a bolt from the

1 Public Record Office AIR 8/435.

blue. We didn't mind if Harris was able to mount a successful repetition on any industrial area, Berlin or anywhere
else, as long as he intended to start towards the specific
targets eventually.'

So the Battle of Berlin opened, with most of those
responsible hoping for swift success, but with Harris prepared to devote the whole winter to the task *if he was not
pulled back from that task by his superiors.* It was, in fact, an
exhilarating time, a time of heady optimism. Much of the
bombing war so far had consisted of long slogs, at best
inconclusive in result, more often costly and disappointing.
But, now, in the past months had come a rush of successes,
with the Battle of the Ruhr, with news of the catastrophe
at Hamburg just reaching England and, in the past week,
the Americans, having carried out their first deep penetration raids of Germany when, on 17 August, following
their directives faithfully, they had attacked the ball-bearing factories at Schweinfurt and the Messerschmitt factory
at Regensburg. The Americans had lost no fewer than 60
out of the 376 B-17s dispatched that day, but serious damage had been inflicted on the targets, particularly at
Regensburg. That same night, the R.A.F. had risked 596
bombers in moonlight conditions in a daring raid on the
German rocket research and manufacturing station at
Peenemünde, setting back the rocket programme by
several months at a cost of forty aircraft lost.[1] Generaloberst
Hans Jeschonnek, the Luftwaffe's Chief of Staff, had to
report these assaults on key points in the German war
industry to Hitler and Goering. Faced by the wrath of his
two leaders over the Luftwaffe's failure to defend Germany, Jeschonnek shot himself. One cannot blame Churchill and the R.A.F. commanders for their optimism over the
Berlin battle which was to open less than a week later.

1 Full accounts of these raids can be read in *The Battle of Hamburg, The
Schweinfurt–Regensburg Mission* and *The Peenemünde Raid,* by the same
author.

2 THE ADVERSARIES

R.A.F. Bomber Command had already experienced four years of war when it was committed to the assault on Berlin. Its front-line strength was higher than at any previous period, with more than 700 four-engined aircraft available. Its bomb-carrying capacity was powerfully effective, as witness the recent successes in the Ruhr and at Hamburg. Morale was high. The training and aircraft replacement programmes were producing a copious flow of reinforcements.

In August 1943, the command was made up of fifty-seven squadrons formed into six bomber groups.[1] These were No. 8 (Pathfinder Force) Group, whose aircraft marked targets for a 'Main Force' consisting of Nos. 1, 3, 4, 5 and 6 Groups. 6 Group was administered and mostly manned by the Royal Canadian Air Force, but every Bomber Command squadron contained a proportion of Empire men among its aircrews. The most efficient of the four-engined bombers was the Lancaster, but more than half of the heavy squadrons were equipped with Stirlings or Halifaxes, sound aircraft but with a poorer height performance, which led to heavier casualties, and carrying less bomb tonnage than the Lancasters. These deficiencies would lead to all of the Stirlings and to the existing models

1 Appendix 1 gives details of Bomber Command's Order of Battle and unit performances during the Battle of Berlin.

of Halifaxes being withdrawn from operations to Germany during the coming period, leaving the Lancaster squadrons to bear the brunt of the battle. 8 Group also had three squadrons of Mosquitoes, this fast twin-engined aircraft being used for various duties. Finally, Bomber Command still contained a few squadrons equipped with the twin-engined Wellington, the last survivor of the pre-war bombers, but these old faithfuls were being phased out of the front-line squadrons and none would take part in the Battle of Berlin.

The main question mark over Bomber Command's efficiency as it entered the Battle of Berlin was its technical ability to find the precise location of its targets in the more distant parts of Germany. In 1939 Bomber Command had been forced to fly by night because its aircraft could not defend themselves against the German day-fighter force. As the war progressed, the German night-fighter force's successes further obliged the bomber force to confine itself to the dark nights of non-moon periods. Bomber Command's perpetual problem was to find its targets in that darkness; it was this problem which had caused the attack on individual industrial premises and transportation targets to be abandoned at the end of 1941 and led to the later much criticized 'area bombing' offensive, when the general built-up areas of large cities became the target. It also led to the creation of the Pathfinder Force, which should really have been called the Target Finding Force.

A relentless search for new devices to beat the darkness had achieved some success. The most important of these were Oboe and H2S. Oboe was a superb device with which small numbers of aircraft could be guided accurately to a point over the target. Mosquitoes were used for this purpose; their greater ceiling enabled the curve-of-the-earth Oboe device to operate at greater ranges from the stations in England which emitted the signals. It was the Oboe-directed markers of 105 and 109 Squadrons which had brought success in the Battle of the Ruhr. The heavy Pathfinder squadrons had backed up the Mosquito marking, and the Ruhr cities had been set on fire one by one. Unfortunately, Oboe's maximum range ran out 250 miles short of Berlin.

The second device, H2S, had no range restrictions because it was a ground-echoing radar set carried in the aircraft itself. The limitation for H2S was the lack of definition over many types of terrain, but the responses from some ground features were helpful. Hamburg had an unfortunate position close to an easily definable coastline which allowed the Pathfinders to fix their positions accurately less than half an hour's flying time from the target, and it was also located on the broad River Elbe which showed up well on H2S. These factors had sealed Hamburg's fate in the recent series of raids. But the further inland the Pathfinders flew, the less advantage an H2S-plotted landfall at the coast became, as unpredictable winds and pitch darkness affected navigation. Built-up areas, forests and lakes gave some indications on the H2S screens, but only indistinctly. Most Pathfinder navigators could be relied upon to find the general area of a city the size of Berlin, but that city gave notoriously bad H2S reception because its sheer size filled an H2S screen. The Pathfinders had been provided with a so-called 'H2S map' of Berlin, but Air Commodore C. D. C. Boyce, Senior Air Staff Officer at 8 Group Headquarters, remembers this as 'soon being found to be of little use and discredited. I remember seeing Bennett screw a copy up and throw it into his wastepaper basket.'

There was, of course, a better way of marking targets than this 'blind marking' based solely on H2S indications. An attempt could be made to obtain a visual identification of the Aiming Point using masses of illuminating flares. This method – given the code-name *Newhaven* by the Pathfinders – sometimes worked well but it required clear visibility. The coming autumn and winter would have few nights with such conditions. Bomber Command had been much impressed by the recent success of H2S at Hamburg and had high hopes that the now fully H2S-equipped Pathfinder squadrons could achieve a similar success over

Berlin. If all went well, the Pathfinder crews would arrive at Berlin on time, would reach the edge of the city at more or less the correct place and would then be able to find the precise Aiming Point and keep that position well covered with accurate marking. *It had been decided that blind marking by H2S would be employed exclusively for the Battle of Berlin.* If that method could be used successfully, the destruction of Berlin was almost guaranteed. The powerful Main Force, carrying more than 1,500 tons of bombs on each raid, half of them incendiaries, would then burn out section after section of Berlin. Nearly 5,000 R.A.F. aircrew would take part in each major raid, but their success would depend upon less than a hundred H2S set operators in the Path-finder marker aircraft.

It would not be easy.

There were many layers of protection for the German cities when under attack from the R.A.F., from the German radio-listening service attempting to obtain early warning of a raid, right back to the German householder with his obligatory buckets of sand and water ready to fight any incendiary bomb coming through his roof. But it was the German armed defences which directly opposed the bom-bers, and, while the local Flak and searchlight defences of a city may have been the most vivid and obvious of these, it was the Luftwaffe night fighters hidden in the dark which were the most effective for most of the war. Approximately 70 per cent of all bomber casualties at this time were caused by the night fighters. There was never any chance that the fighters could turn back a bomber raid from its target, but, if sufficient bombers could be shot down, mounting losses could force the British commanders to break off a particu-lar campaign prematurely. But the blow and counter-blow of war had just swung back in favour of the bombers. The introduction by the R.A.F. of the 'Window' device to jam German radars, just one month before the Battle of Berlin opened, had thrown the Luftwaffe night-fighter defence into disarray. So, just as the R.A.F. would have to solve the problems of target marking over Berlin, the Luftwaffe units were having to find a solution to the setback caused by Window. That autumn period of 1943 was one of great tactical upheaval in the night sky and a period of great interest for us many years later.

A brief résumé of the German night-fighter force may be useful.[1] The basic unit was the *Nachtjagdgeschwader* (*NJG*), containing between thirty and fifty twin-engined aircraft and subdivided into three or four *Gruppen*, each of which usually had its own airfield. In August 1943, the existing *Geschwader* were the veteran NJG 1 based in Holland and Belgium, NJG 3 in north-west Germany and Denmark, NJG 4 in Belgium and northern France and the comparatively new NJG 5 around Berlin. Further *Geschwader* being established at this time were NJG 2, reforming in Holland after returning in a weakened state from the Mediterranean, and NJG 6, a new unit being built up in Southern Germany, though not yet fully operational. The main aircraft in use was the Messerschmitt 110, a converted day fighter, manoeuvrable in combat but of limited range and much slowed down by the various modifications for night work fitted to it. The heavier Junkers 88, a former bomber, was appearing in greater numbers; it had a better endurance and more stability for the rigours of night operations. The Dornier 217, a less suitable converted bomber, was being withdrawn at this time. The first purpose-built night fighter, the fast and effective Heinkel 219, had just been introduced, but the numbers available for operations were minute – two aircraft at the opening of the Battle of Berlin, only one more added in the next three months!

The main feature of night-fighter operations before the introduction of Window had been the sophisticated system of night-fighter 'boxes' (*Raums* to the Germans) which were located all along a coastal 'fighter belt' from Norway to France. The ground radars (*Freya* and *Würzburg*) of each

1 Appendix 2 shows the Order of Battle of the Luftwaffe night-fighter force during the Battle of Berlin.

box guided a single night fighter on to a single bomber. When the night fighter picked up the bomber on the fighter's own radar (the *Lichtenstein*), the night-fighter crew completed the contact and attacked the bomber. It was an effective system but only for the limited number of fighters operating in the boxes through which the bomber stream passed. The local nature of box night fighting must be stressed. NJG 1 in Holland could not intercept a raid on Hamburg or the North German ports unless bombers strayed into NJG 1's area by mistake; similarly, NJG 3 in the north could not help with the defence of the Ruhr. Individual *Gruppen* within their *Geschwader* area would be further confined, their crews rarely operating more than thirty miles away from their own airfield!

Window was first used by Bomber Command on the night of 24 July 1943, in the opening raid of the Battle of Hamburg. The clouds of metallized strips dropped by the bombers blinded most of the German radars. It was a massive setback for the Luftwaffe, robbing the night fighters of most of their technical devices, forcing them back on to visual tactics and restoring to the R.A.F. bombers the benefit of operating in the dark. The Luftwaffe realized the extent of the setback and immediately started planning an alternative system for its twin-engined night-fighter force. A conference held within a week of the introduction of Window laid the plans for a new form of controlled night fighting, not for the use of single aircraft in boxes, but for the whole night-fighter force to be used *en masse* along the bomber routes to and from the target. But the technical devices required for this new tactic, mainly the new *SN-2* radar for the fighters, would take five months to develop.

That five-month gap was covered by a revolutionary, some say desperate, recourse. Until July 1943, the close defence of a target city had been exclusively in the hands of the local Flak units. But then had come *Wilde Sau* (Wild Boar in English). This aptly named tactic was the commitment of single-engined fighters directly over the target. With no ground control and no radar fitted to their aircraft, the Wild Boar pilots simply made use of the various types of illumination over a target city – searchlights, the glow of burning buildings or of British Pathfinder flares and markers – to seek out the bombers by eye and attack them on their vulnerable bomb runs. The local Flak command co-operated by restricting the height of its gunfire, to allow the Wild Boar pilots to operate above that height. The tactic was pioneered by Major Hajo Herrmann, an ex-bomber pilot who had never flown a fighter! In the summer of 1943, he held a staff appointment, and his mind was exercised by the need to expand the German night-fighter defence against Bomber Command's growing strength and effectiveness. The Luftwaffe had plenty of surplus bomber pilots, skilled in blind flying. Production of single-engined fighters made few demands upon German industry compared with the more sophisticated twin-engined night fighters. The new arm was not a rival to the established night-fighter force; it was a cheap addition to it. Herrmann's idea was accepted, and he raised and led the new unit himself. Thus was born Jagdgeschwader Herrmann, which Herrmann later had changed to Jagdgeschwader 300 (JG 300), one reason being that he was aware that most Luftwaffe units were named after dead heroes.

The first Wild Boar operation took place successfully on the night of 3 July 1943 during an R.A.F. raid on Cologne; nine German pilots claimed twelve bombers destroyed over the city. When Window was first used three weeks later and threw the established night-fighter force into disarray, the Wild Boar pilots found themselves thrust to the forefront of the battle. But the twin-engined fighters could also be used as Wild Boars over a target, at least until a technical response to Window was found, and, at a conference of twin-engined unit commanders held in Holland in early August, Major Herrmann explained the new tactic. There was only one opportunity to test the full use of Wild Boar by both single-engined and twin-engined night fighters before the Battle of Berlin opened. That was on the night of 17 August 1943, the night of the Peenemünde raid. A total of 213 German night fighters – three-quarters of them being twin-engined – were committed to action. A successful R.A.F. diversion over Berlin by a handful of Mosquito bombers held most of these fighters back from Peenemünde until the closing stages of the main raid, but then a slaughter of bombers took place over and around the target. Forty bombers were shot down that night. This may not have been a true test because it was a night of bright moonlight, but it seemed that the Germans had found a means of overcoming the Window setback and would be able to employ the whole of their night-fighter force in the defence of Berlin.

The extent of the change for the twin-engined units cannot be overstressed. Crews who had never needed to venture more than a few minutes' flying time from their home airfields, who had been closely controlled from the ground to creep up in the darkness to within a few yards of their bomber victims, now had to fly hundreds of miles across Germany, navigating by radio beacons, flying in poor weather conditions, listening to ground commentaries which were often based on mistaken judgements or were jammed, and then engage in visual combat with bombers in all the hurly-burly and glare of light over the target city. Small wonder that, for the night of the Peenemünde raid, the War Diary of a veteran night-fighter unit in Belgium contains this entry:

17.8.43. Tag der Revolution der deutschen Nachtjagd Völlige Umstellung auf 'Reportage und Wilde Sau'. (Revolution day for the German night-fighter force. Full conversion to commentary and Wild Boar.)[1]

Many of the established crews did not like the change. They had always been given first turn in the boxes through which R.A.F. bombers were flying; a long list of successes and many decorations had followed. Now they were supposed to join in the battle over the target with all the dangers of sometimes uncontrolled Flak, of collision, of return fire

1 Kriegstagebuch of II/NJG 1, St Trond, Bundesarchiv RL/540.

from vigilant bomber gunners, and with no more advantage than the most junior pilot in their unit. One Luftwaffe general let it be known that the defence of Berlin was so important that pilots were to pursue bombers right into the Flak area if necessary and that aircraft casualties through Flak damage were acceptable. Charges of cowardice were hinted at if pilots were judged to be unwilling to press home the Wild Boar attack with sufficient enthusiasm.

But many of the junior night-fighter crews were delighted with the new method, and there are some Germans who believe that the introduction by the R.A.F. of Window actually benefited the Luftwaffe more than the R.A.F. Although many Bomber Command aircraft were undoubtedly saved during the period immediately following Window's first use, the opportunity given to the mass of junior German pilots to show their initiative and play a full part, together with the new technical methods which were forced upon the Germans and would come into play during later stages of the Battle of Berlin, probably did cause Bomber Command a greater loss in the long run.

So the opening of the Battle of Berlin found Bomber Command's chief adversary, the German night-fighter force, at a major crossroads in its development. The great distance inland of Berlin and the long period over the target allotted by Bomber Command to each raid, forty-five minutes being the standard duration, would help the Luftwaffe to get the more distant of its 250 to 300 fighters into action in the target area. But these advantages would be counterbalanced by the darkness of the non-moon periods which Bomber Command would use and the bad weather of the coming winter. The bombers would often use what the Germans called 'backside weather', when conditions were clear for take-off and landing in England but thick cloud covered Germany and hampered the German fighters. The blind bombing methods to which Bomber Command was committing itself for the coming battle meant that the bombers need never see the ground while over Germany!

The night-fighter force had other problems. The lack of purpose-built night fighters left too much to the slow, converted aircraft of other types. Leutnant Günther Wolf, of III/NJG 5, says:

The performance of my Messerschmitt 110 was not particularly good; for example, there was not enough speed advantage to close in on a well flown Lancaster. The Lancaster was vulnerable if it still had its bomb load but, if it had dropped its bombs, I could only gain slowly on it in level flight and not at all if the Lancaster was climbing.

As for our night-fighter training, you can skip it. I had a very good basic training as a pilot, lasting eighteen months, but the so-called night-fighter training unit at Ingolstadt was useless. I was only there for one week, making eleven short daylight flights, a few mock combats, but mostly just fun, flying around – not one night flight, not one radar training flight. Then I went to my new unit which was just being formed. The *Staffelkapitäns* were experienced pilots, but the rest were nearly all new men. My first real operation came when the R.A.F. attacked Berlin on 23 August.

Leutnant Wolf's experience may have been typical of newly formed units, but there was a good concentration of experience in the more established ones, particularly in the élite NJG 1 based in the Low Countries. But here the weakness was the favouritism in box fighting which had been shown to the senior pilots. Leutnant Peter Spoden, of II/NJG 5, has this view:

NJG 1 had a legendary reputation in the night-fighter force. Senior officer pilots either wangled postings there or, if posted away from it to build up other units, tried to get back to NJG 1 as quickly as possible. These officers were crazy for the *Ritterkreuz*. It was often said that they were suffering from *Halsschmerzen* (neck pain) – until they won their decorations. It was a kind of sickness, a craziness, which permeated the whole Luftwaffe. Sometimes, when they eventually got their *Ritterkreuz*, they didn't bother too much with further successes, but were after a staff job.

There was even a saying – only half serious, I suppose – that, after the war, the *Ritterkreuz* holders might be allocated a *Ritterguthof* – a knight's estate in the east, the traditional place for landed estates, just like the Roman legionaries who were given land in France after long service.

They told us that the old system was more or less finished and we were to be sent to fight over the cities. We were pleased to receive such orders. Don't forget that I had been training for three years to shoot at bombers – that's all. I had no ambition to sleep with girls or get drunk, just to shoot at R.A.F. bombers. That was all I thought about, and these new tactics suited us young pilots very much. Until then we had only had second or third turn in the boxes.

The big question mark hanging over the German night-fighter force as the Battle of Berlin opened was, how would the favoured experts and the insufficiently trained rank-and-file crews cope with the Wild Boar tactic which was all that was left to them until the development of a technical reply to Window and which would force them to fly all round Germany in the wintery conditions which Bomber Command would use to attack Berlin?

It was as big a question mark as that facing the R.A.F. bomber force: Could accurate marking over that huge city be consistently provided during the dark, cloudy nights of the winter?

The answers to these questions, hanging over each side, would decide the outcome of the Battle of Berlin.

3 BERLIN: THE CITY TARGET

The 'Battles' of Bomber Command were not fought out between two sets of formed adversaries as in conventional combat. It is true that the Luftwaffe tried to engage the bombers and wear down their strength, but more than nine out of every ten bombers usually reached the target area unscathed, and it was here that the true battle was fought, between the tonnage of bombs dropped and the target city itself. The true German 'side' in the Battle of Berlin were the city's air-raid organization and civil administration, the resilience of its public services and of its industrial and commercial firms and, above all, the spirit and will-power of the civilian population.

There is no need to devote much space to a description of Berlin as it stood awaiting the bombers in August 1943. It was huge, being not only the capital and largest city in Germany, but the third largest city in the world, with an area covering nearly 900 square miles and a pre-war population of more than four million of the tough stock of local inhabitants. Now, in 1943, it was the administrative centre not only of Germany but of the new empire that had been carved out of Europe by conquest. Those massive government departments alone would have been a sufficient attraction for the R.A.F. interest, but Berlin's war factories and its rail and canal communications, standing halfway between the Western and Eastern Fronts, made it both a major arsenal and the hub of Germany's interior lines of communication. The 'big five' in war industry terms were the Alkett factory at Spandau, which produced large numbers of self-propelled guns and half of the Wehrmacht's field artillery; the Borsigwerke, making locomotives, rolling stock and heavy artillery; the D.W.M. and D.I.W. combines, both producing large quantities of small arms, mortars and ammunition; and Siemens, the huge electrical firm not only located in its self-contained 'Siemensstadt', a huge area packed with various factories, but with other plants all over Berlin. A selection of some of the other well known names of firms with premises in Berlin confirms the obvious importance of the city to Germany's war effort: at least ten A.E.G. factories, the Arguswerke where V-1 engines were built, a B.M.W. and two Daimler-Benz motor factories, two Henschel and one Dornier aircraft factories, a Mauser weapons factory, three Rheinmetall and three Telefunken factories, V.K.F. ball-bearings, Zeiss cameras.

Most of this had been hardly touched by the war so far. When Britain rearmed in the mid-1930s a bomber force was planned with the range to reach Berlin. But the first attack was delayed for nearly a year, initially by the general bombing restraint which held until the German offensive in the West in May 1940, and then by the R.A.F.'s preoccupation with the Battle of France and the home invasion threat. The first raid was carried out by about fifty Wellingtons and Hampdens on the night of 25/26 August 1940, in retaliation for a raid on London the previous night. It was a disappointing raid. Strong head winds, thick cloud and the navigation problems which were to hamper the bomber crews for much of the war resulted in only a handful of aircraft reaching the Berlin area to drop a few bombs in the countryside south of the city. But Bomber Command persisted for more than a year. The records for that period do not make it clear exactly how many sorties were dispatched to Berlin, but possibly a thousand aircraft attempted to bomb the city between August 1940 and November 1941. At least sixty-two bombers were lost in these operations. The climax came on the night of 7/8 November 1941, when 169 aircraft were dispatched to Berlin, despite a poor weather forecast. Twenty-one of these did not return. It was the culmination of a disappointing period and the Commander-in-Chief of Bomber Command, Air Marshal Sir Richard Peirse, departed.

When Sir Arthur Harris took over early in 1942, he ignored Berlin for the whole of that year, preferring to build up the strength of his force carefully and to experiment with new tactics against easier targets. Then, in early 1943, came a series of five raids, with 1,415 four-engined aircraft sorties being sent to Berlin. These raids produced moderate results; various residential areas were damaged and about 650 Berliners were killed. By no more than chance, all of these raids hit only the southern districts of Berlin; the administrative centre and the industrial areas which were mainly in the north were hardly touched. Now, in August 1943, after the shorter nights of summer, Harris was ready to start with his main effort against the German capital. The tonnage of bombs he would be able to deliver to Berlin in the coming winter would be more than fifteen times greater than the tonnage dropped in all of the preceding years of the war.

German historians stress how the slow expansion of the British bomber effort over the early years of the war enabled the German authorities to develop both the armed defences of their cities and the local air-raid services without ever being overwhelmed – at least, not until the recent disaster at Hamburg. Berlin, with its gradual introduction to the experience of being bombed and with the priorities afforded to a capital city, was particularly well prepared to meet the coming test.

The preparations received an urgent boost from the experiences of Hamburg three weeks earlier. Evacuation of children before then had been a voluntary matter; the result had not been effective, and many of the children sent away in the early days later returned. But after Hamburg, Goebbels, who besides being Minister of Propaganda was also *Gauleiter* of Berlin, ordered that all children and young mothers were to leave the city. Entire schools, children and teachers together, went off to the east, out of range of the British bombers. The school buildings thus emptied would become valuable emergency hospitals and collecting centres for the people bombed out of their homes in the coming raids. Because of the pressure on the railways, this mass evacuation was not complete by the time the first R.A.F. raids came, but it continued with even more urgency after the first series of raids and would be complete before the Battle of Berlin was resumed in November. A total of 790,000 women and children left, an exodus which saved many lives and reduced the pressure on Berlin's services during the main battle. This was in direct contrast to the recent Hamburg experience, when the children of that city had figured prominently in the huge death toll.

Berlin was and still is a city of flats (apartments to Americans), vast numbers of four-, five- or six-storeyed blocks filling street after street, and it would be in these flats and in their basements and courtyards that the outcome of the battle would be decided. The life of Hamburg had been temporarily stopped because its housing had been destroyed by fire. In those August days, the people of Berlin worked hard to learn the lessons of Hamburg and make their homes as fireproof as possible. Each family in a block had a partitioned section of the building's attic; now, all belongings had to be removed from these, and the Todt Organisation then came and ripped down the partitioned walls of the attics to enable incendiary bombs to be reached. Fresh supplies were added to the sand and water which every family was obliged to have in their flat and corridor. Berlin was particularly well equipped with air-raid shelters. As in London, the underground railway stations – in Berlin the *U-Bahn* – provided deep and safe shelter for thousands of people. But the Berliners had an advantage over the people of London; every block of flats had a large basement area and these became sturdy air-raid shelters for the families upstairs. No German city dweller of the war years will forget the countless hours spent with their neighbours in those basement shelters. To avoid being trapped in a shelter by rubble-blocked exits, holes were knocked through the walls separating each basement. These holes were then re-covered, to preserve the privacy of each shelter, but only with a thin layer of easily removable bricks. In this way, the people in a threatened shelter could move from one basement to another, the whole length of a street if necessary, to find an unblocked exit.

Again, comparison can be made with both London and Hamburg. Berlin was a more modern city, the streets of its residential districts were wider, with more room for an incendiary-bomb attack to waste itself and less chance of the rubble blocking the streets to fire-engines or of fire leaping from one side of the street to the other. There were more open spaces. There were no streets of the flimsy terraced houses which had suffered so badly from high explosive bombs in the London 'Blitz', and the Berlin blocks of flats were acknowledged to be of sounder construction than those in Hamburg which had burnt so fiercely in the Firestorm.

Then there were the Flak and the searchlights – the armed defence of the city. Berlin was known to all Bomber Command men as 'the Big City' because of the extent of that defence. Flying Officer R. E. Luke, of 426 Squadron, was a bomb aimer who had to fly over Berlin.[1]

The murmur which swept through the briefing room when the target map of Berlin was revealed paid tribute to the severity of the defences, which, particularly on a cloudless night, struck fear into the hearts of those crews ordered to attack it. It seemed to us that only the best

1 The ranks and squadrons of R.A.F. contributors are those of the Battle of Berlin period.

German personnel were posted to defend the city. An enormous cone of searchlights ringed the city, which could be seen a long way off, and it did not seem possible to breach them. In all our thirty-three operations we encountered no target more heavily defended than Berlin.

Flight Lieutenant R. B. Leigh was another bomb aimer, in 156 Squadron.

Lying in the nose of a Lancaster on a visual bomb run over Berlin was probably the most frightening experience of my lifetime. Approaching the target, the city appeared to be surrounded by rings of searchlights, and the Flak was always intense. The run-up seemed endless, the minutes of flying 'straight and level' seemed like hours and every second I expected to be blown to pieces. I sweated with fear, and the perspiration seemed to freeze on my body.

A Bomber Command map of the period shows that the Flak area around Berlin measured forty miles across, and the searchlight belt around it was sixty miles wide! Certainly no other target in Germany was better defended than Berlin, though some Bomber Command men say that the Ruhr defences were of comparable strength.

Some aspects of the Berlin defences are of particular interest. The Flak defences had been installed early in the war, with an outer and an inner ring of guns. When the R.A.F. started to use a 'bomber stream' this system was no longer suitable, and the guns now operated under combined control and simply filled various ordered sections of the sky with a box barrage, although bombers which arrived early, stragglers or those caught in searchlights could still be engaged by aimed fire. The main feature of the old inner ring of guns was twenty-four massive 128-millimetre guns mounted in pairs on three Flak towers built in parks in the Zoo, Friedrichshain and Humboldthain districts. These guns had been developed by the local Borsigwerke factory. The eight guns on each tower could fire a salvo every ninety seconds, to a maximum ceiling of 45,000 feet (14,800 metres) and, when the eight shells exploded in the planned pattern, they had a lethal zone of 260 yards (240 metres) across. The gun platform crews on the towers were all trained German soldiers, unlike most German Flak batteries which had many pressed Russian prisoners and German schoolboys in their crews; the only Russians were down in the basement ammunition chambers, loading the shell hoists. Many of the gunners on the towers were from a Hamburg unit with much to avenge.

The construction of the towers themselves, by the Todt Organisation on plans by Speer, had commenced as early as 1940. Hitler wished to show the people of Berlin and of the world that the city was 'Fortress Berlin' which would survive the war and last for ever. Hamburg and Vienna were the only other places to be blessed with such massive edifices. The Flak towers in Berlin were to be the first buildings of the proposed post-war remodelled city named Germania which would replace old Berlin. The towers had thick concrete walls, steel windows, air-conditioning and an independent Daimler-Benz generating plant six metres underground. All had a hospital floor, and the Zoo tower had one level in which the most valuable of Berlin's art treasures were stored. The local residents were, at first, not happy to see their parks disfigured in this way but they were later to be well pleased when certain levels in the towers were thrown open to the public as air-raid shelters. The Humboldthain tower had passages leading to the nearby Gesundbrunnen Station, one of the deepest of the *U-Bahn* system. Up to 21,000 people at a time would take shelter in the combined tower and *U-Bahn* during the coming winter.

Another interesting aspect of Berlin's anti-bomber defences is the extent of the decoy methods employed. Decoy fire sites were a feature of every German city, but Berlin is believed to have had fifteen such sites, including one particularly large one at Staaken, on the western approaches to the city, which was based on the sets of a pre-war film studio. One wartime schoolboy *Flakhilfer* asked me about the wartime rumour that one night several bombers separated from the main stream and dropped some wooden bombs on the Staaken decoy site!

There was another, more serious 'decoy' story I was told in Berlin that I had not encountered before. The Germans realized that the lakes around Berlin were an important aid to the British H2S radar operators. Consideration was given during the summer of 1943 to covering over these lakes to prevent their distinctive radar reflections being used by the bombers. This was not possible because of the amount of material required, but the Germans did produce large numbers of timbered floats, each in a cruciform shape about five metres across, which were moored at about 300-yard intervals, certainly on the Tegeler See and probably on the Havel too. These two large lakes were on the westerly route into Berlin. The effectiveness of these floats – called *Tripel-Spiegel* – is not known, but they may have contributed to the difficulties encountered by the Pathfinders in establishing their positions on the marking runs into Berlin that winter.

So Berlin – with its tough population of mainly Prussian stock, its great war factories and government buildings, its stoutly constructed housing, its gradual introduction to the bombing war, its well established fire and air-raid services, its Flak towers and underground shelters, its powerful gun and searchlight defences, its range of decoy devices – Berlin awaited the arrival of the bombers.

4 THE BATTLE OPENS, 23 AUGUST 1943

The decision taken between 9.0 and 10.0 a.m. on Monday, 23 August 1943, to commence the Battle of Berlin that night was a simple one. Air Chief Marshal Sir Arthur Harris had long ago decided that he would start attacking Berlin as soon as the combination of waning moon, lengthening autumn night and suitable weather conditions presented itself.

The non-moon period available for operations would last for approximately nineteen nights. The current period had actually opened the previous night with a raid on Leverkusen, an industrial town between Cologne and the Ruhr. Harris had committed only part of his available force, dispatching three-quarters of his Lancasters and Halifaxes but resting the Stirling squadrons. It was an unusual raid for this period of the war, with the 462-strong bomber force targeted to attack, not the town centre, but an individual factory, the I.G. Farben works. This attempt to use the bombers in a precision rather than an area role was probably a follow-up to the recent successful Peenemünde raid, though with Oboe Mosquitoes being used to mark the target rather than having a Master Bomber to control the marking as at Peenemünde. This somewhat experimental raid had nothing to do with the coming Battle of Berlin.

The attack on Leverkusen was not a success. A partial

failure of the normally reliable Oboe equipment and the presence of unexpected thick cloud over the target, into which the markers disappeared, led to bombs being dropped over a wide area. Leverkusen suffered only minor damage and four people killed; at least twelve other German towns reported being bombed! Five bombers were lost. Nothing was learned, only that consistently successful night bombing remained elusive.

After listening to the disappointing Leverkusen report, Harris moved on to consider the coming night's operations. He wanted to go to Berlin if the weather conditions were favourable. What he needed was good weather over the English bases and freedom from thick cloud over Berlin. No serious problems were forecast for the bases, but there were doubts about Berlin's weather. Harris did not need completely clear conditions at the target; he was not planning a visual marking attack – a _Newhaven_ – but an H2S-directed ground-marking attack – a _Parramatta_ – in which the 250-pound Target Indicators cascaded at low level and should be visible, even through light cloud. But towering high clouds would force the use of the much less reliable _Wanganui_ method, with lightweight parachute markers being dropped; these tended to drift quickly across the target area in any strong wind. No records were kept of the conference, but, from the timing of certain events later in the day, it is probable that Harris decided that Berlin should be the target, but only if a weather reconnaissance flight later in the morning indicated that the target area was free from high cloud. The group headquarters were advised that a raid was probable, but no target was mentioned at this stage. The meeting broke up. There were no dramatic statements, no rousing Order of the Day. Harris intended to feel his way carefully with Berlin.

A Mosquito of 1409 (Meteorological) Flight took off from Oakington at 12.40 p.m. and flew as far as Kassel; from there the crew was able to have a good look to the east, at the weather which would reach Berlin twelve hours later. There was only some scattered low cloud. The Mosquito

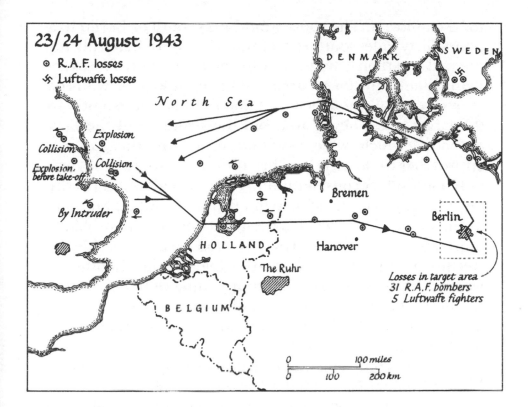

landed just before 4.00 p.m. Harris confirmed that Berlin was to be attacked, and the teleprinters clattered out the plan which his operations staff had already prepared. The groups received these orders just before 4.30 p.m., which did not leave much time for their final preparations; the first aircraft would take off only three hours later.

The details of the plan contained in the orders to the groups will emerge as this chapter progresses. In essence, every available four-engined bomber would carry maximum loads for a raid on Berlin which would open at seventeen minutes before midnight and last for forty-four minutes. An almost 'straight-in' outward route would be employed, crossing the Dutch coast and then turning only slightly to avoid the Flak defences of Bremen, Hanover, Brunswick and Magdeburg. On arriving in the Berlin area, however, an unusual method of approaching the target was to be employed. The route would pass south of Berlin to a point thirty miles south-east of the city, cut back sharply for the raid and then leave the city by the north-east. The extra flying time in the target area would be unpopular with the crews, many of whom believed that the 'back door' entry to the target was a device to avoid the strongest of the Flak defences, which were assumed to be on the western approaches to the city; but this, if thought about at all, was only a secondary consideration. The unusual routing in the target area was partly to help the Pathfinder Blind Markers in a manner which will be described later but was probably more an attempt to destroy a section of the 'far side' of Berlin early in the series of raids, while Bomber Command was still fresh to its task. The route home would be well to the north, out over the Baltic and then across Denmark, a long route which should outdistance the fuel capacity of the German night fighters.

There was only one other tactical novelty – the use of a Master Bomber (still called a Master of Ceremonies at that time). A senior pilot orbiting the target and attempting to improve both marking and bombing had been used only four times before – on the Dams raid by aircraft of a single squadron in May 1943, on a raid to an aircraft factory at Friedrichshafen employing only sixty aircraft a month later, by about the same number of aircraft attacking Turin early in August (this being a rehearsal for the Peenemünde raid) and then the actual Peenemünde raid only a week before this coming operation to Berlin. A Master Bomber had never been used over a German city target; it was obviously hoped that this feature would help bring success in the Battle of Berlin. It was left to Air Vice-Marshal Bennett of 8 Group to select an officer from one of his squadrons for the coming raid. The choice fell upon Wing Commander Johnny Fauquier, the vigorous commander of 405 (Canadian) Squadron; the Deputy Master Bomber is believed to have been Wing Commander K. H. Burns, a flight commander in 97 Squadron.

There would be no diversionary raids to help the Berlin

force; diversions were not yet a feature of Bomber Command operations. Eight Oboe Mosquitoes of 105 and 109 Squadrons would assist by dropping 'route-marker' flares either side of the bombers' outward route as it crossed the German border with Holland. The only other Mosquitoes available – nine aircraft of 139 Squadron – would join in the main raid on Berlin. Forty Wellingtons, which were being phased out of the front-line squadrons, would drop mines off the Frisians and off U-boat bases in France, and a further twenty-two Wellingtons from training units would drop leaflets over various towns in northern France.

The total force dispatched to Berlin was 719 aircraft[1] – 335 Lancasters, 251 Halifaxes, 124 Stirlings and 9 Mosquitoes. The largest contribution was provided by 4 Group, both at group and squadron levels. The group dispatched 156 Halifaxes; of these, 158 Squadron at Lissett provided twenty-eight and 51 Squadron and 78 Squadron at Breighton each provided twenty-seven. 158 Squadron's effort that night would not be exceeded by any other squadron throughout the Battle of Berlin. Together with the aircraft involved in route marking, mine-laying and leaflet dropping, 788 Bomber Command aircraft would be operating practically the entire strength of the command. In addition, twenty-six Mosquitoes and ten Beaufighters of Fighter Command would be flying as Intruders near the bombers' route and over German night-fighter airfields. The total bomb tonnage to be carried was 1,812, made up of 962 tons of high explosive and 850 tons of incendiaries. The Lancasters of 5 Group carried the greatest total load, 490 tons or 3.95 tons per aircraft; but the Lancasters of 1 Group carried the greatest load per aircraft, 4.17 tons. (The bomb-loading policies of these two groups will be discussed later in the book.) The average Halifax could carry only 1.52 tons of bombs to Berlin and the average Stirling only 1.43

1 An aircraft is assumed to have been 'dispatched' if it started its take-off, even if it crashed on or near the runway. Totals quoted in this book have been compiled from a study of squadron records which may vary from the less accurate totals in group or command documents.

tons, which demonstrated why Harris was begging for every Lancaster he could get.

Because of the late confirmation of the target, the crew briefings on the bomber stations could not be held until late afternoon. Many men remember the occasion. Much stress was laid upon Berlin as Germany's capital city, but the importance of this raid as the opening of a prolonged 'battle' like the recent series of raids on Hamburg was not mentioned at most airfields. 'That,' as one Pathfinder navigator says, 'began to dawn on us later.'

Few crews of the Main Force had been to Berlin before. The disclosure of the target produced a ripple of excitement and apprehension. One man says, 'It was the target every aircrew member wanted to see in his log book for the prestige that name gave it, but it also caused the greatest surge of fear', although among the Stirling crews of 214 and 620 Squadrons at Chedburgh, 'Morale was so good, despite our losses getting higher, that there was a great roar of joy at having a crack at the Big City.' Flight Sergeant F. R. Stuart, a young Australian air gunner on 10 Squadron, reflects the feelings of many first-timers to Berlin.

I had done quite a few ops, but never to Berlin. I suppose I knew that it would only be a matter of time before it would come up. However, I'll never forget that briefing, when the curtain covering the map of Europe was swept aside and – there – the tapes ran to that great, evil looking, blood-red blob – Berlin – the Big City!

I remember quite well how I broke out into a cold sweat – and yet a feeling of relief. At last. How would I go? I was fairly confident of my ability as an air gunner by this time, but Berlin! This was different. If I could handle this one, then I could handle anything, whispered the youthful voice of self-confidence – and yet a little more fear than usual ran through me.

That night, before we took off, I know my turret had had an extra polish. My guns were in perfect condition – and that left only me.

The reaction on Pathfinder squadrons was different; most of their crew members had experienced Berlin and its defences before. At least one wireless operator and two air gunners refused to fly. It was probably to counter this nervousness that no fewer than three of the six station commanders in 8 Group – Group Captains N. H. Fresson at Bourn, B. V. Robinson at Graveley and A. H. Willetts at Oakington – placed themselves on the battle order. Only one of them would return.

The first aircraft to take off was Lancaster ED 702 of 49 Squadron, piloted by a New Zealander, Flight Lieutenant R. Munro, who lifted off from Fiskerton at 7.36 p.m. This was half an hour before most squadrons commenced taking off, and Munro was probably carrying out a late air test before setting course for Germany.[1] It was a beautiful August evening, and there were no take-off crashes. There was, however, an accident at Elsham Wolds, while Lancasters of 103 Squadron were preparing to take off. Sergeant John McFarlane, a navigator in one of the Lancasters, describes what happened.

We had just run up the engines of our Lancaster, checked all the equipment and were sitting on the grass chatting and listening to the other Merlins being tested. All of a sudden, there was an enormous CLANG from the next dispersal; the engines of the Lanc there had been started with the bomb doors open (strictly against orders). The whole bomb load had fallen to the ground and the incendiaries were now burning with the Cookie and the 1,000 pound bombs in the middle of the smoke and flames. We threw ourselves to the ground and waited for

1 Flight Lieutenant Munro completed his tour successfully, but ED 702 was lost with another crew exactly one month later, on a raid to Mannheim.

the bang; our Lanc was the nearest, only about 150 yards away. Nothing happened. Then the Wingco tore up in his car and yelled, 'Get your aircraft away.'

All seven of us scrambled into the Lanc. We could not start the two inboard Merlins normally used for taxiing, but managed to get the two outers going. The ground crew who helped us start the engines then disappeared very quickly.

All this time, the incendiaries had been burning, with the Cookie still visible in the middle of the smoke and flames. As we rolled out, we had to turn back towards the burning bombs to follow the peri-track. Just as we were nearest to the fire, the whole lot exploded. Large lumps of exploding bombs came hurtling past and through our aircraft. The blast stopped the starboard outer and swung us round 90 degrees towards the explosion. We felt there were more bombs to go up. We had a full bomb load and were scared that our bombs would also explode, so we jumped out of the front hatch and stopped running several hundred yards away.

Unfortunately, Harry, the wireless op, had been hit in the head by a large chunk of metal and was past all help.

In such unusual circumstances did Sergeant H. S. Wheeler become Bomber Command's first fatal casualty in the Battle of Berlin. The Lancaster whose bomb load had been released was destroyed, but the crew were not hurt.

It started to grow dark as the bombers flew out over the North Sea, converging on the rendezvous point where they would come together to form a continuous stream fifty miles from the Dutch coast. Three bombers never reached that point. The logs of returning crews recorded that one was seen to explode and two more to collide and go down on fire. The aircraft which exploded was probably a Halifax of 102 Squadron, the body of whose pilot was later washed up on the English coast. The collision was in an area through which 1 Group's Lancasters were flying, and the victims were probably two of the three aircraft from that group lost without trace on this night.

The bomber force suffered more serious depletion when no less than seventy aircraft turned back, aborting their flights because of various difficulties. Together with further returns which would be made over Holland, 10.7 per cent of the force were affected in this way. This was well above the normal figure for a raid at this time and may reflect the apprehension of some about pressing on to Berlin. The highest figures for the early returns were in the Halifax and Stirling squadrons.

The first bombers crossed the Dutch coast just before 10.00 p.m. They were making use of a frequently used route, in over a quiet sector between Ijmuiden and Texel, then over the Zuider Zee (now the Ijsselmeer). This approach was a direct challenge to the German defences. The German radar system was plotting the bombers' actual flight without difficulty, but to employ their fighters properly the Germans needed to forecast the bombers' next move. From this position over Holland, the bombers could go straight on to Hanover, Brunswick or Berlin, or swing south to the Ruhr or north to a target such as Bremen or Hamburg. The bomber crews were alert, but there was little action. Wing Commander Desmond McGlinn, flying a Stirling of 214 Squadron, remembers the night:

It was a relief eventually to get off the ground. If there had been a 'war of nerves' before the 23rd, it had impinged more on the R.A.F. bomber crews, culminating in a surprise raid the day before it was expected by the experienced. I shall never forget that evening. It was not fully dark when we crossed the coast on the way in. It was a beautiful night; one could almost see Berlin from the coast.

Another Stirling, from the same squadron, crossed the coast south of track and was coned by the Ijmuiden searchlights. Flight Sergeant H. Triplow twisted his way through but was then picked up by the Amsterdam defences, lost much height, had an engine fail and was forced to turn for home. Two German Flak batteries claimed to have shot the Stirling down into the sea, but it returned safely.

The coastal fighter boxes in this area were normally manned by the best crews in NJG 1, but on this night these crews had been ordered into the Wild Boar operation which was being mounted and would come into action over or near the target if the German controllers could guess this in time. Only a few crews remained to man the coastal boxes. They did not achieve much; Window caused them too much trouble. Only two bombers were lost over Holland. A Halifax of 51 Squadron was caught by a fighter thirty miles north of track and shot down near Groningen. The crew all parachuted to become prisoners. The second loss, a Lancaster of 100 Squadron, came down near the Zuider Zee, exactly on track. A survivor in the crew believes that a technical fault caused the fierce engine fire which led the pilot to give the 'abandon aircraft' order before the wing fell off, but again two local Flak batteries claimed it. The Australian pilot, Warrant Officer Frank Preston, and his English flight engineer, Sergeant Harold Chadwick, were the first Bomber Command men to be killed by enemy action in the Battle of Berlin.

Approximately 635 bombers flew on over the German frontier, course just a few degrees north of due east, with only 250 miles and ninety minutes of flying time remaining before the Berlin area was reached. There were no serious navigational problems; the steady tail winds were almost exactly as forecast. Eight Oboe Mosquitoes had been dispatched to drop a succession of Target Indicators eight miles either side of the route on the German border as a final navigational help to the bomber crews. One Mosquito struck a bird on taking off from Marham and had to abandon its flight, but the other crews all carried out their tasks. This type of operation, 'route marking' at points along the

route, was almost the only contribution Oboe could make
to the Berlin flights.

It was a long, almost straight route from the Dutch coast to
Berlin, with just a small change of course so that the bomber
stream could pass between the Flak defences of Bremen
and Hanover. A belt of cloud was encountered but none
was higher than 15,000 feet. Some of the Stirlings suffered
from icing in the cloud but they cleared this, either by
descending or by pushing through to the clearer conditions
beyond. From the Brunswick area onwards the cloud disappeared, but it was now completely dark. This intermediate area, between the coastal fighter belt and the target, was
not usually a dangerous one for the bombers, at least under
the German defence system which had existed for so long
before the introduction of Window. But on this night the
bombers suffered a steady loss, even though the Germans
would send their main fighter force directly to the target.

It is quite easy to reconstruct the German moves from
entries in the log books of former night-fighter crews and
from the reports of the R.A.F.'s Y Service, which was listening to the broadcasts from the German ground stations to
their fighters in the air. The main strength of the night-
fighter units based near the North Sea coast, from NJG 3 in
the Hamburg area, through NJG 1 in Holland and Belgium
down to NJG 4 in France, was ordered up at 9.40 p.m.
(10.40 p.m. German time), a few minutes after the British
bombers crossed the Dutch coast. As the bombers flew
inland, more fighter units received orders to take off – JG
300, the single-engined unit located at airfields just inside
the German border, and NJG 5, the twin-engined unit
based around Berlin. All of these units were ordered to
orbit one or other of the many radio or light beacons
located throughout Germany, while the controllers tried to
guess the bombers' target. The absence of any diversionary
raids made the plotting of the bomber stream a simple matter. The running commentary warned that the bombers

were approaching Bremen, but the fighters were not committed there, and, when the bombers flew on, the controllers started mentioning Berlin as a possible target. At four minutes past eleven the controllers made a firm decision and ordered all their fighters to Berlin, *thirty-nine minutes before the first Pathfinder markers were due to be released*. This was only the second large-scale Wild Boar operation that the Luftwaffe had mounted, and it had made all the right decisions on a night of perfect flying weather.

The bomber force lost nine more aircraft on the way to Berlin. One, a Stirling of 149 Squadron, was probably shot down when it strayed into the Hanover Flak defences; another, a Lancaster of 207 Squadron, is believed to have turned back with mechanical trouble and this solitary aircraft was picked off by a night fighter as it recrossed the Dutch border. As for the other seven bombers, it is never possible to be certain about these things, but it is probable that they all fell to fighters. The German fighters were supposed to be flying straight to Berlin, but some of the *Gruppen* from NJG 1, the long serving *Geschwader* stationed in Holland and Belgium, were flying almost parallel courses to the bomber stream and, with their superior speed, were overhauling the bombers. Window was jamming their *Lichtenstein* radar sets with false echoes, but the radar operators in the more experienced crews were learning how to overcome this by picking out the moving echoes of aircraft from the fast-closing echoes of slowly falling little clouds of Window. It was these crews who found and shot down bombers on that route across Germany. The names of the following pilots appear on the German success claims for this stage of the night's operations: Major Werner Streib (his 63rd success claim), Hauptmann August Geiger (his 42nd), Oberleutnant Heinz-Wolfgang Schnaufer (his 22nd), Leutnant Johannes Hager (his 12th) and Leutnant Werner Baake (his 11th); all five of these experienced pilots were, or would be, Knight's Cross holders. Some of the established German experts were not over keen to become embroiled in the rough and tumble of the Wild Boar fighting over the target and these crews were probably using their talent and experience to hunt for bombers on the route to the target. They were developing, in fact, a tactic which would later be known as *Zahme Sau*, Tame Boar, a tactic which would supersede the Wild Boar tactic before the end of the Battle of Berlin.

Unteroffizier Erich Handke was the temporary radar operator in Oberleutnant Schnaufer's Messerschmitt 110, which had taken off from Leeuwarden; Schnaufer's regular operator was away on a course.

Firstly we searched for half an hour east of the Zuider Zee and north of the Ruhr. We saw three single-engined fighters, between Münster and Hanover; they were flying with tail lights showing. Then, sudddenly, Schnaufer saw four exhaust flames to the left and above us. The exhausts belonged to a Halifax. Schnaufer opened fire *von unten hinten*, from below and behind, a short burst in the left wing, and then dived quickly away. The wing burned – at first only a small fire – but after two minutes there was a white stream of burning petrol twenty metres long. Shortly afterwards, we saw three men leave the underside and open their parachutes. The bomber turned over on to its back suddenly, reared up, then went into a spin and, still burning, went into the cloud which was at 2,000 metres. There was a red glow and then a bright flash.

Next day we flew to Celle because the crash had been seen by Flying Control there. It was twenty kilometres north-north-east of Celle, so we had an eyewitness.

The Halifax shot down by Schnaufer may have been the 77 Squadron aircraft of Flight Sergeant (posthumous Pilot Officer) Alec Massie. Sergeant Charlie Brister was the mid-upper gunner.

The tail gunner gave a bit of a warning; he reckoned he'd picked up fighters in the area. We kept a good look-out and the pilot started weaving – but not violently. Then, when we thought we were clear and had been flying normally again for a few minutes, we got clobbered underneath without warning. We didn't see or hear anything until the rattle of a couple of good bursts. They hit us in the port wing, somewhere between the two engines, and it was only a few seconds before it burst into flames. The fire in the tanks got gradually bigger and bigger, until it trailed back nearly to the tailplane, passing right by my turret. I shouted to Alec, 'We'll have to get the hell out of here; she's on fire.'

Alec put the nose down and tried to dive the fire out, but it didn't work. I took it for granted that it would be a bale-out, though I never heard the order given. The tail gunner, Charles Rollings, and myself had an arrangement that we would try to help each other if we ever got into difficulties. I only got one side of my parachute clipped on and was on my way down to the rear turret when the plane started to rock about; I think the controls were burning away. I opened the main door as I went down to the tail turret. I got almost to the turret and the nose of the aircraft dropped suddenly and I was thrown back to the cross beam just aft of the mid-upper turret. The aircraft was spinning by now and I couldn't get back to the tail turret. After a struggle, I got the rest of my parachute pack clipped on. I managed to get my feet out of the door, sitting on the floor, and the slipstream actually whipped me out of the aircraft. As I went past the tail, I noticed the whole tail section was on fire; I think the burning petrol had set the tail unit alight. The fin on the port side had practically gone.

From then on it was 'wait a little and then pull the cord'. I was swearing like the devil at the fact that I was having to bale out into Germany; I wanted to go home. Coming down, I saw another parachute canopy below me. I collapsed the air out of one side of my parachute and tried to slide down to this other parachute. I must have come down almost to him, because when I landed in some trees, Croftie, the engineer, was only a few yards away.

The pilot, the bomb aimer and the tail gunner were all killed. (This Halifax, JD 379, crashed in open country near a wood and later appeared in the photograph album of the 8th (Motorized) Flak Division, wrongly described as that unit's 128th success. The picture is reproduced in this book as photograph No. 7.)

Major Streib was flying one of the only two advanced Heinkel 219s yet available for operations. His victim may have been the Pathfinder's first loss of the night, the 35 Squadron Halifax of Australian Pilot Officer Laurie Lahey which came down north of Magdeburg. Flight Lieutenant John Annetts was the bomb aimer.

About seventy miles from Berlin we were two minutes early. From a romantic point of view it was a beautiful night, a clear sky with moon and stars; from a PFF point of view it was awful.

Then the cannon shells hit us. The starboard inner was in flames and there was a big hole in the side of the aircraft. In spite of feathering, diving and fire extinguisher, the fire spread and the captain gave orders to abandon aircraft. All the crew got out and I went back, patted the captain, gave the thumb-up sign, then went myself. I came out in a sitting position, looking up at the starlit sky. I had no feeling of body and it was absolute ecstasy. I had a golden flash and thought that I now knew God. How long it was I do not know, but I suddenly thought, 'Don't be a bloody fool. Pull the cord.' This I did and the ecstasy finished. The harness came up and cut my mouth, the harness creaked in the deadly silence and I suddenly saw the ground approaching fast. I pedalled and made a good roll landing.

It is interesting to note that nearly all of the bombers lost in or near the stream – five Halifaxes and two Stirlings –

were flying in lower height bands. The higher flying Lancasters, which comprised nearly half of the force, suffered only one loss on the route to Berlin and another which turned back and was flying alone. This aspect, the vulnerability of the lower flying aircraft, was not new. The bombers had now lost fourteen aircraft, three crashing in the sea and the remainder shot down over Holland or Germany. The only German casualty so far was a Messerschmitt 110 which force-landed near Hanover with its radar operator wounded after a combat with a bomber.

As the head of the bomber stream passed just south of Brandenburg, twenty-five miles from Berlin, the leading Pathfinders started dropping a series of Red Spot Fires, which were extra-large target Indicators, to act as the final route markers for the bomber force. Of the 710 heavy bombers which had taken off from England, 626 arrived at this gateway to Berlin.

These are the orders given to the Pathfinder crews who would open the attack:

BLIND MARKERS WILL MARK THE AIMING POINT WITH T.I. RED BY MEANS OF THEIR SPECIAL EQUIPMENT. THEY WILL APPROACH THE DATUM POINT (5238.1N 1317.7E) SO THAT IT IS MAINTAINED AT A CONSTANT BEARING OF 331 TRU AND WILL RELEASE AT 9.1 NAUTICAL MILES ON THE 30/30 SCANNER - ONLY IF ABSOLUTELY CERTAIN.[1]

It was a complicated plan. Thirty Blind Marker crews – the best of the Pathfinders – were to fly past Berlin, to a point south-east of the city, then turn to cross the target in a north-westerly direction until a built-up area which jutted out from the northern edge of the city appeared at the top edge of their H2S radar screens as a supposedly distinctive echo among the great mass of featureless returns from

1 Operation Orders to Squadrons from 8 Group Headquarters, Public Record Office AIR 14/3105.

Berlin. Once the position of that suburb had been picked up on their H2S screens, the Blind Markers were to approach it on the course ordered and release their Target Indicators at the range indicated. If all went well, a mass of red T.I.s would cascade over the north-western edge of the central Berlin district known as Mitte, to be more precise in the area around the Oranienburg Tor and the Stettiner Station. (Map 2, on page 63, shows the planned route through the target area.) The Main Force bombing attack would then creep back, slowly it was hoped, across the very centre of Berlin. It was a pure area-bombing plan. There were no major factories in this area. The intention was to destroy the heart of Berlin. It was also a purely radar, blind-marking plan; no Pathfinder crew would attempt or need to see the ground.

Of the thirty Blind Marker aircraft which had taken off from England, none had turned back with mechanical trouble, two had been shot down *en route* and a third arrived in the target area too early and was also shot down. Two more would be shot down on their marking runs. Six more crews held back their markers; five because their H2S sets were not functioning properly and one because the operator was unsure of his position. This left nineteen Blind Markers whose seventy-six red T.I.s should have cascaded over the Aiming Point seventeen minutes before midnight (at 00.43 German time), two minutes before Zero Hour for the Main Force.

The plan did not work. The nineteen Blind Marker crews who did release T.I.s all returned safely to England, and the photographs they took at the end of their marking runs were closely examined because the accuracy of those early markers determined the outcome of the whole raid. There was no cloud to obscure the ground, but because of smoke and ground haze only seven of the photographs could be plotted. All were well west or south of the desired position, with a main group of five photographs being centred four miles south-west of the Aiming Point, and it was around that area that the ensuing raid inevitably developed. The

Operations Record Book of 83 (Pathfinder) Squadron made this comment after the raid:

The success of the attack was not due to our accurate bombing but to the Germans for building such a large city! Failure of Y equipment [H2S] caused 83 Squadron to attack six miles west of the Aiming Point.[1]

Bomber Command's own report says:

The Blind Markers were instructed to bomb on a range and bearing fix from the hooked projection on the north side of Berlin. It appears that this projection, being on the far edge of the city, was not seen, and strong echoes from other areas much nearer to individual aircraft were mistaken for it.[2]

In plain terms the H2S sets available to the Pathfinders had not been able to overcome the size and nature of Berlin on this occasion.

The most important event of the night historically was not the failure of the marking plan but the successful deployment by the Germans of their night fighters in Wild Boar action over the target. The German fighter controllers had performed their task well, although in favourable circumstances. No figures are available, but it is probable that between 200 and 230 German fighters were airborne from bases as far distant as Northern France, 450 miles away. Some of the night fighters were held back for duty in the coastal boxes or to catch the bombers on a return flight, but at least 150 had been ordered to Berlin by a clearly heard running commentary more than half an hour before the first Pathfinder markers were released. There was also good co-operation with the local defences at Berlin for this first Wild Boar operation over the city. The Flak barrage

1 Public Record Office AIR 27/687.
2 Night Raid Report No. 408, Public Record Office AIR 14/3410.

was restricted to about 12,000 feet. There was little cloud, and approximately 200 searchlights were able to operate; the accounts of airmen of both sides stress how useful this mass of light was to the German fighters. The ensuing air battle can best be described by some of the participants, first by the Germans.

Major Hajo Herrmann was the founder of the Wild Boar tactic.

I took off from Bonn/Hangelar in my Me 109. The running commentary gave a constant easterly course for the bombers and I never thought of any other target; I was totally fixed on Berlin. As I approached the bombers' route, I saw some of the 'torches' going down, bombers crashing; they were my 'pathfinders' so to speak. On the frequency of my own unit, I heard Müller reporting that he had found a bomber about 100 kilometres west of Berlin and another of my pilots reported the course was still due east. I heard the ground control order them not to attack but to fly with the bombers and plot the exact course of the bomber stream. We kept being told that the *Spitze* – the vanguard of the stream – had reached a certain point. Then, suddenly, I felt the turbulence of the bombers' slipstream and I knew that I had arrived.

They seemed to turn at Potsdam and go straight into Berlin from the south-west. I think I arrived a bit later than the others. I did not need the glare from the target; it was searchlight fighting that night. It was clear, no moon, and the searchlights were doing a good job. I tried for one bomber, but I was too fast and went past him without firing; I was still a beginner as a fighter pilot.

I came up to the next one more slowly, level, from the rear, but before I could open fire another chap coming down from above me attacked the bomber and set it on fire. I do not know what type of fighter it was; I only saw the tracer.

I circled back over the target and had no difficulty in finding a third bomber. Normally, if a fighter wanted to

attack a bomber in the searchlights, we should have fired
a flare, so that the Flak would cease fire, but we Wild
Boar men rarely bothered to do this. We usually waited
until the bomber weaved or dived out of the searchlights
and then attacked it. I shot that third bomber down.

Leutnant Heinz Rökker's unit, I/NJG 2, had recently
returned from the Mediterranean, where Rökker had
gained five successes, four Wellingtons shot down by night
and a Beaufort by day. Now, flying from Gilze Rijen, he
was carrying out his first Wild Boar operation and seeking
his first success in the West. He was operating on the
approaches to Berlin.

I saw the raid begin. It was the first time I had seen a
German city being attacked. We could see the Flak and
the markers and the city burning. Then I saw my first
bomber, above me, the first four-engined bomber I had
ever seen. It was my method to fire as I came up, then
climb above him and then dive down again to fire a
second burst, so that he had to fly through my fire both
times. So I climbed, pressed the button and gave him
what we called *die Feuergarbe* – 'a bundle of fire' – both
cannons and all four machine-guns.

My fire was quite accurate, although he was much
faster than the Wellingtons I had shot down in Africa.
This one was flying the same speed as myself. I saw my
shots hitting the right wing and fuselage, and the wing
caught fire at once – a fierce fire streaming back. I did
not know whether it was a Lancaster or a Halifax; it had
two tail fins, so I knew that it was not a Stirling.

I pulled to the side and throttled back, to fall behind
and see what happened. He continued to burn and
started to lose height, then he suddenly fell away to the
left. We watched him all the way; my diary, which I still
have, says that it took two minutes for him to crash. I did
not see any parachutes.

The second success came fourteen minutes later. I saw

this second one above me in much the same way, though I think I was nearer to him this time. I attacked him as before and I saw my shots hit but he did not catch fire. It started to go into what you call a corkscrew action but I could follow him easily. I had much more difficult times following other corkscrewing bombers; I think this one was damaged. The rear gunner did not fire; I think he was hit. I followed him and fired two more bursts, both times just as he was changing from one curve to the other. Then both wings began to burn and he immediately fell in a large arc and we watched him hit the ground.

I flew right over the centre of the target then and could see the shapes of the bombers over the burning city, but I couldn't reach them – they were always too far away. I tried diving on them but I never caught one because, by the time I reached their level, they were no longer visible against the ground fires but were hidden in the dark ahead of me.

We landed at Rechlin. We were well satisfied with our success and it was a very impressive operation for us – the long flight in an Me 110, the sight of Berlin under attack and catching two bombers before they could drop their loads.

Unteroffizier Hans-Georg Schierholz was the radar operator in a veteran all-N.C.O. crew of Unteroffizier Rudolf Frank of I/NJG 3, who had flown a Junkers 88 nearly 250 miles from Wittmundhafen; it was the crew's 118th operational flight but, again, their first Wild Boar operation.

Radar had nothing to do with our success that night, only the Wild Boar method in the Berlin area. Our crew was somewhat reluctant to try this new method; a new crew, not so set in their ways, would probably have been more willing. I do not know who saw our first bomber; it was not me, I was looking out of the back. The pilot or the flight engineer saw the Stirling below, against the light of the raid. We were directly over Berlin. I turned round and saw it for myself, a silhouette about a thousand metres below. Frank throttled back and reduced speed. We lost height and attacked it – not in our normal method, *von unten hinten*, but in a dive from above, just like a day fighter, the first time we had ever attacked in this way.

The crew of the bomber must have seen us because it tried to evade us – but too late. When we were sure that its petrol tanks were well on fire, we left it; we knew it would go down and we did not want to follow it down into the Flak.

We caught the second one, a Halifax, at the same height and we attacked it from the right rear. Our fire opened ahead of the bomber and it flew right through it. The right wing caught fire and down it went. The Flak claimed it. We were only three pairs of eyes up in the air but there were hundreds of them down on the ground willing to verify it and the Ministry gave it to them, so we never had it confirmed.

The situation over Berlin was hectic by then. We saw about twenty bombers in a short time; we could have shot down a whole squadron. We fired on three of them but we were being shot at by the gunners from some of the other bombers and we were not able to make careful attacks. We got out of it after a bit, pulling away to find a quiet corner for a while to check our oil and petrol. We went back again to the centre but it was about all over by then.

We did not have enough fuel to go back to our base so we landed at Brandenburg. We had no trouble getting down; it was well organized. We immediately asked for something to eat and where we could sleep. It was early the next day that we talked to the other crews about their experiences. There were also a lot of questions from senior officers about that first Wild Boar night. My own crew agreed that it had been a success, but we were really

Einzelkämpfer – lone operators – and we still did not like being mixed up with this mass of other aircraft.

The next two accounts show how the German crews did not always emerge unscathed. Leutnant Günther Wolf was the pilot of a Messerschmitt 110 of III/NJG 5, a newly formed unit flying from Greifswald, which was only eighty miles north of Berlin.

We were over Berlin in half an hour. We flew about at random for about ten minutes and then spotted a Stirling, below us, with converging course from right to left. We followed for approximately two minutes, then attacked from the right and above. After the first burst, his number three engine caught fire which extended very quickly. It disappeared in a left turn, downward, and we saw the crash fire at 01.01 local time. Turning back to the target area, we saw another four-engined bomber. It was a Lancaster at roughly the same altitude as ourselves. We attacked, again from the rear, this time at the same level. The result was the same, a fire in the right wing and going down. They were two simple attacks. I had no difficulty at all, even though they were my first encounters with bombers.

I thought that if we could get two in six minutes, we could surely get one more, but it did not work out like that because three minutes later we were hanging on our parachutes. Don't ask me who hit us, because I do not know. There was just one loud bang and the right engine was on fire, the canopy shattered. That was enough, I told the radar operator to get out. I heard him release his cockpit canopy and say he was going, and I followed.

Leutnant Peter Spoden was a Messerschmitt 110 pilot in II/NJG 5, flying from Parchim.

I looked around. I had never seen so many aircraft at one time before. There must have been thirty or forty of them. Some were night fighters, but the majority were four-engined bombers. Most of the planes seemed to be flying from south to north but the tracer was going in every direction. There were searchlights – hundreds of them – and they caused me to lose my orientation. I saw one Lancaster in a steep dive, trying to get out of the searchlights, and another which dived steeply and then reared up and actually looped right over – I swear it. It was terrible for a kid like me and I think it must have been just as bad for the British boys. It was the most intensive night battle of the war I ever saw, a terrible inferno, still following me in nightmares in the next decade.

I did not know what to do. I think my blood pressure was going up and my pulse was racing, but then I saw one bomber directly ahead of me, caught in a cone of searchlights only about 400 metres away. He was not taking evasive action; perhaps he was on his bomb run. He had two tail fins. I fired several bursts from about 200 metres' range. I don't remember where I aimed, probably between the engines, at the fuel tanks, my normal method. He didn't go down at once; they usually lasted a few minutes, but then he did fall. I didn't see any parachutes.

I looked left and right to find another. The next contact was over the city again. I fired several times but didn't see any result. He was corkscrewing, but very cleverly, making abrupt turns, not regularly according to the manual, and that saved him. I fired several times but I was too inexperienced and I was particularly excitable that night because of all the light and activity over Berlin. He got away into the darkness.

The next one was a Short Stirling – well ahead of me – and this one was a very clever pilot. The visibility was so good that he saw me as well and turned into me so that I had to open fire from the front. It was the only time I did that in my whole career; that fellow forced me into it. He gave me quite a job. I managed to hit him hard but, as he dived under me, his tail gunner got me. I heard the hit in my fuselage and a small fire started behind me. I checked with the crew but received no answer; the intercom was not working. When the heat of the fire became unbearable, I shouted 'GET OUT!' four or five times, as loud as I could. Then I jettisoned the cockpit canopy and went out myself. It was not easy; I found out later that my left thigh had been hit by a bullet and the bone was broken. Then, when I did get out, I struck the tailplane, my stomach was actually held against it, my head over the top and legs underneath. I was scared to death because I could not release myself and the plane was going down like hell.

Then I was caught in a searchlight but they did not shoot at me. The officer in command came to see me in hospital later and told me that he had recognized the Me 110 and was trying to help me. I got off it somehow, pulled the handle of the parachute and then lost consciousness.

I woke up in the garden of Grunewalddamm 69. I was being walloped by some civilians and an S.S. man until I told them I was German.

Spoden's experience, trapped over the tailplane of his air-craft, was later described and illustrated in the German magazine *Signal*. His radar operator came down safely, but the flight engineer was found dead in the aircraft. Spoden recovered – with a limp – to claim more than twenty more bombers shot down before the end of the war and then to fly for Lufthansa, retiring as a senior captain on Boeing 747 jumbo jets.

It is time for the British view of what was a one-sided battle, described firstly by some of the survivors of the shot-down bombers.

Squadron Leader Charles Lofthouse, of 7 Squadron, was the captain of a Blind Marker aircraft and was carrying his Station Commander, Group Captain A. H. Willetts, as second pilot. His Lancaster was probably the first aircraft shot down over Berlin.

The H2S set had started playing up soon after crossing the Dutch coast and Cayford, the navigator, had been trying hard to rectify it. In retrospect, if we had not had the Station Commander on board, I would have decided halfway to the target that we were not going to be able to mark and would have dropped back then, but I decided to press on and do everything possible to become a valid marker. We actually reached the target about seven minutes early and were flying straight and level, trying to get an astro fix, when we were heavily coned. I couldn't lose them. This was all before the raid started. I shot off the colours of the day, as advised by Intelligence, but it had no effect.

Then, I saw a great, bright 'whoosh' of tracer come past the cockpit on the port side. I don't suppose anyone saw the attacking plane; the gunners must have been blinded by the searchlights. This coloured tracer just raced by us and all the damage was on the port side. The wing and engines were badly hit.

The engineer tried to put the fire out in the engine; I felt that I wasn't getting the proper response from the ailerons and we were losing height. Then Denis Cayford came up on the intercom, asking if he should get out and put the fires out on the wing, presumably by going out through the astrodome and crawling along the wing like the V.C. chap had done on a Wellington once. But we weren't on a Wellington and he had no chance at all; I said, 'No.'

At some stage I told the bomb aimer to jettison the bombs, but not the markers, and soon after this I ordered, 'Abandon.' The flames were very fierce by now, stretching back from each engine, and there was a large hole in the wing between the two nacelles, with flames coming out of it, being beaten back by the airflow.

The crew started going. The flight engineer put my parachute ready beside me. The wireless op came forward and gave me a thumbs-up to indicate that the boys at the back had gone. Cayford came back at that stage, went back to his 'office', and then went forward and out. He told me later that he had come back for a gold signet ring from his girlfriend, which he always took off when flying because it got so cold. That horrified me because I was fighting the controls hard by then, but I managed to get out.

Lofthouse, one arm broken, came down in a tree, hanging from his parachute just outside the window of a wooden barrack building used by a concentration-camp outside working party. He was a prisoner within seconds. All of his crew survived.

Flight Lieutenant Allan Ball was also in a Blind Marker crew; he was 35 Squadron's Signals Officer, replacing a wireless operator who refused to fly that night. Ball, on his fifty-eighth operation, was keen to take the man's place so that he could finish his tour at sixty operations and get married.

We arrived eight minutes early; we knew that our Station Commander was there in another aircraft and we wanted to be on time. The pilot flew an orbit to the south before going in. There were no problems with the bomb run, though there was a fierce defence reaction. We took our photograph. Then, about a minute later, there was a ginormous 'whumpf'. I was looking out of a small blister just behind the H2S set at the time. Something came up at me and smashed my skull open. I remember something on the intercom about fighters and then that the two starboard engines were alight, but I was a bit dopey by this time, stunned. I remember a blinding light and there was another explosion, and I finished up with twenty-three holes in me and I have five bits of metal in me still. The worst bit was the piece of metal which went into my brain. Then I heard on the intercom that we had to abandon the aircraft; we were spiralling down.

I went to the door which was quite near me and tried to jettison it by pulling the emergency toggle at the top, but it just would not fall away because the centrifugal force was forcing it the other way. I could only use one hand because my left arm was knocked out. I just tried and tried until I was exhausted – I didn't see anyone else. In the end, I just sat on the step and gave up. I thought, 'Bugger it; it'll be all over in a minute or two.' But then I went back and tried once more and this time the door fell away beautifully – no trouble at all – and I baled out.

Allan Ball came down outside Berlin, was quickly taken prisoner and was being given medical attention by the time the All Clear sounded. His injuries were so extensive that he was repatriated in 1944 and married his fiancée soon afterwards. Three members of the crew died.

At Chedburgh, home of two Stirling squadrons, two crews had started their tours together earlier in the year and were now joint seniors, each on their twenty-fourth operation. The aircraft of Sergeant George MacDonald, a former Glasgow policeman, met a violent end, described by the navigator, Flying Officer J. D. Sutton.

We were shot down by a Ju 88. Our normal crew rear gunner was sick with flu; we therefore flew with a rear gunner straight from training school. He just didn't have a chance against the Ju 88. He froze. I went back and found him killed by a cannon shell. The pilot said, 'For Christsakes, get out.' The bomb aimer went and as I went out, the port wing dropped off; it actually fell alongside me. I always believed that no one else except the bomb aimer and myself got out. Unfortunately we were giving a Canadian squadron leader an acclimatization flight; he did not survive.

Mr Sutton was amazed when I informed him that the Canadian passenger, Squadron Leader A. P. Philipsen, also survived, but the bodies of the other five crew members could not be identified after the violent crash of the Stirling. Sergeant MacDonald's commission came through just after his death; promotion in 3 Group was slow.

The other senior crew at Chedburgh was that of Pilot Officer Ray Hartwell, whose Stirling was also shot down that night. Sergeant Ralph Elliott was the rear gunner.

We were still among the searchlights. I never saw the fighter; I think he was underneath us. It was a typical August night, dark down below, but lighter above. I still look up into the sky every 23rd of August and remember the sort of light there was in the sky. The first thing I knew was the explosion of the cannon shells. The rear turret was hit underneath me.

There were flames, and the ammunition in the belts was going off between my legs. They got burned – not seriously – and my right ear was singed. I also got some small pieces of shrapnel in my backside. My intercom had gone dead, so I was completely isolated way back there.

I went along to the mid-upper's turret and felt for his legs, but he was not there. Everything was very dark at the back. The night fighter was still attacking and I think the main part of the plane was on fire. I had the impression that I was the only one left so I went back to the hatch and jumped.

When he met fellow survivors later, Elliot realized that the aircraft probably flew on after he baled out and suffered further fighter attacks before crashing. All the crew survived, but two were so seriously injured that they each had a leg amputated.

Sergeant Bert Nixon of 199 Squadron was on his first raid to Germany, also flying in a Stirling.

We had bombed and had nearly got to the edge of the searchlight area; we thought we were over the worst.

Then it was as though a giant hand took hold of us and there was a huge shuddering and shaking sensation, just like a massive dog shaking a rat. That's what laid me out. I came to, lying across the guns, and I was actually gripping the firing mechanism. All four guns were firing, tracer coming out. I tried the intercom but got no response. I rotated the turret so that I could see forward and I could see flames in the fuselage. The hydraulics were still working so I rotated back to the neutral position, opened the doors in the back of the turret and went down into the fuselage. I set out to crawl along the catwalk; I wanted to get up with the others and see if I could help. The aircraft appeared to be stable but there was a fierce fire between me and the mid-upper turret.

I came back and put my 'chute on, mainly because we had been trained not to go about the aircraft without it, and I still intended to get up to the front again. Then, I can only remember letting the escape hatch go and it getting very hot under my feet. The next thing I knew was that I was coming down on the end of a parachute. I thought, 'Blimey; I must be dreaming. Nothing ever happens to me.' I couldn't believe it. I don't know how I got out or how the 'chute opened.

Sergeant Nixon was the only survivor in this crew; the wireless operator, Sergeant 'Stan' Stanley, had been married less than three weeks.

Pilot Officer Alan Bryett was the bomb aimer in Flight Lieutenant Kevin Hornibrook's 158 Squadron crew, flying a Halifax.

We hadn't gone more than a minute or two, still coned, when the rear gunner shouted, 'Fighter approaching!' We never heard from him again. Almost at the same moment there was a burst of machine-gun fire which we heard striking in the mid-upper area and then we started to burn there.

The pilot took evasive action. I went back to the mid-upper area to see what I could do about the fire, which was spreading very quickly. As I got there, the gunner was getting out of his turret. He was in a terrible state, having been hit in the face, and was staggering around in a horrible mess. I think the fighter had aimed at the two gunners and had got them both in the first burst.

We were attacked again. I went back to the pilot. We had our intercom on and he shouted out, 'Don't bale out.' But the intercom was very bad and crackly and I think that some of them only caught the last two words. The wireless operator, the navigator and the flight engineer all went out. So, one gunner was probably dead, the other probably dying and three men had baled out, just leaving myself and Kevin. He tried to control the plane but the fire probably burnt through the control cables and it started to dive, with a terrible screaming sound. Kevin and I realized that we had to get out but, because of the G force, we couldn't get to the hatch in the nose.

I could see that we were going to go down in this bloody plane but Kevin managed to reach the escape-hatch in the nose and pulled it open. He then physically got hold of me, shoved me into the hatch and pushed me out with his feet. He said he was following. I pulled my cord. I couldn't see anything but very quickly indeed I landed in some trees. The plane crashed three or four hundred yards away.

Kevin never got out. We had been too low. I am very conscious that my life hinged on that moment when Kevin pushed me out. When my son was born in 1951, I called him Kevin, as a daily reminder of Kevin Hornibrook, to whom I owed the rest of my life. Never a day goes by without me remembering that he was first at the door and could have saved himself easily.

Twenty-one-year-old Kevin Hornibrook, an Australian, is buried in Berlin War Cemetery alongside his two dead gunners. His brother Keith, a twenty-year-old fighter pilot, went missing on operations a year later. They were the only children of their parents, from Brisbane.

There are other stories, about bombers badly hit over Berlin but managing to get back to England through the skill and courage of their crews. Here are three examples; it is significant that they all involve Stirlings.

The aircraft of Flight Lieutenant Bill Day, a Canadian of 90 Squadron, was coned in searchlights just after releasing its bomb load. Day dived steeply and evaded the lights, but the Stirling's descent had been followed by up to three single-engined fighters. The Australian tail gunner, Flight Sergeant Colin Mitchinson, had cleverly kept one of his eyes closed and covered with a hand while in the searchlight glare and was thus able to spot the fighter which came in first. In the exchange of fire which followed, the Stirling was badly damaged, but the Focke-Wulf 190 was also seen to be hit. The other fighters were evaded, and Day flew out of the target area so low that individual houses in the suburbs were easily seen. The most serious damage to the Stirling was the ruptured tanks which leaked fuel, some of it to slosh along the floor of the aircraft. The lights of neutral Sweden were passed on the homeward flight, and a vote was taken among the crew, with the choice of risking a flight home over the sea with fuel running low or parachuting over Sweden. The result was four to three in favour of England. A safe landing was made at the base of an American fighter unit; two men went to hospital, the wireless operator with cannon-shell fragments inside him and the mid-upper gunner with an attack of shingles brought on by his overnight experiences.

The Stirling of Flight Sergeant Gil Marsh, of 622 Squadron, was attacked and hit in the same way, this time by a Ju 88. Marsh was injured by a cannon-shell explosion which blew a hole in his thigh and cut his sciatic nerve. He managed to evade the fighter by diving steeply. The hydraulics to the rear turret were cut, and an engine was on fire. Pain, loss of blood and bouts of unconsciousness started to affect the pilot, but the Stirling was kept flying, with the help first of the navigator and then of the bomb aimer, who had himself been stunned in the dive. The pilot eventually had to be lifted from his seat, and it was the bomb aimer, Sergeant John Bailey, who flew back over the North Sea and landed safely at Mildenhall, helped by the fact that he had once reached almost to the end of a pilot training course before being 'washed out'. Bailey, a Canadian, was given an immediate commission and the Conspicuous Gallantry Medal.

Once again, a cone of searchlights, a fighter attack, damage and a steep dive left another Stirling in serious trouble. This was the aircraft of Flight Sergeant O. H. White, a New Zealand pilot of 75 Squadron. The tail gunner was killed in the fighter attack, and three other crew members had misunderstood an instruction on the intercom and baled out prematurely. Without a navigator and with much damage to his aircraft, White, his flight engineer and one gunner brought the aircraft home, White using his pre-war experience as a yachtsman which helped him navigate by the stars. Finally, having located their home airfield at Mepal, the Stirling had to be crash-landed without lights, flaps or undercarriage. The three survivors walked safely away from their wrecked aircraft, White also to receive a commission and the C.G.M., the other two well earned D.F.M.s.

There was no relief for the bombers over Berlin. The German fighters which had greeted the first aircraft to arrive would operate throughout the raid and then harry the last bombers into the darkness north of the city. Thirty-one bombers came down in an eliptical shaped area sixty-five miles along the bombers' route. Only five of these fell inside the city limits; the biggest concentration was to the north of the target where some of the victims struggled on a little before crashing and others were caught by German fighters which preferred to engage the bombers when they flew out of the illuminated area.

The Pathfinders had lost heavily, with nine marker air-craft being shot down and a tenth crashing later. Several personalities were in these aircraft. Group Captain A. H. Willetts, D.S.O., Station Commander at Oakington, would become a prisoner of war and later earn the respect of the R.A.F. men who were taken prisoner on this night and gathered at a local Luftwaffe camp for demanding and receiving better conditions for the prisoners. Group Captain B. V. Robinson, D.S.O., D.F.C. and Bar, A.F.C., Station Commander at Graveley, was dead with all of the 35 Squadron crew with whom he was flying; he had earlier in the war made an epic flight from Italy as the sole occupant of a Halifax whose crew he had ordered to bale out when the aircraft appeared to be about to crash. Another Path-finder loss was Flight Lieutenant Brian Slade, D.F.C., a courageous young pilot known on 83 Squadron as 'The Boy Slade', who had set himself the task of flying the 'double Pathfinder tour' of sixty consecutive operations. He died flying the fifty-ninth, just starting his bomb run. (Slade's flight engineer was Flight Sergeant Vernon Charles Lewis, whose Christian names were probably so chosen after the Victoria Cross won by his father in the Welch Regiment in the First World War; the old soldier outlived the airman son.)

The disparity in losses between the various aircraft types in the Main Force is startling. Of the 249 Main Force Lan-casters believed to have reached Berlin, only two were lost in the target area – a rate of only 0.8 per cent – compared with eight Halifax losses from 182 aircraft and ten Stirlings from 109 aircraft – rates of 4.4 and 9.2 per cent. One of the lost Stirlings was hit and set on fire by an incendiary bomb dropped from a higher flying bomber. It is unlikely that the Berlin Flak, well restrained in the height of its fire, could be credited with any success, leaving the other shot-down bombers to be claimed by night fighters. If a further eight bombers which were so badly damaged by fighter attack over Berlin that they crashed at various places on the return flight are added in, the Wild Boar operation could

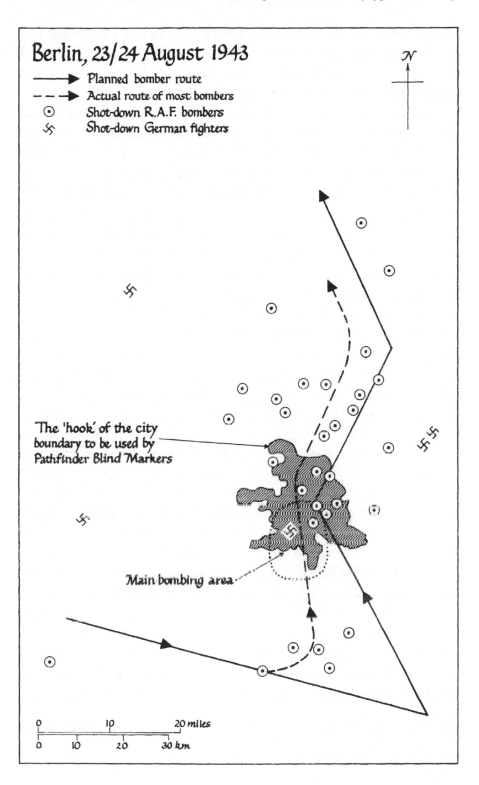

Berlin, 23/24 August 1943

→ Planned bomber route

--→ Actual route of most bombers

⊙ Shot-down R.A.F. bombers

卐 Shot-down German fighters

N

The 'hook' of the city boundary to be used by Pathfinder Blind Markers

Main bombing area

0   10   20 miles

0   10   20   30 km

claim thirty-eight successes. Eleven German pilots gained their first success, four of them scoring twice, a good example of the new tactic allowing the full strength of the night-fighter force to become effective.

This impressive performance by the German fighters was gained for the modest cost of four Messerschmitt 110s and one Focke-Wulf 190 destroyed (four by bombers' return fire and one either by a 'friendly' night fighter or by Flak fire) and seven fighters damaged (four by Flak and three by bombers' return fire). German aircrew casualties in the fight over Berlin were three men killed and one wounded, compared to the British figures of 169 men killed and 53 prisoners just in those aircraft which came down in the immediate vicinity of the target.

The bombing was planned to last for forty-four minutes: four minutes for the Blind Markers, forty minutes for the Main Force. The Main Force, originally 593 aircraft strong but depleted by casualties, was split into six waves, each wave being allocated to a particular aircraft type. Path-finder Backers-Up and Recenterers were to re-mark the Aiming Point throughout the raid. Nine Mosquitoes carried out a 'support attack', dropping much Window and then a few bombs later in the raid. The tonnage of bombs dropped in and around Berlin that night was approximately 1,706: 909 tons of high explosives (including 296 of the 4,000-pound 'Blockbusters') and 797 tons of incendiaries.[1] All of this was routine. The only tactical innovation was the use of a Master Bomber, the first occasion one had been used over a German city target. Wing Commander J. E. Fauquier was carrying out this duty. Air Commodore C. D. C. Boyce, then Senior Air Staff Officer at 8 Group Headquarters, says that 'if anyone could have coped with Master Bomber work it was Johnny Fauquier. He had the ability to impose his will. He was a bright, hard fellow, who

1 In all figures given in this book for bomb tonnages dropped on Berlin, the loads of the aircraft which returned early have not been counted, and it is assumed that half of the missing aircraft bombed before being shot down.

certainly would have made the Master Bomber method work if anyone could.'

Fauquier was flying a standard Lancaster, carrying green Target Indicators, a light load of incendiaries and seventy gallons of extra fuel. His orders were to attempt to control the first ten minutes of the raid, using the call signs of 'Dagin', for himself, 'Skylark' and 'Old Crows' for the Blind Markers and Backers-Up, and 'Ravens' for the Main Force. He arrived over the target on time, released his T.I.s and bomb load immediately after the Blind Markers and then commenced to orbit the target and broadcast his instructions. Squadron Leader P. G. Powell was his navigator.

It was a good, clear night below and we had an excellent view of the city. I was in the bomb aimer's position. My main function was to assess the accuracy of the T.I.s. Johnny would then broadcast the information to all crews: 'Those green T.I.s are short – aim for the red ones further on', 'Disregard the T.I.s on your left', etc. Then he would encourage the Main Force with such comments as, 'Come on in, fellows! The Flak is nowhere near as bad as it looks!' He had an excellent R/T voice which came over loud and clear to all we later talked with. It no doubt helped to calm jittery nerves and, I believe, it helped produce a better concentration of bombs on the Aiming Point.

Fauquier devoted most of his efforts to encouraging the Main Force to press right on into the target and not to release their bombs prematurely. It was not easy. He could deride the Flak, but Main Force crews harassed by fighter attack were not always inclined to listen.

The raid proceeded in no better, no worse, manner than so many raids on targets beyond the range of Oboe. Enough of the forty-nine Pathfinder Backers-Up and Recenterers arrived to produce a steady supply of green T.I.s. The planned route in from the south-east was never achieved. It is clear, from the evidence of bombing photographs, that once the early markers and bombs were seen to go down, both the Pathfinder Backers-Up and Main Force swung in from due south, neither being prepared to spend extra time in the target area flying on to a theoretical turning-point further on. Many of the Main Force crews were bombing the first markers they saw, instead of the centre of the markers as ordered, or were dropping short of the markers; a long 'creepback' developed. The night was clear. Bomber Command's Operational Research Section later examined 468 bombing photographs and concluded that only five aircraft had bombed within three miles of the correct Aiming Point, that only a quarter of the force bombed 'the vulnerable area of Berlin and that most of the remainder bombed lightly built-up suburban areas'.[1] The Main Force groups which produced the best photographs were 1 and 5 Groups, whose Lancasters were flying above the worst of the air battle. 3 Group came in the middle of the accuracy table, despite having the lowest flying aircraft; 6 Group came next, with 4 Group at the bottom of the table.

And so the raid ran its course. Returning crews reported various decoy fire sites; intelligence about these had been accurate. The runway lights of Tempelhof Airport were still switched on for the first few minutes of the raid. Many fires were seen below, and a large explosion was logged halfway through the raid. Sergeant Ferris Newton, a flight engineer in a Halifax of 76 Squadron, wrote this description of the scene over Berlin that night in his diary:

The first thing we have to do is to fly through a wall of searchlights; they are in hundreds – in cones and in clusters. It's a wall of light, with very few breaks, and behind that wall is an even fiercer light, glowing red and green and blue. It is pretty obvious as we come in through the searchlight cones that it is going to be hell over the target.

There is one comfort, and it has been a comfort to me

---

1 Public Record Office AIR 14/3410.

all the time we have been going over, and that is that it is
quite soundless; the roar of your engines drowns
everything else. It is like running straight into the most
gigantic display of soundless fireworks in the world.[1]

The Berliners had ample warning of the raid. Many had
been listening to the broadcast on a special short wave-
length used by the 1st Flak Division in the Zoo Flak tower.
The passage of the bombers through Western Germany
had been reported, and, when Hanover and Brunswick
were passed, people knew that Berlin was the probable target and started to make their preparations. Valuables were
gathered together; knitting, books, food and drink were
collected, ready for what might prove a long night in the
shelters. When the sirens sounded, they went down. When
the first bombers reached the city, the Flak broadcast on
the radio gave the quadrants of the area into which the
barrage should be fired. Those civilians who had Flak maps
then knew exactly over which part of the city the bombers
were.
  The bombing this night was so scattered that no part of
Berlin received a knock-out blow. My appeals in the city
brought only two responses from people affected by the
raid – one in a central area, one in the outskirts. This lack
of eyewitnesses does not matter. The main historical aspect
of this night was the Wild Boar air battle; the turn of the
civilians in Berlin would come later. However, the two
quotations contain some interesting points. The first is
from Käthe Hauch, who was a thirty-five-year-old lady who
acted as secretary to her architect father. Her home was
in the district of Schöneberg, over which the early Target
Indicators fell. Her account shows how the attack never
became concentrated here. 'Christmas tree' (*Christbaum*)
was a popular German name for a Target Indicator.

I had had a few quarrels with some of the other people in

1 By kind permission of his widow, Mrs Dorothy Newton.

the house, so I did not go down into the basement despite the regulations. I didn't like being ordered around. My mother also stayed put and there was an old lady from the fourth floor who also didn't like going to the shelter. She asked if she could come and sit with us. So there were these two old ladies and me.

I opened the doorway to the balcony to see what was happening. I could see the Flak firing and then heard the droning of the bombers' engines. I didn't hear any bombs falling, because of the Flak fire, mostly from those heavy guns on the Zoo Flak tower which was not far away. All of a sudden, I saw incendiary bombs starting to burn, little patches of fire here and there all over the street. It was fascinating. Then I looked up and there was something I had never seen before, but something my cousin from Krefeld had told me about. It had to be one of the 'Christmas trees' she had described to me. It was like a pyramid of balls of red fire dripping down; it seemed to hang in the sky for a long time. Now I knew what it looked like. I was not particularly worried; I didn't know what it meant and had no idea what was about to happen.

We were lucky. None of the houses in the street near us were burning, despite all the incendiary bombs on the roadway. My first impression was that their aiming was not very good, all those incendiaries in the street and none of the houses being hit.

There was a pause before the next wave came over, this time with high-explosive bombs, so I decided to go back inside to make sure that everything was all right. I was just outside the bathroom when there was an explosion; it felt as though the floor jumped about a foot up into the air and the false ceiling came down on my head, but it was only a light wooden ceiling with empty cardboard boxes and suchlike stored above it. I was not hurt but I found myself in a cloud of dust and could not breathe. I tried to get into the bathroom where there was a bath full of water ready for fire fighting. The door frame was twisted but I managed to push it in and got a wet towel over my mouth.

What had happened was that high-explosive bombs had hit two houses across the road and the house next door on my side. The only casualty was an old lady over the road, a Baroness So-and-So, but I don't know her exact name. She was well known for the hats she wore, surprisingly modern considering her age; they were crazy hats with feathers and birds and suchlike stuck on the top. She hadn't gone down to the cellar but had stayed in her flat on the ground floor and been killed.

In a discussion after this interview, it was decided that many of the incendiaries burning in the roadway had cascaded from the particularly steep roofs of the houses in this street, the roofs being intact because the incendiary bombs fell before the high explosives. That was the sort of thing that happened when bombing was not concentrated.

Reinhold Neumann was an eighteen-year-old youth who had been called up into the Labour Service at a camp in the suburb of Lankwitz. This was four miles further back down the bomber's route and would catch the later bombing of the creepback. Neumann was a member of a fire-fighting team.

It was a nice clear night, quite warm. Suddenly, just above us the 'Christmas trees' appeared, four of them, set out in a square, and we were right in the middle. It was the first time I had seen them and I didn't understand what they were for, but I wasn't worried. Then the first bombs fell, high explosives, and we took shelter in the covered trench. The bombs came nearer; the earth shook and sand trickled down between the roof timbers.

When it became quieter we got out. Our main administration building was on fire, smoke billowing out of the roof. We went to our fire unit, a trailer with a big pumping engine mounted on it. Unfortunately, we could not use it because the hoses were all punctured and some were burning. So we had to fight the fire in the roof of that building with the buckets of water and sand which were always ready. There were three incendiary bombs. They had come through the roof and first ceiling and were stuck in the wooden floor of the top room. They had broken open and the core which was burning had a bright, reddish-gold glow, turning to yellow and white and spitting out burning material over a small area, just about a metre around the bomb. We used the sand to cover the bombs – that was the most important thing – and the water was thrown over the floor to keep the fire from spreading. We needed a lot of sand to smother the bombs completely. There were about ten of us at it. We got the bombs covered quickly but the burning floor took a little longer. The whole job was over in about ten minutes. No one was in charge but we didn't get in each other's way. We felt quite proud when we had them all out.

This young man had come face to face with the main weapon of Bomber Command, the 4-pound incendiary bomb, little realizing that he was in the front line of a famous battle and had gained a small victory for his side.

Documents from Berlin record the results of the bombing in great detail. To succeed in its task, Bomber Command needed to produce concentrated bombing, starting so many fires in one area that the fire-fighting units would be overwhelmed by calls and the fires would join up to become widespread conflagrations out of control. Cities were destroyed by fire, not by high explosives. The best verdict would be that this raid was a serious blow, by far the heaviest of the war so far on Berlin, but its scale was not sufficient to be classed as a major success for the bombers and hardly worth the number of aircraft and crews lost. The fires were quickly dealt with, and the after-effects of the raid could be measured in days rather than weeks. Bombs fell over a large area of south and south-west Berlin, with the districts of Mitte, Tempelhof, Mariendorf, Marienfelde, Lankwitz and Lichterfelde suffering serious damage and with seven more western districts being only lightly hit. The number of districts listed is witness to the lack of bombing concentration. Twenty-five villages outside the city limits also reported bombs, most of them in a long line stretching to the south as far as Lückenwalde, twenty miles south of the city and nearly thirty miles from the planned Aiming Point. Six people died in the country areas.

In Berlin itself, 2,611 properties were listed as destroyed or burnt out; 2,115 were classed as *Wohnungen* ('dwellings') and most of these were flats. Minister Alfred Rosenberg, one of Hitler's chief policy advisers, lost his house in Wilmersdorf but he survived to meet his destiny with the hangman at Nuremberg after the war. Every government office building in the Wilhelmstrasse was damaged, and various military buildings were hit, including the Officer Cadet School at Köpenick and the barracks of the Leibstandarte Adolf Hitler Depot in Lichterfelde. Many aviation and engineering workshops were damaged around Tempelhof Airport, where two light aircraft parked in the open were destroyed and where a Stirling bomber crashed.[1] Five industrial concerns are listed as having a complete stoppage of production, the Steglitz Power Station being the most important of these.

The surprising feature of the raid was the large number of deaths. A total of 854 people were killed: 684 civilians, 60 service personnel, 6 air-raid workers, 102 foreign workers (89 of them women) and 2 prisoners of war. Eighty-three more civilians were missing, buried under their collapsed blocks of flats. When the raid reports were examined by the authorities it was found that most of the dead had not been in their air-raid shelters. Goebbels, in

---

1 This was Stirling EH 986 of 218 Squadron, a new aircraft on its first operation; Flight Sergeant W. S. Williams and four of his crew died, two survived.

his capacity as *Gauleiter* of Berlin, is reported to have been furious at this and he gave strict orders that harsher methods were to be used to make sure people took shelter in future.

The bombers' return route was north-west out of the Berlin area as far as the Baltic coast near Rostock, then more westerly to cross the narrow neck of Denmark and reach the North Sea. This long route was chosen in an attempt to outrun the German fighters and avoid Flak areas; nearly three-quarters of the route was over the sea. There were no navigational problems, and the weather was clear until some low cloud appeared over the North Sea.

The air battle ended abruptly when the Berlin area was left. Many of the German fighters were running low on fuel, and fog was threatening the local airfields at which more than 150 aircraft would need to land. At forty minutes past midnight (British time), about the time the last bombers were flying out of the searchlight area, the German fighters were ordered to land. Only four bombers went down on the 250 miles of route to the North Sea coast of Denmark. At least one of these, and possibly another, had been damaged over Berlin. A third was coned in searchlights over Kiel and shot down by a local fighter. The fourth was probably hit by a fragment of Flak as it passed near Rostock; the engines caught fire one by one, and the Lancaster crashed in the sea eighty miles further on, just near the German coast at Kiel.

Two bombers went to Sweden, both Halifaxes from Canadian squadrons. One of these, an aircraft of 428 Squadron, had been badly shot up over Berlin, and the wireless operator killed. The captain, Flight Sergeant H. A. Read, ordered four of the crew to bale out over Germany in case Sweden could not be reached, keeping just the bomb aimer to help him cross the Baltic and crash-land near the Swedish town of Ystad. The other

Halifax to reach Sweden was from 405 Squadron; the circumstances of its journey to that neutral country are not known. The crews were interned for six months and then sent back to England. My research colleague in Sweden, Rolph Wegmann, has listed all R.A.F. aircraft arriving in his country during the war; it says much for the morale of Bomber Command that, throughout the trials of the coming winter, only two more damaged bombers took refuge in Sweden while raiding Berlin, even though routes often passed close by and the lights of that neutral country must have tempted many a crew.

A German fighter also turned up in Sweden that night. Unteroffizier Fritz Ammann, of II/JG 300, was flying a Messerschmitt 109 fitted with an experimental *Naxos* set, a device to home on to the radar transmission of the H2S sets carried by the British Pathfinders. He had taken off from Oldenburg and flown north-eastwards in an attempt to pick up one of the Pathfinders homeward bound from Berlin. He found such a bomber and exchanged fire briefly with it, but then his wireless went dead and he was faced with the problem of how to find a friendly airfield without a navigator. He reported later that he had 'followed two R.A.F. bombers to Sweden', where he baled out when his fuel was nearly exhausted, breaking his arm on landing.

The German fighters were not quite finished. A few mostly junior crews had been held back at their coastal airfields to man the local boxes in case any other raid developed or to catch bombers returning from Berlin. These fighters gained at least six more successes. Two of these were shot down on track, just after leaving the Danish coast. Damaged bombers were now spread out over a wide front, and it is presumed that four of these provided the other fighter victims, two over Holland and two over the sea off the Frisian Islands. Three more aircraft crashed in the North Sea, probably as a result of damage received over Berlin. In one of these incidents, three men from a 90 Squadron Stirling survived a week in their dinghy before

being picked up by the Germans in the Heligoland Bight.[1]
A particularly sad episode was the fate of Flying Officer
John Austin of 78 Squadron and most of his crew. One
engine on their Halifax had failed just before Berlin was
reached, but the target was bombed from 8,000 feet. The
aircraft was then picked up by fighters and was attacked at
least ten more times before reaching the Dutch coast. These
attacks were survived, but another engine failed only a
short distance from the Norfolk coast, the pilot could not
control the Halifax, and it spun into the sea. Three men
survived the crash and were rescued, but two of them later
died from their injuries. When the squadron commander
heard the report of the only survivor, the tail gunner, he
asked for all of his Halifaxes (Mark IIs) to be fitted with
square tail fins instead of the triangular ones which had
not allowed Flying Officer Austin to keep control with two
engines out on one side.

Unlucky 78 Squadron, which had lost two aircraft over
Germany before Flying Officer Austin's Halifax went into
the sea, lost two more aircraft over England. These were
among several aircraft refused landing permission at
Breighton, their home base, because of bad visibility and
they were diverted to Leconfield. This airfield could not
take them either, and they were diverted again, but then
the two Halifaxes collided and crashed. Only one man, mid-
upper gunner John Greet, survived, waking up in hospital
two weeks later with multiple fractures; his recovery took
four and a half years. The two Halifaxes crashed just outside the town of Beverley. When John Greet's wife gave
birth to a daughter, the little girl was christened Beverley.

There was one more bomber casualty. Sergeant Cliff
Chatten of 97 Squadron was flying his Lancaster on the
final stage of the flight over Norfolk when a burst of tracer
struck the Lancaster from ahead and an aircraft was seen
to flash by underneath. Chatten was injured, and his mid-

1 One of the members of this crew has provided an excellent account
of this incident. Its length makes it unsuitable for use here, but it is
included in 'Experiences' at the end of the book.

upper gunner was killed; the Lancaster was badly damaged and on fire. The remaining crew were ordered to bale out and all survived. Chatten then spotted some airfield lights ahead and was approaching these when the lights were suddenly switched off. He hurriedly, and with some difficulty, jumped and was so low that, when his parachute opened, the Lancaster exploded on the ground directly below him and he nearly fell into the flames. Chatten recovered to fly a full tour of operations with the Pathfinders, but three members of his crew refused to fly again after that experience. The identity of the German intruder is not known. A radar contact was followed out to sea, and five Beaufighter and Mosquito night fighters attempted to catch it but without success.

The shooting down of Chatten's Lancaster brought Bomber Command's loss of aircraft for the night to sixty-two: one Lancaster destroyed in a bomb accident before take-off, fifty-seven lost over Holland, Germany or in the sea, two Halifaxes in collision over England, a Stirling written off after a crash landing at its airfield and Chatten's Lancaster. This was the heaviest loss Bomber Command had suffered in one night so far in the war and it represented 8.7 per cent of the heavy bombers dispatched to Berlin. The figures for aircraft types are:

Lancasters – 335 dispatched, 20 lost (6.0 per cent)
Halifaxes – 251 dispatched, 25 lost (10.0 per cent)
Stirlings – 124 dispatched, 17 lost (13.7 per cent)

The heavy Stirling losses were spread evenly through the 3 Group Squadrons. Individual squadron losses were headed by 78 and 158 Squadrons losing five Halifaxes each and 100 Squadron and 35 Squadron losing four Lancasters and four Halifaxes respectively. 5 Group had been extraordinarily fortunate, losing only three Lancasters from 156 sent on the raid.

The total number of aircrew casualties was 298 killed, 117 prisoners of war, nine interned in Sweden, two shot down but evading capture and a small but unknown number of men injured in returned aircraft. There were no aircraft or aircrew casualties among the seventeen Mosquitoes which were supporting the Berlin raid, nor from the Wellingtons which were mine-laying and leaflet dropping over France.

The German night-fighter force lost nine aircraft destroyed – five Messerschmitt 110s, three Focke-Wulf 190s and one Messerschmitt 109 – with four aircrew killed and two injured. The damage and casualties in Berlin have been listed earlier in the chapter. The R.A.F. sent a photographic reconnaissance Spitfire (of 540 Squadron) to Berlin early the next morning, and this aircraft was over the city before 9.00 a.m. A large pall of smoke covered part of the area which had been bombed, but most of the central area was clear and no damage could be seen in that section which had been intended as the target for the bombing.

So ended the first raid of the Battle of Berlin. There would be eighteen more.

5 31 AUGUST TO 3 SEPTEMBER 1943

Bomber Command switched targets for the next two raids, to areas well away from Berlin. After three nights of rest because of unsuitable weather, there was a maximum effort against Nuremberg on 27/28 August, a raid on which there were tactical aspects which are relevant to the Berlin story. A Master Bomber was again used; this was Wing Commander K. H. Burns, a flight commander in 97 Squadron. But his efforts were no more successful than Wing Commander Fauquier's had been over Berlin.[1] There was no cloud over Nuremberg but it was very dark, and the bomber force was under heavy attack by night fighters. A creepback into the open country south of Nuremberg developed, and only slight damage was caused in the city. The second feature of interest is that the Germans added a small refinement to the night-fighter tactics. The twin-engined fighters were ordered to follow the bombers from the target as far as possible on the homeward route. This was a natural progression of the Wild Boar tactic. Bomber losses were again heavy, thirty-three aircraft being lost, but this was not as high a casualty rate as on the recent Berlin raid, probably because the sky over Nuremberg was not as well illuminated as over Berlin and also because the choice

1 In the first edition of my book *The Bomber Command War Diaries* (written with Chris Everitt), we mistakenly stated that Wing Commander Burns was Master Bomber for the Berlin raid of 23/24 August 1943.

of a target deep in Southern Germany resulted in fewer fighters reaching the scene of action.

Three nights later, on 30/31 August, 660 bombers (including 57 Wellingtons) were sent to attack the twin towns of Mönchengladbach and Rheydt, short-range targets just over the German border. This raid had the benefit of Oboe-directed marking, and the ground defences were not strong in these towns, which had never been seriously attacked before. The Pathfinder backing-up was excellent and the bombing of the Main Force accurate. Serious damage was caused in both towns. Twenty-five bombers were lost.

Night of 31 August/1 September 1943

BERLIN 613 aircraft dispatched – 331 Lancasters, 176 Halifaxes, 106 Stirlings, with 9 Oboe Mosquitoes as Route Markers. Abortive sorties: 86, 14.0 per cent of those dispatched.

Time over target: 23.38 to 00.01. Approximate bombs on Berlin area: 1,396 tons – 749 high explosive, 647 incendiaries.

47 aircraft missing – 20 Halifaxes, 17 Stirlings, 10 Lancasters, 7.7 per cent of the heavies dispatched. Aircrew casualties: 225 dead, 108 prisoners of war, 1 evader.

Other operations: 47 aircraft dispatched, no losses.

This was another maximum-effort raid, but, because of the casualties and the maintenance and repair pressures of recent raids, the force available was nearly 100 aircraft less than on the last raid to Berlin. Many of the crews were tired, having had only a few hours' sleep since the raid of the previous night. Another cause of dissatisfaction was the

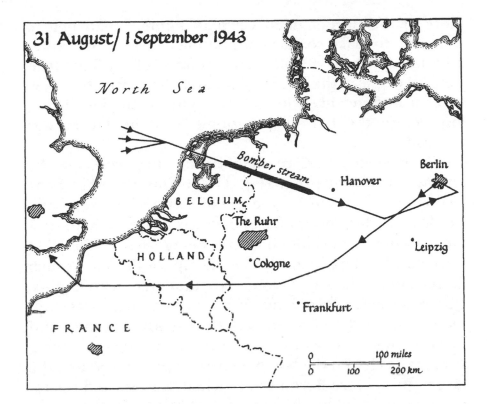

choice of route, crews being asked to fly to a point seventy miles beyond Berlin before turning and attacking from the south-east. The only variation in tactics over the last Berlin raid was a long southerly withdrawal route.

The approach flight to the target area took place in good weather conditions, but eighty-six aircraft turned back. The proportion of the force doing this was the second highest in the raids to Berlin covered in this book. (The only raid with a higher rate suffered a signals mix-up which led some crews to believe that a recall signal had been broadcast.) All aircraft types were affected, with the greatest numbers being from 3, 4 and 5 Groups. This high figure for early returns must have reflected the reluctance of some tired crews to tackle Berlin again.

The German night-fighter force also made a maximum effort. The now standard Wild Boar operation over the target was ordered, but the bomber force was easily tracked on its approach flight over Holland and Germany, and more of the twin-engined German fighters than before were able to make contact with bombers before the target area was reached. A Pathfinder Halifax of 35 Squadron went down near the Zuider Zee, and thereafter the Germans scored steadily, with at least eighteen bombers being lost before the last turning-point into the target was reached.

When the bombers reached Berlin they were met by another tactical surprise. Hajo Herrmann, the Wild Boar innovator, had asked for the use of a unit whose sole duty would be to drop bright flares over the target area, to supplement the various illuminations being used by the Wild Boar pilots and particularly to make up for the loss of such illumination when low cloud obscured the searchlights. I/KG 7, a Junkers 88 bomber unit which was doing development work at Greifswald, was thus made available and carried out its first operation on this night. The high flying Junkers 88s found the bomber stream and tracked it to the target. Just before Berlin was reached, they started releasing long strings of bright flares. Pilot Officer Harry Gowan, a Canadian of 405 Squadron, was the pilot of one of the first Pathfinder aircraft over the target.

That raid will never be forgotten. The Flak was particularly heavy, presumably because it was easy to predict on one aircraft. But, as though this was not bad enough, the fighters were busy laying a flarepath just behind us with white parachute flares. The psychological effect of this action cannot be described. Obviously, they knew exactly where we were at all times and were only allowing us to go in the hope that the Flak would get us. But we didn't know which second would be our last when we had served their purpose of marking the route of the coming attack.

Many British reports pay tribute to the success of these 'fighter flares', mentioning 'the incredible speed at which they got the flares organized' and 'the blinding candle-power'. One bomber man says, 'It was like suddenly coming out of a dark country lane into a brightly lit main street', and another that 'It was like running naked through a busy railway station, hoping no one would see you.'

The introduction of the fighter flares was a timely move by the Germans. Most of Berlin was covered by cloud, and the searchlights were not effective. Not only did the flares make up for this loss of light, but the illumination was extended along the first part of the bombers' return route. The now familiar battle ensued. One German pilot, Hauptmann Telge of II/NJG 1, shot down one Stirling but then collided with a second, the starboard wing of his Messerschmitt 110 catching the Stirling's rudder. The Stirling went straight down and exploded on hitting the ground. The Messerschmitt's wing came off, and the rest of the aircraft went into a spin. The radar operator got out, but Telge did not. Leutnant Johannes Hager of the same unit used up all the ammunition for his forward firing guns in shooting down one bomber; when he found a second, his radar operator shot the bomber down with his rear gun – a rare event at night. Sergeant F. P. G. Hall, a Halifax navigator in 76 Squadron, watched another bomber go down.

Just after bombing, there was a cry from the mid-upper gunner – 'Dive port!' A Lanc was on fire above us, standing on its port wing. As it dropped, we all instinctively put our hands to our faces. It went past – seemingly just yards from our starboard wing. What a fright!

Wing Commander Ken Burns, who had been the Master Bomber over Nuremberg four nights earlier, was blown out of his Lancaster when it was attacked and exploded on his marking run.[1] Twenty-two aircraft, nearly all Stirlings

---

1 Burns lost a hand when shot down over Berlin. After the war he became a transport pilot and he often left his artificial hand attached to the control column when he went back for a rest, which sometimes disconcerted passengers visiting the flight-deck.

and Halifaxes, went down in the target area and over the first seventy miles of the return route.

The Aiming Point was in the same area as on the first Berlin raid, and the 'hook' of built-up suburb on the northern edge of the city was again to be the reference point for the Pathfinders. But the Blind Markers could not find it and they failed to achieve concentration either in time or in accuracy. Most of them were flying south of the planned track and many of them were late. The complicated H2S plan, inaccurately forecast winds and the unnerving mass of fighter flares which suddenly appeared to herald another fierce battle all contributed to the Pathfinders' failure.

This poor start was further complicated by a sheet of cloud covering the centre of the city into which the Target Indicators disappeared. But the southern suburbs were clear. The Backers-Up thus re-marked the T.I.s which were furthest from the Aiming Point. The Main Force, whose planned route passed south of the city, was certainly not inclined to fly another seventy miles further on when markers were going down just a few miles to port. The crews' own bombing photographs and German records show that most crews swung in, bombed the first markers they saw, then got away from the hell of the air battle as quickly as they could. The marking and the bombing 'crept back' rapidly. Sergeant Denys Teare was the bomb aimer in a 103 Squadron Lancaster.

We had become one of the squadron's most experienced crews and been promoted to the first phase of the bomber stream, going in immediately after the Pathfinders.

Over the 'target' we were agreeably surprised to find virtually no Flak opposition and the target markers clearly visible, so the bomb load was most accurately sighted, released and the statutory period of straight-and-level flying for the photo-flash was maintained in textbook fashion.

The following day, however, at the Intelligence Section where I expected to see a 'bull's-eye' picture, I learnt that not only had losses been very heavy but everybody's photos were being plotted in open countryside.

A total of 377 aircraft returned with bombing photographs which showed either ground detail or fires on the ground which could be plotted. It was estimated that only ten of these aircraft bombed the built-up area of Berlin and that most bombs fell in a long spread up to thirty miles south of the city. It is probable, however, that some of the ninety-seven aircraft whose photographs were not plottable bombed the cloud-covered areas nearer the city centre.

The German records are quite clear as to where the bombs fell. The central area, for which the attack was intended, was almost untouched, although the National Police Hospital here was set on fire. There was some industrial damage in the nearby districts of Wedding and Moabit; this may have been caused by the more accurate of the Pathfinders. At the West Harbour in Moabit, a direct hit killed fourteen people at the headquarters office of the Berlin Docks; this seems to have been the most serious incident of the night. The remainder of the bombing which fell in Berlin was scattered over a wide area in the south. Sixty-eight people were killed in Berlin and nineteen more in the country areas. The raid was so ineffective that the Germans estimated that only 150 bombers took part.

The bombers flew home. The long southerly return route and the threat of fog at the German airfields soon caused most of the night fighters to break off the action. Two more bombers soon crashed, possibly having been damaged over Berlin, but there were no more losses until a damaged Stirling of 75 Squadron succumbed 160 miles further on near Bonn, breaking into two parts in the air. The two gunners trapped in the rear portion amazingly survived the crash unhurt, but Flight Sergeant Douglas

Henley, the New Zealand pilot, was not so fortunate and died in the front part. Four more bombers were lost before England was reached.

There were no problems at the home airfields, and the returning aircraft landed without further loss. It had been a disappointing raid. Forty-seven aircraft were missing: 20 Halifaxes, 17 Stirlings and 10 Lancasters, 7.7 per cent of the force dispatched. The Halifaxes and Stirlings had again suffered disproportionate casualties, Stirlings 16.0 per cent, Halifaxes 11.4 per cent. Among the losses were Wing Commander E. J. Little, D.F.C., commander of 623 Squadron, and his crew who all died when their Stirling blew up or crashed so violently south of Berlin that only two bodies could be identified. All this was a heavy cost for the slight damage caused in the Berlin area, where only eighty-seven Germans died compared to the 225 dead R.A.F. aircrew. But this second raid on Berlin now caused Goebbels to order that the evacuation of children and young mothers from the city should be speeded up and must be completed in two weeks. One and a half million people left Berlin.

Night of 3/4 September 1943

BERLIN 316 Lancasters dispatched, with 4 Mosquitoes to act as 'Spoof Markers' outside Berlin. Abortive sorties: 18, 5.7 per cent of those dispatched.

Time over target: 23.13 to 23.29. Approximate bombs on Berlin area: 965 tons – 583 high explosive, 382 incendiaries.

20 Lancasters missing, 6.3 per cent of those dispatched. Aircrew casualties: 130 killed, 10 prisoners of war, 2 interned in Sweden, 1 evader.

Other operations: 111 aircraft dispatched, 3 lost.

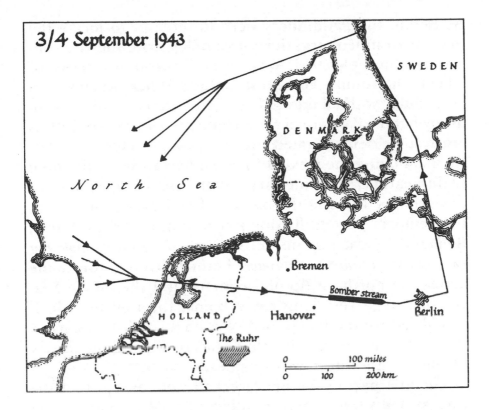

Three nights later, it was Berlin again. It was the fourth anniversary of Britain's entry into the war, and the cheering news that Allied troops had invaded the mainland of Italy that morning showed the bomber crews that the war was progressing steadily in their favour. Harris decided to rest the Stirling and Halifax squadrons which had recently suffered such a mauling, leaving an all-Lancaster force to carry out the raid. The tactical planning contained some bold features, but there was also a helpful element of simplicity. It was obvious that some features of recent raids had been too complicated for the bomber crews.

The outward route consisted of one straight line crossing the Dutch coast and then leading directly to Berlin without any deviation for 350 miles. Such long legs were rarely used, in case German fighters penetrated the stream and were more easily able to follow the bombers, but they could be risked now that the Germans seemed to be concentrating their night fighters over the target.

At Berlin, the Pathfinders were to attempt to locate the town of Brandenburg, thirty-five miles from the city centre, and then plot their way on H2S through a series of lakes to the Aiming Point, a straight-in attack which would be popular with all crews. Four Mosquitoes were to drop decoy fighter flares on a false route out of the target; this last feature demonstrated two things – the speed of riposte in imitating the massed German flares used only three nights earlier, and the first small use of a 'spoof' or diversionary force in the battle. After leaving the target, the bombers were to fly due north, out across the Baltic, then north-west just inside Sweden, *deliberately violating that neutral country's air space*, before turning for home across the northern tip of Denmark and the North Sea. It would be a very long route home, the fuel for which would reduce the bomb load of each aircraft by nearly a ton, but that was a price that Harris was willing to pay on this occasion to save casualties.

The first part of the plan worked well, except that the forecast tail wind veered slightly and caused much of the force to be late at Berlin. But the fast, straight run across Holland and Germany, aided by thick cloud below, hindered the German fighters, and it is possible that no more than five bombers were lost before Berlin was reached. The direct route may also have deceived the Germans. The aircraft of one unit, III/NJG 5 stationed at Werneuchen near Berlin, received orders to fly to the south, the controllers believing that the route pointing straight at Berlin was a ruse; those night fighters arrived back at Berlin too late for the raid.

The bombers were again fortunate when they reached the target. The cloud reaching up to 18,000 feet, which had been present all the way from the Dutch coast, suddenly cleared just as the target area was reached, allowing the Pathfinders to use Target Indicators instead of the unreliable Skymarker parachute flares. Most of the Pathfinders had detected the wind change, and the early markers went down on time. One load was almost directly over the Aiming Point, but most fell in a group between two and five miles to the west, back along the track. If this had been a full-scale raid lasting the normal period of up to forty-five minutes, this marking would have been the prelude to another long creepback with most of the bombing being wasted in the countryside. But the Backers-Up kept that original group of T.I.s re-marked, and the single wave of Main Force Lancasters came thundering in. The raid lasted only sixteen minutes.

One pilot wrote in his diary the next day: 'Great concentration over target; Lancs all over the place.' A squadron leader who had flown a tour of operations earlier in the war and was now preparing for a second tour was flying as a passenger with Flying Officer J. A. Day of 103 Squadron, who remembers that 'he got very excited over the target, his first time over Berlin. Straight and level over Berlin! – as though that was the ultimate in a Bomber Command man's career.' But Berlin's Flak defences were in full action, not giving way on this night to fighters. It is believed that nine bombers were lost over Berlin, five shot down by Flak and four by night fighters.

The shortness of the creepback resulted in most of the bombs falling within the city – if not on the central area, which escaped serious damage yet again, at least on an important area not hit in any previous raid and which contained some important factories. The districts of Tiergarten, Wedding, Moabit, Charlottenburg and Siemensstadt received most of the bombs. Some crews could even recognize the Siemens factory estate by the light of the flares. Several of the Siemens plants were hit, also two A.E.G. factories; many public services were affected. Among other buildings hit were a large brewery, the Opera House, Charlottenburg Town Hall and General Guderian's house, which was destroyed. A total of 568 people were killed, including 123 foreign workers (92 women and 31 men), who were often the victims of air raids because of the poor quality of their air-raid shelters. Among many other items, the precise Berlin records show that 35,030 people were bombed out of their homes for various periods and that four criminals or political prisoners, who could earn remission of their sentences by digging out unexploded bombs, were killed when a bomb exploded. The raid was a modest success, but the lightness of the attack did not produce any of the serious fire areas for which Bomber Command was hoping.

As soon as the bombers left Berlin, their route swung sharply to the north, and a useful tail wind took them quickly to the Baltic coast and out of Germany. Four Mosquitoes of 139 Squadron attempted to disguise the turn at Berlin by flying further east, releasing streams of flares to imitate the German fighter flares. This move was probably successful; the bombers hardly saw a German fighter during the remainder of the night.

The most interesting aspect of the return flight was the deliberate use of Swedish air space. The southern tip of Sweden was crossed, and then the route remained just inside the west coast of Sweden for 120 miles before turning out across Denmark and the North Sea. Flight Lieutenant Ron Munday of 57 Squadron describes the Swedish reaction to this.

Their Flak started as soon as we crossed the Swedish coast but we knew, from our briefing, that there would be no harm in it; there was nothing above 5,000 feet. It looked quite formidable initially but we quickly recognized it as being well below us and it acted as a good route marker for us all the way. At the last turning-point, when we left Sweden, their searchlights were laid horizontally on the sea, definitely laid down as a track guide for us; they had probably detected the path of our leading aircraft. It was a friendly gesture to which we were quite unaccustomed. It was all peace and quiet for the rest of the way home.

Further unusual items for the British airmen were the sight

of lit-up towns and the more spectacular view of the brilliant colours of the Northern Lights.

One bomber went down in this area. It was a Lancaster
of 460 Squadron, captained by an Australian, Flying Officer F. A. Randall. Two engines had been knocked out by a
fighter over Berlin, and one man had parachuted out over
Germany. Randall ordered the rest of the crew out when
he was over the Danish island of Zealand (Sjaelland), very
close to Sweden. One man was never seen again and was
probably drowned in the sea or a lake. Two were taken
prisoner by the Germans in Denmark, and a third who
came down in Denmark later escaped to Sweden. Randall
and one of his gunners, Sergeant H. Bell, came down in the
sea between Zealand and Sweden; both started swimming
towards Sweden and were picked up by a Swedish patrol
boat. The Lancaster flew on a little further and crashed just
inside Sweden. Randall was quickly returned to England,
awarded an immediate D.F.C., and went back on operations, but returning from Berlin in bad visibility on the
morning of 17 December, he and his new crew were all
killed when his Lancaster crashed into a wood near
Binbrook.

There were no landing problems at the end of this operation. Twenty aircraft were missing, 6.3 per cent of the
force dispatched, the highest rate for the Lancasters so far
in the Battle of Berlin because the Stirlings and Halifaxes
were not present to bear the brunt of the German opposition. One feature of the casualties was the high proportion
of deaths in the shot-down crews. The heavily laden Lancasters, with poorly designed escape hatches, always suffered
a higher fatal casualty rate when shot down than other
aircraft, but the deaths on this night were exceptionally
high. Only thirteen men survived in the twenty lost aircraft;
only one man survived from 5 Group's eight lost Lancasters. Among the 5 Group casualties was Group Captain
A. F. McKenna, Station Commander at Langar, and the
second-tour flight commander's crew of 207 Squadron with
whom he was flying. They disappeared without trace.

Three days after the raid, the Swedish Government protested through its London Embassy at the obviously deliberate violation of its air space.

To The Right Honourable Anthony Eden, M.C., M.P.

Sir,

During the night between the 3rd and the 4th of September, 1943, a number of foreign aircraft flew in over Swedish territory, crossing its southern and south-western parts. Details of these flights are given in the annexed memorandum.

It being beyond all doubt that these foreign planes were British, I have been instructed to lodge my Government's firm protest against these repeated violations of Swedish territory.

> *I have the honour to be,*
> *with the highest consideration,*
> *Sir,*
> *Your most obedient,*
> *humble Servant,*
> *C. O. Gisle*

The Swedes had to wait until 18 October for this reply:

Your Excellency,

With reference to Monsieur Gisle's Note, of the 7th September, regarding the alleged violation of Swedish territory by British aircraft on the night of the 3rd/4th September, I have the honour to inform Your Excellency that enquiries made of the competent authorities have revealed that on the night in question a large force of aircraft was despatched on operational duties over Northern Germany. On returning from their target, a number of aircraft took a northerly course and, despite the instructions which, as Your Excellency knows, have been issued to British air crews to avoid flying over Swedish territory, crossed the South West corner of Sweden before reacing the Kattegat.

I have, therefore, to convey to you the expression of His Majesty's Government's sincere regret for this incident.

> *I have the honour to be, with the*
> *highest consideration,*
> *Your Excellency's obedient Servant,*
> *(For the Secretary of State)*
> *C. F. A. Warner*[1]

The intrusion would be repeated again later in the Battle of Berlin, when Bomber Command used Sweden on both its outward and return routes in a raid to Stettin.

There were two nights of rest for the bomber crews before they were off again, but they were finished with Berlin for the time being. The twin towns of Mannheim and Ludwigshafen were the next target, on the night of 5/6 September. It was a maximum-effort raid which achieved outstanding results, with large areas of both towns being burnt out. This area of Germany was beyond the range of Oboe, and the success was due primarily to the excellent use made by the Pathfinders of H2S. The distinctive junction of the wide Rhine and Neckar rivers helped with this. But there was another fierce air battle, and thirty-four bombers were lost, 5.6 per cent of the 605 aircraft dispatched. The next night, Harris sent a smaller force of 404 Lancasters and Halifaxes deeper into Southern Germany to attack Munich. This was a disappointing raid, spoiled by thick cloud which swallowed up the markers. Sixteen aircraft were lost.

Two nights later, Harris decided to go to Berlin again, hoping to achieve at least one major success before the end of the current non-moon bombing period. The orders were sent out to the groups, but the raid was cancelled, presumably because the weather conditions became unfavourable. Exactly the same thing happened the next day, 9 September. Bomber Command documents do not record details of cancelled operations, so it is not known what size of force Harris was intending to send on these raids. The

1 Copies of this correspondence were kindly provided by the Swedish Embassy in London.

new moon period now arrived and that put an end to distant operations for nearly two weeks.

So ended the first phase of the Battle of Berlin. This is a résumé of the major raids carried out during this period:

	Raids	Sorties dispatched	Aircraft lost
To Berlin	3	1,652	125 (7.6 per cent)
To other targets	5	2,805	113 (4.0 per cent)
TOTAL	8	4,457	238 (5.3 per cent)

The squadrons of Bomber Command had thus lost one third of the four-engined aircraft strength and about a quarter of the crews they had held nineteen days earlier. There had been no bad weather to inflate these casualties; they had been inflicted mostly by the German night-fighter force, the Luftwaffe having answered for the time being the question hanging over its future by showing that its first Wild Boar success in the bright moonlight over Peenemünde could be repeated over the German cities in the non-moon period Bomber Command normally used for operations. The Wild Boar expedient was certainly filling the gap in the German defences caused by Window at this time. The bomber casualty figures emphasized two worrying features. First, Stirlings always suffered the heaviest loss; Halifaxes always came next; Lancasters suffered heavily only when they were the only aircraft type operating. The second feature was that the larger the bomber force, the heavier the percentage loss, because the longer time required over the target gave the German fighters more opportunity for success. But Bomber Command needed the maximum bomb tonnage possible to deal heavy blows on distant Berlin, and this required the use of the Stirlings and Halifaxes. It was a vicious circle.

In return for its heavy losses, Bomber Command had carried out two very successful raids – Mönchengladbach/Rheydt and Mannheim/Ludwigshafen – and had caused serious but not critical damage in Berlin on two other nights. The other four raids in this period had been failures. In particular, the major hurdle facing British success at Berlin, the successful application of H2S marking, had not been overcome. But to make these comments is to list only the problems of the British side. The three raids on Berlin, coming after the recent blows on Peenemünde by the R.A.F. and Schweinfurt and Regensburg by the Americans, showed that the Allies were now able to deal heavy blows on distant targets, and this undoubtedly worried the Germans. They knew that Berlin might have to face a winter of heavy bombing and that the British could be expected to improve their performance.

At some time in the week following 10 September, Sir Arthur Harris made the major decision that his command could not continue with the campaign against Berlin under the present conditions and that there would have to be a delay until certain changes were made. The question should now be asked whether Harris had ever intended this to be the true start of the Battle of Berlin or whether he was merely satisfying, in the short term, Churchill's request of 19 August that the city should be raided. Harris's book states: 'The Battle of Berlin, as it came to be called, began on the night of November 18th–19th',[1] and other writers repeat this. There is no way of checking. Harris and his deputy, Saundby, in whom he may have confided, are both dead, although Saundby later wrote: 'in August 1943 the battle began'.[2] Harris had rare powers of independent action and did not consult anyone at the Air Ministry about this. It is my opinion, however, that Harris had intended these recent raids to be the true start of the battle. Three raids in which 125 of his bombers were lost, and the willingness to carry out at least a fourth raid if the weather had

[1] *Bomber Offensive*, p. 186.
[2] *Air Bombardment*, p. 163.

been suitable, are unlikely to have been Harris's way of simply pacifying Churchill. Furthermore, his official reply through the Air Ministry to Churchill in mid-August referred to 'a prolonged attack' requiring 40,000 tons of bombs. I believe that Harris did intend that the raid of 23 August should mark the opening of the battle but, by not making any dramatic announcement to that effect, he was able to break off the battle when forced to by circumstances.

The main reason for a pause was to find some solution to the marking problem. There was sign of improvement. The existing H2S sets were based on a scanning beam of 10 centimetres, but a new set was being developed with a narrower beam of 3 centimetres which was likely to give much clearer definition of ground echoes. This was known as H2S Mark III, but development work was proving difficult, and there was no prospect of Bomber Command obtaining any sets through normal channels for several months, during which time the long nights of winter would be slipping away. But on 14 September, Air Vice-Marshal Bennett of the Pathfinders, Wing Commander Dudley Saward, Harris's radar officer, and scientists of the Telecommunications Research Establishment at Swanage where H2S Mark III was being developed hatched 'a desperate plan' to obtain six sets for the Pathfinders 'in a clandestine operation'; it was hoped that the sets would be delivered in two months' time.[1] This arrangement was made without the knowledge of the Air Ministry, which was treating Coastal Command and the U-boat threat as a higher priority.

A more formal means of helping Bomber Command was the decision by the Air Ministry at the end of September to form a new group in Bomber Command. This would be 100 (Bomber Support) Group, which had the dual role of operating Radio Counter-Measures squadrons to jam German night-fighter communications and Mosquito night fighters to hunt for German fighters near the bomber

1 This incident is recorded in *Bomber Harris* by Dudley Saward, pp. 218–19.

stream, using a device called Serrate which picked up the emissions of the radar sets being used by the German fighters. But this reinforcement, too, would be slow in arriving. 100 Group's first R.C.M. flights would not take place until the end of November, and the first Serrate operations not until mid-December; both types of operation would be on only a small scale until the spring of 1944.

There were other moves, not as important as the new H2S and the new group, but interesting enough to record here. A Master Bomber aircraft had been used on two of the recent raids, but little success had been achieved. Group Captain John Searby, who had successfully used the method over Peenemünde, says:

There was a big difference between a limited 'moonlight special' like Peenemünde and the area attacks which were much more difficult, with the sheer confusion of the bombing, the defences, smoke, fires and, of course, the terrific mass of searchlights. It was not like the relatively easy target conditions at Peenemünde. The Master Bomber on an area attack was a refinement that did not make much difference, because the chap just could not see the ground properly.

And Wing Commander Ken Burns, who had been the Master Bomber over Nuremberg, says:

I think that the reason for the discontinuance of the tactic may have been that on very large areas in poor visibility it was extremely difficult to drop the primary markers accurately, and that most crews of the Main Force and some of the Backers-Up had only one thought in their mind at the target and that was to get in, release their bombs and get out, and not let their own intercom be messed up by incoming instructions.

A Master Bomber was used only once more, in a raid to Montluçon in France in mid-September, before the practice was discontinued for the next six months. But the Public Record Office contains an interesting correspondence [1] concerning a request made by Bomber Command for six special Lancasters, one for each of the Pathfinder heavy squadrons, to be used by future Master Bombers. The date of the first letter is 24 September 1943. The request was for a Lancaster with up-rated Merlin engines which could fly higher than the existing types, presumably to allow the Master Bomber to circle the target safely above the bomber force. Initially, Lancaster Mark IVs were expected, but the best that could be managed were Mark Is with Merlin 85 engines. An initial delivery date of the first aircraft to Rolls-Royce at Hucknall, for final modification before handing over to the Pathfinders, was given as 15 November – again just in time for the late November non-moon bombing period – with the other five aircraft arriving at regular intervals up to the end of February. In fact, the first aircraft did not arrive at Hucknall until 5 December, and then required a further six weeks of work before it was delivered to the Pathfinders, eventually arriving in time for the last raid of the Battle of Berlin. It is interesting to note that 8 Group's attitude to a Master Bomber was to get him up as high as possible; while, in 1944, 5 Group would adopt the technique but by sending the Master Bomber in at low level in a Mosquito.

Bennett made another plea at this time. Another Public Record Office file [2] contains a long letter from Bennett to Harris dated 25 September 1943. Harris had apparently complained about a poor Pathfinder performance over Hanover three nights earlier, the first raid of the next bombing period. The main point Bennett was trying to make, with much justification, was that the crews sent to 8 Group were not the best available. In particular, he asked that he should be able to claim for the Pathfinders all crews starting a second tour of operations in Bomber Command. Recent casualties had hit the Pathfinders badly; thirty-one

1 AIR 14/794.
2 AIR 14/3546.

crews had been lost in the first Berlin raids and the other operations of that bombing period. Bennett pointed out to Harris that the average level of experience of Pathfinder captains now stood at twenty sorties, compared to thirty-two sorties the previous February. But Bennett's request went unheeded. Harris was not prepared to weaken the Main Force groups by taking away the flow of second-tour men who provided the squadron and flight commanders in the Main Force.

6 A NEW START

The 'heavies' of Bomber Command did not visit Berlin during the next two monthly bombing periods, although Mosquitoes of 139 Squadron attacked the city on a few nights. But the offensive was kept up elsewhere. Fifteen major raids on Germany took place during the two non-moon periods, and comparatively undefended French targets were attacked five times on the brighter nights. Most of the German targets were in what might be called the intermediate area between the German frontier and Berlin. The main features were a series of four raids on Hanover, which achieved only poor results, and a raid on Kassel, on the night of 22/23 October, in which excellent Pathfinder marking was followed by very accurate Main Force bombing. There were huge fires, probably a minor firestorm, and severe damage was caused to both industrial and residential areas; it was the second most damaging raid in one night so far in the war, ranking only after the firestorm raid on Hamburg in July.

The breaking off of the raids to Berlin brought a reduction in Bomber Command's losses. The overall casualty rate for heavy bombers during these two months was 3.5 per cent, compared to the 5.3 per cent of the August/September raids. The rate on raids to Germany was 4.1 per cent and to France only 0.7 per cent. The aircraft supply position more than made up for the casualties, and the front-line strength of Bomber Command improved. In particular, eight new Lancaster squadrons either were formed or had completed their conversions from Wellingtons. With other Lancaster squadrons growing from two to three flights, the numbers of Lancasters available for the resumption of the Battle of Berlin rose from 331 to 473. The Halifax squadrons increased by three in number, but the total strength of aircraft available for operations remained steady at around 250. The conversion of the Stirling squadrons to Lancasters was only progressing slowly. The Stirlings had not operated over Germany at all during the second of the recent non-moon bombing periods but they were still classed as front-line aircraft and would have to face the hazards of Berlin again.

There were also technical reinforcements. The six H2S Mark III sets had been produced in the clandestine operation as promised and fitted into new Lancasters made by A. V. Roe's Chadderton factory at Manchester. Three of the Lancasters were flown to Wyton on 13 November and three more on 17 November, just in time for the next period of dark nights. (The six aircraft were JBs 352, 355, 365, 402, 412 and 461.) It was decided that 83 Squadron at Wyton should operate these aircraft because 8 Group's radar workshops were at that airfield. A search took place for suitable crews. Those with a good record of blind marking behind them but with a useful proportion of their tours still to be served were considered. The best of these crews were then approached, told that some interesting new equipment was on the way and asked if they would consider carrying on beyond the normal forty-five-sortie Pathfinder tour limit. But there were not many takers, and that requirement was dropped when the final selection was made. The key men were the navigators, to whom the new device was mostly entrusted, rather than the bomb aimers who were usually the H2S set operators in Pathfinder aircraft. Little extra training was required; the controls were similar to the existing H2S sets. A few practice flights took place over London, so that the features of a large city could be studied. At least one improvement was noted, the clearer definition of woods. There was much interest in the new equipment and high hopes that it would solve the problem of blind marking.

Ordinary H2S radar was now starting to appear in some of the Main Force squadrons. Until now, only a few Stirlings and Halifaxes had been fitted with H2S, to provide a reserve of aircraft for the Pathfinder squadrons operating those types, but ninety-eight aircraft fitted with H2S had now reached the Lancaster squadrons of 1 and 5 Groups and were ready for operations. The equipping of most Main Force squadrons with H2S would be complete within the next few months, although the Lancaster Mark IIs, which had longer bomb bays, would not have room under their fuselage for the large H2S 'blister'.

There had also come an improvement in Bomber Command's Radio Counter-Measures effort. The R.C.M. aircraft of 100 Group had not yet started to operate, but a Main Force squadron, 101 Squadron at Ludford Magna, was now an 'A.B.C.' unit (from the code-name Airborne Cigar). The squadron's Lancasters were fitted with jamming equipment and an extra, German-speaking crew member who listened for the radio instructions to the German night fighters and then jammed the frequency used with a V.H.F. transmitter. These A.B.C. Lancasters were spread throughout the bomber stream on all raids. The weight of the special equipment reduced the bomb load by about 800 pounds, and there was no room for H2S, but A.B.C. would cause the Germans considerable irritation. Another R.C.M. effort was Corona, the transmitting of fake instructions to the German night-fighter crews by German-speaking operators at the radio station at Kingsdown in Kent. Corona, like A.B.C., was introduced in October, and both devices would be fully operational when the Berlin raids were resumed. The Germans responded with more powerful transmitters to break through the jamming and by the use of music played on radio stations, the different tunes indicating various instructions to the night-fighter crews. And so the electronic war went on, an ever growing element in the bombing war.

To face the growing power and range of devices of Bomber Command, the Luftwaffe night-fighter force could show little increase in its effectiveness. In particular, the twin-engined force was no better placed than it had been two months earlier. There was little improvement in overall strength, and the new radar to beat Window had still not appeared. For the next two months, the twin-engined force could only use the Wild Boar tactic over the target and the nearly blind free-lancing along the routes – and all this in deteriorating weather conditions. But there had been a threefold increase in the strength of the single-engined units. Major Hajo Herrmann, who had introduced the Wild Boar technique and formed the first single-engined *Geschwader*, JG 300, describes what happened.

After Hamburg and Peenemünde, which both made a big impact on us, came the first Berlin raids. I have no documents but I feel that it was in one of my regular telephone conversations with Goering that I told him that I did not think the twin-engined units were flexible enough to do proper Wild Boar. So Goering told me to go ahead and create a new division, the 30th Jagddivision. So I became a divisional commander and went from Major to Oberstleutnant and then to Oberst all in two months.

Our headquarters were in the Flak barracks at Döberitz, on the outskirts of Berlin. There were three *Geschwader*, JG 300, 301 and 302, and the Junkers 88 *Gruppe* which dropped flares.[1] Two of the *Geschwader* commanders were former bomber pilots and the third was either bomber or transport.

I had plenipotentiary powers for the recruitment of

1 The original flare-dropping *Gruppe*, I/KG 7, was replaced by III/KG 3 at about this time.

pilots and went the rounds. They came from all over, instructors, staff pilots, transport pilots, pilots in staff positions anxious to get into action 'before the war ended'. In particular, I visited XIV Korps at Tutow and obtained a lot of Junkers 52 pilots. In the end, there were not enough places for all those who wanted to come; we filled up in remarkably quick time. There was more difficulty with the aircraft because of the competition from the fighting fronts and I was a new claimant. But Galland, *General der Jagdflieger*, was also conscious of the danger to the cities from Bomber Command and was particularly understanding and co-operative.

The division formed with tremendous speed. Then we had a little training but not much. The pilots were all 'blind' fliers; they only had to learn to shoot. I think we were complete by the end of October or the beginning of November when the next series of raids on Berlin started. We had an immediate setback when the new commander of JG 301, Major Weinrich, was killed. That was a disappointment; he had been an old bomber pilot colleague of mine earlier in the war.

This increased single-engined force apparently posed a major threat to the continuing British campaign against Berlin, but there were several problems. Herrmann did not get everyone's support; many of the twin-engined night-fighter pilots were scornful of the idea that ex-bomber and transport pilots in single-engined aircraft could become instant night-fighter pilots. Only one-third of the aircraft in each of Herrmann's units actually belonged to those units; the remainder were borrowed from the local day-fighter units with which airfields were shared. And, again, the worst of the winter weather had yet to be faced.

The moon waned, and, on Tuesday 16 November, Bomber Command again stood ready to attack Germany. Harris held his morning conference; the initial weather forecast was favourable, and a raid was planned. But the raid was cancelled later in the day, and it is not known whether this would have marked the reopening of the Battle of Berlin. The only references found for the cancelled operation are in the records of 12 and 460 Squadrons, both in 1 Group, and the raid may only have been of limited size and to a short- or medium-range target. This possibility is supported by what happened on the following night. The operation on that next night, 17/18 November, was an unusual one, with only eighty-three Lancasters and Halifaxes of 8 Group being sent to Ludwigshafen-on-Rhine, just across the river from Mannheim, with the I.G. Farben chemical factory as the Aiming Point. The tactics employed were unique. Although the aircraft involved were all from Pathfinder squadrons, there was to be no 'pathfinding', and no markers were to be dropped. The important feature was that these aircraft were all fitted with H2S, and each crew was to aim its bombs by means of that device. The choice of this target was most favourable for the use of H2S; the factory was on the bank of the wide Rhine, near a prominent junction with the River Neckar.

The raid was reasonably successful. Forty-three crews bombed on H2S; those crews whose H2S equipment was unserviceable bombed fires. The night was clear enough for thirty-five bombing photographs to be plotted. Either two or three bomb loads hit the I.G. Farben factory itself, and at least six more were within one mile; most of the remainder were within two miles. It was a good result but of limited application. The trial was probably laid on at the instigation of specialist radar officers to see whether H2S could be used as a blind bombing device when all of the squadrons of the Main Force were fitted with H2S. But the results showed only that the skilled crews of the Pathfinder squadrons could hit a town with good H2S characteristics, a fact which was already known. The trial had nothing to do with the imminent use of H2S Mark III and could have no immediate application to the resumption of the raids on Berlin, and yet virtually the whole of the Pathfinder Force was risked on this raid just when the Battle of Berlin was due to reopen. The trial was not followed up, and when H2S later reached all of the Main Force squadrons it was mainly used as a navigational device, rarely for blind bombing. Fortunately the experiment was not costly. Only one bomber, a 405 Squadron Lancaster, was lost.

Night of 18/19 November 1943

BERLIN   440 Lancasters dispatched, with 4 Mosquitoes to drop dummy fighter flares. Abortive sorties: 26 Lancasters, 5.9 per cent of those dispatched.

Time over target: 20.56 to 21.12. Approximate bombs on Berlin area: 1,575 tons – 792 high explosive, 783 incendiaries.

9 Lancasters missing, 2.0 per cent. Aircrew casualties: 43 dead, 20 prisoners of war, 4 evaders.

LUDWIGSHAFEN-ON-RHINE   395 aircraft – 248 Halifaxes, 114 Stirlings, 33 Lancasters – dispatched. 23 aircraft missing – 12 Halifaxes, 9 Stirlings, 2 Lancasters, 5.8 per cent of the force.

Other operations: 45 aircraft dispatched, no losses.

At his morning conference on 18 November, Harris decided that the offensive against Berlin would be resumed that night. The weather was favourable; the groups were warned early, and no cancellation took place. But this was to be no all-out effort, and there was a considerable degree of sophistication in the plans produced at High Wycombe that day. The main feature was that Bomber Command was to be split into two forces: an all-Lancaster force to attack Berlin, and a mainly Halifax and Stirling force to attack Ludwigshafen-on-Rhine. These two forces were to

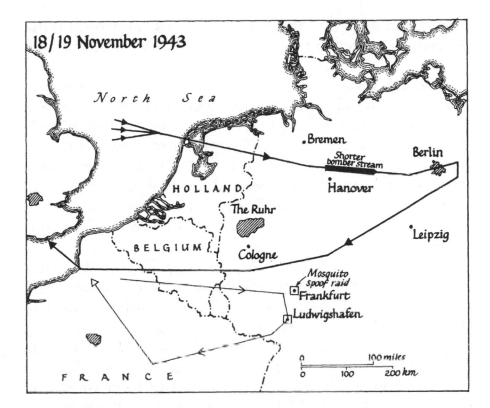

cross the enemy coast simultaneously, but at points 250 miles apart. How to deal with such a situation should pose a major problem for the German controllers. A small force of Mosquitoes would carry out a decoy raid on Frankfurt to divert German attention from the Ludwigshafen operation.

Another important feature of the plan was the shortening of the bombing period over Berlin. Bomber Command had always been reluctant to shorten the duration of the 'time over the target' because of the danger of aircraft colliding or being hit by the bombs of higher flying aircraft. A rate of twelve aircraft per minute in the Thousand Bomber Raid to Cologne in May 1942 had been thought a great risk at that time. This had been increased only to sixteen aircraft per minute until recently, with raids lasting up to forty-five minutes. Now, on this night, the Berlin raid would last only sixteen minutes, and aircraft would attack at a planned rate of over twenty-seven per minute. This shortening of the time spent over the target was Bomber Command's most effective counter to the German Wild Boar night-fighter tactics.

The diary of a Lancaster squadron commander pin-points another change: 'All-up weight has been increased to 65,000 pounds for the first time';[1] this would allow each Lancaster to carry up to half a ton more bombs. But the move was not as effective as might appear. It was soon observed that more crews started jettisoning part of their bomb loads in the North Sea to retain some manoeuvr-ability if attacked by a night fighter before reaching the target.

The crews were briefed. Again there were no dramatic exhortations. The earlier talk in the press of 'Berlin next' had faded, and the aircrews would only slowly realize that they were now committed to a long slog against the German capital. The two bomber forces both made an early start, and aircraft were taking off in clear weather all over Eastern England by 5.00 p.m., the Berlin force to fly out over the North Sea, the Ludwigshafen force flying south, past London and out over the Channel, before turning to cross Northern France. Only two of the six H2S Mark III aircraft had been ready for operations, and one of these was found to have a defect during its air test and had to be withdrawn, leaving only Pilot Officer D. N. Britton and his crew to carry this repository of so many Pathfinder hopes into battle. But his H2S set developed a fault as it flew across the North Sea, and since he had been ordered not to risk the valuable set over Germany if it was not functioning properly, Britton dropped his bomb load on the Dutch island of Texel and returned to base.

The Germans detected both bomber forces, tracking them without difficulty on their separate paths. Part of their twin-engined force (from NJG 3) was not available, having been sent to Norway that day to engage a force of American B-24 Liberators which attacked an airfield near

1 From the diary of Wing Commander G. A. Carey-Foster, 101 Squadron.

Oslo. The available German fighters – about 120 aircraft –
were ordered up and, after some hesitation by the controllers, were split into two groups, each to engage one of the
British raids in Wild Boar action over the target. The
Mannheim/Ludwigshafen area was correctly forecast as the
target twenty-eight minutes before the raid there was
scheduled to open, and Berlin was named with forty minutes to spare.

The flight of the Berlin force from the Dutch coast to the
town of Brandenburg, their gateway to Berlin for this raid,
was without major incident. It seems that only three bombers were lost along that route. There were some navigational problems. The clear weather which was forecast
turned out to be thick cloud, and the forecast winds were
also unreliable. Pilot Officer John Chatterton, on his first
flight to Germany with his own crew, writes of 'hauling our
ancient Y-Yorker up through thousands of feet of thick
cloud, and after hours of vague, indecisive groping, finally
and with great relief breaking through to the reassuring,
ordered pattern of the stars. During all this time we had
not seen a single other aircraft and felt very much alone –
but not for long!'

A total of 411 Lancasters reached Berlin, but their efforts
were not successful. The changes in the wind caused bad
timing; and not only had the only H2S Mark III aircraft
turned back, but no less than eighteen of the twenty-six
Blind Marker aircraft also failed to drop their markers,
either because their H2S sets failed or because they could
not identify the town of Brandenburg from which they
were to make a timed run to the Aiming Point. The situation was worsened by the presence of the thick cloud, with
tops estimated at 10,000 to 12,000 feet, into which the Target Indicators soon disappeared. Each marker aircraft was
carrying a parachute Skymarker for just this eventuality,
but these were too few in number to be a sure guide to the
Main Force. Finally, one Pathfinder Backer-Up released a
yellow Target Indicator which should only have been used
as a route marker. This remained in view for some time

and confused Main Force crews, who had been briefed only to bomb green T.I.s. The Main Force could do little more than scatter bombs all over the city. Berlin documents say that no 'centre point' could be identified, and the Germans estimated that the bomber force numbered only sixty to seventy aircraft! Bombs were recorded as far apart as the Berlin districts of Reinickendorf, in the north-west, and Marienfelde, twenty kilometres away in the south. Four industrial buildings and 169 houses were destroyed, and some small factories were damaged, but no important firms are listed. The number of people killed was 131, with a further 14 missing.

The bomber crews will remember that night for the vicious Flak barrage fired at them, particularly on the run-in from Brandenburg. Whether because the number of fighters available for Wild Boar action over the city was not large, or because liaison between Flak and fighters failed, the guns flung everything they had at the bombers without any regard to height restrictions. The searchlights were no good; they could not penetrate the cloud. Several fighters were seen, but only on the edge of the target area, making half-hearted attempts: some of the fighters were being advised to land for fear of fog at their airfields even before the raid started. The guns reigned supreme. Surprisingly, only three bombers were shot down by Flak, but the very high number of exactly 100 aircraft came back from Berlin with some degree of Flak damage, not one with fighter damage!

The three Lancasters shot down by Flak – from 9, 156 and 460 Squadrons – all crashed in the north of the city, three miles off track. There were no survivors. Léon Butticaz, a Frenchman drafted from Paris as a forced worker in an armaments factory, describes events at his hutted camp in a park in Reinickendorf.

That was the night when the Avro Lancaster which crashed added to the terrible nightmare of the raid. The wreckage fell in and around the camp. It must have exploded in mid-air. The tail part fell upside down on a path near one of our huts; there was no crew member in this part. My friends and I always wondered why the tail wheel seemed to glow; the rubber tyre was a luminous green.

The next morning, we learned that other parts of the bomber had come down outside the camp. I didn't personally see these, because I had to go to work at 6.00 a.m., but many of my friends who were on the night shift were able to go and see the wreckage. They told me that they found the nose section and cockpit, about three metres long, with the front turret and the bomb aimer's 'bubble' stuck in the earth. There were two dead members of the crew, laid back in their seats. The German police were looking for identity papers in the pockets of the two men and were also taking out cigarettes and chocolates.

We talked a lot about the sad fate of this bomber and would have liked to know more, particularly whether the other five men managed to parachute to safety.

Mr Butticaz sent a vivid sketch of the Lancaster tail unit which fell near his camp but with not enough lettering visible to identify the aircraft.

The loss of the 156 Squadron Lancaster over Berlin shows how the Pathfinders were losing some of their best crews. The pilot was Wing Commander John White, a flight commander on the squadron. He had played a vital part in the Peenemünde raid when, as Deputy Master Bomber, he had placed his markers in exactly the right place and drawn the bombing back from a camp for foreign workers on to the correct target. Now White and all his crew were dead; all but one had been decorated for earlier actions.

The increased concentration of aircraft over the target did not produce the feared rash of collisions – there was just one, which resulted in one Lancaster crashing and the deaths of two men. Even this collision was not over the target, but on the run-in just before Brandenburg. The aircraft involved were from 207 Squadron and 9 Squadron (actually a 467 Squadron aircraft with a 9 Squadron crew). The 207 Squadron aircraft struck the tail of the other Lancaster, possibly killing the rear gunner and certainly removing the tops of the tail fins. The 9 Squadron Lancaster lost height rapidly, and Pilot Officer F. J. Lees ordered the remainder of the crew to bale out. The other Lancaster suffered a smashed nose, with the bomb aimer's 'bubble' and the escape hatch, above which the bomb aimer usually laid himself, both disappearing. The propellers and radiators on both starboard engines were also damaged but not seriously. The pilot, Pilot Officer Bill Baker, regained control of the Lancaster, despite a freezing gale of wind coming in through the broken nose. The bombs could not be released because of the damage in the bomb aimer's position, and Baker decided that he dare not lose height because of the danger of light Flak hitting the 4,000-pound bomb still aboard or, if it could be jettisoned, of being blown up by the subsequent explosion. He was therefore forced to fly back across Germany in a temperature of about minus 40 centigrade and in the windflow coming in through the nose.

When the Lancaster's nose compartment was examined, there was no sign of the bomb aimer, Sergeant Jim Shimeild. This poor man's fate can only be surmised. He was not wearing a parachute at the time of his disappearance. His body was not found in the area of the collision near Berlin but close to the town of Schnakenbek, which is near Hamburg and more than a hundred miles away from the location of the collision. A solution to this discrepancy may be found in a study of the map. The River Harvel runs from Brandenburg to join the Elbe, and the Elbe runs past Schnakenbek. Presumably Shimeild's body fell into the river and was washed on to the bank a hundred miles away.

Pilot Officer Baker flew a direct route to England. The Lancaster survived being coned by searchlights and fired

on by Flak, and this lone aircraft was extremely fortunate
not to be caught by a night fighter. The 4,000-pound bomb
was eventually jettisoned over the North Sea, and a safe
landing was made at Spilsby. But Baker's hands were so
badly frostbitten that every finger and thumb had to be
amputated. Two other crew members were also frostbitten
but they had not been exposed to the full force of cold wind
as had the pilot.

There was another lonely death over Berlin that night.
Warrant Officer H. S. Fraser, a New Zealand tail gunner in
a 49 Squadron aircraft, was found dead in his turret, frozen
vomit blocking his oxygen mask.

The main bomber force left Berlin, a sharp southerly
turn and dummy fighter flares dropped by some Mosquitoes to the north throwing off the German fighters. The
long return route was back over Germany south of the
Ruhr and then across Belgium and Northern France to the
Channel. An undetected wind from the south scattered
part of the bomber stream and pushed many aircraft over
the Flak defences of Kassel and the Ruhr. But luck was
riding with the bomber force that night; several aircraft
were peppered by Flak but not one was lost on the 400-
mile stretch from Berlin to Belgium, although two bombers
were lost over that country.

The 395 aircraft sent to Ludwigshafen were not so fortunate. The German fighters allocated to this raid successfully
engaged the bombers, and twenty-three aircraft were shot
down.

So ended the first night of the resumed Battle of Berlin.
The raid on Berlin had been a failure, due to the old
problem of blind marking. The only redeeming feature
had been the partial outwitting of the German defences
and the low casualties in the Berlin force, which lost only
nine aircraft, a 2.0 per cent loss rate which would be the
lowest during the Battle of Berlin.

Night of 22/23 November 1943

BERLIN 764 aircraft dispatched – 469 Lancasters, 234 Halifaxes, 50 Stirlings, 11 Mosquitoes. Abortive sorties: 68, 8.9 per cent of those dispatched.

Time over target: 19.58 – 20.20. Approximate bombs on Berlin area: 2,501 tons – 1,153 high explosive, 1,348 incendiaries.

26 aircraft missing – 11 Lancasters, 10 Halifaxes, 5 Stirlings, 3.4 per cent of those dispatched, and 6 aircraft were lost in crashes and accidents in England. Aircrew casualties: 167 killed, 25 prisoners of war.

Other operations: 38 aircraft dispatched, none lost.

After a raid by a force mostly made up of Stirlings and Halifaxes to Leverkusen on the night of 19/20 November, and then two nights of complete rest for Bomber Command because of bad weather, Harris's morning conference held on Monday 22 November found better prospects for a resumption against Berlin. There were two important pieces of information. The first was a near perfect weather forecast. Conditions would be reasonably clear over the bases in England; much of Germany would be covered with low cloud or fog which would hinder the German night-fighter effort, but Berlin itself was expected to have no more than broken, medium-level cloud. The second piece of good news was that the Pathfinders promised that four of the H2S Mark III aircraft could be made available; this number would actually be increased to five by take-off time.

Harris decided to make the best of these favourable conditions. He ordered a maximum effort; every front-line squadron was to fly, the only exceptions being the two Oboe Mosquito squadrons and the specialist 617 Squadron. The total of 764 aircraft eventually taking off for Berlin would be a record. To capitalize on this, and in the hope that the

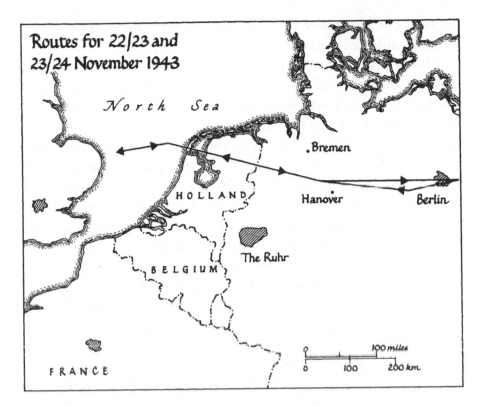

Routes for 22/23 and 23/24 November 1943

bad weather over their bases would keep down the German fighters, he ordered a route that was as near 'straight-in, straight-out' as possible. This and the increased number of Lancasters now available allowed bomb loads which were 788 tons greater than the previous best to Berlin (on the night of 23/24 August). To avoid casualties to night fighters over the target, this great effort was to be further concentrated in its bombing time. Only twenty-two minutes were to be allowed for the raid, a density of thirty-four aircraft per minute, compared with twenty-seven on the previous raid and only sixteen in the August raids. One method of achieving this was to abandon the long-standing system of allocating different aircraft types to different waves of the attack. On this night, the types were all spread evenly over five waves, the most experienced crews at the front, new ones at the rear. This new arrangement was bad news for the Stirling crews who had always been given their own exclusive wave; now they were in even more danger of being bombed from above.

The bombers took off in the gloom of a dull, late afternoon, quickly climbing into cloud. Two Lancasters crashed on take-off, but there were no casualties in the crews. The total number of aircraft turning back early was no more than average, but no less than twelve of the fifty Stirlings on the raid returned. A further loss was the return of three of the five H2S Mark III Pathfinders, all with technical problems on the new sets. The three crews obeyed orders, bombed Texel and came home, annoyed because this could not count as a completed operation under existing rules; these crews were soon given a special dispensation to count early returns due to H2S failure as part of their tours. The weather became worse than expected, with cloud at all levels and some icing. The bomber stream became a little scattered; most crews did not see the route markers dropped by the Pathfinders halfway across Germany. But the bad weather kept most of the German fighters on the ground. A few experienced German crews took off and met the bombers at the Dutch coast but they scored no more than two successes there. Flak may have picked off one or two more bombers which strayed away from the stream, but Berlin was reached with negligible loss.

The first markers were due to go down just east of the centre of Berlin at 7.58 p.m. The importance of what happened in those first few minutes cannot be overstressed. Harris would be unable to gather a force as strong as this for another two months. There were some German fighters about, but not many. Thick cloud was rendering the searchlights useless. Two of the H2S Mark III aircraft and nine ordinary Blind Marker aircraft arrived to drop seventy-nine Target Indicators and sixty-eight parachute Sky-markers on time. It is worth examining what happened in some detail.

There were three new elements in the Pathfinder plan. The H2S Mark III crews were now designated 'Special Blind Markers' and each carried four red T.I.s, four yellow

T.I.s and sixteen Skymarkers. The ordinary Blind Markers were split up into two groups, one to open the raid and the other to carry on marking by H2S throughout the raid. All of the marker aircraft were to drop both T.I.s and Sky-markers regardless of the cloud conditions. This new method, dropping both T.I.s and Skymarkers whatever the conditions, became known unofficially as 'the Berlin method'. The three new points were, therefore, that the Special Blind Markers had their own coloured T.I.s, yellows, which were to be judged by the Backer-Up crews as being the most accurate markers available; that H2S blind marking would be available throughout the attack and not just to open the attack; and that both T.I.s and Skymarkers would be used, so that whatever the state of the cloud some markers should be visible, the more accurate T.I.s being bombed if they could be seen, if not the Skymarkers being used. How did it go?

Sky Marking & Target Indicators

Berlin was completely cloud covered, with the cloud tops reaching up to between 10,000 and 16,000 feet. The Target Indicators quickly disappeared into the clouds; the Sky-markers were needed. It was as good a test as any for blind marking and the new H2S sets. Particular care had been taken over the Pathfinders' run-in to the target area. Flying Officer Bernard Moorcroft, the navigator in Flight Lieutenant A. C. Shipway's crew, was working one of the H2S Mark III sets. After the war he kept his navigational logs, and these enabled him to provide exact details of that important flight.

We got a succession of good fixes on the outward route at Leeuwarden in Holland, at Lingen on the Rhine, at two lakes west of Hanover and then a distant fix – sixteen and a half miles – on Hanover itself. On the last phase of the route in we used the town of Stendal; we went right over the top of it. What you wanted was a solid, medium sized town, but not one which spread itself out.

Then we came to the town of Rathenow which was the start of our final run to the Aiming Point. I got two good fixes on Brandenburg, twelve miles off to starboard, it had a distinctive lake just outside the town. We were late, because of the lighter than forecast winds, so we lost height from 21,000 to 18,000 feet and increased speed from 140 to 155 Indicated Air Speed. Coming up to Berlin itself, we passed between two wooded areas [the Spandau and Tegel forests to the north, and the Grunewald to the south], which were fairly distinctive on either side of us, and then it was a timed run to the Aiming Point.

We were due to mark at 20.01 but were still a little late and did not drop our markers until 20.05. We did not know exactly where we were, because of the cloud, but we believed we had done well and had marked in the right place.

The second H2S Mark III aircraft was captained by Pilot Officer R. A. Hellier, who had on board Flight Lieutenant G. H. Wilson, a gifted H2S operator whose tour was over but who had come back to help on this important operation. This crew also arrived safely and on course; they marked at the same time as Shipway's crew, eight distinctive yellow Target Indicators thus going down at the same time. In view of what is known to have happened under the cloud, those yellow markers must have been right over the Aiming Point. It was a success for the new H2S, but the yellow markers soon disappeared, and credit should also be given to the other Blind Markers and the Backer-Up. There were no gaps in the marking, and the marking never became scattered. The Main Force responded well; 2,500 tons of bombs went down on those Pathfinder markers. A massive explosion was seen right at the end of the raid, and the red glow of extensive fires could be seen reflected on the cloud; this glow would be still visible from eighty miles away on the return flight. Because the target area was totally cloud covered, there were no bombing photographs to study after the raid, and the photographic reconnaissance Spitfire sent out next morning was also unable to obtain evidence.

Bomber Command could do no more than guess at the results. In fact, the raid was an outstanding success. It will be more suitable to study the results and to hear from the eyewitnesses on the ground in a later chapter.

The shortening of the time spent over the target reduced the effects of a vicious Flak barrage. No bombers were lost to collision or falling bombs, and only four were shot down, Pathfinders from 83 and 156 Squadrons, a Lancaster of 50 Squadron and a Halifax of 51 Squadron – no Stirlings. The 83 Squadron aircraft was captained by Pilot Officer Ralph Henderson, D.F.M., who had only just returned to his squadron via Spain after evading capture after being shot down on an earlier raid. Henderson and his crew were all killed. The shot-down Halifax contained the commander of 51 Squadron, Wing Commander Christopher Wright; he was killed when his aircraft was shot down into the Grunewald on its run up to the target, but two of his crew parachuted safely.

The bombers flew right through the target area, swung round south of the city and flew straight back to Holland and home. The cloud continued; no member of a bomber crew saw any part of Holland or Germany that night. Navigation suffered, and several aircraft were shot down by Flak, but hardly a fighter was seen. Further aircraft came down in the North Sea due to unknown causes. Five men from a Stirling were picked up by the air-sea rescue service. Two Halifax crews died when their aircraft collided over Yorkshire; another Halifax was wrecked when it crashed – all of this in its own terrible way was routine stuff.

Twenty-six aircraft were lost over enemy territory or in the sea, and a further six written off after crashes and other accidents. It had been a remarkable raid, an all-out, all-risks-taken effort by Harris, with every possible aircraft sent out by the shortest possible route, with maximum bomb loads and with every kind of marker thrown down over Berlin. And it had worked. It was the first real success for the R.A.F. in the Battle of Berlin.

There was one subsequent development of interest. Only fifty Stirlings had taken off for the raid. Twelve had turned back early; three were shot down. The tonnage of bombs dropped by Stirlings on Berlin had been negligible. In the three raids of the Battle of Berlin in which they had so far participated, 280 Stirlings had taken off, 46 (16.4 per cent) had turned back early, and 37 had been lost, a casualty rate of 13.2 per cent of those dispatched and 15.2 per cent of those which had reached the enemy coast. Harris decided that the Stirlings were a spent force and he was not prepared to force them to suffer further heavy casualties for such slender results. He ordered that the Stirling squadrons no longer be used on raids to Germany. Ten squadrons thus ceased to be part of Bomber Command's front line. This decision reduced 3 Group, one of the finest groups in Bomber Command in the early war years, to a strength of only two effective squadrons, both operating Lancaster IIs. Some of the Stirling squadrons were posted to Transport Command, where they would take part in the invasion of Normandy as glider tugs; others started a conversion to Lancasters which would be painfully slow because most of the Lancaster production would be needed to replace losses in existing Lancaster squadrons as the Battle of Berlin progressed.

Night of 23/24 November 1943

BERLIN   383 aircraft dispatched – 365 Lancasters, 10 Halifaxes, 8 Mosquitoes. Abortive sorties: 46, 12.0 per cent of those dispatched.

Time over target: 19.58 to 20.15. Approximate bombs on Berlin area: 1,377 tons – 734 high explosive, 643 incendiaries.

20 Lancasters were lost, 5.2 per cent of the force, and

6 Lancasters were destroyed in crashes and accidents. Aircrew casualties: 127 dead, 24 prisoners of war.

Other operations: 6 Oboe Mosquitoes dispatched, none lost, but one crashed on return, its crew being killed.

When Harris heard the preliminary reports of the successful attack on the night of 22 November, he ordered an immediate follow-up raid, but by a mainly Lancaster force. The previous night's plan was hardly changed. The routes and the Zero Hour at Berlin would be exactly the same, although the smaller bombing force would spend less time over the target. The decision to go to Berlin again so soon required a lot of work at the squadrons. Two raids in two nights was hard work at any time, but two operations to a target as distant as Berlin in consecutive nights was unprecedented. The strain told. Of the bombers which had just returned from Berlin, nearly a hundred could not be made ready for this new raid. At Ludford Magna, the task of fully bombing up nineteen Lancasters proved beyond the station's resources, and each aircraft would take off 2,000 pounds short of its proper bomb load. The operation caught 514 Squadron at Foulsham just about to move to a new airfield at Waterbeach. Sergeant Peter Twinn describes what happened·

The target was, as usual, the Big City, but with a difference; on our return we would land at our new base. How or why it was ever allowed, I never knew, but all kit had to be taken with us! So, apart from the full bomb load, the fuselage was crammed with trunks, cases, boxes and two bicycles! Luckily, all the squadron returned, but I hate to think what German Intelligence would have made of a crashed Lancaster complete with all that kit.

The bombers took off. A cross-wind was so strong at Elsham Wolds that only fourteen of 103 Squadron's twenty-seven Lancasters got away before take-offs were stopped. The bomber force suffered further major depletion as it flew out towards Germany. The first sign was a rash of 'Cookie' explosions as bomb loads including 4,000-poun-ders were dumped into the North Sea from aircraft turning back. Forty-six crews decided that there was something wrong with their aircraft and returned. This high rate of 'early returns' mainly resulted from the pressure of servic-ing aircraft for this raid. But there was another factor. The figures of early returns for raids in the Battle of Berlin show that Lancasters often experienced higher rates of return when their crews knew that the lower flying aircraft, Halifaxes and Stirlings, were not operating. The combi-nation of this factor and a second raid in two nights for many of the crews undoubtedly persuaded some who were tired or nervous to turn back when, on another night, they might have continued. The highest return rate was in 1 Group, with 18 per cent early returns. This group was pur-suing a policy of loading its aircraft with the maximum possible bomb tonnage; its average Lancaster on this night was carrying 10,050-pound loads compared with 9,600 pounds for the 5 Group Lancasters that were operating under identical conditions. Wing Commander Carey-Foster's diary contains an interesting comment; his 101 Squadron had detailed twenty-three aircraft for the raid but had four aircraft 'cancelled' during the day after air tests by the crews and five more returned early from the raid itself. 'All the abortives, with the possible exception of Sergeant Trotter, were black shows; cancellations were also rather shaky. All the pilots concerned have been given a very severe talking to by me.'

The Luftwaffe mounted a major effort despite the low cloud over many of the night-fighter bases. At least ten bombers were lost on the outward route. The controllers' instructions to the German pilots were clearly heard in England. A large number of fighters were sent towards Berlin, and others were obviously 'working the route'. The British 'ghost' controllers were successful in interrupting the German broadcasts, so the Germans suddenly switched to a female voice. But the British had a German-speaking woman standing by for just this eventuality, and she immediately came on the air with false instructions to the German pilots. I spoke with two German night-fighter men who remember the women's voices being introduced that night. Obergefreiter Hermann Vollert was a radar operator in a I/NJG 1 fighter.

I heard first the German man's orders, then the British man interrupting him, then a German woman, then the British woman. She was telling us to fly to the south, towards the Kassel area I think. I do remember both women accusing the other of lying. I think we knew which was which and went to the right place, but we didn't shoot anything down because we were still only a new crew.

Leutnant Wilhelm Seuss was a Messerschmitt 110 pilot of IV/NJG 5, flying from Erfurt.

I was flying somewhere near the Harz Mountains. I think I was waiting for the return flight of the bombers. The call sign of our *Gruppe* was '*Kolibri*' humming bird – that night. I heard a woman's voice using the call sign. '*Machen Sie Reise. Reise zum Bahnhof*', or perhaps she said '*Lucie Anton*'; both of those were our landing instructions. The voice seemed to come through loud and clear without interference and without any counter-instructions. I went home, very pleased to do so I may say. I think I was the only one to come back in the two *Staffels* based at Erfurt; the ground staff were astonished to see me.

When the bombers arrived at Berlin, they found the target covered by cloud again. The glow of the previous night's fires could be seen through the cloud. The Pathfinder plan was exactly the same as on the previous night. The success of the raid would again depend on the ordinary Blind Marker crews, because both of the available H2S Mark III aircraft had been forced to turn back. A long description of what happened is not needed. The opening Pathfinders arrived on time and marked accurately; their markers were well backed up by later Pathfinders. The Main Force came in well, and nearly 1,400 tons of bombs fell into roughly the same area of Berlin as on the previous night. (Again, the effects of the bombing will be described in a later chapter.)

The bombers were fortunate. A large number of German fighters had been sent to assemble over Brandenburg, just outside Berlin, the Luftwaffe being axious to protect the capital from another heavy blow. But either the fighters were slow in arriving or the liaison with the Flak command failed, because the Flak was allowed free rein over the target for the first part of the raid. Four bombers were shot down during this period. The Flak fire was then restricted in height, and the fighters came in. All the familiar elements of a Wild Boar operation were seen, including a Focke-Wulf Condor which was dropping fighter flares, a Lancaster crew clearly identifying the swastika on the tail of this four-engined aircraft. The Lancaster gunners opened fire on it but missed. But the German fighters were slow in coming into the target area and they shot down only four bombers there. The short period of the raid ended the Wild Boar action abruptly, and the bombers flew off into the darkness. The weather worsened on the return flight, and the night fighters achieved little further success.

The bombers returned to England, six Lancasters crashing at various places, with eleven crew members being killed and fifteen injured. There were not enough bombing photographs for Bomber Command to build up a picture of the raid. Two Spitfires flew to Berlin the following morning but neither was able to photograph the city. However, the raid had again been very successful.

Three features of this night's operations were worthy of comment. Twenty aircraft – all Lancasters – were missing, 5.3 per cent of those dispatched. This was not as high a casualty rate as on any of the August raids to Berlin but it was the highest of the present series despite the fact that the bad weather, the British 'ghost' controllers and the shortness of the time spent by the bomber force over Berlin had all caused difficulties for the German night fighters. The Pathfinders suffered the heaviest proportional loss, with seven aircraft being shot down and two crashing in England. Three of the lost Pathfinder crews were senior ones, including that of Wing Commander Raymond Hilton, D.S.O., D.F.C., the commander of 83 Squadron, who had held that position for only three weeks. He and all his crew were killed when shot down on their bombing run. The second feature of interest was the high rate of early returns in the Main Force squadrons when they felt they were being asked to do too much in carrying out two raids in two nights, although the Main Force did very well over Berlin when presented with good marking. The third feature was the increasing number of crashes when the bomber force returned to England.

Night of 26/27 November 1943

BERLIN 443 Lancasters dispatched, with 7 Mosquitoes in supporting roles. Abortive sorties: 28, 6·2 per cent of the force.

Time over target: 21.13 to 21.27. Approximate bombs on Berlin area: 1,624 tons – 889 high explosive, 735 incendiaries.

28 Lancasters were lost, 6·3 per cent of the Lancaster force, and 14 Lancasters were destroyed in crashes and accidents. Aircrew casualties: 196 dead, 35 prisoners of war.

STUTTGART 157 Halifaxes and 21 Lancasters dispatched. 6 Halifaxes lost, 3·4 per cent of the force.

Other operations: 38 aircraft dispatched, no losses.

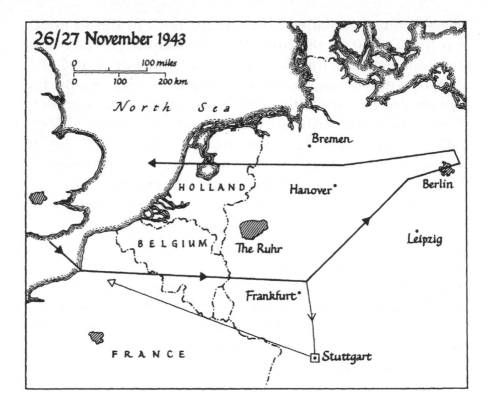

The heavy bomber squadrons were all rested on the next night, but six Mosquitoes bombed Berlin and disrupted the city's sleep. Bomber Command was ready to operate again the following night, that of 25/26 November. The Lancaster force was warned for Berlin and the Halifaxes for Frankfurt. But doubtful weather conditions in the Berlin area caused the Lancaster raid to be abandoned, the cancellation order not reaching squadrons until 10.00 p.m. The Frankfurt raid went ahead with 236 Halifaxes and 26 Pathfinder Lancasters; twelve bombers were lost. On the morning of 26 November, the weather conditions were more favourable. The Lancaster force and the Mosquitoes of 139 Squadron were again warned for Berlin. Part of the Halifax force with twenty-one Pathfinder Lancasters would attack Stuttgart, the real object of this operation being to provide a major diversion for the Berlin raid.

The bombers took off, again an early start. A Lancaster of 83 Squadron blew up at its dispersal at Wyton. Three of the aircrew and several ground personnel, including 'Ginger', a popular Waaf driver, were killed. But this was the only mishap, and the two bomber forces were soon safely on their way; they flew out as one bomber stream, a southerly route out across the Channel, then easterly over France and Belgium and into Germany.

The first part of the route was covered by cloud and all was quiet. The bomber stream was routed to fly just north of Frankfurt, with the intention of threatening to bomb that important city again, and the Germans reacted to this. The weather was clear over most of their airfields, and a large number of night fighters were up, being advised by ground control to make for Frankfurt. The first clash came north-east of that city, when fighters of NJG 1 from Holland, making for Frankfurt, crossed the path of the bomber stream. The first combats soon took place and these attracted further fighters to the scene. Flight Sergeant Les Bartlett of 50 Squadron describes the action:[1]

Suddenly, as we came within range of Frankfurt, the cloud disappeared like magic and there was a sight which to me was new and rather alarming. Dead ahead and on our starboard beam were masses of searchlights. Already many kites had been coned and were being shot at in no mean fashion, and to make matters worse enemy night fighters were putting down two lines of flares bang across our track so we just had to go straight in, neck or nothing so to speak. Still, we made it okay, but I saw two Lancs who didn't and went down in flames. Needless to say, we went flat out over that area, and were jolly glad to be able to turn on to the last leg to Berlin.

Five bombers were lost here.

The bomber stream divided thirty miles past Frankfurt, the Stuttgart force turning due south and the Berlin force flying off to the north-east. The German controllers were

1 Bartlett's pilot was Flying Officer Michael Beetham, later Chief of the Air Staff; Beetham's crew went right through the Battle of Berlin.

confused by this. Their attention remained focused on the Stuttgart force, which was the first to make its move. They remembered a ploy used by Bomber Command on a recent raid to Mannheim, when the bombers had flown beyond that city, then, turning back, had attacked from the east. They still believed that Frankfurt was the main target and thought that the British might be using the 'Mannheim trick' again. So the night fighters were ordered to remain in the Frankfurt area. Both bomber forces were thus able to shake off the fighters and get well away on their separate routes. The Germans were plotting the progress of the bombers at many control rooms. The officers on duty at *Oberbefehlshaber Mitte* in Berlin (Supreme Headquarters, Central Region), suddenly realized that a separate bomber force detected in the Gotha–Erfurt area was approaching Berlin, the numerous H2S indications being picked up from it confirming that it was a force of heavy bombers. Urgent orders went out that all fighters were now to fly to the capital. But it was too late. Most of the fighters would have neither the time nor the fuel for a high-speed flight to Berlin. Even the aircraft of NJG 5, the *Geschwader* whose units were all based around Berlin, were absent in the south.

The bomber crews had been told that Berlin would be covered by cloud, but the area was quite clear and they had to face the city's formidable searchlights and the Flak. A new feature was introduced at the opening of the raid. Three Mosquitoes flew over the city four minutes before the first Pathfinder aircraft, dropping a few bombs but releasing as much Window as they could to disrupt the radar-predicted Flak which always greeted the first bombers over a target. This duty was carried out efficiently, and the Pathfinders suffered fewer casualties than on recent raids. These Mosquito 'Window Openers' would now become a regular feature of Bomber Command raids. 139 Squadron, with its dropping of dummy fighter flares, its harassing attacks on Berlin when the heavies were not operating and now this new duty, deserves much praise for its contribution to the Battle of Berlin.

Despite the clear visibility, the marking plan was again purely 'blind', relying on H2S. The route into the target was more from the south-east than on recent raids, with a final H2S approach over the Harvel Lake and the wooded Grunewald. Only two H2S Mark III aircraft had arrived, but contributions are available from the set operators in both of them. Bernard Moorcroft, a twenty-two-year-old navigator very conscious of the responsibility resting on his actions, was in Flight Lieutenant Shipway's crew. Again his navigation log helps to provide an accurate description.

We were due to be the first of the 'Specials', marking at Zero minus 2, that is at 21.13. Our final run-up appeared to be very, very good and we estimated that we would mark on time. We were on our run-up over the wooded area and were lined up nicely for the Aiming Point which, on this night, was well over to the east of the city. So we still had quite a long way to go over Berlin to reach our release point.

Then we were picked up by what appeared to be every searchlight in Berlin and the pilot started weaving; he was very good at throwing the aircraft about. Some pilots would have kept it straight and level and won a posthumous V.C., but we were all young lads and wanted to live. We didn't mind him weaving. I expected him to shake the searchlights off and get back on to the run which I had been very happy with. But we didn't get rid of the searchlights; I logged that we were held by them for six minutes and the bombing run was completely spoiled. I didn't know where we were. As Special Markers, if we had dropped our T.I.s in the wrong place, we would have spoiled the attack so, dead on time, at 21.13, we just dropped our 4,000-pound bomb, not the markers. My log shows that our air speed was 180 m.p.h. at 18,500 feet – we had started at 140 m.p.h. at 20,000 feet.

After we had bombed and had lost the searchlights, I came out of my compartment to have a look and there, way off to the north-west, there was a whole bundle of yellow T.I.s from another 'Special'; he was a long way out. We were cursing then that we hadn't been able to drop our T.I.s; we would have been the only ones from the Special Markers to have been in the right place.

The other Special Blind Marker was Pilot Officer R. Hellier's aircraft, in which Flying Officer Charles Haynes, the bomb aimer, was operating the H2S on this flight.

We arrived on track and on time at the final turning-point, probably some forty miles from Berlin. During the couple of minutes after our turn on to the approach course, we must have unknowingly crossed a front and become subject to a wind that was almost the reciprocal of that with which George Baxter had navigated accurately up to the turning-point. I can well remember working to try to improve the not very good picture on the screen and searching for a lake which was due to show up. Just as it seemed that it was not going to appear, I located a dark patch on the screen at roughly the expected distance and bearing from us. I was not sure that this was the lake that we wanted, but it was quickly followed by another dark area just where one should have been and I then considered that we were justified in dropping our Target Indicators.

As we left Berlin, I was able to get a definite navigational fix which indicated that we must have put our markers down some miles from the Aiming Point. Back at base, I slept poorly for an hour or two and then went down early to see the photographs. That confirmed how far astray the raid had gone but it showed at least that we had accidentally hit an industrial district.

This aircraft had come in well north of its intended track. Its clear photograph showed that the yellow markers went down a mile and a half north of the head of the Tegel Lake, right on the outskirts of the city and nearly nine miles north-west of the Aiming Point. These were the first Target Indicators to go down in the raid and they remained visible for several minutes in the clear conditions. This was a potentially disastrous situation, because even the most modest of creepbacks would take all of the bombing from that position out into the open country.

But once again, the ordinary Blind Marker crews retrieved the situation. Several of these crews made good approaches and dropped their red T.I.s along a line leading up to the centre of the city, although somewhat short of the exact Aiming Point. The first of the Backers-Up were thus faced with a triangular set of markers, a long base line of reds and a northern point of yellows. Most of them dropped their green markers into the centre of that triangle, and a good concentration of marking was kept going in this place throughout the raid. The Main Force responded well, and most of the bombing fell into the centre of that triangle. It was still five miles from the Aiming Point, but, by chance, the most important industrial area of Berlin lay below. The size of the force was not large enough, nor was the bombing concentrated enough, for terms like 'devastation' to be used, but this was undoubtedly a successful raid, with serious damage being caused. A later chapter will describe the effects of the bombing in more detail.

The searchlights, exploding Flak shells and fighter activity over the target looked frightening, particularly to those new crews whose only experience of Berlin had been the last three raids, when the city had been completely covered by cloud. Flying Officer I. R. Richardson, an Australian in 460 Squadron, sums it up well.

Our morale was strengthened, if that was possible, when our first three operations, all to Berlin, were carried out over extensive cloud cover, bombing on Skymarkers. New crews who started operations at the same time as ourselves reported gleefully that Berlin was 'a piece of cake'. Alas, on the next raid, skies were clear and these new crews were visibly shaken when they encountered Berlin's Flak and searchlight defences at full stretch for the first time. But I would not suggest there was any lowering of morale – rather there was a mood of grim resolution.

But appearances were deceptive. The Flak seemed to be firing up to only 18,000 feet. This height was an unsuitable one for the German defence, probably a compromise between the Flak units which wanted their turn at the bombers and the few fighters which had arrived. Most of the Lancasters could fly just above the Flak, yet the exploding shells were high enough to deter the fighters. Returning crews carefully logged nine bombers shot down, seven by Flak, two by fighters. There were two collisions over the target, but three of the aircraft involved managed to get back to England; the fourth probably went down over Berlin but cannot be identified.

The bombers flew home, taking a direct route across Germany and Holland. The variable wind led to a scattering of the force, and several aircraft were shot down when they left the bomber stream and flew over Flak areas or were caught by night fighters. A 405 Squadron aircraft drifted as far north as Hamburg, where it was coned and vigorously engaged by Flak. The pilot dived steeply and warned his crew to prepare to bale out. Two gunners anticipated the order and went out by parachute, but the aircraft recovered; it was so badly strained that it never flew on operations again. Another Canadian aircraft was not so lucky. Wing Commander A. C. Mair, the commander of 408 Squadron, and all of his crew were never seen again, probably crashing into the sea.

The bombers faced a serious problem when they reached England. Fog and mist had appeared over all of the bases south of Yorkshire. The Lancasters of 6 Group were the only ones able to get down at their own airfields. The remaining Lancasters, possibly 350 aircraft, were sent to land at the Yorkshire bases or to more distant airfields, or were forced to attempt landing in the fog because of shortage of fuel. Many of the Yorkshire bases were overwhelmed. I have many accounts from men involved in various difficulties, but unfortunately the balance of this book does not allow much space to be devoted to what was becoming a frequent feature of the Berlin raids. Between twenty and thirty Lancasters crashed or crash-landed; fifteen were wrecked completely or so badly damaged that they never flew again. Thirty-nine aircrew were killed, and a farmer and his wife died when a Lancaster crashed on their farmhouse near Pocklington. Three Halifaxes from the Stuttgart force and two Stirlings which had been out mine-laying also crashed, the crew of one all being killed. The experience of trying to get down in fog was a terrifying one, often affecting crews more seriously than combat with night fighters or being caught by searchlights over a German city. A wireless operator in a 57 Squadron crew was found to have been so frightened on this, his first operation, that he had not made any entries in his log and had not passed the diversion signal to his pilot; he went 'L.M.F.' ('Lack of Moral Fibre', the form of words recorded in the record of aircrew refusing to fly on operations). A more experienced navigator, on 408 Squadron, suffered a nervous breakdown after his aircraft crash-landed in a field near Lincoln; he was sent home to Canada, a sick man. One sad little incident resulted indirectly from the fog; this was the death of a young Waaf van driver at Stradishall, to which several Lancasters were diverted. Stradishall was a Stirling base, and the Waaf's van could safely drive under the turning propellers of a Stirling, not so under a Lancaster's propellers.

So the fourth raid on Berlin in the November bombing period ended. The Stuttgart diversion and the clever tactics of the outward route had confused the Germans and saved casualties, but twenty-eight Lancasters were missing, this 6·2 per cent loss reflecting an ever rising casualty rate during this period, and there had been the further loss of all the aircraft crashing in England. The Stuttgart force had lost only five aircraft.

Night of 2/3 December 1943

BERLIN   458 aircraft dispatched – 425 Lancasters, 15 Halifaxes, 18 Mosquitoes. Abortive sorties: 43, 9·4 per cent of the force.

Time over target: 20.04 to 20.24. Approximate bombs on Berlin area: 1,600 tons – 840 high explosive, 760 incendiaries.

40 aircraft were lost – 37 Lancasters, 2 Halifaxes, 1 Mosquito, 8·7 per cent of the force. Aircrew casualties: 228 dead, 60 prisoners of war, 2 evaders, together with 2 war correspondents killed and 1 taken prisoner.

Other operations: 35 aircraft dispatched, 1 Mosquito lost.

It had been a hectic first half of the current non-moon bombing period, with major operations on seven out of ten nights. The second half would be quieter. There were three nights of stand-down after the last raid, then two nights when raids were organized but then cancelled. There remained time for just two more raids before the moon rose. The first of these took place on the night of 2/3 December, and Berlin was again the target. The tactics employed were so similar to those of the recent series that the main aspects of this raid can be described more quickly on this occasion.

The raid was planned as a maximum effort for the front-line squadrons, but most of the Halifaxes, about 210 air-craft, were withdrawn from the raid late in the day because

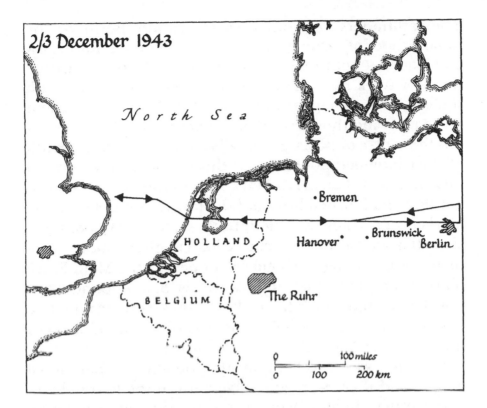

2/3 December 1943

of fog which was forming at their Yorkshire airfields. The number of Mosquitoes on the raid was increased to eighteen, with the newly formed 627 Squadron carrying out its first operation to Berlin. Take-off was in the late afternoon. A towering front of cloud over the North Sea had to be climbed through; many aircraft suffered from icing, and nearly a tenth of the force turned back. The bad weather continued over Holland and Germany, with variable winds affecting navigation and scattering the bombers. German fighters were up in strength, and the spread of the bomber stream resulted in bombers losing the protection of Window; many bombers were attacked. The German controllers were heard warning their crews to ignore fake broadcasts to land because of fog and they forecast Berlin as the target seventeen minutes before the raid started.

The bombing at the target proved to be a failure. Many aircraft, both Pathfinders and Main Force, were late, and the variable winds had pushed most of them south of track.

The Pathfinders were supposed to run into Berlin on the radar echoes of a line of three towns – Stendal, Rathenow and Nauen – but those marker aircraft which had drifted south of track used the echoes of three other towns with similar radar characteristics – Genthin, Brandenburg and Potsdam – and thus arrived at a point which they thought was the centre of the target area but was fifteen miles south of their intended position, and this is where they released their markers. Four H2S Mark III aircraft had taken off, but three had turned back and the fourth was not carrying markers of a distinctive colour because, with so few of these aircraft available, one inaccurate load might do more harm than good. Among the bombs dropped by the Main Force on or near Berlin that night were six 8,000-pounders; it was the first time these huge blast bombs were dropped on Berlin. They were carried in the extra-large bomb bays of the Lancaster Mark IIs of 115 Squadron.

Visibility was excellent at the bomber's operational height, and there were extensive gaps in the lower cloud. The German fighters were given priority over the target area, and there were the usual elements of a Wild Boar operation: searchlights, fighter flares and many combats. The German fighters were helped by the early identification of Berlin as the target and by the prolonged period in which the scattered bomber stream arrived in the target area. Casualties mounted still further when the many aircraft which were bombing south of Berlin turned left and left again, as ordered after bombing, and found themselves flying back through the northern part of the Berlin defences.

It was an unsatisfactory, tough and confusing time for the crews. One man says that 'the last twenty minutes to the target was one continual illumination of fighter flares, with bombers blowing up every few minutes'. Two Lancasters, from the same squadron by coincidence, collided over the target but both limped home. One of the air gunners, on his first operation, had seen the other Lancaster brush just above his head; he refused to fly again.

Several men have provided good accounts of that frightening time. Wing Commander Eric Nelson had recently returned to England after a long attachment with the Royal Australian Air Force. He was now in command of 103 Squadron and was carrying out his first raid to Berlin, flying as a passenger in one of his squadron's Lancasters.

A Lancaster exploded very fine on the port bow on the run in to the target. It suddenly appeared – a huge ball of waves of fire rolling over each other and overtaking each other. For many years I had in my log book, 'Just missed by scarecrow Flak', but years later I discussed this with other aircrew and after reading books I amended it to, 'Exploding Lancaster'. The pilot turned slightly to starboard and our port wing actually appeared to pass through the ball of fire, but we didn't suffer any heat damage.

I remember timing our flight through the defended zone – twenty-five minutes. That flight to Berlin sent up my admiration for the pilots and crews who had to go to Berlin so often that winter. The defences were certainly a tough nut to crack.

Sergeant H. Hannah, of 9 Squadron, was making his first flight to Berlin.

We were thrown in the deep end; what a terrifying introduction to a tour it was. I don't think it was the Flak – I think that was mostly below our level, steadily building up a cloud layer of its own, with its smoke puffs. It was the awesome sight of the fighter flares at our level, the searchlights, the streets delineated by fires, the explosions on the ground and, most of all, the immensity of the city and our excruciatingly slow progress across it. Doubtless that is how it came by its nickname 'The Big City'.

Flight Sergeant K. G. Thompson, a navigator on 101 Squadron, was another first-timer.

We were twenty miles south of track when the route markers went down near Hanover and we had to go through the Hanover Flak and searchlights. We lost time there, with weaving and with navigational problems, and reached the Berlin area thirty minutes after the end of the proper time. We saw a few lights and activity on the ground but not enough to identify it as the target. We flew on and I took two astro shots; these showed us to be well beyond Berlin. We came back and eventually bombed the activity we had seen earlier, but more than an hour late. The navigation officer later back-plotted my results and said that we had bombed at Cottbus, fifty miles south-east of Berlin.

We came back by guess and by God and came out over Antwerp, a hundred miles south of the proper route. We landed at Bradwell Bay. We had plenty of fuel left and could have got home, but we had a few Flak holes and we were tired.

The battered force flew home, the bomber stream being spread over a 200-mile frontage by the time it reached the North Sea. More bombers were lost. When they reached England, they did at least find their airfields clear and only one bomber, a 9 Squadron Lancaster, crashed on a farm in Nottinghamshire, killing six aircrew and fifty of the farmer's sheep. It was the end of a bad night. Bomber Command had suffered its heaviest loss since the resumption of the Battle of Berlin two weeks earlier. The heaviest casualties were in 1 Group, which lost eighteen Lancasters, a casualty rate of 12·5 per cent. The Australian 460 Squadron, based at Binbrook, lost five aircraft. The only Mosquito lost was from the newly formed 627 Squadron, but the crew parachuted over France and eventually returned to England, and this turned out to be the only Mosquito lost in the nineteen major raids of the Battle of Berlin. There were three unusual casualties. The recent successful raids on Berlin had induced the Air Ministry to send no less than four press and radio correspondents on the raid as passengers in Lancasters. Captain Nordhal Greig and Mr Norman Stockton, an Australian, were both killed when the separate 460 Squadron aircraft they were in were shot down in the Berlin area. Lowell Bennett, an American, was also shot down but became a prisoner of war. The only one to return was the famous American broadcaster, Ed Murrow.

The results of the bombing were negligible. It is probable that three-quarters of the bomb loads fell in open country south of Berlin. Some scattered damage was caused in various parts of Berlin, but there was no concentration or large fires. Between 100 and 150 people were killed. Among the buildings listed as damaged were two Henschel aircraft factories and a Daimler-Benz works, the last possibly being damaged by a crashing bomber, and also the Marstall, a famous old Berlin building which had once housed the Imperial horses but was now being used as a library and museum.

The last raid of this important month's bombing period was on the night of 3/4 December, when all of the available Halifaxes, and 307 Lancasters attacked Leipzig. This was a large and important city, nearly as distant as Berlin and hardly yet touched by bombing. It was also high on the list of targets associated with German aircraft production which Bomber Command was being urged to attack in the current combined Allied bombing plan. It is believed that Berlin was first chosen as the target that morning, but Leipzig was substituted later in the day.

The raid was a complete success for Bomber Command. The bomber stream flew straight out on the familiar route across Holland and Germany as though to attack Berlin, but then turned abruptly southwards to Leipzig when only eighty miles from Berlin, leaving nine Mosquitoes to fly on to Berlin and drop Target Indicators there. The Germans were completely fooled, sending all of their fighters to Berlin and none to Leipzig. The Pathfinders performed well at the target, aided by two accurate loads of markers dropped by H2S Mark III aircraft, the first time these scarce aircraft were risked in a target other than Berlin; it was their best performance so far. Leipzig suffered its heaviest blow of the war. A great area of the city's property was hit, 41 per cent of all housing being destroyed or damaged to some degree according to German records. A large pre-war exhibition hall, now being used to assemble Junkers aircraft, was among the important buildings hit. The bombers suffered only four losses at Leipzig, but a good night's work was spoiled when part of the stream wandered into the Frankfurt Flak defences on the way home, losing about twelve aircraft there. The total loss for the night was twenty-four aircraft, 4·6 per cent of the force.

Thus ended for Bomber Command a satisfactory, seventeen-night-long bombing period. There had been eleven major raids on nine nights.

	Raids	Sorties dispatched	Aircraft lost
To Berlin	5	2,499	123 (4·9 per cent)
To other targets	6	1,677	72 (4·3 per cent)
TOTAL	11	4,176	195 (4·7 per cent)

The results of the five raids to Berlin can be classed as: one very good, two good, one medium and one poor. This was an excellent start to the resumed Battle of Berlin, and Harris and his staff must have felt quietly confident about the prospect for eventual success. The two-month wait for H2S Mark III had made little contribution to the successes at Berlin. This is an analysis of its use on the five Berlin raids:

Aircraft prepared for operations		20
,,	taking off	15
,,	returned early	10
,,	reaching Berlin	5

,,   dropping markers   4

,,   believed to have marked accurately   3

No criticism is intended here; there had been no time for proper development or testing of the new sets. But it must be said that the credit for the successes at Berlin belonged to the ordinary Pathfinder Blind Markers who had performed so well and to the Backers-Up and Main Force crews who showed that they were willing to come right in over the target when good, concentrated marking was established.

But there was anxiety when the casualty figures for the recent period were studied. The overall loss rates were an improvement on the raids to Berlin in the first phase of the Battle of Berlin, but the individual loss rates for the recent raids on Berlin showed an alarming escalation during this period:

18/19 November − 2·0 per cent

22/23 November − 3·4 per cent

23/24 November − 5·2 per cent

26/27 November − 6·2 per cent

2/3   December − 8·7 per cent

7 UNDER THE BOMBS

This chapter will describe the effects of the most important of the raids on Berlin in the period just ended. Two unsuccessful raids – on the nights of 18/19 November and 2/3 December – can be ignored, but three raids in five nights, on the evenings of 22, 23 and 26 November, caused severe damage. The R.A.F. statistics are easy to present. Of 1,590 bombers taking off from England for the three raids, approximately 1,450 reached the Berlin area and dropped 5,500 tons of bombs, made up of almost exactly equal quantities of high explosive and incendiaries. The bombing success was mostly due to the Lancasters, which flew 82 per cent of the sorties and dropped 93 per cent of the bombs.

Bomber Command realized that these raids were successful, but no firm details were known because photographic reconnaissance was not successful until 20 December, by which time there had been three more raids. But the German authorities compiled a mass of reports, and most of these survived the war. Extracts of these were obtained for me by my Berlin research colleague, Arno Abendroth; he examined up to seven different files for each raid.[1] His

1 The reports were from the *Oberbürgermeister* of Berlin, the Chief of Police of Greater Berlin, the Greater Berlin Fire Brigade, Major General Hampe (a senior air-raid services officer), the *Technische Nothilfe* (Emergency Rescue and Relief) of both Berlin and Mark Brandenburg and a file of Berlin district reports.

reports now enable me to identify where the bombs dropped on these three raids and with what effects. In addition to this documentary material, personal contributions were obtained from thirty-one people who experienced the raids – twenty-five civilians, five Flak men and one French forced worker. It is believed that this is the first time that these raids have been described in detail, either in Britain or in Germany.

The first of the three raids, in the evening of Monday 22 November, was the most severe; in fact, it was the worst raid of the war for Berlin. More than 700 bombers came straight in from the west and dropped just over 2,500 tons of bombs. This was a record tonnage for a raid on any capital city so far in the history of air warfare and a record which would stand for Berlin for nearly three more months of continuous bombing. Very few of the bombs fell outside the city. The raid lasted for only half an hour, from 7.55 to 8.25 p.m. local time. There was thick cloud, and the only bombers seen by Berliners that night were crashing ones. It was a gloomy night, at least before the bombs fell, with mist and drizzle.

The main bombing was concentrated into a four-mile swath covering the districts of Mitte, Tiergarten and the eastern part of Charlottenburg. This was basically the centre and west-central part of the city, which contained many public buildings and a mass of streets of four-, five- and six-storeyed blocks of flats, mostly residential but often having shops and small businesses on the ground floor. These were just the type of district where area bombing could be most effective, although the large Tiergarten Park was an open space in the middle of the most severely bombed area. The worst of the property destruction and fires and the heaviest casualty figures were in this area.

Among the long list of public buildings hit here were many of the government buildings, including Albert Speer's private office and his War Industry Ministry, the

Naval Construction Headquarters, many embassies on and around the Unter den Linden, ten churches including the Kaiser Wilhelm Memorial Church at the end of the Kurfürstendamm (the ruins of this church were partially preserved, and this place is now a major tourist attraction in West Berlin), the Ka De We department store (described as 'the Harrods of Berlin'), the Romanisches Café (a well known meeting place of intellectuals), the barracks of a famous guards regiment (the Garde du Corps on the Spandauer Damm), the Technical University, two hospitals, the Berlin Zoo, important railway stations, theatres, museums and so on; the list is almost endless. An interesting small item was the destruction of Hitler's private train in a railway siding. Hitler was not present in Berlin at this time, he was at his headquarters in East Prussia throughout the Battle of Berlin.

There was an outer ring of less severe damage. Housing was always the worst affected, but it was in some of these areas that various industrial premises and public utilities were hit. There was a spectacular explosion at the Neukölln Gasworks; this was the large explosion seen and reported by many bomber crews. Overall casualties were not so high in these districts, but by chance the two worst incidents of the night were in such areas. There was a panic at a public shelter in Neukölln, and 105 people were crushed as they tried to get down the steps to the shelter in a disused section of underground railway tunnel. A much higher death-toll occurred at a public shelter in the basement of the Joachimstal School; it is said that 500 people were killed, probably by blast from a 4,000-pounder which dropped just outside the building.

Overall statistics were carefully compiled, although, with another heavy attack falling on the next night, there may have been some misallocation between the two raids. The number of individual buildings in the housing and commercial classifications destroyed was 2,791, with another 2,835 seriously damaged and 23,000 slightly damaged. Most of those 'slightly damaged' buildings suffered broken windows and roof tiles blown off by 4,000-pounders; these bombs caused vast quantities of damage of this type, and the Germans had special mobile 'window-and-roof' gangs which did nothing else but repair such damage and make property habitable again as quickly as possible. But fire, as Bomber Command well knew, was the biggest destroyer of property, and the buildings classed as 'destroyed' usually finished up as burnt-out shells. The records of the Berlin Fire Department show that 950 local fire-engines and mobile pumps, together with another 1,550 brought in to help from outside Berlin, deployed 5,000 hoses, the total length of which was 660 kilometres. Ten fire-boats were also used. The Fire Department later counted up 2,720 separate fires reported during this and the next night. But of all the incidents described to me in personal interviews, only one person saw a fire-engine in action, and that was fighting a blaze in an official building. Factories, large commercial premises and public buildings had first call on the fire-engines, and most of the fires in domestic buildings were either tackled by the inhabitants, who had been trained for this duty, or left to burn themselves out. This failure to control fires in domestic property was aggravated by the fire service's own casualties. The important Moabit Fire Station, in a key area, was badly damaged; a total of fifty-one fire-engines or pumps were destroyed by the bombing, including eighteen main control vehicles fitted with radio, and a further seventy vehicles were badly damaged. This situation was a good example of what Bomber Command planners called 'overwhelming the fire services'. There was another feature of the fire damage. One man, from the heavily populated lower-middle-class area of Moabit, walked from his home towards the centre, coming into the Hansaviertel area. He found the same proportion of buildings affected by fire in both areas, but more buildings were completely burnt out in the Hansaviertel because, he thinks, there were not enough civilians in this much wealthier area to put out the fires.

Many of the Berlin personal accounts mentioned 'firestorms'. There was nothing on the scale of the Hamburg and Dresden firestorms; there were undoubtedly strong, gusting winds caused by some of the larger fires, but these never joined up to make a major firestorm. And, although people found much difficulty in passing through some streets, there were no significant 'firestorm deaths' caused by people being unable to breathe.

There are statistics available for industrial, military and transportation buildings destroyed and damaged, but no major company was put out of action, and none of the major war-industry factories was much affected.

It was not easy for the authorities to be certain how many people died on this night, again because of the heavy raid on the next night before rescue work was complete. The figures usually quoted are 1,737 people killed, 6,923 injured and a round-figure estimate of 180,000 people 'bombed out' of their homes. But the more carefully prepared overall figures for deaths during the three raids in five nights come to one-fifth more than the figures for individual raids, so that a death-roll of about 2,100 may be more accurate for the raid of 22 November. The worst incidents, accounting for 600 deaths in just two places, have already been mentioned. Most of the remaining deaths occurred when old, frail or stubborn people died lonely deaths in their flats having refused to take shelter, or when larger numbers of people died, twenty to forty at a time, when high-explosive bombs penetrated their shelters or collapsed a block of flats and crushed a basement shelter. There were not many deaths by fire; buildings burnt slowly enough for most people in the basement shelters to find an exit to the street after the raid. Very few people died in the streets; there was hardly anyone out of doors during the raid. The figure of about 2,100 deaths was not excessive considering the volume of the destruction, and is a tribute to the strict air-raid discipline imposed on the Berlin civilians. Comparisons with the Hamburg firestorm, when 40,000 people died in one night, are not appropriate. Three other places had suffered higher casualties earlier in 1943 than Berlin suffered on this night: Kassel (5,599 people killed on the night of 22/23 October), Cologne (4,377 on 28/29 June) and Wuppertal/Barmen (3,400 on 29/30 May).

The next raid followed exactly twenty-four hours later, during the evening of Tuesday 23 November. The weather was clearer, but many fires were still smouldering from the previous night. Berlin was a tired, smoky, miserable place. Spirits were always at their lowest when it became dark on the day after a heavy raid, with fears of another raid to come. This time only the Lancasters came, and the bomb loads were thus reduced to about 1,400 tons, with a lower proportion of incendiary bombs.

There is no need for such a long description of this night, because many of the features of the previous raid were repeated and because the Berlin records do not contain so much specific information. The bombing was again concentrated, but with its centre point being located a little further to the west. The central district of Mitte was not hit quite so hard as on the previous night, but Tiergarten was again heavily bombed, and Charlottenburg, particularly the western end, suffered more severely.

The numbers of domestic and commercial buildings hit are recorded as 1,989 destroyed, 2,442 seriously damaged and 20,000 slightly damaged. These figures are higher, in proportion to the tonnage of bombs dropped, than the previous night and probably indicate that the raid was more concentrated. Among the public buildings destroyed or seriously damaged in this raid were the Kaiser Wilhelm Museum, the former British Embassy, the administrative offices of the Waffen S.S., the State Printing Press, the State *Kriminalamt*, the Hertie department store and the Schloss Brewery. One eyewitness remembers seeing the Hertie store with 'fire coming out across the street like a flame-thrower; I would like to have been in the glass and porcelain department when the bombs hit, to hear all the glass smashing'. The list of damaged industrial concerns contains some important war-industry names: three of the Siemens plants, B.M.W., Felsch aero-engines and the Arguswerke, which made V-1 engines. It must be stressed again, however, that most of the destruction was to the blocks of flats in the city streets.

The number of human casualties is given as 1,315 killed and 6,383 injured. These figures, while lower than the previous night, are again higher per ton of bombs dropped. The number of people who had to leave their homes for various periods is given as 180,000, but this is probably a rough estimate. The evacuation of bombed-out people broke down, and many people spent up to a week, during which there were two more night raids, in all sorts of places. Manfred Spielberg, a schoolboy allowed to stay in Berlin with his mother because his father had been killed at Stalingrad, describes how they took refuge after being bombed out.

We found protection in a public shelter at the Moabit Courthouse and Prison. It was packed. There was no proper evacuation for a week. Thirst was the major problem; there was no water in the pipes and we had to fetch water in buckets from reserve water tanks; it was old water in brick-built pits. Army lorries brought food but only the younger people dared go outside to get it; the older ones were scared to risk their place in the shelter. During this time some of the older people died from strain and delayed shock. There was no organization; there were no men to organize anything and the women were not able to wield any proper authority.

There were no heavy raids on the next two nights, but a few Mosquitoes came to cause the sirens to sound and to disturb the sleep of the tired citizens of Berlin on both nights. The results of the few 500-pound bombs dropped are not known.

Every Lancaster available was sent on the next night, Friday 27 November. They arrived over Berlin just after 9.10 p.m. and dropped more than 1,600 tons of bombs at the rate of about a hundred tons a minute. This was the night on which the Blind Markers dropped their red Target Indicators in a line leading into the centre of the city, but the solitary H2S Mark III aircraft of 83 Squadron dropped its load of yellow markers more than seven miles to the north outside the city limits. The Pathfinder Backers-Up, faced with the two groups of different coloured markers, dropped their green markers halfway between the reds and the yellows, and the Main Force bombed the greens. The result of this was that most of the bombs did not fall on the intended area in the south-west-central part of the city, which would have created a new area of devastation if all had gone according to plan, but fell in an area between three and five miles further north. The southern part of this area was taken up by the Tegel Forest and by Tegel Airport, and many bombs fell harmlessly in those places. But the remainder of the bombing area took in the districts of Reinickendorf and Borsigwalde. The residential parts of these districts made poor bombing targets, with wider streets and more open spaces, but by chance the most important war industries in Berlin were all in this area. A large fire was started at the Alkett tank factory, possibly the most important factory in Berlin. Albert Speer describes how Hitler heard of the fire and ordered every available fire-engine to be sent to Alketts. The fire was extinguished in reasonable time, but no one dared to countermand Hitler's order, and the surrounding streets became jammed with idle fire-engines, while many other fires were ignored.[1] The Rheinmetall–Borsig works were hit by twenty-one high-explosive and more than 10,000 incendiary bombs; later, somebody carefully calculated that 59,386

1 From *Inside the Third Reich*, p. 289.

square metres of factory floor space were destroyed and 144,656 square metres were damaged. The Mauser weapons factory and some nearby workshops lost 37,661 square metres of factory space. The very important D.W.M. (Germany Weapons and Munitions Works) was hit by three very large bombs, possibly 2,000-pounders, and by one 4,000-pounder which did not explode. Other factories not so badly hit were: Arguswerke again, Elz Armourplating, Dürener Metalworks, Borsigwalde Oxygen, Siemens and Halske (radar sets), Dornier Aircraft, B.M.W. motors, some railway repair workshops and the Tegel Gasworks. It was a goodly haul of valuable industrial destruction, and all because Flying Officer Haynes, operating the H2S set in his Lancaster, mistook his route over Berlin.

The statistics for the night are: housing – 981 buildings destroyed, 6,347 seriously and 55,000 slightly damaged; casualties – 470 killed, 2,091 injured and 25,000 bombed out. The much lower figures for housing and for casualties on this night are due to the less dense nature of the area bombed. If it had not been for the unexpected bonus of the war-industry damage, this raid would be classed as having been a near failure. Ninety-two of the dead are reported to have been in a shelter underneath a large corner block of flats when an R.A.F. bomber crashed on to the building.

Thus ended three raids in five nights which would turn out to be Berlin's greatest bombing ordeal in the war. The diligent city officials eventually compiled a comprehensive set of statistics covering those five nights, including the two small Mosquito raids. The report was completed on 24 January 1944; it was only for official use, of course, but it survived the war. It listed the number of bombs dropped, then, district by district, the damage to buildings, damage to flats, human casualties and the numbers of people bombed out. A total of 8,701 buildings containing 104,613 individual flats/apartments were completely destroyed. The total number of people killed is given as 4,330, but this does not appear to include the 105 people crushed to death in the panic at the air-raid shelter at Neukölln. The numbers killed include 574 people whose bodies were never recovered from the ruins, and the deaths are also known to include 157 foreign workers, 79 servicemen, 54 policemen and 26 prisoners of war. Over 400,000 people were bombed out. The district of Tiergarten, which contains the sub-district of Moabit, is at the head of every table. This was an area situated immediately west of the city centre, containing a large number of streets of flats – but good-quality flats, the smartest shopping areas in Berlin and the large open space of the Tiergarten Park. It was similar in character to London's West End and had the misfortune to lie in the path of the bombers every time they approached the city from the west.

The Battle of Berlin was not yet won, but the first success in it had been gained. Two questions may be asked: how did this success compare with other 'battles', and what were the chances of Bomber Command gaining complete victory at Berlin as the winter progressed? To answer the first question, Berlin had undoubtedly been hit hard. The contributions from survivors will show how the city's services were overwhelmed. Fires in private housing were not tackled by the public fire services. The relief and evacuation services could not cope with the bombed-out people; no official help was seen in the bombed streets in the day between the two heaviest raids. The hospitals rapidly filled with wounded, and many people had to wait for treatment.

But, to gauge the true degree of success, one must study the effects of fire and compare the recent raids on Berlin with those on other cities. The area badly hit on the two evenings of 22 and 23 November measured roughly ten miles by seven miles. Most of the 2,720 fires recorded in Berlin were in this area, but the area was too large, the streets were too wide and the buildings too soundly constructed. Individual buildings hit by incendiary bombs often burnt out, despite the effort of the householders. But there were very few examples of fire spreading from a building on fire to an undamaged one next door or across the street. The Bomber Command successes in the battles of the Ruhr and Hamburg were gained because fire spread from house to house and from street to street. This hardly ever happened in Berlin and probably never would, however concentrated the bombing. Bomber Command was going to have to burn Berlin out house by house. Moreover, although the bombing had been concentrated, it had not been concentrated enough. The bomb loads had been heavy but not heavy enough. At Hamburg and in the Ruhr, bomb loads which were greater in total (because of the shorter distance to the target) had been dropped into much smaller areas than the ten-by-seven-mile main bombing area at Berlin. That bombing area at Berlin had certainly had great chunks of property torn out of it, the shells of the buildings now standing like black skeletons, but there had been complete destruction nowhere, and the gapped nature of the damage would make it more difficult for Bomber Command to set fire to Berlin when the battle was resumed; those burnt-out buildings would act as fire-breaks.

Behind the statistics there were a myriad of personal experiences and just a few of these can be described here, in the words of the ordinary Berliners. I spent ten days in Berlin, talking with people who volunteered to help. It was hard work; the Berliner is a great talker, and I had to listen to hours of conversation and then make sure that I had my interpreter's translation correct for the few paragraphs I needed in each case. But it was a valuable experience because not only was I talking to a cross-section of the people in the worst bombed area but I was actually in that area for much of the time, with people who were often still living in the same flat as in 1943. I was taken down to see the basement in which they sheltered; I was shown where the incendiary bomb came through the roof; I was taken to the window and shown the place along the street where a block had collapsed, killing so many people. I came to realize what a Target Indicator looked like from underneath, how the make-up of the R.A.F. bomb loads contributed to the success of a raid, how high-explosive bombs cut water mains, cratered or blocked streets with rubble to stop the passage of fire-engines and forced firefighters to stay under cover during a raid, how 4,000-pounders blew off tiles and allowed the 4-pound incendiaries to lodge in roofs instead of clattering down into the street, and how the same 4,000-pounders smashed windows and allowed in air to fuel the fires, how 30-pound incendiaries penetrated to lower floors so that a flat could burn from the bottom upwards and from the top downwards at the same time, eventually to burn out, the roof and floors falling in, leaving only an empty shell which no amount of wartime repair could make habitable. I learnt of the great fear the civilians had of two elements in the attack: the blast effects of 4,000-pounder *Luftminen* which could crush the lungs, and the eleven pounds of phosphorus contained in the 30-pound incendiaries, partly as an 'anti-morale' weapon. The Germans were terrified of this phosphorus, the fire of which could not be put out by water and the burns from which were almost impossible to treat.[1]

And so, let me present the best of the personal accounts from these days, or rather nights. The contributions are all from what the Germans called 'the double blow', the raids in the evenings of 22 and 23 November; those well remembered nights took their prominent place in Berlin's history. The accounts reflect, with one exception, the balance of the population inhabiting Berlin at that time. There were Flak troops, a few men in essential positions, some soldiers on leave, two foreigners, a lot of young women without chil-

1 The British Official History fails to mention the 30-pound incendiary with its phosphorus in a five-page survey of wartime bombs (Vol. IV, pp. 31–5), but Sir Arthur Harris did not shrink from writing about it and its 'marked effect upon the morale of the enemy' in his book *Bomber Offensive* (p. 162).

dren.[1] But one large element of Berlin's 1943 population is not represented, because the old people of 1943 have since died.

Many people commented how the Flak batteries did not open fire when the bombers arrived over Berlin on the first night. There was thick cloud over the city, and it was a familiar tactic to restrain the guns in the hope that the bombers were unsure of their position and would fly on further. Leutnant Heinz von der Hayde was Fire Control Officer at a Flak command post in the west of Berlin whose four batteries were well within the range of the bombers being tracked by radar.

The batteries were ringing me up, begging for permission to fire. But, because of the thick cloud, 1st Flak Division at the Zoo Flak tower ordered an absolute restriction. I called up my local headquarters; that was Flak Regiment 5, but they said we could only fire when the bombs started dropping. So then I called 1st Flak Division again and asked them the same question but I got the same reply, 'Permission to fire will only be given when the first bombs fall.'

   Then a very strange thing happened. Reports came in from the batteries that the first markers were coming through the clouds; the reports said that the markers were actually dropping through the clouds and turning the clouds green and red. So I called Division again, and asked for permission to fire. The men out at the batteries were very angry at not being allowed to open fire and, on the other hand, Division and Regiment were very annoyed. They repeated, 'You can fire only when bombs are dropping, not markers. Don't play the lawyer with your fine differentiations.' But the bombs started a few seconds later and the gunners were happy that they could open up. They shot so fast that the barrels got red hot

1 Married names are shown in the Acknowledgements.

and they could only handle the guns with asbestos gloves. We had to resupply each battery with 900 rounds the next day and nearly every barrel had to be changed. Some were bent with the heat; others had the rifling worn out. Division told us later that we had shot down seventeen bombers over the Berlin area.

By the next night, we knew the bombers were able to find the city, even through thick cloud, and we were allowed to open fire as soon as we had them on radar.

Heinrich Möller was a *Flakhilfer*, one of the thousands of German boys who combined school lessons and gun drill by day with helping to serve the Flak batteries by night. He was manning a range-finder for the Zoo Flak Tower gun battery; his position was not on the main tower but on the smaller control tower nearby. The towers were right in the middle of the bombing area.

The bombers were reported near Hanover and their course was directly aimed at Berlin, almost directly at us in the Zoo Flak towers. When they reached Stendal, we received orders to hold our fire. The guns were following the incoming bombers, all loaded, but not firing. That made us very nervous. The guns eventually reached maximum elevation; we knew then that the bombers must be directly over us. There was this deathly silence over the whole city.

Then we ducked. There was this horrible shrieking, the like of which I have never heard before, as the hail of bombs came down on to us. They seemed to fall all over the surrounding area at once. There were thousands of incendiaries; a whole lot of them fell on top of both our tower and the gun tower, about 300 on each. Across at the gun tower, it looked just like a firework display. There were at least ten just near me; I was lucky not to be hit by one. We threw most of them over the edge. We had two gunners killed on the gun tower. One had his head bashed in by an incendiary bomb falling right on top of his steel helmet; that scattered his brains. The other one was hit by an incendiary bomb on the shoulder. I think that was the only time we had men killed on the top.

After this inferno of incendiary bombs came the high explosives and then the whole area round us was on fire, getting redder and redder as far as I could see. Then a small hurricane of wind came; it was so fierce that we had to tie ourselves to the rails to avoid being blown over the edge. Over on the gun tower they had to give up firing because the wind was so strong and also because a phosphorus bomb dropped right in among the electrical equipment and put the Giant *Würzburg* radar out of action. That only left the other two Flak towers; they got all the medals that night.

Günther Lincke was another *Flakhilfer*. His battery position was near the Olympic Stadium.

We picked up a target coming in. Through my headphones, I was ordered to elevate the gun. The elevation was set electrically and my job was to keep the manual dial exactly on the electrical dial. My school friend had to do the same for the line of sight. Pjotr, our Russian loader, already had the shell in the breech, ready to fire. Unteroffizier Sturmegger, who came from Vienna, pulled the firing cord – one round every eight seconds. We kept on firing but then there was the dull clang of a bell. What had happened? Someone had allowed a shell to hit the tower of the stadium and strike the bell which had called the youth of the world to the Olympic Games in 1936. The 'someone' was me. I had allowed the elevation of the gun to drop too low. The barrel had knocked away the wooden wall which would have stopped us firing in that direction.

My battery commander was nearly disciplined for this mistake, but he was deemed not responsible for the error of a high-school boy who was a keener artilleryman than a Latin student.

During the fighting in Berlin at the end of the war, the bell tower was destroyed. The bell itself was recovered and today it stands beside the main entrance to the stadium, still with a hole in it from an 88-millimetre shell. The angle of the hole in the bell is the same angle at which we were firing on 22 November – 24·25 degrees.

Turning now to the civilians, the first of the two bad raids, coming early in the evening, found many people out and about. Léon Butticaz, a French forced worker, and some friends heard news of the bombers' approach on the radio and left their camp (at Schönholz Park), hoping to travel by *S-Bahn* to find a better shelter than those in the camp. But the trains stopped running just as they reached the station.

All the lights went out. Everyone ran in panic down the street to any shelter they could find. My friends – two Frenchmen and three Poles – kept together. We could hear voices in the dark and see the shapes of people. We didn't want to go back to the camp so we followed the three Poles towards some trenches they knew in a patch of waste ground near by.

A long, slow, gloomy, throbbing noise, like organ crescendos, broke the silence – the engines of the first wave of bombers. It was a sinister sound. Then we saw a multitude of bright lights coming through the cloud, like bunches of grapes of different colours, and our whole area became as bright as day. Hardly thirty seconds later, a young army officer and his wife or girlfriend came running across to the trench holding hands. These two, like us, arrived out of breath and stood in the entrance, chatting in German and looking at the lit-up clouds. I could see their faces perfectly in the light; they were only young.

We waited, in a perpetual torment of anxiety. All of a

sudden there was the sensation of a violent blast of wind blowing the trees, then a crushing sensation. It was the bombs. We threw ourselves to the floor of the trench and huddled together, the German officer and his girl all mixed up with us foreigners. A series of heavy blows hammered the ground, just like an earthquake. Soil trickled through the planks of the shelter walls and roof, just like sand in an hourglass; it went down our necks. Blasts of hot air struck us, whipping our faces, blowing our hair about and going up the legs and sleeves of our clothes. Through the half-open door we could see that the dark of the night had given way to a bright orange red glow in the distance. The young German woman in the officer's arms was trembling with fear and sobbing and some people were overcome with a sudden bout of diarrhoea.

Ellen Slottgo was a student.

It was my nineteenth birthday and I had skipped college. It was miserable, travelling a long way there each day and then working at serious and difficult technical studies, coming home cold and then waking up the next morning still cold. There wasn't much fun. I remember one girl in my class suddenly shouting, 'I would give five years of my life for one good ball!' That was what it was like. I wish they had bombed the college.

So, I had set off that morning as though to go to college, but my friend Eva-Maria and I were not going to college; we were going to have a grand day out. We went to a cinema in the afternoon and then had something to eat. The food was pretty terrible but it was a treat to eat out. Then it was time to go home. I had tickets for an early performance of the opera. I was going to go there with another friend, Ursula, and my cousin Fritz who was a cavalry officer passing through Berlin from the Eastern Front. The opera was *Tosca*. We had good seats and everything was fine.

The alarm sounded as we were on our way home, changing trains at the Nollendorf Platz Underground Station. The trains all stopped and we were ordered into the shelter on the lowest platform. We were right in the middle of the bombing area. The room was shaking; it was almost like sitting on a swing. Ursula was very frightened; she kept saying that she knew something was happening at home. Fritz was calm of course.

We came out at the end of the raid. The trains weren't running, so we went up to the street level. We tried both exits but we could see nothing but fire on both sides. I hadn't heard the word 'firestorm' until then, but that's what it was. I saw masses of sparks and burning particles being carried along in the wind; it made it look as though the air was burning. I think that if Fritz had not been there we might have done something silly and gone out into that storm, but he knew what to do. Someone must have announced that there would be no more trains that night, so we set off to walk along the underground track. I remember it was very tiring, stepping from one sleeper to the next – we were dressed for the opera and certainly didn't have the right shoes for walking along a railway. They were my best shoes, low heels, flat pumps, black patent with some suede at the front and your foot just slid in. They were my Confirmation shoes.

We walked for three kilometres before coming up. When we got to Ursula's house the roof was on fire and Ursula was very upset. All the people were working hard, getting their belongings out into the courtyard. Everything was a mess but no one was saying anything; that seemed strange. Ursula's parents were safe. We helped them as much as we could, then Fritz and I set out to walk home.

There wasn't much damage at home but the electricity was cut off. Mother was sitting up with a candle, very worried about me. We had planned to have a little birthday supper after the opera. We didn't have much of an appetite, but I remember we sat round this table – the very same table that you are writing your notes on – and ate this little snack.

It was back to school next morning. I found then that Eva-Maria had lost her home. She had a favourite dress; we called it the 'daisy dress' and I asked her about it. 'Oh yes,' she said, 'I saved the daisy dress.' Every place I went to on that day of my birthday was destroyed that night: the flats of both of my friends, the cinema and the Opera House; that was something that made me very sad. Fritz, the cavalry officer, disappeared in the last weeks of the war; both of his brothers were killed as well.

Karl de Haas was a Dutch teacher who gave private tuition to the children of wealthy families. He had just given a joint lesson to the daughter of the manager of the Berlin branch of Opel and to another boy whose first lesson this was. He was taking this new boy to his parents' home when the raid started. Their journey by underground train was halted at the Kaiserdamm Station.

All the passengers were ordered to go to the passage connecting the lowest platforms. We heard a faint and dull roar, like a roll of thunder, and the earth seemed to tremble and rock. The people in the passage turned pale and some began to cry and moan. Then they brought some wounded people down and the crying got louder. One girl had a bandage round her lower jaw; she was absolutely soaked with blood and shocked by her injury. She kept shouting for an apple but one of the people who brought her in told us not to give her an apple because a bomb splinter had taken off the lower part of her jaw.

My pupil now began to cry, seeing all the despair around him. He was terrified and became worse and worse. I was not able to stop him crying so I gave him a spanking; that gave him a real reason to cry. After some time he stopped and did as I told him. We were told when the All Clear siren went but, on reaching the street, we found burning and demolished houses everywhere

and the air suction made it very dangerous. I took my
pupil by the hand and began to hurry along the
Bismarckstrasse. A light rain was falling and this was
blown about by the wind and mixed with the ashes and
the brick dust from the ruined houses to become a silty
mud in the street. We tried to hurry – I wanted to get my
pupil home – but we could only make slow progress.

When I reached the boy's home, his father's butcher's
shop and flat were not damaged. I took my pupil in and
found the boy's mother sitting in the office. I told her we
were back but she fainted; I don't think she believed her
son would return. She had been listening to the radio and
knew that we had been in the bombing. The boy's father
was an old soldier of the First World War and he came in,
having been fighting a fire in the next house; he also
looked surprised to see his son. I told him we had found
our way home and also that I had been forced to give the
son a spanking.

Most people were at home when the raid started and
went down to the basement shelters under their blocks of
flats. Else Wolter was a book-keeper who lived with her
parents on the Hansaplatz, an elegant area close to the
Tiergarten Park. Her parents were out of town, at their
summer home to escape the raids, but she had come back
to visit a friend on her birthday.

I was just having a cup of coffee before setting off when
the alarm went. I was frightened. Most of the raids were
late at night when you were asleep, but being awake this
time I had more time to become afraid. I gathered
together my personal documents and packed them into a
little case with an eiderdown, some coffee and meat, and
a tablecloth which my sister and I had embroidered, it
was an old favourite. We had a good shelter in the cellar.
It had a curved roof from olden times and was
particularly strong. There were about twenty families

there, mostly women, only one child and only about six or eight men.

The first bombs must have been incendiaries because the air-raid warden came down shouting to a family living in the second storey that their flat was on fire and they should go and fight it. The man and woman and all the other men went up but, when they got there, the blast of a *Luftmine* which fell about 800 metres away blew in the doorway of the hall. The glass in the door caught the lady in the face; she lost an eye and the other eye was injured. The cellar started to become very smoky and it was difficult to breathe, but we were able to go up then because the All Clear sounded.

I was a bit dazed because of the smoke. We couldn't get out to the courtyard at first because burning debris and beams were falling from above, but we eventually made our way out into the street where all the houses were on fire on the fronts; the fires had taken hold very quickly. We found that in our house an incendiary bomb had come all the way through to the ground-floor flat. The lady of that flat had a big store of coal and coke and timber in the cellar underneath; they were coal merchants and there was some valuable anthracite imported from England before the war. I found out later that the coal burned for three months.

We ran to the open area of the Hansa Platz and took shelter under a large stone bridge over the River Spree; we felt much safer there. There were about fifty of us. I kept vomiting every few minutes all through the night because of the smoke I had inhaled. We lost absolutely everything in our house; all I saved was the tablecloth and those other things I took to the cellar. I had a black woollen coat on and later found that the outer part had been badly scorched. My orange pullover was all black, but a good woollen hat which I had pulled down over my head kept my head safe. A neighbour's little boy attached himself to me, holding on to my dress. He hung on all night. He was crying at first, but was quiet when his parents turned up later, carrying their suitcases.

Renate Nigmann, a young secretary, had just come home from playing table tennis.

We had to go down to the cellar. We put the supper into the oven. It is still perfectly clear in my mind because it was venison, one of my favourite dishes. We put on our warm clothes and took our small air-raid suitcase and a book to read, probably one of my travel books. I remember all this clearly because those were the last memories of my home. We all had our own regular seats in the shelter. We sat there, with our little cases and our hot coffee or tea, because there was no heating in the shelter. It is difficult to describe one's feelings – somewhere between anxiety and hope. Sometimes someone would try to cheer things up with a little joke, specially for the children, but really, you couldn't do anything except listen for the bombs and hope that you would be spared.

The bombing was so heavy on this night that we dared not leave the shelter when the fires started. Bombs were coming down all around us and then we heard the moaning of a *Luftmine* coming down, not the whistling sound of the ordinary high-explosive bombs; the blast blew dust and sand into the shelter, even though the steel door was firmly closed. Our house was also hit by several incendiaries.

Eventually, we decided that we should try to get out. We knew that the house next door had collapsed; we couldn't open the connecting door into its cellar. If our house, which we knew was on fire, and the one on the other side collapsed as well, we would be trapped. So we decided to go; we were directed by the warden through the openings in the wall. Some of the exits were blocked but we managed to get out into the street. Our house was well alight, the burning beams in the roof were falling down inside, into the next floor, the fire spreading steadily downwards. It was all inside; there were not many flames to be seen, only a deep glow from the fire inside. But when the fire reached the ground floor where my mother's grocery shop was, the provisions caught fire – things like oil, butter, fat and sugar. Then the big windows smashed and fierce flames leapt out and roared upwards.

The burning things in the house and the interior walls must have all collapsed into the cellar after that because, when we went back some days later, there was my piano, upside down in the cellar, with all the insides hanging out. If we hadn't got out when we did, we would all have been killed.

We gathered in some little gardens near by. No one was doing any firefighting; it was too dangerous for householders to go into the houses and the fire brigade couldn't get to us because of the rubble in the streets. We could only stand and watch helplessly as our home completely burnt down. I will never, ever, forget that picture of giant flames roaring out of the shop windows.

That night changed all of our lives. It wasn't just the material loss. There was the problem of finding a new home; my father caught pneumonia; my mother was in shock. We got a few things together but then got bombed out again. After that we moved our remaining possessions out to Thuringia, but the Russians got those. My twin brother died as a soldier. All our troubles seemed to follow that night.

Alice Wawrzyniak was a nineteen-year-old typist.

I was ill in bed with a high fever which turned out to be diphtheria. We never went into the shelter; we had a ground-floor flat with no proper basement. I stayed in bed. There were some high-explosive bombs near by and the windows blew in, quite violently; the curtains came in too. I wasn't frightened; we'd had all that before. We had

some sheets of cardboard all ready in case this happened.
I tried to put these up over the broken windows. Mother
was up in the attic with some of the other families,
fighting incendiary bombs. But they couldn't put them
out and she came down and told me to get dressed at
once and stop that nonsense of putting up the cardboard.

We talked it over with some friends and we decided
that we should all leave. We couldn't imagine that we
would never come back. We assumed that the fire brigade
would soon be round and put the fire out. We just could
not believe that it was so bad everywhere. We just
thought an odd house here and there had been hit, as in
earlier raids, but then someone went out into the street
and came back a few seconds later reporting that there
were fires everywhere. Mother got some wet towels and
we wrapped these round our mouths and noses, because
of the acrid smoke and the sparks out in the street. We
managed to walk along to a house at the end which was
not on fire. My mother rang the bell of one of the flats
and asked for a glass of water for me because I was so ill.
They took us in. There was a loud and jolly party going
on with music, because a Knight's Cross man was home
on leave. It was amazing.

They let me have a bed in a little room; people were
usually willing to help in those circumstances. Mother
went back to our home three times to fetch some of our
belongings but I went to sleep. Next morning, I was so ill
that I never thought to thank those people for their help.

Gerda Ganschow, a sales lady at a printer's, took shelter
in the Humboldthain Park Flak tower.

I lived alone. Dinner was ready but not yet eaten. I put it
on the top of the stove; it was rabbit, a nice one. I ran to
the shelter and got there before the raid started. The
place was packed and I had to sit on the floor. It was so
stoutly built that you couldn't hear anything, maybe it just
shook a little. It was completely safe and it wasn't until

they let you out at the end that you knew what sort of raid it had been.

When we did come out, it was just fire and smoke all over the place from the houses around. There was a lot of wind and I had to walk down the middle of the street. I had a fur coat on; I had only had it for two months. My boss had loaned me the money to buy it; he was going to deduct it from my future pay. I was walking with my arms around my face when someone grabbed me, pulled me down and rolled me along the ground. I screamed; I thought someone was robbing me, but he said, 'Lady, you are on fire. You are stupid; you should have worn the coat inside out.' So, I had lost my coat and I hadn't even paid for it properly. When I got home I found that our house was the only one still standing but the windows had been blown in and the rabbit I had ready for supper was decorated with glass. I couldn't eat it.

But the houses on both sides were on fire and the caretaker came and told me I had to get my possessions out because there was no chance of the house surviving. We started to take what we could down to the hall but then someone in a uniform came and ordered us back to the shelter. He said it would be safer there with the fires all around us. Back in the Flak tower, everything was working well. The field kitchen was there and we got some soup and some sandwiches.

We stayed in the tower all the next day. I went out several times to have a look. There were no fire-engines; they just let the fires burn themselves out in that area.

There was another raid the next night and they got our house this time. There was one old lady who was too old to get to the shelter and no one seemed to be able to help her. She was killed. When I went to see my home later, the whole building had collapsed. The only thing I found belonging to me was the twisted name-plate which had marked our flat.

My boss was very good. He gave me two weeks' holiday, let me off the money he had lent me for the fur coat and

gave me 200 Reichsmarks. Later, the post-war
Government gave me an official compensation of 500
Deutschmarks for losing my home – it was nothing, like a
penny in a bucket.

Wilma Hauck was a schoolgirl whose parents had managed to keep her at home when her school was evacuated.

The blast blew me into the basement. It was the first time
I had felt them so near. Everyone was praying; even the
Russians who had come in. I was squatted down on my
knees, with my head down, just like a foetus; I
instinctively, like an animal almost, felt that was the safest
position.

   As soon as the bombs finished, Papa Schülke, the old
retired policeman who was the house warden, and I went
up the stairs; I, the sixteen-year-old schoolgirl, was his
deputy. It was our duty to see if there were any fires. We
went out, round to the back of the block. The front and
one side wing were on fire in the roof and the top floor.
My first thought was that we needed help to get water
and I went back to the cellar and told everyone who was
able to hold a bucket to come and help. They all came,
even the Russians, because most of the women had
treated them well, giving them extra food and cigarettes
because their rations were so small.

   At first, the taps were running and we were able to
make a chain of buckets. Papa Schülke had to leave to
report to the local police post, leaving me, the schoolgirl
with a steel helmet and overalls, in charge. We found
what we thought was the most dangerous fire and we got
on well to start with, although I got wet through because
the Russians were so enthusiastic passing the buckets to
me. Then I noticed something I will always remember,
something was dripping down the wall, burning so
fiercely with a bright white light. It seemed so unrealistic,
I think it was phosphorus – the water made no
impression on it. It was about then that the water

pressure started to drop and I realized that we had no chance of putting out the fire.

I managed to get a few items of furniture out, but then, down in the street, I saw something I thought was impossible. There were two or three lorry loads of soldiers and some firemen. And what were they doing? Trying to save the building over the road. It was the office building of the Arbeitsfront, the party organization which took the place of the trade unions that had been disbanded before the war. There were only offices filled with papers.

I shouted out, 'What are you doing there? What about saving our house, not all that paper?' One of the officers called back, 'Boy, come here!' I told him I wasn't a boy. He gave me just one Hitler Youth boy and a hose-pipe, a size C hose, the biggest size of all. It was pumping water out of the River Spree. The boy and I worked for the rest of the night with that hose, taking it in turns to hold it, and we managed to put the fire out. I was delighted that we had saved our flat. My mother took me into her arms. It was a wonderful feeling. The Arbeitsfront burnt down; burning papers were floating all over the place. The boy did well; I never asked his name.

But all our work was wasted. The whole building was destroyed on the next night when Mother and I were away visiting some friends in the next street. Eight of the people in our flats were killed, including poor old Papa Schülke who was squashed flat by a heavy door. That was a terrible night.

This lady was in tears at the end of the interview.

Horst Hartwich was at his parents' home. The men and some women had to give up fighting a fire in the upper part of the flats.

We went back down to the shelter and told the people that, barring a miracle, the house would burn down. So most of the people came out and started rescuing their

belongings. Several other houses were burning and the
street was full of smoke. That smoke was the worst; it bit
your eyes – that and the smell of burning wood. It was
psychological, very depressing, that smoke and the smell
of burning. There was a sports ground behind the house
and there must have been between fifty and a hundred
fire-bombs there, all burning with a bright, fierce white
light. I had never seen them before, only in training
films. But it wasn't like the films at all – much more
frightening, much more lively.

It was just like moving house. We took out the parakeet
first and then all the carpets because they were valuable
and also easy to move. Then we took the chairs and table,
then the beds, dismantling them. We didn't think the
whole street would burn down, someone would surely
find room for us. We wanted to have a bed at least. Those
were the basics. Then we took some china, already
packed in a case, some paintings and some valuable
books. Those were things that we could not replace.

That took about three hours. We put it all in the
middle of the street. The fire was slowly working its way
down the house; no one was fighting it. The water mains
were broken and the emergency water tank was empty by
now. The street was full of people, some helping, but a
lot of them just watching. Some of them were crying and
screaming, but we were happy. My father was Jewish and,
for the first time, those Nazis were being hit. The only
one I felt sorry for was an old blind man who sat in the
middle of the street, on a chair among the belongings
they had saved, while his home burned down. That
picture, of that old, helpless, blind creature in the
firestorm, made me feel very sad. Another scene I
remember was that of a man who was beating his wife
horribly, with his fists. I don't know why; probably it was
a sign of his nervousness. That was just one street; there
would be the same scenes in many other parts of our
area.

Ursula Reimann, convalescent from an attack of infantile paralysis, lived in a large flat with her mother and her grandfather, who was an architect.

When the All Clear sounded, Mother went up and found that the upper two storeys were on fire and that burning phosphorus was running down the stairs. The whole place was full of smoke. Mother was so dazed that she only saved some shoe boxes containing some silverware. That was all we saved from that expensive, five-roomed flat. Herr Pohl, the air-raid warden, came then and told us that we had to get out because the house could not be saved. I could only take small steps, because of the paralysis, but managed to get down to the street.

All around, every house in the street was ablaze and there was so much smoke that we could hardly breathe. Then a storm started, sucking at our bodies, and we had to hold on to each other for safety. We managed to get round the corner into the Ranke Platz where there was a large restaurant, the Zigeuner Baron, which had not been hit. A lot of people gathered there. Everyone was covered in black soot and I felt so helpless with my handicap that I couldn't stop crying. Mother was in shock and could do nothing. Grandfather tried to quieten me. He told me he would repair the windows of the flat and that everything would be all right again. But then there was a big crash round the corner. We knew exactly what it was; our flats had collapsed.

We were in that restaurant all that night and the next day. People were wandering around aimlessly, not knowing what to do. No one came to help us in our area at all. I heard that the officials had decided to concentrate all their efforts on saving the Kaiser Wilhelm Memorial Church. I thought that was insane, but you dare not say anything. You always thought the next person to you was a police informer.

It wasn't until late afternoon that some strangers came and told us that there were some people in the Ranke

Strasse who would be willing to take me in for a night or
two.

Ingeborg Spie, whose husband was a soldier in Denmark,
was with her new baby in the basement shelter under her
parents' flat. The reader might like to contrast her description of what happened that night with the photograph
showing this lady and other carefree young women carrying out fire-fighting training (see photograph number 8).

We heard the first bombs and counted them – one, two,
three. That last one hit the house next door and we
waited for number four. It never came; but we could
hear the clattering of the incendiary bombs. There was
dust everywhere. The other women, all older than me,
started crying and some of them were praying.
    When the alarm ended, I went up to the flat first to put
the baby to bed, then I went outside. The houses all
around were burning in the upper storeys. There was
only our house on one side and two houses opposite
which were not on fire. We got the old people into the
three undamaged houses where they were making tea
and coffee. They were shaking all over and some were
badly burned. I was very upset when a married couple, a
nice, elderly couple I had made friends with while in the
park with my baby, were trapped in their flat on the
second floor and jumped because there were fires above
and below them. They fell close to me; it was a noise you
cannot describe, when people splash down like that; they
lay there like broken dolls. They were the first dead
people I had ever seen. There were thirty or forty people
who were hurt. I had a first-aid kit; but it was soon used
up. When all the bandages were gone, I tore up
bedsheets. People were trying to get their belongings out
into the street so I helped them. We put everything on
the pavement near those three houses that were not
burning. No one could fight the fire; there was no water
in the taps. It was a nightmare.

We worked like that the whole day and, by evening, we were dog tired. We were desperate for a good night's sleep but then another raid came. They got us this time. The last three undamaged houses in the street were hit and burned out.

Gerhard Hansa was an official at an important war factory.

We breathed a sigh of relief that our area was spared on the first night, but we were hit the next night. I wasn't in the Army or any party organization but I had to do something, so I was the house warden. It was a four-storey block with twenty-four apartments and about sixty people in all. We had no basement shelters because the basements were being lived in. We had to go to a good, concreted shelter in the cellars of a nearby market hall. We shared this with the families from two other blocks; it was a very large gathering. There were three Jewish families who were not allowed to go into this shelter. The horse-stable cellar where they should have gone was too wet, so I allowed them to stay in their flats, although I would have been in trouble if the police had found out. They survived the bombing but they disappeared in May 1944, deported to Poland.

My post was with seven other men in a special outer room with double steel doors which separated the main shelter from the street. It was useful, because we could smoke there; it wasn't allowed in the main shelter. It was my duty to stay under cover but to keep watch outside. We had to keep the outer door open for this. Looking up, I saw all around these 'Christmas trees' – bright red. I was frightened then; I knew it would be our district which was for it.

We closed the outer door and were still going down the stairs when the first bomb exploded just outside. I can remember it as though it was yesterday. I am pleased that these things are being recorded, because the younger generation do not know about them and they should be written down. There was a hell of a bang and the lights went out. We eight men all huddled together. Then we scrambled through to the main room and managed to close the heavy fastenings – just in time, because the next bomb hit directly over that outer room and blew an army lorry standing above it down into the chamber we had just left. We would all have been killed.

All hell broke loose. The main shelter was specially strengthened with pieces of timber, actually tree trunks, holding the roof up. I flung my arms around one of those trees because of the dreadful concussion. We were scared stiff of those *Luftminen*. Then some smoke came in, I don't know how, and the women and children started to scream. I had to shout to get order in this chaos, telling them to wet their handkerchiefs and hold them over their mouths. Because the main exit was blocked, everyone had to get out through one narrow gap in the wall through to some more cellars and then on to another exit. Because I feared a crush, I made everyone stand in a queue, a thing German people don't normally do, but everyone behaved like children in this situation and did as they were told.

Eventually we got everyone out. I was the last, climbing over heaps of rubble. I found that most of the people had disappeared, many of them running off to a place where there were some open trenches and they were huddled together in these. The All Clear had not yet sounded. A cow stall had been hit and the cows were running around, some of them falling into the trenches.

My wife was not there. I was desperate to find her; she had gone out of the shelter ahead of me. I went to our home first. The houses on both sides had been hit and were on fire from the roofs to the cellars. I went on to where there was a collection place. The fires were so strong that the air being pulled into the burning houses was buffeting me from one side to the other. I passed some people who were trying to get their belongings out but there were already some looters there, helping themselves to the stuff that had been brought down into the street. It seems impossible that people could steal the last belongings of fellow human beings just bombed out. I didn't stop; I just wanted to find my wife. I looked into the basement of a church where there were people sheltering. My wife was not there but an elderly couple from my block of flats were. They asked me what things were like outside. I hadn't the heart to tell them that their home was gone; I only said, 'Don't hope for too much.'

It took me hours to find her. She was at the flat of an acquaintance. We just fell into each other's arms; neither of us could say a single word. We had lost everything but, it's funny, I couldn't bring myself to throw away the keys to my flat.

8 THE NEW YEAR

Not one heavy bomber flew on operations for twelve nights from 4 December, because of a combination of full moon and bad weather. Even the Mosquitoes left Berlin alone. It was a time for Bomber Command to draw breath and for Sir Arthur Harris to consider how the campaign was progressing. He would have to wait until 20 December before receiving any reconnaissance photographs of Berlin, but there was sufficient information from other sources for him to realize that Berlin had been hit severely in the recent series of raids. There could have been no doubt in his mind that the battle must be resumed as soon as possible. Harris's doubts would have been over the ability of his squadrons to deliver sufficient tonnages of bombs to Berlin. Now that the Stirlings had been taken off operations to Germany, the problem of heavy casualty rates had transferred itself to the Halifax squadrons. Harris was obviously in two minds whether the Halifaxes should continue to be sent to Berlin at all. In a letter to the Air Ministry at this time he refers to 'the increasing difficulty of finding suitable targets and conditions for the Halifaxes'. The improved Mark III version of the Halifax was eagerly awaited, and the first two squadrons – 35 Squadron in 8 Group and 466 Squadron in 4 Group – would start operating these aircraft during the coming series of raids, but it would be several months before the entire Halifax force would be re-equipped.

Unfortunately for Harris, the strength of the Lancaster force remained static at this time, because of recent casualties, and no new Lancaster squadrons would become available in the coming period.

Harris was always vigorous at gathering in the aircraft, equipment and support for the task his squadrons faced. The story of the earlier subterfuge employed to obtain the H2S Mark III sets is a good example. A few more of these sets would soon start to come through by normal channels, but H2S Mark III was not to solve many problems. Another move by Harris had been to write to Churchill, on 3 November, stating in dramatic terms his case for persuading the Americans to join in the Battle of Berlin: 'We can wreck Berlin from end to end if the U.S.A.A.F. will come in on it. It will cost between us 400–500 aircraft. It will cost Germany the war.'[1] It was quite improper for Harris to communicate with the Prime Minister in this way. His letter should have gone to the Air Ministry, but he knew that Portal, whatever his private views on concentrating on Berlin, would be obliged, in any official correspondence, to defend the joint Allied decision about strategic bombing, and Berlin had no prominence in such plans. It is not known whether Harris's plea to Churchill was ever passed on to the Americans. Even if they had been willing to change their policy, which is unlikely, the Americans were in no tactical position to help. Their first deep daylight penetration raids in the autumn of 1943, without long-range fighter protection, had suffered heavy casualties. Less than three weeks before Harris's letter, on 14 October, 291 B-17s set out to make a second raid on the ball-bearing factories at Schweinfurt. Sixty of the bombers did not come back, and that was the end of the American theory about self-defending 'Flying Fortress' formations. They would have to abandon such distant raids for nearly five months. In his 3 November letter, Harris was perhaps hoping that the Americans would abandon daylight bombing and turn

1 British Official History, Vol. II, p. 190.

to night bombing, R.A.F. style, but this never happened, at least not in Europe.

Returning now to the run-up to the next series of raids, Harris realized that he had made a good start on the task of destroying Berlin, but that the bomb tonnage he could effectively deliver might fall. The Americans were not going to help; H2S Mark III was a disappointment; the Stirlings could no longer be used, and the Halifaxes were becoming a doubtful element; the Lancaster force was not growing. He composed a further letter, this time to the Air Ministry, pleading for increased production of the Lancaster. It was a well reasoned case, pointing out that the current production of Lancasters did little more than replace losses. To reinforce his case, he included statistics which showed the amount of destruction in German cities achieved with the tonnage of bombs so far dropped in the area-bombing offensive, and he projected forward what might be achieved by 1 April 1944 if he could keep up the monthly tonnage. He added the second of the famous statements he made at this time: 'From this [his calculations] it appears that the Lancaster force alone should be sufficient, but only just sufficient, to produce in Germany by April 1st 1944 a state of devastation in which surrender is inevitable.'[1] Harris never mentioned Berlin once in this long letter, because Berlin was not an Air Ministry priority target, but it was undoubtedly against Berlin that the Lancasters would be used.

Any increase in Lancaster production which this letter might produce could not arrive in time to affect the next monthly bombing period. Harris would have to continue the battle with no immediate reinforcement of either aircraft or equipment. The only consolation, if Harris had known it, was that the German night-fighter force was also stagnant in its development at this time. There was no expansion in the twin-engined night-fighter force, although several units were moved from bases in France

1 British Official History, Vol. II, pp. 54–7.

and Denmark and concentrated around Berlin. A new radar set, the *SN-2*, which could 'see' through Window, had at last been produced but in such small numbers that it would not yet affect either the German success rate or the development of tactics. The battle would resume after that twelve-night gap with both aerial contestants virtually unchanged in strength, but with the city of Berlin unlikely to be able to withstand another round of raids as damaging as the November ones.

Night of 16/17 December 1943

BERLIN 483 Lancasters and 15 Mosquitoes dispatched. Abortive sorties: 30, 6.2 per cent of those dispatched.

Time over target: 19.58 to 20.12. Approximate bombs on Berlin area: 1,773 tons – 925 high explosive, 848 incendiaries.

25 Lancasters were lost, 5.2 per cent of Lancasters dispatched, and 34 Lancasters were wrecked in collisions or crashes or abandoned by their crews in bad weather over England. Aircrew casualties in both missing and crashed aircraft: 294 killed, 14 prisoners of war, 7 interned in Sweden.

Other operations: 91 aircraft dispatched, 1 mine-laying aircraft lost.

Harris lost no time. On Thursday 16 December he ordered that Berlin should be attacked that night, but only by the Lancasters and Mosquitoes. It was almost a premature resumption; a three-quarter moon would appear later in the night. Steps were taken to avoid the effects of the moonlight; there was the earliest possible take-off time – soon

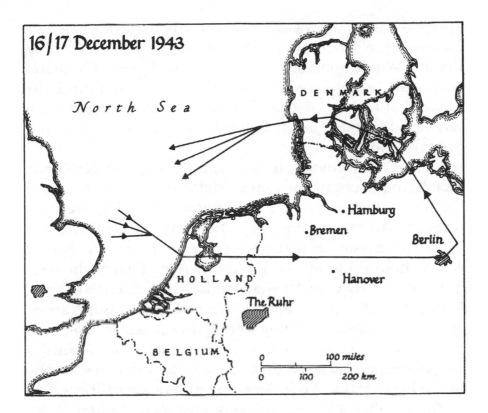

16/17 December 1943

North Sea

DENMARK

Hamburg

Bremen

Berlin

HOLLAND

Hanover

The Ruhr

BELGIUM

0   100 miles

0   100   200 km.

after 4.00 p.m. – and a direct route to Berlin, and then a long northerly return route over the Baltic and Denmark when the moon rose. These plans were helped by a weather report which forecast that the German night-fighter bases would be closed in with fog, but there was a fear that fog could also appear over the bomber airfields during the night. There were thus three dangerous elements present in this operation: the moon, the use again of a long, straight approach flight over Holland and Germany and the fog which might not appear over the German airfields but might descend over England.

There was obviously some anxiety and hesitation over these factors. The Met Officer at Bourn stated at briefing that he was sure the raid would be cancelled because of the possibility of fog. The diary of a Canadian pilot at Linton-on-Ouse shows that take-off time there was suddenly brought forward by twenty minutes, and his Lancaster took off without its full bomb load. But the operation went ahead. There was a bad start when two Lancasters collided and crashed near their airfield at Elsham Wolds and fourteen men were killed. The bombers soon broke through the low cloud and found the unusual situation, at this time of the year, of having a setting sun going down behind them as they flew out over the North Sea.

The Germans detected the approaching bomber force, identifying it as a major raid by detecting the emissions of the increasing number of H2S radar sets being used. As forecast, there was fog over the German airfields, but orders were issued that the most experienced night-fighter crews should attempt to go into action. Fifty-eight such crews took off. One Messerschmitt 110, of III/NJG 5 at Königsberg/Neumark, took off into the murk, but crashed at once, probably becoming iced up in the cloud. The crew were killed. The pilot was Oberleutnant Ulrich Wulff, a *Staffelkapitän*, described in an unofficial war diary as 'one of our best'. Many of the German fighters were directed on to the bomber stream, and long strings of fighter flares were seen from the Dutch coast all the way to Hanover. This was a disturbing feature for the British, a sign that the Germans were again extending their operations to the long routes to and from Berlin. A flurry of combats started as soon as the Dutch coast was crossed, and at least fourteen bombers were shot down on that section of the route. An account is available from Unteroffizier Fritz Rumpelhardt, who was radar operator in Oberleutnant Heinz-Wolfgang Schnaufer's crew of IV/NJG 1. Their Messerschmitt 110 took off from Leeuwarden into a cloud base of only thirty-five metres and climbed hard, but with its wings coating heavily with ice. 'The emergence into a radiantly star-studded sky at 5,000 metres caused us quickly to forget that dangerous climb.' They were in touch with the ground control in the local fighter box, named *Polar Bear* and were directed on to the bomber stream. Rumpelhardt does not say whether his aircraft was fitted with a new *SN-2* radar, but, since Schnaufer was one of the aces, it probably was.

Rumpelhardt picked up his first contact at a range of 4,000 metres. The aircraft was also fitted with the *schräge Musik* installation of two upward firing cannons, a device which allowed a night fighter to attack from the blind spot underneath a bomber. That first contact was swiftly shot down. It was the 7 Squadron Lancaster of Warrant Officer W. A. Watson; there were no survivors. The burning Target Indicators from this Pathfinder aircraft caused Schnaufer to believe that he had shot down a Master Bomber. This crew went on to shoot down three more bombers: an A.B.C. Lancaster of 101 Squadron, a Lancaster of 49 Squadron, then a Canadian Lancaster of 432 Squadron which spotted the fighter and nearly shook it off by vigorous corkscrewing. The relatively safe *schräge Musik* attack method normally allowed German pilots to shoot at the petrol tanks in a bomber's wings, starting a fire but allowing most of the bomber crew to survive by parachute, but there were no survivors in Schnaufer's first three victims and only four in the last.[1] The exultation of the German crew was now dampened by the need to descend through the cloud and find somewhere to land. Schnaufer decided to return to his home airfield. A radio bearing brought them to the approximate area, but four approaches were unsuccessful, Rumpelhardt stating that 'the nerves of the crew were stretched to breaking point, but then, a miracle, a hole in the cloud and Schnaufer put it down smartly' Schnaufer was later heard to say that never again would he take off in such conditions. Several aspects of Schnaufer's operation are significant: the usefulness of the SN-2 radar in enabling the Germans to operate on the bomber routes, the deadly effect of the upward firing *schräge Musik* and the ability of some of the German fighter crews to operate in the worst weather conditions; this all boded ill for Bomber Command fortunes as the Battle of Berlin progressed.

1 Details of Schnaufer's successes on this night were researched by a Dutch writer, Ab Jansen, for his book on wartime operations from Leeuwarden, *Wespennest Leeuwarden*.

The section of route from Hamburg to Berlin was quieter, although there was one incident which was a bad omen for the German night fighters. 141 Squadron, flying Beaufighters, had developed a device called Serrate which could home on to the emissions of the radar sets used by the German night fighters. The squadron had been operating near the bomber routes in this way for several months, gaining successes now and again, but only within the limited range of the Beaufighter. Now 141 Squadron had moved to West Raynham, to come into Bomber Command's newly formed 100 Group, and was starting to convert to Mosquitoes. Two Beaufighters and two Mosquitoes flying on this night represented the first of the Bomber Command Serrate operations, which would grow in intensity and effectiveness as the war progressed and prove a steady cause of irritation and loss to the German night-fighter force. The two Mosquitoes were ordered to ignore any Serrate contacts picked up over Holland and to press on through to the Berlin area. Squadron Leader Freddie Lambert and his set operator, Flying Officer Dear, picked up a contact near Berlin, and a long encounter followed. The German fighter, a Messerschmitt 110, was aware of the Mosquito's presence, and both aircraft jockeyed for position, partly visually and partly by radar. Several bursts of fire were exchanged. The Mosquito was not hit; Lambert claimed the Messerschmitt as damaged.

Conditions for the bombers on their arrival at Berlin were favourable. The German fighters, which had assembled at nearby Brandenburg, had not been sent to Berlin itself, because the controllers were worried that the approach flight to Berlin might be a feint before a turn-off to another target as had happened on the recent Leipzig raid. The Flak batteries were in action, but cloud was preventing the searchlights from reaching to the bombers' height. The German fighters were eventually committed to action over Berlin but they were too few and too late. Some half-hearted attacks on bombers took place in the closing minutes of the raid, but not one bomber was shot down by

Night-fighter attack methods

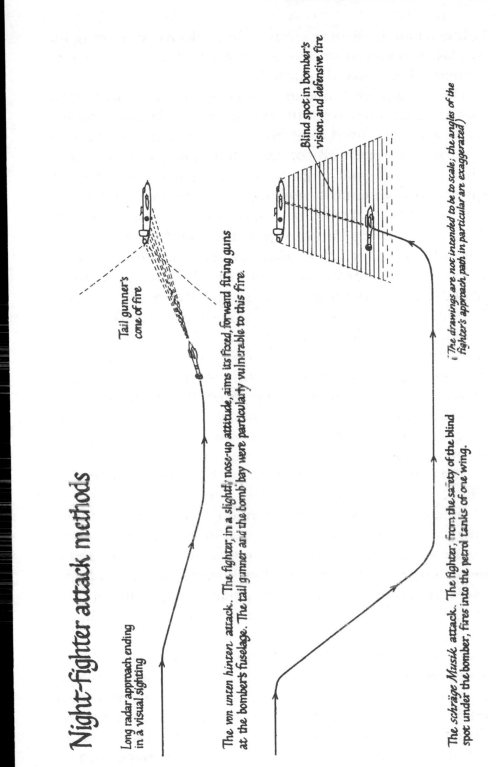

Long radar approach ending in a visual sighting

Tail gunner's cone of fire

The *von unten hinten* attack. The fighter, in a slightly nose-up attitude, aims its fixed, forward firing guns at the bomber's fuselage. The tail gunner and the bomb bay were particularly vulnerable to this fire.

Blind spot in bomber's vision and defensive fire

The *schräge Musik* attack. The fighter, from the safety of the blind spot under the bomber, fires into the petrol tanks of one wing.

(The drawings are not intended to be to scale; the angles of the fighter's approach path in particular are exaggerated) fighters. One Lancaster was seen to go down after being hit by Flak, and there were two collisions, with four Lancasters definitely being lost through this cause.

The Pathfinders came in exactly on time, and four H2S Mark III aircraft were among the Blind Markers which made what appeared to be good marking runs. The initial Skymarkers were well concentrated, and there was little wind, but later marking and bombing were observed to spread both west and east along the route through the target. The spread of the attack to the east, forward from the Aiming Point, was an unusual feature and a considerable bonus for Bomber Command, because few bombs had yet fallen in the eastern parts of the city. No useful bombing photographs were taken because of the cloud, and Bomber Command could only hope that this was a successful attack, although no big fire glow was seen. The German records show that it was an effective raid, not as severe as the November raids, but still a success for the bombers. The early markers fell about a mile short of and south of the centre of the city. The worst damage was caused in a rectangular area four miles long and about half as wide in the south-central area of the city.

The German records contain some interesting features. There were no large fires, partly due to a lack of concentration, partly because there were now many gaps of burnt-out property from earlier raids and partly because the weight of bombs dropped was not sufficient. Harris really needed those Halifaxes with their mainly incendiary bomb loads. A number of industrial premises were hit but the biggest emphasis in the German reports was on railways. Two passenger stations, a goods station, the Ostbahnhof marshalling yards and the headquarters offices of the State Railways were all badly damaged. This, and the cumulative effect of earlier raids, caused over a thousand railway truck loads of weapons and munitions intended for the Eastern Front to be blocked in the city. But, as always, it was housing accommodation which suffered the worst damage, and for the first time 'living huts' are included in the list of property hit, reflecting the large amount of housing destroyed in earlier raids, with the essential work-force increasingly being housed in hutments which were easier to burn down or blow away with bombing than the pre-war housing. The German records also show that 175,000 flats had now been destroyed in Berlin, and a further seventy to eighty thousand were seriously damaged and unlikely to be repaired as long as the raids continued. This amounted to one-quarter of Berlin's pre-war living accommodation. My German colleague, Herr Abendroth, wrote: 'These are the official, top-secret reports. I hope you use them.'

The human casualty list was a heavy one; 720 people were killed or missing. Only 438 of these were Germans; the remainder were 279 forced workers and three prisoners of war; 186 of the dead foreigners were women. There was a particularly horrifying incident at the Halensee Station when a train load of forced workers from the East (probably from Poland or the Ukraine) was hit, and at least seventy people were killed. By contrast, three young Ukrainian men were killed when they left their shelter to steal food during the raid.

The bombers flew off to the north, into a growing moonlight, but the German fighters were unable to follow, and there were few difficulties on the homeward flight. The crews of two damaged aircraft considered making for Sweden. A 426 Squadron Lancaster had lost so much fuel when damaged over Berlin that England could not be reached; this decision was an easy one. Pilot Officer A. C. Davies and all his crew baled out over that neutral country and were interned. The second aircraft in distress was the Lancaster of Warrant Officer Mervyn Stafford of 460 Squadron. It had suffered considerable blast damage by the explosion of a strange projectile over Berlin, and the aircraft's controls were almost unmanageable. Stafford asked his crew to vote on whether to make for Sweden or risk the hazardous flight across the North Sea to England.

The pregnancy of the rear gunner's wife swung the vote four–three in favour of England, but Warrant Officer Stafford was one of many pilots forced to crash-land on reaching England, and that same rear gunner was killed in the crash, the only member of the crew to die.

The trouble facing the returning crews was extremely low cloud, which, as feared, had descended over England. This was so extensive that the only clear airfields were far away in Scotland or the west of England, and the bombers had insufficient fuel to reach these places. Most crews had little choice but to orbit above their home airfields, waiting their turn to land, but delayed from doing so by the numerous overshoots as other pilots felt their way gingerly down through the cloud. A very serious situation developed. Some aircraft crashed at their airfields while attempting to land. Others ran out of fuel, and their crews had to decide whether to bale out and lose a valuable aircraft or attempt crash landings in open country.

These are a selection of experiences. Flying Officer Harry Darby was the bomb aimer in a 514 Squadron Lancaster, on his first operation. 'FIDO' was an oil-burning installation alongside a runway which dispersed fog.

We struggled back to Waterbeach on three engines but were diverted to another airfield equipped with FIDO. On arrival, Crombie called up the control tower and was told, 'You are turn three-six; circle the (radio) beacon at 18,000 feet.' This meant that thirty-five other aircraft, stacked at intervals of 500 feet, were waiting to land before us. Hoping for some degree of priority, Crombie informed control that we only had three engines, but that cut no ice.

After what seemed an eternity, our turn came round and we made our approach. The bomb aimer was supposed to come up on to the main flight-deck for the landing but I always stayed down in the nose in case the pilot needed any last-minute guidance. The total gloom gave way to a diffused glow ahead and then, suddenly, I

1 The Stirling. First of the four-engined bombers but becoming obsolete at the time of the Battle of Berlin because of its low ceiling and, hence, heavy casualty rate. These are aircraft of 7 Squadron at Oakington, which operated Stirlings until July 1943.

2 The Halifax – a Mark II of 405 (Canadian) Squadron at Gransden Lodge. The container under the nose is an overload fuel tank, fitted in the bomb bay for long flights such as those to Berlin.

3 The Lancaster. An aircraft of 101 Squadron at Ludford Magna with a typical 'area' bomb load in late 1943 – a 4,000-lb 'Blockbuster', four 1,000-lb H.E. bombs and containers of 4-lb stick incendiaries.

4 Stirlings of 90 Squadron lined up at Wratting Common for the 31 August 1943 raid to Berlin. Eighteen Stirlings took off; one was lost.

5 Lancaster crews of 101 Squadron, well prepared for the cold of a winter flight, about to board the truck which takes them out to their aircraft for a Berlin raid in December 1943.

6 Debriefing, 24 August 1943. Warrant Officer Martin Callaway (with forage cap), a twenty-year-old 'veteran' Stirling pilot of 90 Squadron, and his crew give details of their flight on the first night of the Battle of Berlin. Callaway and most of his crew were killed when shot down near Berlin six nights later.

7 A Halifax of 77 Squadron, captained by Pilot Officer Alex Massie, shot down by a night fighter on the way to Berlin on 23/24 August 1943. There were four survivors, including Sergeant Brister whose account is in Chapter 4.

8 and 9 The women of Berlin, upon whose resilience the outcome of the battle would partly depend. These scenes are of air-raid practice earlier in the war. The women fire-fighters were equipped with light-weight, air-raid service steel helmets; those with white overalls were auxiliary nurses. The lower photograph was taken in the communal shelter in the basement of a typical block of flats.

10 and **11** Night-fighter aircraft. A Messerschmitt 109 (top) pressed into action as a Wild Boar fighter and a Messerschmitt 110 fitted with the *SN-2* radar which proved so effective in the Tame Boar operations later in the Battle of Berlin.

12 and **13** Night-fighter crews. The experienced crew (top) of Major Wilhelm Herget (left) who made 700 operational flights in the war, claiming 57 night and 15 day successes. In the lower picture, Herget distributes Iron Crosses to one of his 'young' crews which has just shot down its first R.A.F. bomber.

14 and 15 Flak towers in the Berlin Zoo park. The upper picture shows the control tower with its Giant *Würzburg* and smaller *Freya* radars, and an observation cabin from which 'notables' could view raids. The lower floors contained the headquarters control rooms for all of Berlin's Flak and searchlight units. The gun tower (lower picture) has four twin 128-mm guns; some of its lower floors were used as public air-raid shelters. The zigzag patterns were for aiming practice for the crews of the smaller 20- and 37-mm guns located on the lower platforms.

16 Off to work. A familiar scene in Berlin after a raid in which public transport had been disrupted. This scene was in the morning of either 1 or 3 September 1943.

17 Bombed-out people collecting food and documents at a relief centre at a local Nazi Party H.Q. All relief work was handled by the party, which was thus seen to be the friend of distressed people. The girl serving at the table wears the uniform of the Bund Deutscher Mädchen, the female equivalent of the Hitler Youth. This scene was on 24 August 1943.

18 Bombed out. A typical street scene after people have removed their belongings from their burning homes. This was also taken on 24 August 1943.

19 An injured survivor of a bombing incident thanks his rescuer after one of the December 1943 raids.

20 A good illustration of typical blocks of Berlin flats. A high-explosive bomb, possibly a 4,000-lb 'Blockbuster', has collapsed the flats in the foreground, and rescue workers are searching for bodies. The blast of the bomb has stripped the tiles off the surrounding roofs, making them vulnerable to the mass of 4-lb stick incendiaries dropped on every raid, although there are no signs of fire damage here, an example of a lack of bombing concentration.

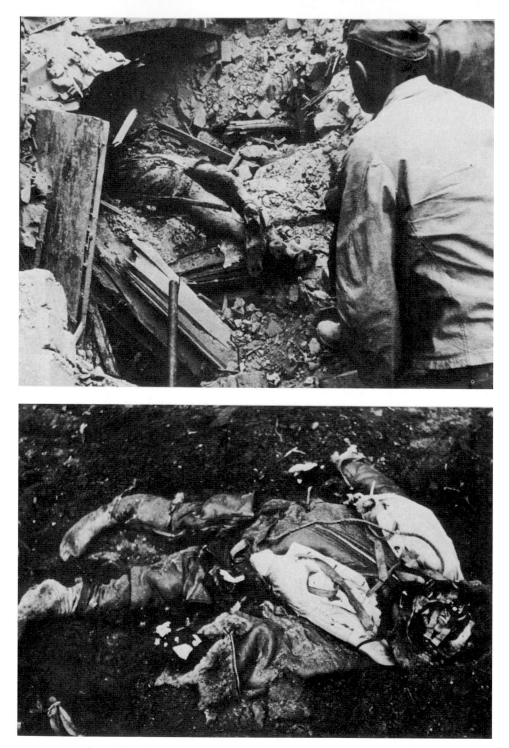

21 and **22** The victims of the battle. The body of a woman is recovered from the ruins of her home in August 1943, and (below) a dead R.A.F. man has fallen into Berlin on one of the December raids; he probably died at once when his bomber exploded, because he still wears his oxygen mask and flying helmet, and the oxygen and intercom leads are severed. His flying boots have disappeared.

23 Unexploded bombs were normally surrounded by bales of straw until they could be rendered safe. This one, in a Berlin street, has exploded, scattering the straw.

24 Bombed-out people forced to leave their homes in a modern block of flats have left messages for relatives and friends about their temporary whereabouts.

25 A senior Nazi local official pays homage to nineteen public-transport workers killed in one of the early Battle of Berlin raids.

26 and **27** The Flak towers, post-war. The French try for the third time
to blow up the tower in their sector. The attempt failed and rubble from
wrecked buildings was later built up around this tower; only the top
platform is now visible in the Humboldthain Park. In the lower photograph, the tower in the Zoo park, in the British sector, succumbs slowly
in May 1956.

28 The painstaking work of building up one of the *Trümmerberge* to dispose of wartime rubble. Work on this one, in the Grunewald in West Berlin, has been going on for so long that the lower slopes have become overgrown.

29 The British War Cemetery in West Berlin. Approximately 2,000 of the 3,576 men buried here died during the Battle of Berlin. The series of seven-grave rows running up to the Stone of Remembrance and on as far as the Cross each contain a seven-man bomber crew, many in communal graves.

could see the FIDO flares along both sides of the runway.
I realized at once that we were too high and informed the
pilot. About halfway along every runway was a bar of
seven red lights, set across it at right angles, and if you
hadn't touched down by the time you reached it, you
were supposed to open the throttles and go round again.
I shouted to Crombie that we were about thirty feet up
when we crossed the bar but he yelled back, 'I'm
buggered if I'm going to overshoot on a night like this.'

He just dropped the old kite on to the runway with an
awful bump. We ran off the end into what looked like a
cabbage field but, miraculously, Crombie swung her
round on to the perimeter track and we were safely
down. We had been in the air for over nine and a half
hours and the flight engineer said we had just about
enough fuel left to fill a cigarette lighter.

Pilot Officer G. R. Fawcett was a 101 Squadron pilot.
'SBA' was Standard Beam Approach, a useful form of radio
approach guidance but very time-consuming while other
aircraft were waiting to land.

The FIDO at Ludford was operational, I think, but flying
control could handle only a limited number of kites
coming in on SBA and, being well down the field on
return, I was diverted to Leconfield.

En route thither, with barely enough juice left to fill a
lighter, my bomb aimer spotted circuit lights through a
hole in the murk and, on the 'bird-in-the-hand' principle,
I let down over the glow of the lights, broke cloud at
something like 250 feet, saw the circuit clear and lobbed
down. It turned out to be Grimsby. The final approach
was well lit by the burning remains of a Lanc that didn't
quite make it; this accounted for most of the glow already
mentioned. I found out later that this contained the C.O.
of 100 Squadron, Dave Holford, who had been Chief
Instructor at my Conversion Unit when I passed through.
I don't think any of the crew survived.

Two severely injured members of Wing Commander Holford's crew did survive.

Flight Sergeant Ron Buck was the rear gunner in a 97 Squadron Lancaster. 'QFE' was the setting on an altimeter to allow for pressure changes at an airfield, essential information for a blind approach.

I saw the glow of fires beneath the fog and knew that aircraft were going into the deck. We were tired and tensed up. It had been a long trip and we were keen to land and get to bed. A discussion broke out among the crew whether to attempt to land or abandon the aircraft. Pete Drane, the pilot, cut the discussion short, 'I'll take her up to five thousand and anyone who wants to bale out has my permission to do so.' There were no takers and we all decided to stay and take our chances. It was our eighteenth 'op' and I'm sure we all felt a little ashamed of ourselves.

At last came the order, 'A-Able, you may pancake.' Pete Drane said, 'Right, everyone; I'll put this cow down if it's the last thing I do.' I settled down as best I could and concentrated all my attention on the blackness below. We banked and straightened up. Suddenly, I saw the ground and I screamed over the intercom, 'Pull up!' There was no hesitation. The nose lifted and we climbed into the night sky to overshoot. Pete Drane came on the intercom and told me we couldn't have been on the deck; he had 300 feet on the clock when I shouted. It turned out that we had the wrong QFE and I believe that many others did the same that night, but they never lived to find out. Pete called up the control tower, they gave him a new QFE and we started our approach all over again. We were lucky the second time. The wind exposed part of the flare-path and Pete was able to line the aircraft up.

As I felt the wheels touch the runway, I turned the rear turret on the beam, sat back and watched the runway lights flashing by. We seemed to run down the runway for a long time and then, to my horror, there were no more lights. We began to bump and bounce about and I knew we were on the grass. After what seemed an eternity we came to a halt. It was an experience I shall never forget.

Sergeant John Arthurson was the navigator in another 97 Squadron crew.

We were stacked high, circling, as other planes attempting to land using SBA were making more than one try. Two crash-landed. The flight engineer said that at this rate we'd run out of petrol before we landed so the pilot called on 'Darkie' for assistance. We were given a course and time to fly to another 'drome and, when over this one, a flare was fired to fix the area – but none of the crew saw it. We then flew around at 'x' feet with wheels and flaps down, and the bomb aimer in the nose giving instructions, 'Up a bit, down a bit, etc.', amid exclamations of relief at something or other just missed.

We came upon FIDO and momentarily glimpsed a runway – cheers – and the pilot did a turn which should have lined him up to approach for a landing, but we came upon it sideways. Other 'split-arse' turns failed to find it and when the flight engineer said that we only had enough petrol for fifteen minutes' more flying, I said, 'Let's get up and bale out.' The rear gunner followed in agreement. The pilot said he was loath to do so but, after a few minutes more trying to find a runway, agreed.

He set the plane on an easterly heading at about 8,000 feet and checked that all the crew had jumped before he did so himself. The rear gunner hit somewhere at the back of the plane, probably the tail wheel, and was knocked out. He doesn't remember pulling the rip-cord but got down safely. When he came to, he 'knew' he was in Germany and set about 'escaping'.

Thirty-two Lancasters were lost because of that bad weather, twenty-eight crashing and four being abandoned by their crews. Conditions were worst in 1 Group, which lost fifteen aircraft, and 8 Group, which lost twelve. 97 Squadron lost seven aircraft, with forty-eight men being killed and six injured. Total aircrew casualties in the bad weather were 127 killed and 34 injured. These were the worst bad-weather landing casualties in Bomber Command during the war, and it became known as 'Black Thursday', the crashes occurring at and around midnight of Thursday 16 December.

So ended another eventful night. It had been a good raid for bombing results and not too serious for the number of aircraft lost on the raid itself – twenty-five – but the crashes in England brought the number of aircraft losses to fifty-nine, a 12.2 per cent casualty rate for the Lancasters involved, the heaviest rate so far in the Battle of Berlin. The losses among Pathfinder crews were particularly severe; six crews had been lost on the raid, and the equivalent of eight more crews were killed or injured in the crashes. The Pathfinders would find it increasingly difficult to replace such crews as the Battle of Berlin progressed.

Night of 23/24 December 1943

BERLIN   390 aircraft dispatched – 375 Lancasters, 8 Mosquitoes, 7 Halifaxes. Abortive sorties: 32, 8.2 per cent of those dispatched.

Time over target: 03.58 to 04.12. Approximate bombs on Berlin area: 1,265 tons – 697 high explosive, 568 incendiaries.

15 Lancasters were lost, 3.9 per cent of heavies dispatched. Aircrew casualties: 104 killed, 16 prisoners of war.

Other operations: 42 aircraft dispatched, 1 Serrate Beaufighter lost, the first loss of a 100 Group aircraft; its crew were killed.

There were three nights of rest after the accidents incurred while returning from the last Berlin raid, and then a heavy raid was carried out by both Lancasters and Halifaxes on Frankfurt on the night of 20/21 December, with a smaller raid on Mannheim as a diversion. The German fighters were up in force and again attempted to intercept the bombers on their approach flight. Forty-one aircraft from the Frankfurt force were lost. The diversion to Mannheim had no effect; the fighter action was on the outward route, not over the target. The main tactical feature of this considerable air action was the way the Germans assembled their fighters at radio beacons or flashing light beacons ahead of the bombers and waited for the bomber stream to arrive. The orders to the German fighter crews were clearly heard by the radio listening station in England. To minimize the effect of this new tactic, Bomber Command would have to make much bigger course changes on the way to targets; the implications for the Battle of Berlin were that smaller bomb loads would be carried and that crews would have the fatigue of flying longer routes.

These factors came into play when the next Berlin raid took place three nights later, on the night of 23/24 December, although a take-off time after midnight would result in the entire operation taking place in the early hours of 24 December, Christmas Eve. Harris decided that once again the Main Force Halifax squadrons would be rested. There would be a long southerly approach, the route of which would threaten first Frankfurt again and then Leipzig, where a small diversionary raid by nine Mosquitoes would take place as the head of the bomber stream passed close by. The longer route and the smaller number of Lancasters available on this night after recent operations would reduce the bomb loads dropped in the target area to 1,265 tons, the lowest figure since the Battle of Berlin was resumed.

This raid was originally planned for a late afternoon take-off, but a forecast of worsening weather over the bomber bases caused the raid to be set back by seven hours

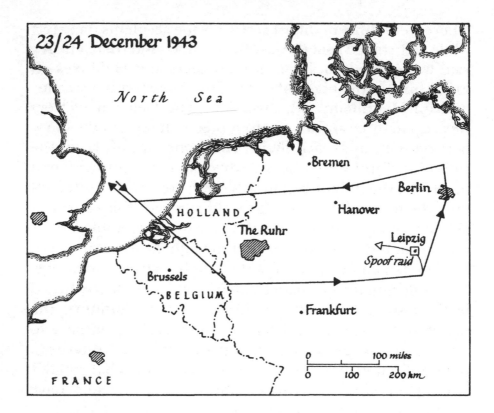

to allow the bombers to return in daylight. Two Lancasters of 12 Squadron collided while taxiing at Wickenby; one broke in half, but no one was hurt. Two more Lancasters of 550 Squadron crashed after colliding near their base at Grimsby, and both crews were killed. There were no problems on the outward route; there was clear weather over low-level cloud. A new navigational aid – 'Windfinding' – was introduced on this night. Selected experienced navigators, mostly Pathfinders but some from the Main Force, calculated their 'found winds' as the flight progressed and radioed these back in brief coded messages to their group radio stations in England. The average of these wind estimates was then retransmitted to the entire force. This process was repeated at half-hourly intervals. The main purpose of Windfinding was to persuade all navigators to use the same wind and thus keep the bomber stream more concentrated.

The radio listening stations in England were able to hear

all of the German night-fighter moves and also carried out their now routine attempts to frustrate those moves by interfering with the German broadcast. The recent trend in German tactics continued, with more fighters being sent to engage the bombers on the outward route. But little success came the way of the German fighters on this night. Bad weather over their airfields and icing conditions in the cloud through which the night fighters had to climb reduced their effort, and the fake instructions and jamming from England were particularly successful this time. It is probable that no more than five or six bombers were lost on the long route to Berlin. Neither were the German efforts to identify the target successful. Frankfurt was, as expected, the object of early attention, but the bombers flew past the city. Then, as the Bomber Command report states: 'The controllers seemed to be loath to decide that Berlin was to be attacked and selected some comparatively insignificant objectives – Weimer and Auerbach – before finally deciding, at a late hour, on Berlin.'[1]

The bombers thus arrived over Berlin under favourable conditions – no fighters, few searchlights because of scattered cloud, no high cloud, only a light wind. It should have been a good opportunity to hit a new part of Berlin. But little advantage was taken of all this. The early Pathfinders, which had performed so well in recent raids, did not do so on this occasion. Thirty-nine Blind Markers were on the raid; all turned up at Berlin, but only eleven released markers, the remainder suffering H2S problems or abandoning their straight-and-level marking runs because of the German defences. Five H2S Mark III aircraft were present, each with a massive load of eleven green Target Indicators, but only one of these aircraft dropped its markers, and these were later found to be six miles south of the Aiming Point. The Main Force thus found only a few scattered markers at which to aim. The Pathfinder Backers-Up concentrated the marking later in the fourteen-minute bomb-

1 Public Record Office AIR 24/262A.

ing period, but it was too late; most of the Main Force had bombed and gone by then. Only seventy bombing photographs showed ground detail or fires through gaps in the cloud; not one was in the main built-up area of Berlin.

The German records show that bombs fell in southern and eastern districts of the city, but many of the bombs fell in suburbs, where there were many open spaces and woods, or in open countryside. Only four important places in Berlin were classed as severely damaged: the Neukölln Gasworks, one small factory, the Frankfurter Allee Goods Station and the tarmac and a hangar at Tempelhof Airport. The number of people killed was 178, probably by high-explosive bombs in the suburbs, but only 600 people were bombed out. The wayward bombing achieved one unexpected success. Four bomb loads fell at Erkner, just outside Berlin and fifteen miles east-south-east of the Aiming Point. By chance, these bombs fell on and around an important ball-bearing factory and caused much damage. This was a nasty surprise for Albert Speer, who was keeping a close watch on the vital ball-bearing industry. He was worried that these stray bomb loads might represent a new form of night precision bombing.

For most of the people of Berlin, the raid passed as another disturbed night and it was not considered a serious attack. I received only two personal contributions. The first was from a lady, Ingeborg Minter, whose soldier boyfriend had brought her a duck for Christmas.

The whole family was excited; it was such a good, fat duck. Mother cooked it on the evening of the 23rd and left it on a table by the kitchen window. A high-explosive bomb fell on a nearby house and the blast blew in our kitchen window. We found the duck full of splinters and quite uneatable. It was very sad; all we got for Christmas dinner were the giblets.

The second contribution was from a Luftwaffe man who complained about the large number of delayed-action bombs dropped on the raid, timed to explode the following evening: 'We thought that was a particularly mean trick to play on Christmas Eve.'

Only four bombers were lost in the target area, two on the run-up to the city and two over the target, the Flak and the night fighters probably sharing these successes between them. Flying Officer Harold Chadwick, of 57 Squadron, watched one of the bombers go down.

We were on our bombing run when I saw a Lancaster just above us on the port side with its two port engines on fire and the rear door on the starboard side of the fuselage wide open. As I watched, three of the crew members appeared at the door and then jumped out into the night. I saw their parachutes open and they floated down into the flames below. As this was almost Christmas Eve, we had a very sad flight back to base, thinking about that unfortunate crew, with the pilot diving down away to port trying to keep his aircraft level enough for his crew to abandon it.

The shot-down Lancaster may have been the 207 Squadron aircraft of Pilot Officer G. E. Moulton-Barrett, who survived with five of his crew, the tail gunner being the only man to die.

One German night fighter was itself shot down over Berlin, probably hit by Warrant Officer Fidge, tail gunner in a 514 Squadron Lancaster. The Lancaster crew had spotted the Junkers coming towards them and about to pass overhead. They warned Fidge, and he was all ready to give it a quick burst as it passed over him. Unteroffizier Hans-Georg Schierholz was the radar operator; it was a Junkers 88 of I/NJG 3 which had flown from its base at Lüneburg to Frankfurt and then on to Berlin, about 450 miles.

The reason we were hit was simple; we weren't awake. The first thing I knew was that I saw tracer going past us and upwards. The attacking aircraft must have been below and behind us. The pilot reacted as a day-fighter pilot would. As soon as he saw the tracer, he dived away, really sharply. We saw that the oil tank in the port wing was on fire. The pilot dived as fast as he could, trying to put out the fire. We went down to 4,000 metres and left Berlin in an easterly direction. We lost a lot of altitude.

At 2,000 metres, the fire was still there so we decided it was time to get out. The pilot didn't want to; it was myself and the flight engineer who decided it. We wanted to be gone before pieces of aircraft started flying around our ears. The aircraft was still manoeuvrable but the flames could reach the petrol tanks and ammunition at any moment.

We had the time to go out through the door in the fuselage. The door was let down. The flight engineer went first. It was his first time; the pilot and I had done it twice before. The flight engineer stood there, clinging on, unwilling to go. I put my foot to his stomach and pushed him out; that made his mind up for him. I went next. The pilot put it on to automatic before he went and we found out later than the plane flew on and crashed near Posen, which is about 170 kilometres away. I came down near Frankfurt-on-Oder.

It was not a good night for the Luftwaffe. The bombers had a long, slow flight home against head winds, but only three more bombers were shot down between Berlin and the Dutch coast, although one or two more may have then crashed in the North Sea. The entire night-fighter force could claim only eleven successes at a cost of six of their own aircraft lost. One radar operator in NJG 1 says that 'Our prima-donna *Geschwader* only had two victories.' In fact, just one German pilot had accounted for more than a quarter of the Luftwaffe successes. This was Oberleutnant Paul Zorner; a *Staffelkapitän* in I/NJG 3. Zorner had received a new Messerschmitt 110 equipped with an *SN-2* radar at the end of November and he immediately shot down five bombers on his first two nights of operations, two on the night of 2/3 December and three on this night. His account shows the increasing versatility of the German night fighters, ranging over large areas of Germany and making use of that excellent new *SN-2* radar which was not affected by Window.

I took off from Lüneburg at 01.39 against a raid coming in far away in the south-west. At first, we thought the target would be Frankfurt, which had been bombed four nights earlier, but the bombers flew further eastwards. At 02.46, we picked up a Lancaster flying at 5,500 metres and attacked it four minutes later from a range of a hundred metres, firing into the right wing. I stood off then, flying alongside on the right, but the fire didn't seem to spread. The bomber held its course but seemed to be going down in a glide. I had the feeling that the pilot was trying to put out the fire, but he didn't succeed. Then, after several minutes, I saw parachutes opening down below and finally the bomber went down in a steep dive, plunging burning into the clouds, and crashed east of Giessen.

During the sixteen minutes we had been in contact with that bomber, we had lost touch with the main stream. I didn't have enough fuel to chase after them all the way to Berlin and started to think about finding an airfield, refuelling and then catching them on the return flight. So I put down at Gütersloh, refuelled and was off again in forty minutes. Gütersloh turned out to be a fortunate choice because the bombers flew straight back, westwards, from Berlin. Thirty-five minutes after taking off again, we had another *SN-2* contact, at a height of 6,300 metres. Our attack hit it in the right wing; it spiralled down, went into the cloud and then we saw an explosion. Eleven minutes later, we got another contact – height 6,100 metres, two attacks, fire in the right wing, then an explosion in that wing a few seconds later and down it went.

They were my seventeenth, eighteenth and nineteenth successes.

Zorner and his crew had covered about 700 miles in their two flights, being airborne for a little over four and a half hours. The bomber he shot down on his first flight was a 576 Squadron aircraft (the pilot was Pilot Officer R. H. Hughes) from which three men survived; the second and third victims were from 44 and 50 Squadrons (the pilots were Sergeant R. L. Hands and Flying Officer D. W. Herbert), but there were no survivors.

The bombers flew home, all to land safely in daylight. The raid had cost only fifteen Lancasters missing and two more which crashed after take-off in England, but the bombing results had been poor.

Night of 29/30 December 1943

BERLIN   712 aircraft dispatched, 457 Lancasters, 252 Halifaxes, 3 Mosquitoes. Abortive sorties: 45, 6.3 per cent of those dispatched.

Time over target: 19.58 to 20.18. Approximate bombs on Berlin area: 2,222 tons – 1,026 high explosive, 1,196 incendiaries.

20 aircraft lost – 11 Lancasters, 9 Halifaxes, 2.8 per cent of the force. Aircrew casualties: 81 killed, 53 prisoners of war, 1 evader.

Other operations: 43 aircraft dispatched, no losses.

Christmas came and passed. The diary of a flight commander in 12 Squadron shows that on Christmas morning the crews were warned for operations that night, but the order was cancelled half an hour later. There must have been much jollification during the remainder of the day; the same officer's diary entry for the next morning reads:

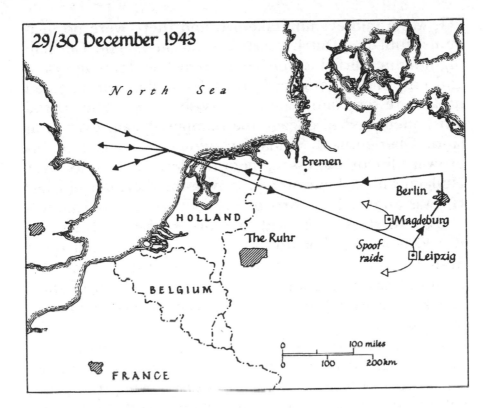

29/30 December 1943

'Stand down 09.45. Everything down; we drop 'em. Day of rest. Serviceability: aircraft – seven; crews practically nil.' The next raid was ordered for the night of 29 December, Berlin again, a maximum effort with the Halifaxes being brought in for the first time for more than a month. It would be the tenth raid of the Battle of Berlin, the third largest for the number of aircraft dispatched and the second largest for bomb tonnage carried, with the Halifaxes adding a great mass of incendiaries to the bomb loads. An ingenious feature of the tactical plan was a 'double spoof' by Mosquitoes. There would first be a diversionary raid on Magdeburg, which was intended to look like a diversion, but this would be followed by a second Mosquito raid on Leipzig which, it was hoped, would look like the opening of the main raid and draw off the German fighters while the bombers flew on to Berlin.

1 From the diary of Squadron Leader J. G. Woollatt.

It was a mid-evening take-off, and there were no incidents until the Dutch coast was reached. The German
night-fighter airfields were covered by low cloud and rain,
and only the experienced crews from the twin-engined
units were sent into action – sixty-six crews. The coastal
units attempted to engage the bomber stream over Holland. Oberleutnant Schnaufer added two more to his
growing list of successes, shooting down a Halifax over
Holland and a Lancaster just over the German border.
He was awarded the first of his four grades of Knight's
Cross two days later, with a score so far of forty-two
R.A.F. bombers shot down.[1] The route was then quiet
until the bomber stream reached the area of the two
Mosquito diversions, when there were a few more fighter
attacks. Sergeant John Barnes-Moss of 61 Squadron was
the close witness of one aircraft lost here. 'I was in the
astrodome on fighter look-out when I saw, to my horror,
over the top of us, only just over the top, passing from
starboard to port, a complete Lancaster wing, the props
still turning, probably just windmilling.' But the bomber
force reached Berlin in good order, having lost no more
than seven or eight aircraft. It is not known whether any
of the single-engined German fighters were in action,
but none was seen by the bombers. The Germans were
definitely confused by the two Mosquito raids, the controllers falling for the first of the two bluffs and ordering the
fighters to Magdeburg. The fighters were later switched to
Berlin but they did not arrive until the twenty-minute
raid was almost over. Only one bomber was observed to
be shot down by Flak over Berlin, but German records
show two aircraft crashing in the Berlin area. Bomber

---

1 Heinz-Wolfgang Schnaufer became the most successful night-
fighter pilot of all time, credited with 121 successes, all by night against
British bombers. He was one of only two night-fighter pilots awarded
the highest grade of Knight's Cross – Oak Leaves with Swords and Dia-
monds. He died after a road accident in France in 1950. The tail fin of
his Messerschmitt 110, with its painted tally of R.A.F. roundels, is now
in the Imperial War Museum in London.

Command would never pass through the Berlin target area with such ease as on that night. About 660 aircraft, carrying over 2,200 tons of bombs, would never have a better chance of success than this.

But the raid was again a failure, although the British did not realize this at the time because of the cloud which prevented any successful bombing photographs being taken. Conditions were almost perfect for skymarking, and the Pathfinders should have been able to mark without difficulty. There seems to be no clear reason why a successful attack should not have taken place.

The German records confirmed the raid's failure. Scattered bombing occurred over a huge triangular area, the sides of which each measured about twelve miles. More than half of the districts in Berlin reported some bombs, but none reported any serious damage, although more bombs were dropped in the south of the city than elsewhere. Bomber Command's records show that 385 4,000-pounders were dropped on the raid; the Germans counted only ninety in the city area. It is probable that most of the bomb loads were dropped outside the city limits on the run-up to the target. The number of people killed was 182, but the relatively high figure of 10,600 people were bombed out of their homes for various periods.

One unusual observer of the raid was Flight Lieutenant Bill Harrison, a pre-war bank official who was now an Intelligence Officer with 466 (Australian) Squadron at Leconfield. He was flying as a passenger in a new Halifax Mark III fitted with H2S.

I flew on the raid with a chap called Baldwin, an Australian who had been on the squadron a long time but who went missing on his next raid.[1] I had to get the A.O.C.'s permission to go. I wanted to do it because I

1 Flight Lieutenant W. G. Baldwin, of Bexley, New South Wales, was killed with all of his crew and a 'second pilot' passenger on the night of 20/21 January 1944, on a Berlin raid. He is buried in the Becklingen War Cemetery.

thought it would make me a better Intelligence Officer I'm sure it was a help. Up till then, I think crews felt I was reading it all out of a book, but they had more confidence in you if you went on raids. I went four times with permission and once without.

This one was a long, quiet trip; my colleagues said I had fixed it up with the Führer. The Flak was not too bad; I was more concerned about the fighters. I remember thinking on the bombing run, 'What's all this nonsense about port, port, starboard. Why don't they get rid of the things?'

On that trip I learnt how difficult it was to interpret flashes and lights seen when the T.I.s had gone into the cloud and there were only Skymarkers. I understood how crew members got muddled up over these. I also realized that navigating on H2S wasn't nearly so simple as it sounded, when there weren't any good, sharply defined coastal or river images.

There was little opposition on the return flight; it is possible that four or five more bombers were lost. The long North Sea crossing had, as so often, to be faced, and at least two bombers did not make it and crashed into the wintry sea. Six members of a 50 Squadron crew died in the first of these aircraft, with just the rear gunner being picked up later by a naval vessel. The pilot of the other ditched aircraft was Flying Officer Lou Greenburgh, before the war an out-of-work Canadian 'hobo' who sailed to England on a cattle boat, was eventually accepted into the R.A.F. as an A.C.2 and was now captain of a 514 Squadron Lancaster whose fuel tanks had been holed by a Junkers 88 on the way to Berlin.

We lost a lot of fuel but I decided to carry on and we dropped our load on Berlin. We were again attacked on the way back. The flight engineer said that we had lost too much fuel and could never reach England. I ordered the crew to bale out but they decided to stick with me and the ship, and I didn't intend to bale out over Germany with a name like Greenburgh.

Coming back, a hundred miles away from England, I found that I had four dead engines and we fell like a rock. I knew we would all be dead in a few minutes. The altimeter unwound fast. I couldn't see a thing; everything was black.

When the altimeter registered zero, I heaved back on the wheel. The bomber hit a wave, nosedived into the heavy sea and broke in two. I was knocked cold. The crew were in forward crash positions and jumped into the half-inflated dinghy. Two of them pulled me out of the water-filled cockpit.

That night was sheer hell. The waves tossed the dinghy all over the place and, by next day, we were completely exhausted and felt hopeless. Pat, the navigator, said he intended to join the Navy to see the world. Strommy, the wireless operator, said, 'So you joined Lou's crew and you'll see the next world.'

Hours later, the dinghy was half-filled with water and leaking. Connie, the rear gunner, saw a flicker in the sky. I shot off our last Very cartridge. The flicker turned out to be a Lancaster. The rescue operation was very tricky and took several hours. My crew showed fantastic courage.

Fortunately the weather was clear over England, and there were no crashes on landing. It had been a disappointing raid, with only poor bombing results in return for the enormous expenditure of bombs, fuel, aircraft flying hours and crew fatigue. The only consolations were the low casualty rate and the poor performance of the German defences. Eighteen bombers were missing, and two crashed in the sea; a loss rate of 2.8 per cent. At least three German night fighters were shot down or crashed in bad weather.

Night of 1/2 January 1944

BERLIN   421 Lancasters dispatched. Abortive sorties: 29, 6.9 per cent of those dispatched.

Time over target: 02.58 to 03.12. Approximate bombs on Berlin area: 1,351 tons – 741 high explosive, 610 incendiaries.

28 Lancasters were lost, 6.7 per cent. Aircrew casualties: 168 killed, 34 prisoners of war.

Other operations: 58 aircraft dispatched, no losses.

After two nights of rest, Harris chose Berlin again for a raid on the first night of 1944. The original take-off time was planned for mid-evening of 1 January, but there was a delay due to doubts over the weather, and take-offs did not commence until midnight; so the whole operation took place in the early hours of Sunday 2 January. The delay also caused a change to the route, which was originally planned as a wide northerly approach over Denmark and the Baltic and a long southerly withdrawal south of the Ruhr and over Belgium. The late take-offs would not allow enough hours of darkness for this long flight, and the bombers were ordered to fly to Berlin on the much used direct route across Holland. The German fighters had been more active on this route during recent raids, but the bomber stream would have the advantage of a strong tail wind. It would be an all-Lancaster raid. The Halifaxes were rested, and the Mosquitoes were sent to carry out a diversionary raid on Hamburg. It was the first time since the resumption of the Battle of Berlin, nine raids earlier, that no Mosquitoes at all flew with the main raid to Berlin.

The bombers started taking off at a bleak midnight. Spirits were not high; the prospect of flying to Berlin again along that increasingly dangerous route did not appeal. Lancasters ran off the perimeter tracks and caused block-

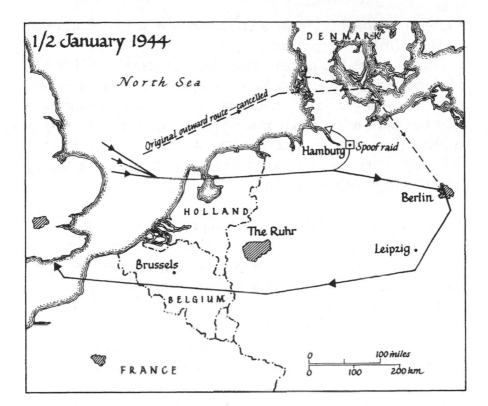

1/2 January 1944

DENMARK

North Sea

Original outward route – cancelled

Hamburg □ Spoof raid

Berlin

HOLLAND

The Ruhr

Leipzig •

Brussels

BELGIUM

FRANCE

0   100 miles
0   100   200 km

ages at two airfields – Ludford Magna and Graveley. This prevented three A.B.C. aircraft and two Pathfinders from taking off. A violent, multi-coloured explosion was seen while the bombers were flying over the North Sea, and it was presumed that a Pathfinder had exploded, possibly after colliding with another Lancaster.

The 400-mile flight from the Dutch coast to Berlin took less than an hour and a half. Thick cloud below the bomber stream gradually rose in height until the bombers were flying in and out of the tops. The German controllers had little difficulty in plotting the progress of the bomber stream. The Mosquito diversion to Hamburg was completely ignored; it might have been given more attention if the original, northerly approach route was being used. Despite their fast progress, the bombers could not evade the night fighters. It is not known whether all German crews were operating or only the experienced ones. Sixteen bombers were believed to have been lost along that flight to Berlin. Some may have been shot down by Flak, but most were night-fighter victims.

One German pilot was particularly successful. This was Major Heinrich Prinz zu Sayn-Wittgenstein, a handsome, twenty-seven-year-old aristocrat. After 150 sorties as a bomber pilot in the early war years, he had transferred to night fighters late in 1941 and proved himself brilliant at this new work. He has been described in these terms by another night-fighter pilot:

He was an individualist, very concerned for personal success. He kept his aircraft near the control room at whichever sector headquarters he thought would be best for that night's operations, watching the situation carefully and judging the best time to take off. He was the perfect example of a successful individualist night-fighter pilot. He did not like working in the night-fighter boxes; he liked to operate on the bomber routes.

Only that morning he had been promoted to command NJG 2. Now he was using the best combination of aircraft and technical equipment available: a Junkers 88 with a long fuel performance, a new *SN-2* radar and the upward firing *schräge Musik* cannons. Major Wittgenstein found his way into the bomber stream and shot down no less than six Lancasters in quick succession. The identity of his victims is not known, but Bomber Command's Operational Research Section later estimated that a high proportion of the bombers lost on the outward flight were Pathfinders flying at the front of the bomber stream.

We move now to another newly appointed unit commander. Wing Commander William Abercromby, D.F.C. and Bar, was a thirty-three-year-old Scot who had recently moved from the command of 619 Squadron in 5 Group to take over 83 Squadron at Wyton, a Pathfinder squadron. Earlier in 1943 there had been an exchange of views between Bomber Command Headquarters and the group commanders over the merit of encouraging bomber gunners to be more aggressive when they spotted German night fighters. Air Vice-Marshal Cochrane of 5 Group had urged that the gunners should open fire at every opportunity, even if this disclosed the presence of the bomber. Air Vice-Marshal Bennett of 8 Group objected to this policy, believing that it would draw attention to the bombers and increase casualties.[1] Now Wing Commander Abercromby had moved from 5 Group to command an 8 Group squadron, and he brought Cochrane's aggressive-gunner policy with him. His new squadron had been encouraged by a previous commander, Group Captain John Searby, to bank or weave gently at all times while flying over enemy territory. This practice, although tiring for the pilot, allowed the gunners to search below the aircraft for night fighters which would otherwise be in the 'blind spot' below the bomber. 83 Squadron had achieved a good run of operations with lower than average casualty rates using this method. Soon after his arrival at Wyton, Wing Commander Abercromby ordered that the practice of weaving had to stop; pilots should fly straight and level so that their gunners would have a stable platform to open fire as soon as they spotted a fighter. There was much resentment at this order, and many of his pilots ignored it. Wing Commander Abercromby was flying on this raid. His own crew were on leave, and he was flying with a new crew captained by an Australian flight sergeant. The aircraft was flying as a 'Supporter', a non-marking Pathfinder aircraft flying at the front of the bomber stream. Just after crossing the Dutch frontier, this Lancaster was shot down. Abercromby and six members of the crew were killed; only the flight engineer survived when the Lancaster blew up.

Flying Officer Harry Bentley was an Australian air gunner in a 467 Squadron Lancaster. He described an unusual combat along that stretch of route.

I recall that night very vividly. Fighter flares had been

[1] Details of the debate are in the British Official History, Vol. II, p. 139.

released ahead of our track. The first indication of the night fighter's presence was a stream of tracer from below our aircraft, port quarter. The target was a Lancaster flying some 100 feet higher, on the same heading as our aircraft and located approximately fifty yards on our port bow. In less than two seconds, both wing tanks of the Lancaster were ablaze. The night fighter was still not seen by our rear gunner. A second attack almost simultaneously by the night fighter was directed at a Lancaster also some 100 feet above our altitude on the same heading, but on our starboard bow at a distance of also approximately fifty yards. The fate of the second Lancaster was exactly the same – both wings ablaze. The sky was now like day. This attack had also originated below and astern of our aircraft. The fighter was still not seen by our rear gunner and myself in the mid-upper position.

I was about to instruct the captain to commence corkscrewing when the night fighter, a silver Messerschmitt, appeared immediately below the fuselage of our aircraft, slightly on our starboard beam and some twenty feet below our altitude. It was actually formating on us. I immediately took action to engage him with my own guns but he was too close and I was unable to depress my guns sufficiently to bring his aircraft into my range of fire. The German pilot was aware of his safe position. He wore a black helmet and black goggles. He immediately made a smart salute to me. I had already requested the skipper to lower our starboard wing in an endeavour to be able to bring the fighter into my line of fire. At that instant, he, the German, dived away to our port side and was gone in a flash. I felt great anger and frustration. Two Lancasters had been destroyed in less than five seconds.

The Pathfinders experienced much difficulty in marking the target properly when Berlin was reached. Up to eight marker aircraft had already been lost, and another exploded when hit on its marking run. The cloud had now built up to 18,000 feet, and there was a strong wind. A modified marking plan was being employed, with the H2S Mark III aircraft being spread through the fourteen minutes of the raid and carrying extra large loads of Skymarkers. The marking started well, but the Target Indicators immediately disappeared into the cloud, and the Skymarkers were scattered across the target by the wind. There were many gaps in the marking because of the Pathfinder casualties and H2S difficulties. There was little opportunity for a successful raid to develop.

The German records confirm the scattered and relatively ineffective nature of the bombing, which was mostly in the southern districts, spread along the whole width of the city from the Grunewald Forest in the west to the suburbs of Köpenick seventeen miles further east. Much of the bombing fell in open country south of Berlin. There were no large fires. The list of buildings and premises hit contains some interesting items, but there was no major destruction. Among the places mentioned are the Army Ministry main offices, two goods stations, a Flak battery with one man killed, a searchlight battery, the Main Post Office, the Rheinmetall–Borsig factory, a church and a hospital. A lock gate at a canal junction was also hit, causing a large hold-up of barge traffic.

The number of people killed in Berlin that night was seventy-nine, one of the lowest totals of the Battle of Berlin. The number of people bombed out was 1,270, also a very low total. I have only two accounts from people in Berlin for that night; they represent extremes of experience in a bombed city. Ulrich Bley was a schoolboy *Flakhilfer* at a battery position on the Wannsee golf course.

We had a battery party for New Year's Day, this time a special one to celebrate three shot-down bombers credited to our battery. We boys had been given a bowl of punch and, later in the evening, wine. The battery commander said that it was officially forbidden to give the boys alcohol but he allowed it on this special occasion. Also present were the ballerinas from Babelsberg where the U.F.A. film studios were; a nephew of the famous film producer Wolfgang Liebeneiner was a member of the battery and he had probably arranged it. Unfortunately, there was another big raid that night and many of us had thick heads.

By contrast, there was a tragic accident at a public air-raid shelter in the Neukölln district. The shelter was in a very deep section of a proposed underground extension. It could hold 3,000 people and was much used by the people of the densely populated area near by. Unfortunately, the entrances were narrow. Friedrich Quapp was a young infantryman, wounded in Russia and now home on leave at his father's shop. He describes what happened.

I think the alarm came later than normal. There was a heavy Flak barrage and bombs were already falling while the people were still out in the open street on the way to the shelter. I was on the way with my parents but we couldn't go fast because Mother was handicapped. When we reached the shelter, we found both entrances blocked with people. The stairways were absolutely jammed and, as more people arrived, they all tried to squeeze in somehow.

I went to the left entrance and, with some other men, tried to pull some of the people out of the mass to clear it from above. We pulled a few out but the noise of the bombs and the Flak made them panic and they all rushed back in again. The bombs were not close; it was the lateness of the alarm that caused the trouble. Normally we had fifteen minutes clear and the police had impressed upon everyone that they must not be out in the street when the raid started. That was the cause of all the trouble.

I pulled out my pistol and fired it into the air to try to stop the panic, but it had no effect; they were more afraid of the bombs than of my pistol. So I tried to get down the steps and actually scrambled over the heads of the people to stop them, but they were like a cork in a bottle at the front. A few people had fallen and those on top and behind were so tangled up that no one could move. The situation was made worse because everyone had their air-raid suitcases containing their papers and valuables.

It took about ten minutes for myself and some other men to get the entrance clear and then things improved and the people flowed in, but back on the steps there were a lot of people trampled to death and others who were injured, all mixed up with broken suitcases and possessions, papers, and so on. I remember seeing a lot of coffee beans spilled on the stairs. You know we Germans are great coffee drinkers and those coffee beans were the real thing, someone's prize possession; they probably had connections on the black market.

They laid out the dead on the platform. There were twenty-one bodies, mostly women, children and old people. I heard later that some police officers were demoted and transferred for allowing all this to happen. 'Transferred' at that time meant the Russian Front.

The official records show that twenty-five people died here. Ironically, no bombs fell in the vicinity.

The bombers left Berlin, facing a long, tiring flight home against head winds. A few more bombers were shot down on the return route, but the exact figure is not known. A Lancaster of 12 Squadron ran out of fuel and had to be abandoned over Germany, and another, from 7 Squadron, suffered the same fate through engine failure and icing.

The very tired Lancaster crews reached England, to be greeted by snow showers and a little fog. Two Lancasters were wrecked in bad landings, but no lives were lost.

Twenty-eight Lancasters were missing. The Pathfinder losses were particularly severe, ten crews missing from the eighty-one who had taken off for the raid. 156 Squadron, at Warboys, lost four aircraft, with not a single survivor in the four crews.

Night of 2/3 January 1944

BERLIN   383 aircraft dispatched – 362 Lancasters, 12 Mosquitoes, 9 Halifaxes. Abortive sorties: 60, 15.7 per cent of those dispatched.

Time over target: 02.43 to 02.56. Approximate bombs on Berlin area: 1,066 tons – 624 high explosive, 442 incendiaries.

26 Lancasters were lost, 7.0 per cent of the heavies dispatched. Aircrew casualties: 168 killed, 31 prisoners of war.

Other operations: 64 aircraft dispatched, no losses.

It was late to bed for the men just back from Berlin that morning of Sunday 2 January. It was snowing. Then, to everyone's amazement, orders arrived that Berlin was 'on' again for that night. Harris had decided to mount another raid, by a mainly Lancaster force. Some alternative aircrews were available, but many of the men who had celebrated heartily on New Year's Eve two nights earlier, and had just come back from an eight-hour trip to Berlin, now had to go again, not in the early evening but on another midnight take-off. The runways would be cleared of snow during the day. Wing Commander Philip Patrick, a flight commander in 7 Squadron at Oakington, remembers the briefing there.

That was the nearest thing I ever saw to mutiny in the

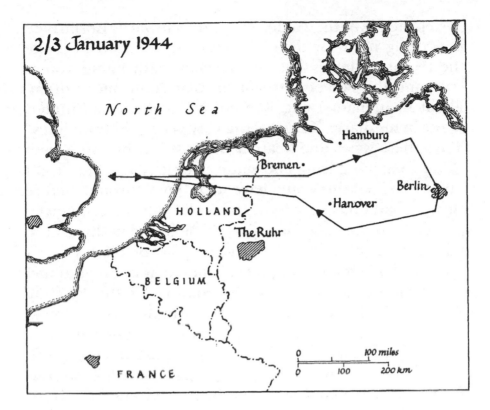

R.A.F., when the guys walked in and saw the map showing Berlin again. There was a rumble of what I might call amazement, or horror, or disbelief. The Station Commander quietened the chaps down and there was no trouble, but you can imagine what it was like to be dead tired and then having to go again. Fatigue was the main problem; I always think that it was worst for the gunners, having to stay awake and keep a look-out for seven or eight hours at a time.

There were also tactical features of the raid which caused dismay. There would be no diversions of any kind. A long, evasive route was originally planned, but this was later changed to an almost straight-in, straight-out route, with just a small 'dog leg' at the end of it, to allow the bombers to fly into Berlin from the north-west, to take advantage of a strong following wind from that direction. But that approach flight across Holland, crossing the coast near

Texel, then over the Zuider Zee and on towards Berlin, was now being used for the eighth time in ten raids, despite the recent evidence that the German night fighters were engaging the bomber stream on that route more often. Flight Lieutenant Doug Renton, a Canadian Pathfinder, wrote in his diary: 'Target – Big City via ye old tram lines.' Then there was a foul weather forecast for the route, with cloud containing icing and static electricity reaching right up 28,000 feet; this would have to be flown through before clearer conditions were found at Berlin. The forecast given to crews was that 'good lanes' could be found in that cloud. Pilot Officer John Chatterton, a 44 Squadron pilot, says: 'It was a hell of a job finding those lanes. It was a typical met man's phrase, given out in the comfort of the Briefing Room, with his feet squarely on the ground. We reckoned they were figments of the imagination to cheer us up a bit.'

Midnight came, and the bombers started taking off. The Lancaster squadrons could prepare only 362 aircraft for the raid, fifty-nine less than the previous night's effort. Two Lancasters crashed, and their crews were all killed; these aircraft were from 460 and 550 Squadrons, both in 1 Group, which loaded its aircraft more heavily than other groups. Thick cloud was met over the North Sea. Sixty bombers turned back. This was the highest rate of early returns in the whole of the Battle of Berlin. Fifteen of the returns were the result of a signals error. 1 Group had eight Wellingtons out mine-laying off the Bay of Biscay U-boat bases, and a signal was sent diverting them to land near Exeter on return. Unfortunately, this coded signal used the same prefix as that being used for the group's Lancasters bound for Berlin. Fifteen crews assumed the signal was a general recall, jettisoned their bombs in the sea and came home. Even without this factor, the number of aircraft returning was unduly high, the normal mechanical causes probably being added to by a combination of bad weather, fatigue and low spirits among the crews. If the 'false recalls' of 1 Group are left out, the worst rate for the early returns was, unusually, among the Pathfinders of 8 Group.

Even those crews which flew on sometimes dropped part of their bomb load into the sea to lighten their aircraft. Sergeant Doug Harvey was a Canadian pilot, flying a Lancaster Mark II of 408 Squadron. He describes what happened to his aircraft over the North Sea that night.

The C.O. had said, 'If you can't get to 18,000 feet, pick out a few cans of incendiary bombs and drop them to lighten your load.' After a steady climb from base we were at 17,000 feet just ten minutes from the Dutch coast. Flying in solid cloud, with ice building on the wings, the straining Lanc couldn't give us any more height. I had the throttles almost wide open but we hung there almost on the stall. I called Steve and told him to select three cans of incendiaries so we could drop them. Our load consisted of one 4,000-pound Blockbuster as well as cans of various sized incendiary bombs.

Steve, after a long delay, said, 'Bomb doors open.' I slammed the lever down and heard the roar of the slipstream vibrating the huge bomb doors as I eased the stick forward to maintain speed.

'Bomb doors open,' I called.

Whomp. The Lanc jumped, as though lifted by a giant hand, and began to climb rapidly.

'Bombs gone,' said Steve, quickly. 'Bomb doors closed, skipper.'

'Bomb doors closed,' I repeated, yanking up the lever. Silence. No one said a word as I set about retrimming the controls. After perhaps five minutes, Eric called on the intercom, 'Steve, did the big bomb drop?'

'No, no,' replied Steve. 'Just the three cans of incendiaries.'

'Felt like the big one to me,' Stan said.

I said nothing. There was no mistaking when a 4,000-pound bomb left the bomb bay. The Lancaster would literally jump up, the controls becoming light and responsive.

We got to an unbelievable 24,000 feet that night over Berlin. The Lancaster never jumped when Steve said, 'Bombs gone.' We just dropped some air over Berlin.[1]

Flying conditions remained bad until half an hour before Berlin was reached. Some of the German airfields were closed completely because of the weather, but a large effort was mounted from other airfields. Between 150 and 200 night fighters took off, the largest force for some time. Many fighters were held at radio beacon *Marie*, near Bremen, but the German controllers got their timing wrong, and the bomber stream flew past without these fighters being released. This was a great opportunity missed for the Germans, because the bomber stream was weakened by the early returns and much broken up by the bad weather. There would have been plenty of lone bombers to be picked up away from the protection of the stream's Window, although the cloud would have hampered the fighters at that stage.

The bomber stream duly dog-legged out to a point fifty miles north-west of Berlin and there found clearer conditions, although there was a smooth layer of lower cloud completely hiding the ground. The Pathfinders set to once again at the difficult task of marking Berlin. It was a new route in for the Pathfinders. The last turning-point was over a large lake, the Müritzsee, which gave a good H2S response. A good intermediate check between there and Berlin was the town of Neuruppin, which was situated on a smaller lake six miles off to one side of the run into Berlin. It was a fast run in, with an 80 m.p.h. wind almost directly behind. It was no good. Of the fifty Pathfinder aircraft which had taken off, eight had turned back, six were shot down (though some of these may still have been present

---

1 This quotation (slightly shortened here) is from Doug Harvey's own book, *Boys, Bombs and Brussels Sprouts*, pp. 125–6.

at this time) and most of the remainder were not able to concentrate their marking. It was an even more disappointing raid than that of the previous night. The Main Force, equally depleted and in many cases arriving late because of the bad weather conditions, could not find any concentration of markers at which to aim. The Berlin local report is one of the shortest of the Battle of Berlin. It estimated that no more than seventy bombers dropped their loads at various places in central, eastern and south-eastern districts of the city, but with no specific building damage mentioned and with only seventy-seven people being killed. Most of the bombing must have missed Berlin.

In addition to all these problems, German fighters were present in great strength. With no diversionary raids, the Germans had simply sent all of their fighters to Berlin, and the dog-legging of the bomber route to the north-west of the target enabled the German fighters to arrive at Berlin in time. The Flak was restricted to 21,000 feet, and a good Wild Boar operation took place. The smooth, low cloud was not thick, and searchlights playing on the underside lit it up so that the bombers were silhouetted against it. The listening radio station in England heard orders for twenty-four aircraft of III/KG 3 to operate as flare droppers. There was plenty of light for the German fighters; at least ten bombers were shot down in the Berlin area and more on the first part of the route home. Among the six Pathfinder aircraft shot down in the target area was the first of the H2S Mark III aircraft to be lost. This was Lancaster JB 355. Flying Officer F. C. Allcroft, a Canadian, and his crew were all killed. This was a very experienced crew; the navigator, Flying Officer Alec Blakeman, was on his fiftieth operation, perhaps having agreed to fly extra operations on the new H2S set.

The bomber force struggled back to England, losing a few more aircraft to night-fighter action and having to fly through the cloud again. There was bad weather at some of the bases in England, and many aircraft were diverted, but there were no crashes, despite the exhausted condition of some of the pilots. Sergeant K. F. Scott of 101 Squadron describes how his Lancaster landed at a strange airfield, taxied to a dispersal area and found to the crew's horror that the surrounding aircraft were all German!

The rest of the crew cast doubts on my abilities as a navigator in no uncertain terms but the tension was broken when a large, coloured American drove up in a jeep with the greeting, 'You all been on a mission?' We had landed at Molesworth, where German aircraft captured in the Middle East were kept to help the Americans with aircraft recognition.

Twenty-six Lancasters were missing, and two had crashed in England on take-off. The poor bombing at the target was a dismal result for the expenditure of these aircraft and for the deaths of 168 aircrew. The Pathfinders had once more suffered the heaviest casualties, nine aircraft and their crews being lost, making nineteen Pathfinder losses in two nights. 156 Squadron at Warboys again suffered severely, now having lost ten aircraft in the last two raids, a 28 per cent loss rate. Only four out of the sixty-four men in these aircraft survived as prisoners of war.[1]

The non-moon period was drawing to a close. There were

1 There was an unusual sequel to the loss of one of the 156 Squadron aircraft on this night. Lancaster JB 640 did not return from the raid, and the Germans found no trace of the aircraft or crew. The names of Pilot Officer John Cromarty and his crew were commemorated after the war on the Runnymede Memorial to the Missing. But in 1976 some aircraft wreckage was discovered in East Germany, presumably at a construction site, and five crates of this wreckage and the remains of four unidentified bodies were delivered to the R.A.F. at Gatow airfield. An R.A.F. man, Warrant Officer Bill Sparkes, a former Bomber Command flight engineer who had flown in the Battle of Berlin, was sent to examine the crates of wreckage and found that these were the remains from Pilot Officer Cromarty's Lancaster. The remains of the four bodies were buried in the Berlin War Cemetery (Plot 7, Row C, Graves 20 and 21). Warrant Officer Sparkes's report is reproduced as Appendix 4.

two nights of rest for the bomber squadrons, and then a raid was ordered to the Baltic coastal port of Stettin, the first raid to that distant target for more than two years. A force of 348 Lancasters and 10 Pathfinder Halifaxes flew out across Denmark and then over the southern tip of neutral Sweden before turning almost due south on a route pointing straight to Berlin. They were preceded by a force of thirteen Mosquitoes which flew on to Berlin and carried out a decoy raid, dropping many Target Indicators. The Germans were completely deceived. Long lines of fighter flares were seen on the approaches to Berlin, and all the German night fighters were ordered there. The bombers were able to carry out an effective raid on Stettin, only a few fighters turning up at that target towards the end of the raid. Sixteen aircraft were lost, a number not considered to be excessive for such a distant target. The Operations Officer at Luftwaffe Central Region, who had ordered the fighters to Berlin, although with Goering's approval, was transferred to other duties.

That was the end of a three-week period of bombing operations. This is a résumé of the raids to Germany:

	Raids	Sorties dispatched	Aircraft lost
To Berlin	5	2,404	114 (4.7 per cent)
To other targets	3[1]	1,062	57 (5.4 per cent)
TOTAL	8	3,466	171 (4.9 per cent)

The five raids on Berlin had started with an attack of medium success on 16/17 December, but the following four raids were all failures. There was no apparent reason why all four should have been unsuccessful. The German opposition had not, on average, been as fierce over the target as on earlier raids when better bombing results had been

1 The diversion to Mannheim by fifty-four aircraft on 20/21 December, when Frankfurt was the main target, has not been counted as a separate raid, but the sorties have been included.

obtained. The problems of blind marking remained but these had been overcome on earlier raids. The causes of the disappointing results were probably threefold. The first was that not enough bombs were being delivered to the targets. The reluctance of Harris to press the Halifax squadrons into action had resulted in only one 'maximum-effort' raid, leaving the other raids to be carried out by a Lancaster force which started the bombing period able to produce 483 serviceable aircraft but finished with 362 on the last raid, of which 56 turned back after taking off. Then there was a lowering of efficiency in the Pathfinders caused by such a rapid loss of senior crews that the general level of experience in the Pathfinder squadrons was falling. The final cause of the failures was probably a general loss of enthusiasm in all of the bomber squadrons for this continuing slog against Berlin. Many crews were tired and could not see any evidence that their efforts and the losses of their squadron comrades were achieving anything worthwhile. The high rates of early returns were a sure sign of falling morale. Pilot Officer G. R. Fawcett, a Lancaster pilot of 101 Squadron, describes the feeling at this time.

Aircrew fatigue increased noticeably as the period progressed. This was evidenced by an increasing interest in sleep, to the detriment of mess parties, booze-ups and the like. Crew and squadron colleagues became noticeably quieter, more serious and introverted.

Morale deteriorated towards the end of 1943 and I remember Christmas being a very low-spirited affair, with very few aircrew letting their hair down. There were three Berlin trips in the so-called 'holiday period' and losses were quite high. Morale was noticeably higher when we felt we had really pranged the target, but there were unfortunately several nights when we returned without this feeling and – inwardly at least – started questioning the strategy.

The casualty rate on the Berlin raids was almost exactly the same – at 4.8 per cent – as in the previous bombing period, although bad-weather crashes made the overall loss rate much higher. Surprisingly, the operational casualty rate was higher on the non-Berlin raids, mainly due to heavy Halifax losses on one raid to Frankfurt. Other than this, the Halifax squadrons had been fortunate. The Main Force Halifax squadrons had flown only two raids in the recent period, compared to the seven raids flown by the Lancaster squadrons, which had suffered 133 aircraft lost and 38 crashed, compared with only 38 aircraft lost by the Halifax squadrons.

There were three more months of long nights remaining.

9 JANUARY – PRESSING ON

There were no major operations while the moon was full between 6 and 13 January. This provided another period of rest for the bomber squadrons and of reflection for their commander. Harris's decision-making was simple. No one at the Air Ministry was stopping him continuing with his campaign against Berlin, and he had no intention of giving up yet. It was not known in England how ineffective the last raids had been.

There was only slight improvement in Harris's resources. Two of 3 Group's squadrons – 15 and 622 – had finished their conversion from Stirlings; this would bring the maximum number of Lancasters available for operations during the coming period to 515 aircraft, but this was only 32 more than the previous highest Lancaster effort. To bring more weight to bear on Berlin, Harris would have to use the Halifax force, which had benefited from the recent respite to form three new squadrons – 578 and 640 in 4 Group and 433 in 6 Group. These squadrons were all equipped with the improved Halifax Mark III. But many of the other Halifax squadrons would have to be withdrawn from the front line to convert to the new type, so the overall Halifax strength would not change. There was a welcome addition to 100 Group's strength with the arrival of two new Serrate Mosquito squadrons – 169 and 239 – and the completion of 141 Squadron's conversion from Beaufighters to Mosquitoes.

These squadrons would be able to dispatch up to twenty Mosquitoes on nights of big bomber raids, but there would be little expansion beyond that figure before the end of the Battle of Berlin. A few more H2S Mark III sets had arrived in the Pathfinders, and each of the five marker squadrons now possessed at least one aircraft fitted with such a radar set. Finally, a new 'floater' Target Indicator had become available; it was able to burst at a higher altitude, but Bomber Command's operational records make hardly any mention of this new marker, and it is believed to have had little effect upon the Pathfinder performance at Berlin.

In contrast to Bomber Command's lack of major reinforcement at this time, the Luftwaffe night-fighter force was fast emerging from its post-Window decline. The basis for this resurgence was an airborne radar set, the *SN-2*. Its use by some of the senior German crews has already been noted, but now the set was being produced in such numbers that more than half of the night-fighter force was equipped with it. *SN-2* worked on a frequency, 90 megacycles, which could not be jammed by Window. The British had no idea of its existence, which meant that the Serrate sets in the Mosquitoes of 100 Group were still calibrated to the frequency of the old *Lichtenstein* radar sets, and this led to a dearth of successful contacts for the Mosquitoes.

The arrival of *SN-2* allowed the Germans to put into operation a tactic which had been planned long before. As far back as 29 July 1943, in the first week of the Window setback, there had been a conference held under the auspices of Feldmarschall Erhard Milch, the Luftwaffe's Director-General of Equipment. Milch's night-fighter specialist, Oberst Viktor von Lossberg, had set out the long-term tactical plan to counter Window. It was to be called *Zahme Sau* – Tame Boar, as distinct from the *Wilde Sau* or Wild Boar method developed by Hajo Herrmann. Briefly, Tame Boar was to bring the large force of twin-engined night fighters, whose radar sets had hitherto been 'blinded' by Window, into action along the bombers' routes to and from the target. But the introduction of Tame Boar had to wait until the necessary radar sets, free from Window interference, became available. The arrival of the *SN-2* in sufficient numbers now made that possible, and the twin-engined fighter units were released from Wild Boar.

The first essential of a successful Tame Boar operation was the ability of the ground controllers to track the main bomber stream throughout its flight; the identification of the target was not so important. The general progress of the bomber force, even one dropping Window, could be plotted by German ground radars. A ground-based device called *Korfu* and an airborne device called *Naxos* could detect if a bomber force contained aircraft using H2S. Since Bomber Command used H2S only on major raids at this time, the identification of which raid was the main raid and which might be a diversion was not difficult, and the progress of the former could be tracked and reported on a running commentary broadcast on multiple radio channels to the night fighters. This enabled the fighter crews to find the general area of the bomber stream. They flew long distances over the night sky of Germany, navigating by means of radio or light beacons, sometimes being held at those beacons until bombers came nearer or the R.A.F.'s intention became clearer. Some night-fighter units moved around Germany in formation, being led by a leader whose aircraft was equipped with a *Y-Gerät* for more accurate control, but most night fighters flew independently. Then, when the time was right, the fighters were 'sluiced into' the bomber stream, and thereafter it was every crew for itself. The fighter crews felt for the slipstream of bombers, looked for vapour trails, used the fighter flares being dropped, concentrated hard on their radar sets and, when all went well, finally sighted and attacked a bomber. The tactics used by Bomber Command at this time, a single stream to one target, with aircraft using H2S, suited Tame Boar perfectly; and the deeper into Germany the target lay, the greater the chance of success. The increasing numbers of long-range Junkers 88s and of the upward firing *schräge Musik* cannons gave the German crews even more oppor-

tunities to increase their scores. *Schräge Musik,* whose cannon shells used only dim tracer, was a danger unsuspected
by Bomber Command for many months. The reports for
this period make references to many bombers observed
being shot down by 'predicted unseen flak'[1] which was
really *schräge Musik,* and returning crews believed that some
of the bombers they saw blow up without evidence of
fighter attack were 'scarecrows', shells fired by the Germans
to affect morale among the bomber crews.

It would not be correct, however, to suppose that all
was going perfectly for the Germans. The attacks of
Bomber Command on German cities are blamed for holding up *SN-2* production through the destruction of small
workshops making the twenty valves which each set
required. So, although Tame Boar was now officially
instituted, some night-fighter units were not yet equipped
with *SN-2,* and the newer crews on all units were still
operating the older radars. Then, the fast Heinkel 219s
and Junkers 188s which von Lossberg had envisaged as
being an essential part of successful Tame Boar were not
appearing; the Junkers 188 was still not operational, and
there were only three Heinkel 219s flying by mid-
November. The American daylight bombing of German
aircraft factories can claim some of the credit for holding
back these more advanced night fighters.

The new bombing period opened promptly on the night of
14/15 January 1944 when 498 aircraft, mostly Lancasters,
were sent to Brunswick, a medium-sized target in Central
Germany about 100 miles less distant from England than
Berlin. Brunswick had never been the object of a major
raid before but it contained two Messerschmitt factories
and was the type of place which the Allied planners were
urging Bomber Command to attack. The raid was a minor
disaster. An almost straight-in route was chosen, pointing

1 Interceptions/Tactics Report No. 2/44, 2/3 January 1944, Public
Record Office AIR 24/263.

towards Berlin, but with the bombers then turning abruptly towards Brunswick. Mosquito diversions were sent on to Berlin and also to Magdeburg. It was the type of route and tactic which had, until recently, usually misled the Luftwaffe. But now, with Tame Boar being used, the fighters were quickly into the bomber stream and simply followed them to the target and then back to the North Sea coast. Bombing results were poor; most of the attack missed Brunswick. Thirty-eight Lancasters were lost, 7.6 per cent of the force. It was the heaviest loss for six weeks. Eleven of the lost aircraft were Pathfinders; five of these were from 156 Squadron, which was suffering an appalling run of casualties, having lost fourteen aircraft and crews in the last four raids out of seventy aircraft dispatched. Flight Lieutenant Peter Coldham, an Australian pilot on the squadron, had been on leave during this period.

On my return to the squadron at the end of January about seventeen aircraft had been lost. I was a virtual stranger in the Mess. The operations on Berlin continued unabated and the gloom was complete. I was glad to get away, having concluded my second tour of operations. Crews operating time and time again to the 'Big City' could see little chance of survival.

A raid was ordered for the next night – 15/16 January – but it had to be cancelled because of bad weather. It is believed that the target would have been Frankfurt. The bad weather continued, and there were no operations of any kind for five nights, an unusual run in Bomber Command. Then, on the morning of Friday the 20th, conditions improved, and a major raid became possible. Harris decided it would be Berlin again, the Halifaxes being recalled for a maximum effort.

Night of 20/21 January 1944

BERLIN 769 aircraft dispatched – 495 Lancasters, 264 Halifaxes, 10 Mosquitoes. Abortive sorties: 75, 9.9 per cent of the heavies.

Time over target; 19.33 to 19.53. Approximate bombs on Berlin area: 2,348 tons – 1,137 high explosive, 1,211 incendiaries.

35 aircraft were lost – 22 Halifaxes and 13 Lancasters, 4.6 per cent of the force. Aircrew casualties: 172 killed, 75 prisoners of war, 10 evaders.

Other operations: 79 aircraft dispatched, no losses.

The recent successes of the German night fighters on the routes at last forced the abandonment of the straight-in routes which had been used so frequently. From now onwards, the bomber stream would take longer and longer routes to targets, requiring more flying time and thus causing fatigue for the crews and a reduction in aircraft bomb loads. But the number of heavy bombers now available – 759 on this night – would be able to take off with 2,456 tons of bombs, the heaviest loads since the highly successful raid on the night of 22 November 1943, when the Stirlings had been available. The plan for the coming night was completed with the addition of two small Mosquito diversions to Kiel and Hanover.

The bombers took off in late afternoon of a fine day. The only setback was at Middleton St George where a new pilot on his first operation ran off the perimeter track and held up eleven other Halifaxes until two bulldozers appeared and cleared the blockage. It was a heartening experience for the crews to start out in daylight and to see the strength of the force flying out over the North Sea. The bomber force ran into the cloud of a cold front over Germany; the temperature was extremely low. But the German night fighters were on the move long before that. The reports of the British radio listening service, supplemented by some details in Ger-

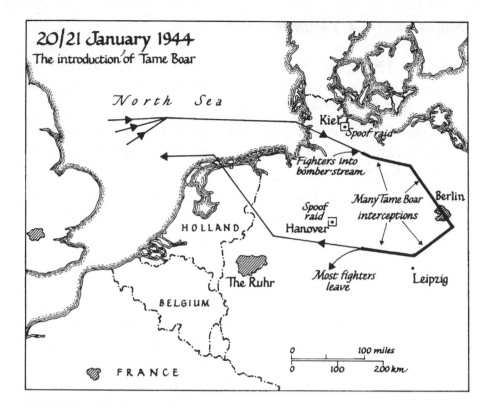

20/21 January 1944
The introduction of Tame Boar

North Sea

Kiel
Spoof raid

Fighters into
bomber stream

Many Tame Boar
interceptions

Berlin

Spoof
raid
Hanover

HOLLAND

Leipzig

Most fighters
leave

The Ruhr

BELGIUM

0   100 miles
0   100   200 km

FRANCE

man records, show us exactly how the German operation developed. The bomber force was detected 100 miles out at sea from the Dutch coast, possibly by a radar ship, the *Togo*, which the Germans were using. A few night fighters with old-fashioned radars were ordered up to man the coastal boxes, in the hope of catching the odd bomber outside the protection of the stream's Window. The orders from the ground radar stations to these fighters were clearly heard, but no success claims were forthcoming, and the bomber stream probably penetrated this first line of defence without loss.

Bad weather forced the Germans to restrict their main twin-engined effort to ninety-eight experienced crews, but the new Tame Boar operation unfolded. The units based in France, Belgium and Holland were ordered to radio beacon *Ludwig* near Osnabrück, then on to *Marie* south of Bremen and then, when the bombers failed to turn south-east as expected, they flew further on to the *Richard* beacon near the

Baltic coast. The long northern approach route being used by the bombers delayed the final contact between fighter and bomber, but the fighters eventually caught up the stream. Aircraft from other units were also joining in the operation as they arrived. It was not a perfect Tame Boar interception, but it was reasonably effective, considering that it was a new tactic and that the British had used an unexpectedly indirect route. The bad weather also limited the number of night fighters the Germans could send into action. The Mosquito diversions on Kiel and Hanover were completely ignored; they were far too small to be effective, and the Germans knew where the main stream was all the time. Berlin was broadcast as the probable target with more than half an hour to spare, but the twin-engined night fighters were not sent there yet; their duty was to continue searching for bombers along the route.

The head of the bomber stream arrived over the Müritzsee, sixty miles from the centre of Berlin, and the Pathfinders ran into the target area from there and attempted yet again to solve the problems of blind marking. There is little evidence in the normal sources to show how the marking and bombing progressed. Bomber Command's Operational Research Section, with no photographic help available because of the cloud, simply stated: 'The timing of the Blind Markers was excellent, and a good concentration of Skymarkers was maintained throughout the attack. The crews of H2S aircraft thought the attack fell on the eastern part of the city.'[1]

German sources[2] confirm that the main bombing was in the eastern parts of the city, in an eight-mile-long spread from the district of Horst Wessel (now called Weissensee)

1 Public Record Office AIR 14/3411.
2 The Berlin city records have no details for this night, but there are reports in the War Diary of Speer's Rüstungs-Kommando I (War Industry Ministry Sector No. 1), held by Bundesarchiv, Freiburg, as file RW 21-2/7, and other Bundesarchiv documents in RM 7/300 and RL 4 II/24, together with one Berlin document captured by the British at the end of the war.

in the north as far as Neukölln in the south. The usual damage to residential property was listed; 243 people were killed and an estimated 10,000 made homeless for various periods. Five industrial buildings were destroyed and forty-one suffered varying degrees of damage. Railways were damaged and the Lichtenberg Power-Station put out of action, which left the main railway line to Hamburg cut and several eastern districts of the city without electricity the following day. There were several large fires. All of this would indicate a raid of medium to good success in areas of Berlin not damaged much in earlier raids. The War Industry Ministry report would have given great satisfaction to Bomber Command. The small firm of Roland Brandt was put out of action completely by a direct hit from a 4,000-pounder; it had been making radar components for the Luftwaffe. And three other nearby firms making military electrical equipment and artillery and Flak fire-control systems were also badly hit, good examples of how area bombing often knocked out important small segments of German war industry.

But the German records also show that a considerable quantity of bombs were dropped outside Berlin. Forty-five communities reported damage, with thirteen people being killed. The bombing stretched in a wide arc around eastern Berlin, from Neubrandenburg seventy miles to the north, right round to the south. The more distant of the northerly bombing may have been the result of aircraft jettisoning their loads under fighter attack, but much of the remainder must have been bombs dropped by crews not prepared to fly through the centre of the target area. Yet again a lucky hit in this wayward bombing caused considerable damage when a Todt Organisation depot and workshops more than thirty miles away from Berlin were hit.

Liaison between the German defences over the target was not good. Conditions were ideal for Wild Boar type fighter action; there was a smooth sheet of cloud at about 12,000 feet which was well lit up from below by searchlights and against which the bombers were clearly silhouetted.

Some single-engined fighters were present, but the Flak was thundering away without any height restriction; forty-six bombers returned with Flak-inflicted scars. Most of the twin-engined German aircraft were seen well below the bombers' height, being content to pass quickly through the target area and recommence their Tame Boar operation later. But some German fighters did come in over the target. Flight Sergeant Keith Thompson, navigator in a 101 Squadron Lancaster, describes one encounter.

It was one of those occasions when we didn't keep our heads down. The tail gunner reported that he could see a night fighter attacking a bomber whose engine was on fire. The tail gunner wanted to open fire. The skipper said, 'Yes.' The mid-upper, instead of watching out for us, joined in as well and the next thing we knew was that we were attacked by three fighters which came bolting across to have a go at us one after the other. We had the bomb doors open at the time, literally being on the bombing run, and we didn't bomb. When the fighters left us, the bomb aimer said could we go round again. The skipper replied, 'Not bloody likely. Drop the buggers now.'

We flew home with the bomb doors open all the way; the hydraulics were shot up. Also we had one fin and rudder badly damaged and a huge hole in the port wing. We had no air-speed indicator and the pilot could only calculate our speed from the engine settings, but we made a good return.

Nine bombers were shot down in the Berlin area.

The twin-engined German fighters resumed their attentions when the bombers turned for home and scored further successes, but most had to give up after about seventy miles and find somewhere to land before their fuel was exhausted. But a feature of the Tame Boar operation was that there was no longer one mad dash for the target but a step-by-step deployment of German units at various places along the route. More night fighters came into the bomber stream near Münster; these were probably aircraft of NJG 6 from Southern Germany. Finally, at the Dutch coast, the box night fighters were waiting again. The bomber stream was by now well spread out, with a strong wind pushing many aircraft south of track. There were further bomber losses.

The weather was clear over the English airfields, but many aircraft were damaged or short of fuel and faced difficulties. Two Halifaxes crashed in Norfolk, and five men were killed or died later. Two more Halifaxes were abandoned by their crews.

It had been a raid of mixed fortunes. Useful damage had been caused in Berlin but at a cost of thirty-five bombers missing. There were wide variations in the spread of these losses. 5 Group suffered only one loss from 155 Lancasters on the raid, and 1 Group only three losses from 144 Lancasters. The Halifaxes did not seem to be able to avoid suffering heavy casualties. Twenty-two Halifaxes were lost and five more crashed in England, 4 and 6 Groups both suffering casualty rates of nearly 10 per cent. 102 Squadron at Pocklington had five Halifaxes missing and two crashing out of sixteen aircraft dispatched. The first full-scale German Tame Boar operation on a Berlin raid had been reasonably well conducted, although there was some initial hesitation, and only about a third of the available German crews had been allowed to operate in the bad weather. But there was every reason to suppose that the Germans would improve their new tactic; it was one to which Bomber Command would be able to find little effective answer.

The favourable weather continued, and Harris ordered the bombers out again on the next night – 21/22 January – but he switched targets to Magdeburg. It was the first raid to this city, which was situated sixty miles west of Berlin. To help with the raid, 5 Group was ordered to send twenty-two Lancasters with twelve Mosquitoes of 8 Group to carry out a substantial decoy raid on Berlin, a prospect that alarmed the Lancaster crews chosen. The main raid turned

out to be a disaster for Bomber Command. Magdeburg was
not seriously damaged, and fifty-five bombers were lost.
The Halifaxes, with 35 aircraft lost from 224 dispatched,
suffered a 15.6 per cent loss rate. The German fighters
ignored the Berlin diversion. One Lancaster crew arriving
at Berlin actually saw German fighters leaving the Berlin
area for Magdeburg, and another man describes his flight
to Berlin on that night as one of the most uneventful of his
tour. But the Berlin defences, probably Flak, shot down
one Lancaster over Berlin; Flight Sergeant John Homewood of 630 Squadron and five members of his crew died.

The Magdeburg raid is remembered for the deaths in
action of two famous German pilots. Major Heinrich Prinz
zu Sayn-Wittgenstein was the leading night-fighter pilot at
that time, with eighty-three successes in the West and in Russia. Wittgenstein's radar operator survived to describe how
Wittgenstein shot down four bombers on the way to Magdeburg but then was shot down while attacking a fifth. The
exact manner in which Wittgenstein's aircraft was lost was
never established. No British bomber returned to claim him,
and some German sources say that the famous man was
caught by a Mosquito night fighter. But no Mosquito claimed
him, and a fortunate account sent to me from New Zealand
probably solves the mystery. Flight Lieutenant Alfred Muggeridge, bomb aimer in a 156 Squadron Lancaster shot
down that night near Magdeburg, describes how his aircraft
was attacked by a night fighter. On the German's second
approach, the Lancaster rear gunner held his fire until the
range was very close. The fighter was seen to be hit and go
down. This more or less coincides with the version of the
German radar operator, so the man who may have
accounted for this famous German pilot was that Lancaster
rear gunner, Flight Lieutenant T. R. Thomson from Edinburgh. The Germans were very upset by the loss of the
legendary Wittgenstein; after his death, his Knight's Cross
with Oak Leaves was up-rated to the rare Oak Leaves with
Swords.

Another German ace to die that night was Hauptmann

Manfred Meurer, the commander of the premier unit of the Luftwaffe night-fighter arm, I/NJG 1 based at Venlo. Meurer, a holder of the Knight's Cross with Oak Leaves, was the third highest scoring German night-fighter pilot, with sixty-five successes, and he was the first pilot to fly the still rare Heinkel 219. But Meurer died when the bomber he was attacking in the Magdeburg area blew up above him and caused his He 219 to crash.

Night of 27/28 January 1944

BERLIN 515 Lancasters and 15 Mosquitoes dispatched. Abortive sorties: 38, 7.2 per cent of those dispatched.

Time over target: 20.28 to 20.42. Approximate bombs on Berlin area: 1,704 tons – 1,036 high explosive, 668 incendiaries.

33 Lancasters were lost, 6.4 per cent of Lancasters dispatched. Aircrew casualties: 172 killed, 55 prisoners of war, 4 evaders.

Diversionary and support operations: 80 Stirlings and Wellingtons mine-laying, 21 Mosquitoes on various tasks, 21 Pathfinder Halifaxes bombing Heligoland, 9 R.C.M. sorties and 12 Mosquito Serrate patrols. 1 Stirling was lost.

Other operations: 27 aircraft dispatched, no losses.

There were three nights of rest after the bad experience of the Magdeburg raid. Then an operation was ordered for the night of 25/26 January, but this had to be cancelled, and it was not until the night of Thursday 27 January that the squadrons were out again. It was to be another Berlin raid, but Harris continued his 'on-off' attitude to the

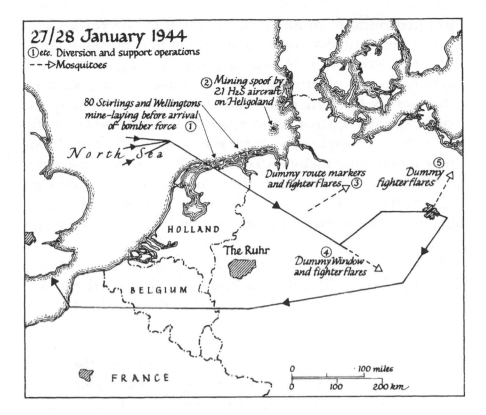

27/28 January 1944
①etc. Diversion and support operations
- - - ▷Mosquitoes

② *Mining spoof by 21 H2S aircraft on Heligoland*

80 Stirlings and Wellingtons mine-laying before arrival of bomber force ①

North Sea

Dummy route markers and fighter flares ▷ ③

⑤ *Dummy fighter flares* ▷

HOLLAND

The Ruhr

④ *Dummy Window and fighter flares* ▷

BELGIUM

FRANCE

0 · 100 miles
0   100   200 km

Halifaxes by sending only Lancasters and Mosquitoes. The planning for the raid contained several new and useful features, with Harris's staff obviously responding to the latest German tactics. It must have been realized that small diversions by Mosquitoes not using H2S were being ignored by the Germans and were a waste of effort. So a mixed force of Stirlings and Wellingtons, accompanied by twenty-one Pathfinder Halifaxes equipped with H2S, went out ahead of the main bomber force into the German Bight. The Stirlings and Wellingtons laid mines in various places, and the Halifaxes bombed Heligoland. The Germans fell for this clever move, and part of the night-fighter force was sent out to sea, attempting to make early contact with what they believed to be the main raid. One Stirling was lost, believed shot down by a fighter near Heligoland.

The real bomber force followed the diversion towards the German Bight initially but then turned south-east to take a well planned indirect route to Berlin; six Mosquitoes dropped dummy route markers north of the route. The course being held at that stage threatened places such as Hanover, Brunswick, Magdeburg and Leipzig, but then the bomber stream abruptly changed course north-eastwards preparatory to its final run into Berlin. When that sharp course change was made, three Mosquitoes continued on the old course, dropping as much Window as possible. All of these moves were made with the benefit of a strong tail wind, and the speed at which the various moves unfolded increased the pressure on the German controllers. It was by far the cleverest tactical plan yet employed on the Berlin raids.

Only a few of the German fighters caught up with the bombers before Berlin was reached. One of them was piloted by Unteroffizier Bruno Rupp, flying a Junkers 88 of II/NJG 3 from Schleswig.

It was nearly two hours before I caught up with the bomber stream. The running commentary was loud and clear but my *Lichtenstein* radar was no good; I didn't have an SN-2 yet. I always had my flight engineer up in front, not watching the control panel but looking out ahead. He saw the bomber first – the exhausts gave it away – about 400 or 600 metres in front, perhaps as much as 800 metres.

I pulled away to the right and lower, to keep under the horizon. I went to the right because I felt that most pilots would react by pulling away to the left in an emergency and not to the right. I waited to see if I had been spotted or not. There was no reaction; he carried on straight and level.

Then I closed in, still out to the right and under its horizon. I wanted to get in to at least 120 metres and, on this occasion, I got very close in. I wanted to hit it in the right wing, in the fuel tanks between the two engines. I put my nose up and aimed in front of the wing, opening fire and reducing my speed so that the cannon shells would pass back through the wing. When I saw my fire reach the rear of the wing, I pulled away to the right at once, to get away from the flames which started immediately and also to be on the safe side if that pilot reacted by pulling away to the left as I expected. It happened exactly that way. I pulled to the right; he pulled to the left and I don't think the bomber crew ever saw me. I watched it fall away on fire and disappear into the clouds.

The next night I did almost exactly the same thing and got two bombers on the way to Berlin. It was a sensation on the unit. We were only a new crew. We had some crews who hadn't been successful in seventy flights. They gave me an aircraft fitted with *SN-2* and *schräge Musik* after that.

Rupp's success on the route to Berlin was an isolated one. Two bombers were seen to collide and go down, but the careful planning resulted in the stream arriving at Berlin in good order and without serious loss.

Again the target was cloud covered, again there were no bombing photographs, and again Bomber Command's report of the marking and bombing is only a brief one. The Skymarkers appeared to be accurate, but the strong winds blew them rapidly along the line of the bombers' route. This was not a bad thing; the onward drift of the markers should counter any tendency for the raid to 'creep back'. The German records show that the bombing was spread right across Berlin; seventeen districts reported damage, and fifteen suffered fatal casualties. The usual cross-section of city buildings was hit; 413 people were killed, and about 20,000 bombed out. Of the dead, 132 were foreign workers. But so scattered was the bombing that sixty-one communities outside Berlin, most of them downwind to the east, were affected by the bombing, and a further twenty-eight people were killed in those places.

Another new feature of this raid was the use for the first time over Berlin of 'Supporters' from non-Pathfinder squadrons. Until now, Supporters were all from 8 Group. They were aircraft whose crews were still learning the Pathfinder methods and had not yet been accepted as full marker crews. They were sent out at the front of a raid with the primary marker aircraft, to help thicken up the Window and jam the radar-predicted Flak which could be such a danger if only a few aircraft arrived at the target at the start of a raid. Supporters carried only high-explosive bombs, so that early fires would not start and be mistaken for markers or cover the target area with smoke. Now 1 Group was ordered to send twenty-eight of its most experienced crews to act as extra Supporters. The tactic seemed to be successful; no Pathfinders were lost over Berlin, and of the two 1 Group Supporters lost, one is known to have been shot down well away from the target. 1 and 5 Groups would alternate in providing a small Supporter force in future raids.

The Flak barrage was noted as being particularly feeble that night; but a large number of fighters, both single- and twin-engined, reached the area of action, and the bomber casualties started to mount over the target and on the return route. Flight Sergeant James Brown was the mid-upper gunner in a 50 Squadron Lancaster attacked over Berlin.

The attack badly damaged our Lanc, starting a fire in No. 1 starboard petrol tank. I opened fire on the Ju 88 and actually saw him nosedive into the blazing target area, badly hit, but as we were more concerned about our blazing petrol tank, nobody witnessed my claim for a 'kill'.

My view of the tank on fire from the mid-upper position was of a colossal flame stretching from the wing trailing edge, right past the fin and rudder, and of a furnace of sparks coming from a great hole in the petrol tank. I reported this to the skipper and I remember him saying that Lancs had flown back with only one wing, which I thought was a bloody stupid remark, considering the 'shit' that was flying about; from his position he could see very little. Nevertheless he did ask me what he should do. This was after we had got rid of the bombs and I said that all he could do was a vertical dive to see if the wind force could abate the fire. In a split second the nose went down and we screamed from 22,000 feet to 15,000 feet

and pulled out. This had a great effect on the fire but it
didn't go out completely. I told him to do it again quickly.
The nose went down again; the wind noise was
deafening. I never thought the Lanc would stand so
much air-frame pressure in a dive.

The skipper said that the altimeter showed 11,000 feet
and, by a sheer miracle, the flames and sparks subsided
and he pulled out straight and level at 10,000 feet with
not a spark to be seen.

The skipper and engineer nursed the Lanc back to
Skellingthorpe where it was placed in the graveyard, a
complete write-off. The four officers in the crew got
D.F.C.s but the three N.C.O.s got nothing.

The bombers flew a long southern return route into a
head wind, the planners hoping that all the earlier activity
in the north would have exhausted the fuel endurance of
the night fighters. Twelve Oboe Mosquitoes which had
made a raid on Aachen tried to confuse the German fighters by releasing decoy route markers thirty miles north of
the main route. These measures were only partially successful. Bomber casualties mounted steadily. But the Germans
also suffered losses; this account by Leutnant Wilhelm
Seuss, of IV/NJG 5, shows how the limited endurance of
the Messerschmitt 110 was a liability and how the night-
fighter force suffered a steady stream of non-action
casualties.

I thought to start with that the bombers were attacking
Magdeburg again, but I found nothing there and tried
looking for bombers further south. We found nothing,
gave up and decided to go back to Erfurt. Then we got
into trouble. Normally, all I had to do was to fly at 210
degrees from Magdeburg for thirty to forty minutes and
always picked up the beacon. But I think there was a
strong wind against us and we could not contact Erfurt.
We tried to get other airfields but my radio receiver had
failed and we heard nothing. The ground was completely

cloud covered. We were lost and had been up for three
and a half hours; the red lights came on.

We lost as much height as we dared but I had to leave
room to bale out. I thought it out – better to go while the
engines were still running. I decided to order the bale-
out at about 1,200 metres. I put the flaps down – not all
the way – but enough to reduce the speed and help hold
it steady. I trimmed the aircraft to fly itself and told the
radar operator and rear gunner to bale out. I thought
they had both gone; I had no way of seeing behind me.
Then, I stood on my seat, sat on the bulkhead behind me
ready to go, but heard one of my chaps calling. The
gunner had opened his parachute too early, actually
while still in the cockpit. The parachute was streaming
behind him but he was trapped in the cockpit, possibly by
the parachute harness or the lines. I couldn't think what
to do; there was absolutely nothing I could do to help
him. It was terrible. I would rather not speak about it.

I kicked the stick forward, partly to push myself out
and partly to make the aircraft dive a little and catapult
me out; I was very worried about being caught on the
tail. I came down in some raspberry bushes in a garden in
the town of Merseburg, eighty kilometres east of my
airfield. All I had was a sprained ankle. The aircraft flew
itself down and nearly made its own landing in a field.
The aircraft was in quite good condition but the tail
gunner was dead, probably with internal injuries.

There were no crashes when the bombing force reached
England, but at least two bombers were lost in the sea. In
the first of these, a 61 Squadron crew had three members
drown when their Lancaster ditched heavily, but the other
four men were saved. In the second incident, Binbrook
airfield heard a distress signal from a 115 Squadron Lancaster, the bearing of which was out over the North Sea, north-
east of the Lincolnshire coast, a huge distance off track for
the time of the radio message. The crew may have mis-
judged the strength of the west wind, turned north too

early and, instead of flying up England, were flying up the
North Sea. Flight Sergeant Arthur Morris, on only his third
operational flight, perished with his crew in the sea.

The bomber force had lost thirty-three Lancasters in
return for a raid of medium success on Berlin. The heaviest
casualties were in 1 Group, which lost 12 Lancasters from
124 dispatched, and in 6 Group, where the three Canadian
squadrons operating Lancaster IIs lost no less than 8 aircraft from the 48 sent on the raid.

Night of 28/29 January 1944

BERLIN   677 aircraft dispatched – 432 Lancasters,
241 Halifaxes, 4 Mosquitoes. Abortive sorties: 66, 9.7 per
cent of those dispatched.

Time over target: 03.13 to 03.33. Approximate bombs
on Berlin area: 1,887 tons – 1,050 high explosive, 837
incendiaries.

46 aircraft were lost – 26 Halifaxes and 20 Lancasters,
6.8 per cent of the force, and 5 Halifaxes were destroyed
in crashes. Aircrew casualties: 254 killed, 67 prisoners of
war.

Diversionary and supporting operations: 63 Stirlings
and 4 Halifaxes mine-laying in Kiel area, 18 Oboe Mosquitoes bombing night-fighter airfields in Holland, 6
Mosquitoes to Berlin before the main raid and 4 on a
decoy raid to Hanover, 6 Mosquito Serrate patrols.
Losses: 2 Stirling mine layers and 1 Serrate Mosquito.

Other operations: 16 O.T.U. Wellingtons leaflet-drop-
ping over France, no losses.

Harris immediately ordered a maximum-effort raid
against Berlin for the next night with a full range of diver-

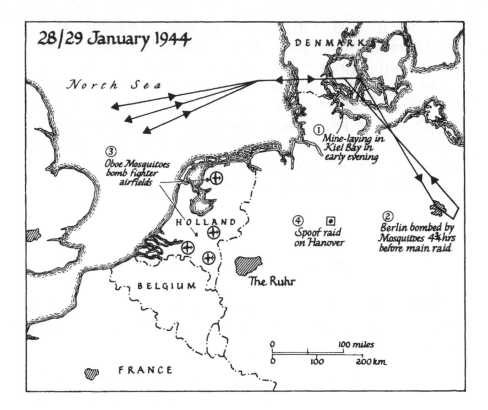

sionary operations. A total of 775 aircraft would be involved. The Battle of Berlin was now approaching its climax, although few realized that at the time. The main features of the planning were long, northerly outward and return routes over Denmark and the Baltic which would be well away from most of the German night-fighter bases but would also reduce the bomb tonnage carried by the raiding force, and raids by Oboe Mosquitoes on four of the most important night-fighter airfields in Holland, this support being provided for the first time.

The first move was a raid by three Mosquitoes on Berlin early in the evening. Flight Sergeant Jim Marshallsay of 627 Squadron was one of the Mosquito pilots; he describes the purpose of the raid and the effect upon Lancaster crews at his airfield.

We took off very early and flew to Berlin by direct route. Our four 500-pound bombs were dropped and we were

back at Oakington after a quiet round trip of three hours
and fifty-five minutes. After interrogation, we walked to
the Mess for our operational egg. Just inside the door we
met crews of 7 Squadron waiting for transport to the
flights – white sweaters, Irving jackets, flying boots,
scarves, whistles on collars. One bomb aimer said, 'Are
you going tonight, Jim?' 'No. I've been,' I said. 'Where?'
he asked. 'Berlin,' said I.

You can imagine the language of the Lancaster crews
as they ambled through the doors – off to the Big City.
Our unusually early attack had been a new type of spoof
– hoping the Germans would decide that, as the
Mosquitoes had been, the heavies would not come that
night.

The mine-laying operation in Kiel Bay and the Oboe bombing of airfields in Holland also took place in the early evening, all hoping to convince the Germans that no major raid
was to take place that night. The mine-laying force
encountered thick cloud, icing and some German fighters;
two Stirlings did not return.

All of these operations were well over before the Berlin
force and the Mosquitoes for the more orthodox Hanover
diversion left England. Even then, there was some doubt
whether the main operation would take place at all because
of bad weather; take-off was twice delayed, and the bomber
force did not get away until midnight. This may have helped
to lull the Germans but it further tired the bomber crews,
many of whom had made the long trip to Berlin the previous
night as well. The 'all-up' weight of the aircraft of at least
some Halifax squadrons was increased just for this raid,
from 63,000 pounds to 64,300 pounds. A Halifax of 76
Squadron crashed on taking off from Holme-on-Spalding
Moor, and two men were killed. When the bomber force set
out over the North Sea nearly one in ten of them turned
back. The Lancaster figures were again very low, despite this
being the second consecutive night's flying for many of the
crews. The Halifax figures were much higher; the worst rate

was in 4 Group, which had 30 aircraft turning back out of 134 taking off.

The Germans had no difficulty tracking the large force of aircraft approaching Denmark. Local fighters were sent out to engage the bombers as early as possible, and the first combats took place sixty miles out at sea. But very little action followed on the long approach route to Berlin, probably because the route over Denmark was too far north for most of the night fighters and probably also because the operations earlier in the night may have caused the Germans to believe that no major raid would develop, and their night-fighter crews had been 'stood down'. The following two accounts from men in bombers which were attacked on that outward route seem to show that the night-fighter crews operating in the stream at that stage were not experienced ones. Sergeant Maurice Ransom was the mid-upper gunner in a 76 Squadron Halifax.

We were attacked by a Ju 88 which knocked out one engine. We managed to lose him but we were losing height and the navigator informed the skipper that we could never make it, so we jettisoned our bomb load near Rostock (we think). After this, we decided to go back the way we had come, the navigator being quite confident he could make it.

Our lone aircraft was harried by Flak, and another twin-engined fighter appeared ahead of us and slightly above. Our navigator claims he could see the enemy observer's head looking around everywhere except below him. He must have been guided on to us by radar and it seemed a long, long time before the enemy crew must have told their ground control that they had boobed, and they broke away from us. We got home okay.

Flight Sergeant Phil Dubois was the Canadian tail gunner in a 420 Squadron Halifax. 'Monica' was a fighter detection device.

As we approached Berlin, we were attacked by a fighter. We had picked him up on Monica and I had my guns fully depressed, searching the lower half of the sky where most attacks came from. I heard Johnny yell, 'There he is, dead astern, up.' I looked up to see the enemy fighter banking not more than fifty yards away, a point-blank shot. I pulled back on my control stick to elevate my guns, but before they were halfway up he was gone. He made two more attacks from the beam but I was unable to bring my guns to bear. Each time he came within fifty yards but, as we were doing evasive action, he could not bring his guns to bear on us. I think we were fortunate that we had come up against a very green night-fighter pilot.

But the relative immunity from fighter attack ended abruptly when the bombers reached Berlin. The single-engined Wild Boar fighters had already been sent to the city, and most of the twin-engined fighters obviously decided to fly straight to Berlin and wait there, rather than flog northwards against the wind. Also present were many flare-dropping aircraft, four-engined Focke-Wulf Condors being clearly identified carrying out this duty as well as the regular flare droppers. The Flak fire was restricted to a lower altitude, and a fierce air battle took place, particularly as the bombers were leaving the target. These are the experiences of some of the men in the shot-down bombers. Flight Sergeant Ivan Taylor was the Australian bomb aimer in a Blind Marker Lancaster of 7 Squadron.

The first of our markers cascaded right below us and caused everything possible to be thrown at us. The gunners shouted that there were three Messerschmitt 110s approaching from behind and I spotted a fighter approaching us from the front, firing tracer. There was then a terrific jolt and the port wing became a mass of flames. The skipper gave the order to bale out. I remember putting on my parachute; then I must have become temporarily unconscious, as the next thing I remember was a dead silence and seeing my knees in front of me and my chute handle. Then I must have blacked out again, because I cannot remember pulling that handle, but I did of course, as the next thing I remember was hearing ammunition exploding and seeing myself still strapped in my chute harness which was hanging from a tree. Not many yards away was what was left of the burning aircraft, hence the exploding ammunition.

There were only two other survivors in this crew.

Flight Sergeant Peter Balderston, another Australian wireless operator in a 466 Squadron Halifax, describes the swift transition from being a member of a bomber crew to becoming part of the bombed population.

It was my job to pass the pilot his parachute, which I clipped on to him as he was struggling to keep the plane level. He had been hit in the face and had suffered other injuries as well. I then went back down past my position; I can recall having trouble clipping my chute on but eventually got both hooks clipped. I lost no time getting out. I can recall free falling for a while, as I did not know how much height we had lost and I wanted to be clear of the bomber stream. I pulled the D-ring and passed out.

I came to at what I judged to be about 6,000 feet and seemed to take a long time to come down. I was in the middle of Berlin; bombs falling all around; fires were everywhere. As I neared the ground, the hot air from the fires must have kept me up just enough to clear them; my trousers were charred and fell to pieces from the thighs to the top of the boots. I just had time to see an unbroken roof approaching and, making sure I kept my feet together, I swung for it, going clean through and landing in the attic of a three-storeyed house. I was standing in the room with my head and shoulders out of a three-foot hole in the tiles. As I had no chance of hiding my parachute, I took it off and threw it up on top of the roof. The house next door was burning fiercely, so that must have been the fire that burnt my pants. I had a torch in my flying boot, so I took this out. It worked and I shone my way down the stairs and out the back door of the house. It was as I was trying to open the side gate that a German civilian with an armband put a gun in my back and asked whether I was an *Engländer*. As I did not want to dispute the issue and say that I was an Australian, I agreed and said, 'Ja.'

I was then taken to an air-raid shelter where I am sure I would have been killed by the civilians but for the protection of a policeman and the gentleman who had caught me.

Pilot Officer D. Shipley was yet another Australian, tail gunner in a 10 Squadron Halifax.

We were attacked on the bomb run and one of our engines caught fire. Our skipper, Flight Lieutenant N. W. Kilsby, never panicked. We immediately dived and successfully put out the flames. He then did another circuit to bring us back on to the bombing route again; he was a beauty.

Then, all of a sudden, there came the same chatter of the fighter's cannon which I will never forget till my dying day. He hit us from underneath and ignited the overload tanks carried in a portion of our bomb bays. The skipper, strict commander and split-second thinker as he was, knew of the immediate danger and gave the command to bale out. I threw myself backwards to get out of this burning hulk. To my horror, I was caught up by my right leg which was trapped in the wall of the turret. This was a terrifying experience to me, because at that time the flames and the slipstream were overpowering. Even though I clawed at the sides of the turret, I was prevented from gaining entrance to free my trapped legs.

I was faced with death. I can assure you it is a

frightening thing. The last things I can remember are the frantic attempts to get back in, the flames which were engulfing me, the slipstream and my despairing appeal to God who, I hoped, would do something to spare my life. As we have heard many times before, my life passed before me; people and events of years gone by were graphically depicted. It was so real. My darling mother, father, fiancée and family, all flashing before me. I knew my number was up.

The next thing I can recall is seeing enormous flames and my first thoughts were that I was in hell. But, all of a sudden, silhouetted against the flames, was a Jerry helmet and a soldier standing guard beside me. I had come down by parachute right next to the runway of an airfield. Five of us got out; only God knows what happened to our poor, brave skipper, Bill Kilsby, and our newly and happily married wireless operator, Syd Daggett, whose charred bodies were found huddled together in the wireless operator's section in the remains of our burnt-out Halifax.

Seventeen Halifaxes and ten Lancasters came down in the Berlin area.

The factors experienced so far – fatigue, many early returns, a long route, heavy opposition at the target – often resulted in poor bombing, but not so on this night. The Pathfinders overcame all the problems of blind marking and performed excellently, arriving promptly, with serviceable H2S sets, and producing concentrated and accurate marking which was maintained throughout the raid. The Main Force attack was not so tidy, and seventy-seven communities outside Berlin reported bombs, but the majority of crews pressed on to the middle of the marked area and bombed there. A strong following wind resulted in the bombing 'creeping forward' rather than, as so often, back up the line of approach. It will be more convenient to describe the results of the bombing later in this chapter, but it can be stated here that this was a very successful raid and that most of the bombing fell in the south central, southern and south-eastern districts of Berlin.

The bombers faced a long flight back across the Baltic and Denmark before reaching the North Sea. The crews were cold, tired and had to face head winds, thick cloud and icing for much of a flight lasting nearly four hours. An unknown number of aircraft crashed into the sea, but three of them, all Halifaxes, were close enough to the English coast for some of their crew members to be rescued. Two Canadian Halifaxes ran so short of fuel over England that their crews abandoned their aircraft by parachute; two more men were killed in doing this. Finally, two further Halifaxes crashed while landing, and another man died. The all-up weight for Halifaxes was reduced after this raid. The arrival over England was in daylight, and many of the R.A.F. men saw the assembly of a large force of American Fortresses and Liberators setting out to attack Frankfurt.

It had been a successful raid, a fact quickly known at Bomber Command Headquarters because there were gaps in the cloud over Berlin and many crews brought back good bombing photographs. But the cost was heavy. Forty-six bombers were missing or lost in the sea; six more crashed in England or were written off after serious damage. Harris's decision to risk the Halifaxes had brought heavy losses to the squadrons flying that unlucky type. The heaviest losing squadrons were 434 Squadron based at Croft, with four Halifaxes missing and one abandoned over England, followed by 10 and 77 Squadrons, each with four aircraft missing. Among the Lancasters lost were the aircraft of the commander of 630 Squadron, Wing Commander John Rollinson, killed with all of his crew near Berlin, and another of the original H2S Mark III aircraft, Lancaster JB 412, shot down over Denmark, with three of the crew being killed.

Night of 30/31 January 1944

BERLIN   540 aircraft dispatched – 446 Lancasters, 82 Halifaxes, 12 Mosquitoes. Abortive sorties: 43, 8.0 per cent of those dispatched.

Time over target: 20.13 to 20.27. Approximate bombs on Berlin area: 1,896 tons – 1,029 high explosive, 867 incendiaries.

33 aircraft were lost – 32 Lancasters and 1 Halifax, 6.2 per cent of the heavies dispatched. Aircrew casualties: 193 killed, 53 prisoners of war.

Other operations: 76 aircraft dispatched, no losses.

Harris allowed his men one night of rest before ordering them to Berlin yet again. Those squadrons equipped with the older Halifaxes – Marks II and V – were not included in the order, but it was a maximum effort for everyone else. The tactical plan was much simpler after the elaborate diversions of recent raids. There would be no preliminary operations and no Mosquito bombing raids on German airfields. There would be only a tiny diversion by five Mosquitoes on Brunswick. The outward route was again a northerly one, though not as far north as on the previous raid. This, and a direct route home, would allow as many bombs to be carried as by the much larger force of the last raid. It was the end of the dark-night bombing period, and there would be a quarter- to half-moon during the outward flight.

The crews were unhappy. The third Berlin raid in four nights was the ultimate in intensity, with the prospect of moonlight to complete the dismay. Sergeant Stan Carter, a flight engineer in 207 Squadron, says:

The ops were hard on the nervous system; boys became men in a hurry. I remember one flight engineer, Sergeant Chalklin, who after his first trip seemed to be convinced he would not return from his next. After the

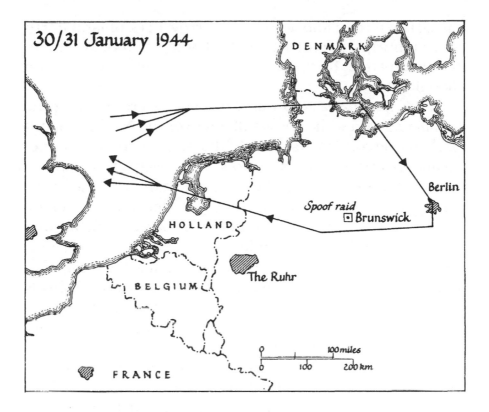

briefing for this raid, Sergeant Chalklin came to me with a large cardboard carton addressed to his mother. He asked me if I would please mail the carton when I returned the next day. I told him to mail it himself when he returned. His reply was, 'I wish I could believe I would be coming back.' The parcel was there when I returned; 'Chalky' didn't return. Hopefully, he became a prisoner of war.

The body of Sergeant Chalklin lies in the Berlin War Cemetery.

Take-off was in the late afternoon of a fine, clear day. It was what the Germans called 'backside' weather, clear conditions over England for the take-offs and landings of the bombers but thick cloud with icing over Germany to hamper the night fighters. There were few problems for the bombers over the North Sea, and they were able to gain altitude before encountering the cloud. They flew on over the German coast and across the narrow neck of land north of Hamburg. It was so clear that some bombers flew in companionable formation with each other in the thin moonlight.

The German reaction was slow. They were tracking the bomber stream while it was still out over the North Sea, but perhaps the controllers thought that this was another mine-laying diversion. Perhaps, too, they were reluctant to believe that Berlin would be attacked again with the moon rising. There is even documentary evidence from the log book of a German night-fighter pilot based at Schleswig/ Jagel, which was directly under the bomber's route, that his unit had been transferred to Holland that afternoon. This unusual event indicates that the Germans were probably trying to outguess the Bomber Command planners, believing that if the bombers were to come this night, they would not use the northerly route again. But the bombers did come in from the north. The Germans eventually responded and sent up their twin-engined units, firstly to radio beacon *Marie*, south of Bremen, and then on to a more general gathering point, at beacon *Quelle* which was near the mouth of the Elbe. The crews who had earlier flown down to Holland arrived back in their home area hungry; they had missed their operational meal at both places. One of the German fighters coming up from Holland was the Messerschmitt 110 of Oberfeldwebel Hallenbruch of I/NJG 1, which was based at Venlo. His radar operator was Unteroffizier Hermann Vollert, who describes what happened to them near beacon *Quelle*.

We thought that we were off too late to catch the bombers but we picked up a contact on radar; it was ten to thirteen kilometres away. I guided the pilot on to it. We thought it was a bomber but we were surprised to see that it only had two engines when we came into visual contact. We had strict orders not to attack any twin-engined aircraft unless we were absolutely sure that it was an enemy. We argued about it. I thought it was a

Beaufighter because it had a thicker fuselage than a Junkers 88, but the pilot thought it was a Junkers 88. He said it's another *arme Sau* – another 'poor devil' – like us.

We were behind it for about two minutes, discussing all this. We decided to turn away and leave it alone. We did so and were flying back to Venlo when, a few minutes later, possibly five minutes, we were suddenly attacked. He hit us in the right wing, between the engine and the fuselage; the whole wing broke off. I tried to get rid of the cockpit cover at my end and managed to do so. The plane was spinning and I kept being pushed into the back end of the cabin. I could hardly get my arm over the edge of the cabin but I knew that I mustn't give up. I tried again and again and got out in the end. I opened the parachute at once because I believed we were over the sea and that the strong west wind that was blowing would carry me nearer to the coast, but I came down in the water about two kilometres off shore. I was lucky; the water was so shallow that I could stand up.

The aircraft came down about ten kilometres out at sea. I don't know what happened to the pilot; they only found a hand and part of his body.

The Operations Record Book of 141 Squadron[1] shows that the Mosquito of Flight Lieutenant C. J. Rice and his Serrate operator, Flying Officer J. G. Rogerson, claimed a Messerschmitt 110 destroyed in this area. They were a new crew to this type of operation, and this was their first operational Serrate flight.

The slow German reaction allowed the bombers to get well on their way to Berlin before encountering serious opposition, but the night fighters then caught up, and the last seventy miles to Berlin saw the familiar sight of combats and bombers being shot down. The Mosquito diversion at Brunswick was too small and too distant to be of any use.

Several contributions are available from men involved in

---

1 Public Record Office AIR 27/971.

that hectic action on the approaches to Berlin. Unteroffizier Otto Kutzner was the Messerschmitt 110 pilot who had transferred to Holland that afternoon and then been ordered back north when the bombers approached.

I thought it would be another raid on Berlin so I decided to ignore the orders about radio beacons and fly direct to the north of Berlin and wait for the bombers there. As I approached Berlin I saw the Flak firing and markers falling. I think it was the beginning of the raid.

I believed that the bombers had equipment which warned them if a night fighter was behind them so I didn't use my radar, but went searching for them in the area above where the markers were falling. It wasn't long before I spotted one. First, it was just a dark shadow but, when I came up behind it, I could see the eight exhausts and I recognized it as a Lancaster by the two egg-shaped tail fins. He never saw me; he just flew straight on. Every pilot had his own method of attack. Mine was from directly behind so that I could put the tail gunner out of action to start with. I made sure I was in exactly the right position, at about fifty metres range, with at least the two outer engines in my gun sight. I gave it two bursts with my four cannons – a mixture of tracer and armour-piercing incendiary – all around the tail. The tail gunner must have been hit; he never fired back.

The tail began to burn and I think the ammunition for the tail turret exploded. I didn't watch it any more because I wanted to look for another bomber, but my crew watched it crash on the ground somewhere north of Berlin.

Flight Lieutenant Ron Munday was the pilot of a Lancaster taking evasive action from a fighter attack.

We went into a diving turn to port but, at the change-over point, on the climbing turn to port which was the next phase of the corkscrew, I yanked the control column back a bit hard in my heightened state of anxiety. In a normal stall, the Lanc would simply drop its nose and regain speed and not fall away on a wing or anything unstable, but this was a high-speed stall and one wing went down – the port one I think – and we found ourselves on our back. All the blind flying instruments toppled. The packets of Window stored behind my seat all went floating freely up to the inverted roof, along with the flight engineer – who was known as 'Upside-down Simmonds' for the rest of his tour – and all the dust and corruption of ages in the floor of the aircraft went sailing up into the roof and gave the impression of smoke inside the aircraft.

I instinctively started to roll the aircraft out of the inverted position by applying aileron. We lost height and gained airspeed. I think we lost about 10,000 feet. As the aircraft resumed its normal altitude, all the dust and corruption, plus the packets of Window, descended on to the floor again. One bundle hit me on the side of the head; I thought it was a lump of Flak at the time. The flight engineer was reunited with his duties and this rapid dive was converted into a climb which eventually got us back to about 19,000 feet. I don't think the whole thing took longer than a minute or a minute and a half, though the pulse rate and adrenalin levels took a little longer to achieve normality. We did not, of course, see the fighter again and we went on to bomb.

Flight Sergeant Robert Fenton was the New Zealand bomb aimer in a 100 Squadron Lancaster which was not so fortunate.

The bomb run had commenced, with bomb doors open, when streams of cannon and machine-gun fire passed through the fuselage. The aircraft immediately filled with smoke and fell into a spin to the left. The intercom was out of action and the engineer was making his way through the forward escape hatch. He called out, 'Fire!

Out!' Meanwhile I had jettisoned our bomb load and released the escape hatch. The centrifugal force was so great that I was unable to throw the hatch out. I recall going forward over the bomb sight and realizing that the Perspex was smashed by cannon fire. For a while I was halfway out of the aircraft, and then suddenly found myself falling. I had always made it a rule to wear my parachute on the bomb run.

After pulling the ripcord, the chute opened with a sound like a pistol shot and I was able to look down on the city on fire, with explosions taking place at regular intervals. The searchlights and Flak were still very active and, as I descended, a multiple cannon position fired briefly in my direction. My immediate reaction was to pull on the parachute cord and turn around – a futile gesture of survival I suppose. Shortly after this I became aware of a strong ground wind and, at several hundred feet, I crossed a large canal or river and passed by warehouses or commercial buildings. A firewatcher had a shot at me as I passed by but thank heavens his aim was not the best. I landed in a tree in a small park, my feet dangling about three feet off the ground, and found myself surrounded by about twenty Hitler Youth lads, all armed and obviously anxious to finish me off.

Fortunately a German soldier came along and took control of the situation. My troubles were not yet over as he quickly bundled me into the nearest air-raid shelter where a large gathering of civilians left no doubt of their feelings towards me. Once again the soldier handled the situation, although he felt obliged to put on an act for the civilians. I was extremely frightened.

More than twenty bombers were shot down on the approaches to Berlin, over the city and on the first part of the return route. Among these was another of the original Mark III H2S aircraft, Lancaster JB 352, in which Flight Lieutenant Albert Sambridge and his crew all died.

But the bombers were rewarded with another effective

raid, the bombing being even more concentrated than two nights earlier. The crews brought no photographs back, because of the thick cloud, but the glow of many fires was seen, and a Mosquito flying over the target later found a column of smoke rising high through the cloud. Details from German records will be given later, but it can be said that severe damage was caused in the districts immediately south of the city centre and less severe damage in a big spread to the north-west.

There is not much more to tell. The bombers flew out of Berlin to the south, then turned west and took a direct route home, reaching England just over two hours later. Several crippled Lancasters made crash landings at various airfields, but the only deaths were in a 640 Squadron Halifax which crashed at Catfoss, killing all of its crew.

Thirty-three bombers were missing. Unusually, most were Lancasters; a Canadian Halifax of 433 Squadron lost near Berlin was the only missing Halifax, a blessing which was probably helped by the reduction in their all-up weight that night. The Pathfinders lost eight aircraft, three of them from 405 (Canadian) Squadron. Other heavy losers were 463 (Australian) Squadron, with four aircraft lost, and 100 and 207 Squadrons with three each. 100 Squadron, based at Grimsby, had flown eighty-six sorties without loss in the previous six raids. Sergeant Harry Widdup, a flight engineer in the squadron, writes:

The 'Reaper' reached out and took three of our crews that night and evened the odds. We were back to being mortals again. One feeling of which I was aware at this time was that of the hopelessness felt by aircrews. No one talked any more of when they would finish their tours; it would have been tempting fate too much. Our rear gunner had gone L.M.F. on being posted to the squadron and our mid-upper did the same after this raid. Our skipper met him later in the war and the gunner told him, 'I never expected to see you again.'

The authorities and the ordinary people of Berlin had to deal with the effects of three raids in four nights. It was midwinter, snowing, freezing, gloomy and smoky. Everyone was tired. There had now been seventeen heavy raids since the start of the Battle of Berlin, fourteen of those raids in less than three months. The city officials were no longer able to compile their air-raid reports so carefully. In particular, they were unable to prepare separate reports for the last two raids, those of the nights of 28/29 and 30/31 January. On both nights the bombers had approached from the north-west and produced a long area of destruction along their route. The following description must, therefore, be of a more composite nature, dealing mainly with the last two raids but also including some details of the raid on the night of 27/28 January.

These attacks were the most damaging since the serious November raids, but the degree of fire damage in particular fell well short of that suffered in November, mainly because there was not the concentration of bombing in these last raids. Nearly every district in Berlin had been hit in at least one of the three raids, the only exceptions being Horst Wessel and Lichtenberg in the north-east of the city and Zehlendorf in the south-west. Another reason why the damage had not been so severe was that the earlier destruction in the areas bombed did not allow the spread of fire. The ability of Bomber Command to destroy Berlin by fire had now disappeared.

The total number of domestic buildings destroyed in the three raids was 2,923, with 4,116 severely and 4,576 'medium'-severely damaged; this meant that over 40,000 flats were destroyed or rendered uninhabitable. The number of 'barrack accommodation' units destroyed was given as 3,603. The number of people bombed out on the three raids was 171,000, of whom only 15,169 would be able to return to their homes quickly. It took several weeks for the numbers of dead and injured to be counted. One early return, for the second of these three raids, says: 'The casualties are still not known but they are bound to be considerable. A vast amount of wreckage must still be cleared; the rescue workers are still among the mountains of it.'¹ It was not until 8 March that a report was prepared showing that 1,341 people had definitely died, that a further 1,090 were 'missing', their bodies presumably being abandoned under collapsed buildings after all hope of rescue from under those mountains of rubble had passed, and that 4,061 people were injured. These statistics suggest that the three recent raids were roughly between 50 and 75 per cent as destructive as the November raids. The worst affected districts appear to have been Charlottenburg and Schöneberg (both hit badly in November as well) and Kreuzberg.

The main war-industry areas were not seriously damaged. Although scattered bombing affected most of the big firms, there were no major incidents and little direct effect upon production. Many smaller firms, however, were knocked out, and this would have an effect upon Berlin's overall contribution to the war effort. A more serious setback must have been the widespread damage to public utilities and transport; these were often more severely affected by scattered rather than by concentrated bombing. Six gasworks were hit and three of these had to close down. The West Power-Station blew up with a blinding flash on the night of 28/29 January. The city's rail network – both on the surface and underground – was also badly hit in the recent raids. The last attack, for example, caught the *U-Bahn* depot at Kreuzberg, destroyed 94 carriages and badly damaged 239 more. The railway report stated that the other main depot, at Grunewald, had been destroyed in the November raids.

Finally, a large number of public and cultural buildings were badly hit, another regular result of successful area bombing raids. A few details of interest can be taken from the lists to illustrate this type of damage: the Propaganda Ministry, the Hermann Goering Luftwaffe Barracks and the Leibstandarte S.S. Barracks, the Town Halls at Wilmersdorf and Friedenau, the Charlottenburg Opera

---

1 *Technische Nothilfe*, Gau III (Berlin–Bradenburg).

House, the Moabit remand prison, the University, six hospitals, three bridges, five embassies. An amusing comment comes from Gerhard Eichel, a young *Flakhilfer* who was ordered to carry out rescue work in the vaults of a bank on the Unter den Linden (probably the Preussische Staatsbank): 'What was on fire was the priceless and irreplaceable stockpile of a tobacco wholesaler and consisted mainly of some five million good cigars. We all pulled out soon with smoke poisoning and became instant non-smokers for life.'

I received only two other useful personal accounts from this period, again reflecting that these raids were not as serious as those of November.

Werner Schlecking, a technical inspector in an important war-industry firm (the Hollerith Werke), took shelter in the Nollendorf Platz *U-Bahn* station shelter on the last of the recent raids.

It was very deep and secure; it was the best shelter in the district but we realized that we were in the middle of the target area. The ground began to shake and heave from explosions all around us. Then the lights flickered and went out. Our nerves were near breaking point. Then there was a tremendous concussion; a heavy bomb must have gone deep into the ground near by. People began to scream. The emergency lights came on but they still left most of the corners in the dark. Then panic broke out. We heard a gushing and gurgling sound – coming nearer – and the terror was complete when someone shrieked, 'My God – WATER!' This cry of horror swept over the whole platform, which was packed tight with people. The panic-stricken mass raced like mad to the stairways leading to the upper platform. What had happened was that the big water main, lying deep underground, had been broken. The stairs up to the upper platform became blocked with people. Parents tried to hold their children above their heads so that they would not be trampled on. The panic was made worse through people having a lot of pets which they had taken into the shelter, strictly against orders. People always seemed to behave irresponsibly. So utter chaos reigned and it was almost impossible to get up to the next platform.

Because I had grown up in this area, watching and playing as a kid there when they built this underground system, I was able to use this boyhood knowledge to save our lives. I held my wife back and told her that first we had to go down into the rushing water which was gurgling over the rail tracks and getting higher every minute. We went into the tunnel and waded against the rushing water which came up to my waist, rising slowly but steadily even further. We went along the dark passageway of the underground tunnel. My plan proved to be right because I knew that the tunnel gradually ascended in that direction.

The water was ice cold and numbing, but very slowly we came out of it and finally it only reached up to our knees. We were able to reach an air shaft which had an iron ladder and somebody helped us out on to the street. We were wet all over; outside it was bitterly cold. In only a few moments our clothes began to freeze on our bodies but everywhere around us fires were raging and that helped to dry us out a little.

I never went back down into that underground station and so I don't know how many people died there. There was no news about disasters like that in the papers in those times; everything was hushed up and kept strictly secret.

When we got home we found our home was on fire, so we were bombed out – for the second time.

The last account is from a nineteen-year-old typist, Cecilia Schellhase, whose home was in the now so often bombed district of Schöneberg. She describes the raid of 30/31 January; several Berliners mention their fear of a raid on this night because it was the anniversary of Hitler's accession to power.

Because Hitler had taken over power exactly eleven years earlier, the people were worried that the R.A.F. would send a special present to us on that night. I was due to be evacuated by the Health Insurance Department to Bavaria the next morning, because we had been bombed so often that I had breathed in too much smoke and had breathing problems. Because of this we took all our stuff down to the shelters in good time. That coming journey was foremost in my mind and my suitcase was ready packed in the shelter. None of us went to bed; we all sat in the flat listening to the radio, waiting to get the earliest possible warning of a raid. We heard that bombers were in the Hamburg area; then I think they mentioned they were near Lübeck, so it was time for the cellar. We sat that raid out, hoping for the best, and we survived it.

But the raid was so bad that I couldn't leave for Bavaria when the time came for me to travel next day. I got as far as Zoo on the *U-Bahn*. I stood alone, among the ruins and the snow, with my heavy suitcase. It was dark, with the pall of smoke, and everyone was walking with handkerchiefs over their mouths. The streets near by were still burning fiercely. I felt helpless and was full of despair. A man told me that there were no trains so I started walking; I don't know where I was going to. I couldn't manage that big suitcase so I took off my belt, tied it round the handle of the case and started to pull it along the snow.

I hadn't got far when an army lorry pulled up. The driver asked me where I wanted to go. I told him I wanted to go to any station where trains were still running, because I wanted to catch a train for Munich. He told me he had come from his camp at Potsdam and that the trains were still running from there. I got up and they let me sit in the front where it was nice and warm. I was there all day. The two soldiers spent the day cruising round Berlin, looking up their relatives and stopping to drink coffee. I finally reached Potsdam at 8 p.m. Everything was normal there. There was even a train standing at the station going in the right direction. I reached the clinic in Bavaria the next day, covered in soot.

So ended a much more successful month for Bomber Command. There had been only four raids on Berlin, but there were no failures; the first two raids can be classed as of medium success and the last two as very successful. This better performance can be credited to two factors: an improvement in blind marking by the Pathfinders and the greater weight of attack brought to bear by the inclusion of Halifaxes in three of the four raids. This table shows the major raids of the past dark-night period.

	Raids	*Sorties dispatched*	*Aircraft lost*
To Berlin	4	2,516	147 (5·8 per cent)
To other targets	2	1,146	95 (8·3 per cent)
TOTAL	6	3,662	242 (6·6 per cent)

The casualties of the two raids to other targets, to Brunswick and Magdeburg, were contrary to the trends in earlier periods of the Battle of Berlin; the Berlin raids were less costly and produced more successful bombing results.

Sir Arthur Harris had a further two periods of monthly darkness remaining before Bomber Command's operations would be subordinated to the need to prepare the way for the Normandy invasion.

10 FEBRUARY – TURNING AWAY

After the Berlin raid of 30/31 January, many of the bomber squadrons were told that they would not be required for operations for nearly two weeks. Squadrons could normally expect a rest during a moon period, but such a long formal stand-down was unusual. With the exception of a small mine-laying operation by fifty Halifaxes on the night of 2 February, not a single major operation took place for thirteen nights. Existing crews were sent on leave or carried out training. New crews arrived. Many men remember this period as one of easing of tension and fatigue and of reinvigoration. An unusually large number of new aircraft were delivered. In First World War phraseology, the squadrons were being 'fattened up'. This rest period was further prolonged by a heavy snowfall. Everyone at the bomber bases was out clearing snow from the runways and perimeter tracks; and, on the morning of Sunday 13 February, Harris decided to recommence operations. It was to be Berlin again, with every available Halifax and Lancaster. But this raid had to be cancelled because of the weather. The operation was laid on again for the next day, but again had to be cancelled. Finally, on Tuesday 15 February, Bomber Command's war started again.

Night of 15/16 February 1944

BERLIN 891 aircraft dispatched – 561 Lancasters, 314 Halifaxes, 16 Mosquitoes. Abortive sorties: 75, 8·4 per cent of those dispatched.

Time over target: 21·13 to 21·35. Approximate bombs on Berlin area: 2,643 tons – 1,230 high explosive, 1,413 incendiaries.

43 aircraft were lost – 26 Lancasters, 17 Halifaxes, 4·8 per cent of the force. Aircrew casualties: 265 men killed, 54 prisoners of war, 5 evaders.

Supporting operations: 43 Stirlings and 4 Halifaxes mine-laying in Kiel Bay, 24 Lancasters in a diversion raid to Frankfurt-on-Oder, 23 Oboe Mosquitoes bombing night-fighter airfields in Holland, 14 Mosquito Serrate patrols, 9 R.C.M. sorties. One Serrate Mosquito was lost.

Other operations: 62 aircraft dispatched; one Stirling was lost while dropping supplies to a Resistance group.

The squadrons made a major effort to get every available aircraft off the ground, and this was a record-breaking night in many ways. The total numbers sent to Berlin, the number of Lancasters, the number of Halifaxes and the bomb tonnage were all record figures. The Halifax figures were boosted by two Canadian squadrons – 420 and 424 – which were now ready to operate after returning from the Middle East; another Canadian squadron – 425 – would be ready for the next raid. The increased Lancaster effort – forty-six aircraft more than the previous best – all came from existing squadrons. 5 Group in particular made a huge effort, providing 226 Lancasters, a record by any group during the Battle of Berlin.

There were several novelties in the planning of the operation. The now standard items of Oboe Mosquitoe attacks on night-fighter airfields and a preliminary mine-laying

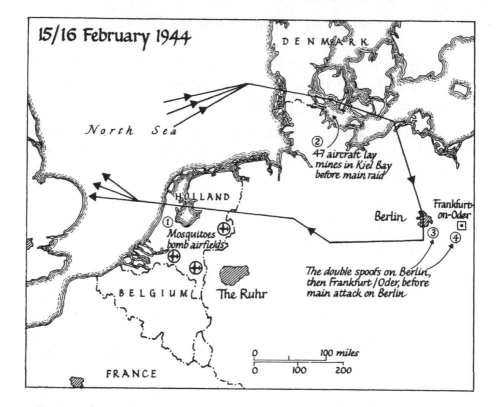

15/16 February 1944

D E N M A R K

North   Sea

② 47 aircraft lay mines in Kiel Bay before main raid

HOLLAND

Berlin

Frankfurt-on-Oder

① Mosquitoes bomb airfields

③ ④

BELGIUM   The Ruhr

The double spoofs on Berlin, then Frankfurt/Oder, before main attack on Berlin

FRANCE

0 ____ 100 miles
0   100   200

force flying to the Kiel area were employed, but some subtlety was used in the tactics for the Berlin area. A force of Mosquitoes was to precede the main bomber force to Berlin, dropping Target Indicators, bombs and fighter flares, but this was intended to be taken by the Germans as a decoy. Next, twenty-four Pathfinder Lancasters *using H2S* were to simulate the opening of a major raid on Frankfurt-on-Oder, fifty miles further on to the east of Berlin, hoping to convince the German controllers that this was the main raid just before the huge main attack actually fell on Berlin. The weakness of this plan was that these moves were mainly designed to outwit a German defence based on Wild Boar operations in the target area. If the Germans mounted a good Tame Boar operation on the outward route, the bombers would be under attack long before this Berlin/Frankfurt-on-Oder/Berlin plan unfolded. Finally, the bombers were to use a split route on the homeward flight, different halves of the force flying routes about forty miles apart.

Again, there was a weakness in this part of the plan. Given the standard of navigation of the average bomber crew, this was likely to result in a broad spread across the two routes, with concentration nowhere. The truth was that Bomber Command was unable to develop a good response to the Tame Boar route-fighting tactic.

The bombers took off in the early evening. There were no crashes. The Halifaxes of 4 Group suffered a rash of early returns, but the other groups pressed on well. Another 4 Group Halifax reported being fired upon by a four-engined German aircraft over the North Sea, but the fire probably came from a nervous British rear gunner. The narrow mainland of Denmark was safely crossed, but then a standard German Tame Boar operation developed.

The Germans detected the bomber force while it was only a quarter of the way across the North Sea. The night-fighter crews were ordered to cockpit readiness; they were as well rested as the British aircrews and most had enjoyed a recent leave. The mine-laying operation in Kiel Bay was ignored. The units based in Holland and Belgium were ordered to take off and told to fly north; those in Germany were able to stay on the ground longer and thus conserve their fuel but those too were airborne before the bombers crossed the Danish coast. The running commentary followed the bomber route in careful detail. British jamming attempts were unsuccessful. Every German fighter which sighted a bomber was ordered to fire a green flare to help his comrades find the bomber stream. The first contacts were made near the east coast of Denmark, and numerous combats took place from that point all the way to the outskirts of the Berlin Flak defences. Most of the action was in the rear half of the bomber stream. At least twenty bombers were shot down.

There are no contributions from the crews of bombers shot down in that battle; much of the action was over the Baltic, and there were not many survivors. Oberleutnant Paul Zorner describes how he took off from Lüneburg, climbed through layers of cloud and found himself in clear visibility between 'towers of cloud'. Listening to the running commentary, he flew over Hamburg, then eastwards over the Baltic where he saw two burning bombers plunging down, and after a final spurt of speed he caught up with the bomber stream. His radar operator brought him into visual contact with a Lancaster, which had to be attacked with forward firing cannons because his *schräge Musik* would not work. The starboard wing of the bomber caught fire; the rear gunner fired back and missed. The fire spread so rapidly that Zorner could 'sit back on his right side in peace and wait'. He saw the Lancaster go down in a steep spiral and crash into the Baltic. Regaining height, he saw Flak fire and bombing in the distance, chased off in that direction and shot down a second bomber north-west of Berlin. He tried for a third success on the return route but soon had to land. It was a typical Tame Boar flight by an experienced German crew; the two bombers shot down were Zorner's twenty-fifth and twenty-sixth successes. He had a personal interest in defending Berlin; his newly married wife lived there.

Leutnant Wilhelm Seuss, a Messerschmitt 110 pilot, was not so fortunate.

We found the bomber stream and gained a contact north of Berlin. I saw a bomber above me and I came up, behind and below him, and tried to get into a firing position. I was flying a new aircraft. I tried to keep it steady but couldn't stabilize it. I flew as slowly as I could but the bomber was going even more slowly and I kept pulling ahead, the bomber falling back and me not being able to fire. I don't know whether they had seen me and were being particularly clever by slowing right down or whether there was something wrong with my aircraft, but it was very strange, quite unreal to see this big bomber just above me and I couldn't do anything about it. Eventually I lost him behind me.

The Flak was given priority over the target when the bombers reached Berlin, and most of the night fighters kept out of the way – but not all of them. Unteroffizier

Benno Gramlich was a Junkers 88 pilot who had been posted to NJG 10 at Werneuchen, near Berlin, where various technical equipment was tested. When a raid was expected, most of this unit's aircraft were sent into action. Gramlich was one of the many night-fighter pilots who managed to pick up only an occasional success. His only one before this night had been six months earlier.

We saw, from a long way out, Berlin burning – at least the glow in the clouds, red and yellow. I decided to fly into the Flak. The earlier night-fighter crews had gained their successes in the box fighting but we 'young crews' had to find our bombers wherever we could. We all wanted to get successes and perhaps even the Ritterkreuz, so we were willing to risk our lives and those of our crew to gain success. We could always fire recognition flares if the Flak got too close.

I flew into the Flak area and there we saw a bomber ahead of us against the illuminated cloud, just like a shadow on a screen. The first bomber I had ever attacked had got away because I didn't open fire as soon as I saw it and I had sworn then that I would always open fire as quickly as possible. I went into a shallow dive and opened fire at once. Unfortunately, my three cannons – my best weapons – didn't work, so I only had my three machine-guns. The tail gunner and the top gunner returned my fire and we were hit in the front of our aircraft, but that wasn't serious because we had armour plating in the nose and bullet-proof glass in the cockpit.

My first job, however, was to knock out those two gunners. That was no problem; our small Ju 88 was more manoeuvrable than this heavy bomber, although I think he had already dropped his load. I closed right in. I think I got the top turret first, aiming in front of it and then pulling my fire back through it; then I did the same with the tail gunner. I fired at the fuel tanks between the engines next. He surprised me. He could have got away by diving into the cloud which was not too far below but, instead, he seemed to be trying to turn into my attack. But we were too manoeuvrable and I saw my tracer striking him. I kept hitting him in the wings but they didn't burn so I started aiming at the cockpit. Then my crew saw three or four men jumping out by parachute. The bomber suddenly reared up, turned on to its back, and went down, not quite vertically.

It was sad for that brave bomber pilot. He had behaved like a day fighter. He had tried to shake me off rather than take cover in the cloud.

Unteroffizier Gramlich's success over Berlin was an isolated one. The Flak barrage was fierce, but it is believed that only three bombers were shot down over the city from approximately 775 Lancasters and Halifaxes which reached the target. One factor contributing to this low casualty rate was the intense concentration of the attack. The planned bombing time was only twenty minutes, with a density of nearly forty aircraft per minute; this was four times greater than some of the raids at the start of the Battle of Berlin. Some of the newer crews at the rear of the bomber stream failed to reach the target on time and were late, but there is no evidence that they came to much harm.

Berlin was completely cloud covered, and the Pathfinders had to use Skymarkers. German records show that the heaviest of the bombing fell in the familiar, well bombed areas to the west and south of the city centre. More than 3,000 individual fires were reported. There was much new damage to all types of property, but the city authorities were no longer so diligent at recording details. The number of people killed is given as 320, including 80 foreign workers and one prisoner of war, but a further 260 people were still under the wreckage when those figures were compiled. The raid should probably be classed as being of medium-good success, mainly because of the record loads carried by the large bomber force. It was the heaviest raid of the war on Berlin; the 2,643 tons of bombs estimated to have been dropped in the area were greater than the tonnage which had caused the Hamburg firestorm. Among the bomb loads were no less than 470 4,000-pounders and fifteen 8,000-pounders. But a substantial part of the effort was wasted. The German records list forty-seven communities where bombs dropped, in a great spread thirty miles away from Berlin in all directions; sixty-one people died in these places. Oberleutnant Zorner's wife wrote to him: 'Last night's raid mostly went astray. Much of the attack fell in open country.'

The night fighters rejoined the bomber stream when it left Berlin, but most of the fighters were getting low on fuel and soon had to land. The diversionary raid to Frankfurt-on-Oder was completely ignored, and the twenty-four Pathfinder Lancasters carrying out that raid returned without loss. The main bomber force had the unusual benefit of a tail wind from the east and made a fast flight back to the Dutch coast. But part of the night-fighter force had been retained in this area, and there was a further flurry of action. Between ten and fifteen more bombers were shot down.

The North Sea was crossed and took its usual toll of solitary, crippled bombers. Two Halifaxes and a Lancaster crashed near their airfields in England, with thirteen crewmen being killed. Two more Halifaxes were abandoned due to petrol shortage. The crew of one of these came down safely by parachute, but the other crew, from 78 Squadron, was unlucky. The veteran operational pilot, Flight Lieutenant R. N. Shard, D.F.C., D.F.M., instructed his crew to bale out, thinking and hoping that the aircraft was over land. But the Halifax was still over the sea, and only one man came down close enough to the shore to survive.

The raid cost forty-two bombers missing and five crashed or abandoned in or near England. Most of the losses were spread evenly through the groups and squadrons. The unluckiest squadron was 7 Squadron at Oakington, which lost four aircraft containing very experienced crews. The lists of the men in these aircraft contained a wing commander and two squadron leaders, and the following decorations: two D.S.O.s, one C.G.M., eight D.F.C.s, seven

D.F.M.s and one O.B.E. Only three men survived in these four crews. The Pathfinders would find it hard to replace such men. Another experienced man to go was Wing Commander E. J. Grace, the commanding officer of 169 Squadron, killed when his Serrate Mosquito was shot down in the Hanover area. His navigator survived.

Harris tried to follow up this raid as quickly as possible. A raid on Berlin was ordered on each of the following three days – 16, 17 and 18 February – but on each occasion the operation had to be cancelled because of unfavourable weather conditions, usually bad weather over the home airfields. But the weather improved on Saturday 19 February, and the raid planned for that night went ahead.

There followed an operation which was probably the most important of the Battle of Berlin. But the target was not Berlin; Harris decided to change destinations and go for Leipzig, an important city almost as distant as Berlin and high on a recent list of priority targets because of its aircraft assembly factories. A maximum effort was ordered, and 832 bombers took off among snow showers, taking an outward route across Holland and Germany pointing straight to Berlin, before turning sharply south towards Leipzig. There were two diversions: a mine-laying operation to Kiel Bay in the north and a Mosquito raid on Berlin. It would have been a good plan if the only necessity had been to deceive the German controllers about the identity of the target, but the long legs across Holland and Germany were ideal for the new Tame Boar tactics.

Two things went wrong and produced the catastrophe which followed. The forecast winds which had been given to crews allowed for a steady head wind, but the actual wind encountered turned out to be only a light wind from the north. These conditions prevailed almost from the beginning of the flight and immediately broke up the cohesion of the bomber stream. Some navigators realized at once what was happening, and their aircraft carried out a series of time-wasting manocuvres to avoid reaching Leipzig before the raid started. The navigational log of a Path-finder navigator who was on his fifty-fourth operation shows how an experienced man coped with the problem. He detected the new wind within seven minutes of setting course from above his airfield and he advised his pilot to 'dog-leg' four times in order to lose time before reaching Leipzig. He was forced to waste a total of thirty-one minutes in this way but he arrived over the target within half a minute of his allocated marking time.[1]

But less experienced navigators failed to detect the strength of the new wind and approached the target too early because the 'broadcast winds' system did not detect the change of wind accurately. This led to the length of the bomber stream being grossly extended. The German controllers meanwhile had ample time to direct their fight-ers into the slow moving, well spread bomber force and carried out their best Tame Boar operation to date. Various Flak batteries joined in and scored successes as single bom-bers flew through their areas, and four more bombers were probably lost through collisions while dog-legging on the way to Leipzig.

Conditions over the target were chaotic. Many crews had arrived early and were orbiting the area; the Leipzig Flak did not open fire, and the searchlights remained doused. Some Main Force aircraft refused to wait for the Pathfinder markers and bombed before Zero Hour, using their H2S. When the Pathfinder markers did go down, there was a wild scramble as several hundred bombers came in from all directions, anxious to bomb quickly and get out of the area. There were more collisions. It is not possible to give details of whether the bombing was successful, because American Fortresses followed up the raid next day, and the Leipzig reports do not allocate the damage caused to the aircraft factories and other parts of Leipzig and the casualties – 969 people killed, 51,380 bombed out – between the two raids,

1 From the navigation log of Flight Lieutenant H. J. Wright, 156 Squadron.

but the high figure of bombed out probably indicates that Bomber Command's area attack was successful.

Bomber Command lost seventy-eight aircraft on this raid, by far its highest loss of the war so far. The overall loss rate of heavy bombers was 9·6 per cent. The most severe losses were in the Canadian squadrons of 6 Group, which lost 18 of their 129 aircraft on the raid.

The experiences of the Leipzig operation caused three immediate changes.

The first was the comparatively minor tactical move of introducing a 'movable Zero Hour', so that, if a bomber force was ever again pushed forward too fast in enemy territory by a change of wind, the timing of the raid could be changed by a simple message added to the regular wind broadcasts.

The second change was the decision by Harris that the older types of Halifax – the Marks II and V – would no longer be required to take part in raids against German targets, a decision which removed eight squadrons in 4 and 6 Groups from the front line. A pilot of 10 Squadron, who had taken part in recent raids to Berlin and survived the Leipzig operation, says, 'I should think that the sigh of relief could be heard all over Yorkshire.' In fact, Harris's decision was not the result only of the Leipzig raid. The casualty rate on that raid for the newer Halifax IIIs was twice as great as for the older Halifaxes. The decision was based more on the results of other raids during this period, when heavy casualties had led to a loss of morale among crews which was reflected in a high rate of early returns.

The third decision was one of outstanding importance. Sir Arthur Harris decided to abandon the campaign against Berlin. He had persevered with his resolve to destroy the city and bring about a German collapse, sending eighteen major raids to Berlin since mid-August, but it is apparent that Harris's vision of a bombing success against Berlin bringing an end to the war had now died. This major decision was Harris's alone; he received no orders from above on the matter. He does not comment upon it at all in his post-war memoirs. Why did Harris pull back from Berlin? This is not difficult to answer. What had happened to the bombers on the Leipzig raid was just as likely to happen again on a Berlin raid and, given the recent evidence of German night-fighter successes, was likely to happen on any operation taking the bombers into that part of Germany. Bomber Command had no answer to the current German night-fighter tactics, and the experience of the Leipzig raid confirmed that bomber losses to targets like Berlin were likely to increase, leading to a further loss of morale among the aircrews and to a delay in the conversion of his squadrons to better types of aircraft and also in the overall expansion of Bomber Command. Although there had been an improvement in Pathfinder marking, and the damage caused in recent raids to Berlin had been substantial, Berlin was obviously still functioning as a seat of government and as an arsenal and hub of communications in Germany's war effort. Also, there was no evidence that the morale of Berlin's civilian population was about to crack.

Harris realized that any continuation of the campaign against Berlin was unlikely to break the city, but was more likely to break Bomber Command. The morale of most of his squadrons was holding, but he was shrewd enough to judge that any further rise in casualties might break the spirit of his men. He had been forced to withdraw first the Stirlings and then the older Halifaxes from the battle, and the crews of the newer Halifaxes showed signs of shakiness; the Halifax IIIs had suffered the heaviest early returns in the Leipzig raid. One can only be amazed at the way the Lancaster crews had stuck to their task, with no respite of any kind in any of the recent operations. But if the Lancaster squadrons were pushed too hard, then Bomber Command might be in no fit state to support the invasion and, far from receiving the credit for breaking Germany, might bear the blame for letting down the Allied armies during the invasion period.

But there was still a way forward. The historical period now known as the Battle of Berlin would continue for another six weeks, until the end of March. In surveying the major industrial cities of Germany which he considered suitable for area attack, Harris found that he could do little more against targets in Northern or Central Germany, north say of a line from Cologne to Leipzig. The Ruhr, Cologne, Hamburg, Hanover, Brunswick, Magdeburg, Leipzig and Berlin had all been hit as hard as his squadrons could manage under the current tactical circumstances. But there were other German cities, south of that line, still in comparatively undamaged condition. Bomber Command could tackle those targets by way of routes across France which were often hundreds of miles away from the airfields of the main night-fighter units.

So, far from abandoning the principle of area bombing and the hope of destroying Germany's industrial cities, Harris switched to Southern Germany. He started the very next night with a raid by 598 aircraft to Stuttgart which was carried out with the startlingly low cost of only nine missing aircraft. For the remainder of that dark-night bombing period and the first half of the next period, Harris kept it up: Augsburg, Stuttgart twice more and Frankfurt twice. Three times he tried to attack Munich but was prevented from doing so by the weather. He also bombed the ball-bearing town of Schweinfurt, but this was not a target of his own choice; he was given a direct order to carry out this raid. The casualty rate on these raids was less than half that of the recent series of raids against Berlin and other targets to the north. And the switch to the south brought success. The attack on Augsburg, on the night of 25 February, was outstandingly effective; Frankfurt was hit very hard; only at Stuttgart, difficult to find in a long, narrow valley, was success elusive.

11 ONE MORE TRY

The non-moon period of the second half of March 1944 represented the final stage of a distinct, year-long section of the bombing war. It was the last dark-night bombing period of what Harris would call his 'Main Offensive', the sustained area-bombing campaign against German cities which, it had been hoped, would break Germany before the invasion of Normandy. That aim had clearly not been achieved, though no one should take away from Harris and from Bomber Command the credit for severely weakening the German war machine and diverting weapons and man-power away from the invasion coast.

The raids carried out during that last period of eighteen nights were of a mixed nature. There were six raids to French railway targets in preparation for the invasion. These were mostly carried out by the Stirlings and older Halifaxes; these did not entail deep penetrations of German defended air space, and the bomber casualties were light. During the first half of the period, the Lancasters and newer Halifaxes, a bombing force now more than 800 aircraft strong, continued the campaign against cities in Southern Germany. But Harris was planning to have one last attempt to gain a success at Berlin. He realized that blind marking was unlikely to produce that success, so he waited patiently for a weather forecast which gave clear conditions over Berlin. At his morning conference on Tuesday 21 March the weather forecast appeared favourable, and the raid was ordered. He even sent one of his rare appeals out to the squadrons:

Although successful blind bombing attacks on Berlin have destroyed large areas of it, there is still a substantial section of this vital city more or less intact. To write this off, it is of great importance that tonight's attack should be closely concentrated on the Aiming Point. You must not think that the size of Berlin makes accurate bombing unimportant. There is no point in dropping bombs on the devastated areas in the west and south-west. Weather over the target should be good. Go in and do the job.[1]

But a later forecast showed that cloud would probably cover Berlin, and the raid was cancelled at 6.00 p.m. Harris had to wait for another three days, until Friday the 24th, before better conditions were promised, and this time the operation went ahead. It would prove to be one of the most eventful raids of the Battle of Berlin.

Night of 24/25 March 1944

BERLIN 811 aircraft dispatched – 577 Lancasters, 216 Halifaxes, 18 Mosquitoes. Abortive sorties: 53, 6·5 per cent of those dispatched.

Time over target: 22.25 to 22.45. Approximate bombs on Berlin area: 2,493 tons – 1,070 high explosive, 1,423 incendiaries.

72 aircraft were lost – 44 Lancasters and 28 Halifaxes,

1 From Alan W. Cooper, *Bombers over Berlin*, p. 185.

9.1 per cent of the heavies dispatched. Aircrew casualties: 392 killed, 131 prisoners of war, 4 evaders.

Supporting operations: 147 aircraft from training units on a diversionary 'sweep' to Northern France, 11 Mosquitoes on a 'spoof' raid at Kiel, 19 Oboe Mosquitoes bombing night-fighter airfields in Holland, Belgium and France, 10 Serrate patrols, 19 Mosquitoes of other commands on Intruder patrols. 1 Serrate Mosquito was lost.

Other operations: 17 aircraft dispatched, no losses.

There was still a doubt about the weather. Frontal cloud was moving eastwards and this might not clear Berlin before the raid, so an alternative target, Brunswick, more likely to be clear of cloud, was included in the orders. But the weather reconnaissance Mosquito sent out that morning did not examine the movement of the frontal cloud; it made only a short flight to Denmark, to inspect the weather on the outward route. No further information came in about the weather, and just before take-off Berlin was confirmed as the target. This would be the first time Bomber Command had ventured into this part of Germany since the Luftwaffe inflicted such heavy losses in the fateful Leipzig raid more than a month earlier, but the Americans were planning a heavy raid on Schweinfurt during the day, and this, it was hoped, would draw much of the Luftwaffe down to Southern Germany. Considerable attention was given to Bomber Command's tactical planning. The approach route was a northerly one, over Denmark and the Baltic, with a small Mosquito attack on Kiel as a diversion. But this was all to be preceded by a flight over France by 147 aircraft from Bomber Command's training units. Hopefully, this would appear to the Germans as the outward flight of the main bombing force on another raid to Southern Germany and would draw the night-fighter units down to the south. It is a measure of how the need to divert German attention had escalated since the opening of the Battle of Berlin that 205

Bomber Command aircraft were this night engaged on diversionary and support operations, compared with none on the first raid of the battle in August 1943.

The tactics to be used at the target were also to be quite different to those used in all the preceding raids of the Battle of Berlin. The Pathfinders were to make every effort to identify the Aiming Point by eye – visual marking – and to use blind H2S marking only as a last resort. There were also to be two Master Bombers, the first time such a feature was employed since the previous August. The reader may remember the reference earlier in the book (see page 96) to the six special Lancasters with Merlin 85 engines ordered for each of the Pathfinder heavy squadrons for Master Bomber work. The first of these aircraft was now available, and Wing Commander R. J. Lane of 405 Squadron would fly as one of the Master Bombers in that aircraft. The choice of the second Master Bomber and of his aircraft shows another interesting development. Wing Commander E. W. Anderson, a very experienced ex-operational navigator now on the staff of Pathfinder Headquarters, was sent as the Deputy Master Bomber, lying on some cushions in the nose of a Mosquito of the Meteorological Flight. Master Bombers were going to be needed for many of the pre-invasion targets, where Aiming Points would often be close to French and Belgian civilian areas. Air Vice-Marshal Bennett was obviously considering using a Mosquito as a Master Bomber aircraft on these coming raids and was using this Berlin raid as an experiment. (This should not be confused with the low-level Mosquito Bomber work later carried out by 5 Group; the Berlin Mosquito would not be allowed to fly below 20,000 feet. Bennett did not believe in low-level marking or raid controlling.)

The bomber force took off in mid-evening, into a dark but clear and starlit sky. The outward route consisted of long legs across the North Sea, Denmark and the Baltic, and this would have been a routine part of the operation but for one factor: the wind. The navigator in every crew was given before take-off the best possible forecast of the wind to be expected on various sections of the night's route. New winds were found during the flight by using Gee or H2S (only over land), by listening to the broadcast winds from England or by taking star sights – all in complete darkness and with the bomber rushing ever onwards while the navigator made his calculations.

Gee was an excellent aid based upon a grid of signals broadcast from England. These were available from the moment of take-off until the Gee signals became jammed by German interference about halfway across the North Sea. The winds forecast before take-off for this part of the flight are shown in navigators' logs as '340/21' and '358/44', that is 21 miles per hour from 340 degrees for the first part of the flight across the North Sea and then increasing to 44 m.p.h. and coming further from the north as the coast of Denmark was approached.[1] The wind was expected to become even stronger as the bombers flew further east.

But many navigators started picking up on their Gee sets much stronger winds than forecast as soon as they set out from England. The 'Windfinder' system started operating. The navigators in the selected aircraft reported their 'found winds' back to England, in short coded messages, and the staffs in England started to calculate revised forecasts. These were retransmitted to all aircraft on the raid. The revised details sent to crews were in two parts: an estimate of the wind for the past half-hour and a forecast for the next half-hour. It was a process that would be repeated throughout the raid.

The first difficulty with that outward flight was the gap over the second half of the route over the North Sea, after the Gee signals became jammed by the Germans and before the coast of Denmark appeared to provide an image on the bombers' H2S screens. No new information could be

1 For these and other details on this night, I am grateful for the use of the navigational logs of Flight Sergeant K. G. Thompson of 101 Squadron and Pilot Officer T. R. Lister of 158 Squadron.

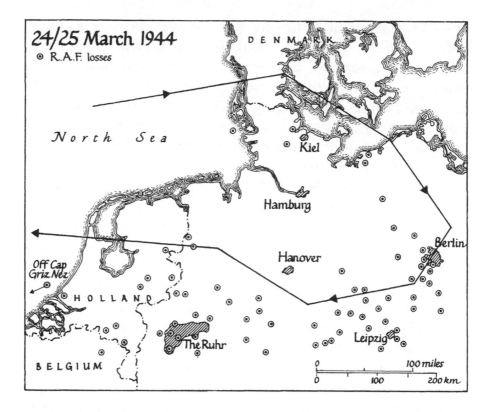

obtained for about an hour. During this time the direction
of the wind from almost due north remained steady; the
wind direction was never any trouble that night, only its
strength. Most navigators had adjusted their course for the
winds detected earlier but had then flown on blindly, waiting for a landfall on the Danish coast. This was supposed
to be fifteen miles north of the island of Sylt; but when
that long, thin and distinctive island appeared on the H2S
screens of many aircraft, navigators were horrified to find
that they were over the south of Sylt, thirty miles south of
track. The reason for this was simple; the wind from the
north was far stronger than anyone expected, probably
above 100 m.p.h. One man says that when the matter was
discussed the next morning it was the first time he heard
the expression 'jet stream'.

The navigators were now in trouble, even the more
experienced ones beset by doubts over their ability, all concerned at how reliable their calculations were in finding

wind strengths far in excess of anything they had ever experienced. Their problem was to get others to believe it. One experienced Lancaster pilot, Flight Lieutenant O. V. Brooks of 15 Squadron writes: 'I recall a furious argument with my navigator. He gave me a wind of 130 m.p.h. and I told him he was a bloody fool; you don't get winds like that in this part of the world. But he was dead right and, to this day, never stops reminding me of it.' The Windfinder navigators calculated their new winds and had to transmit them back to England. Many did not quite believe the high figure of the wind speeds they had found and scaled it down a little. The winds were received in England, where the group staffs probably did the same before sending their figures to Bomber Command. Bomber Command then probably repeated the procedure before sending back the overall forecast to be retransmitted to the whole force. In this way the majority of ordinary navigators received an estimate of wind strength which was much lower than the actual strength of wind being encountered.

The effect of all this was that the bomber stream arrived at the Danish coast well scattered and was then given further inaccurate wind forecasts. Many aircraft tried to regain their proper track and turned north to fly up the Danish coast to the correct landfall, making only slow progress into the teeth of the wind. Others flew on, some hoping to regain the proper track later but others unaware of the seriousness of the situation and actually flying over Germany instead of Denmark. The bomber stream never again became concentrated, and the majority of aircraft would be south of the intended track for the remainder of the night. It became known in Bomber Command as 'the Night of the Big Winds'.

The Germans were attempting to mount a full-scale Tame Boar operation but were hampered by the northerly approach route of the bomber force and by the wind. The local units of NJG 3 were soon in action, being sent from

beacon *Quelle* near Hamburg out to Heligoland and then
north again in search of the bombers. But other units were
held back by the wind in their northerly flight. Emil Nonnenmacher, a Junkers 88 pilot of III/NJG 2, describes how
he coped with the situation.

When we took off from Gilze Rijen we had no idea of the
target. I think we were advised to fly towards beacon
Quelle, which we often used. Nothing useful happened
there because the bombers were still too far north. So I
turned inland, keeping inside the circle which the
bombers were flying; we knew they had to turn inland at
some stage. Berlin seemed to be quite likely as a target,
although the exact location of the target was not all that
important to us.
   We actually reached the Berlin area before the raid
started, so we waited there. There was nothing else to do
until a raid developed somewhere. The running
commentary was not forecasting any targets at all at that
stage. It really wasn't much good that night, perhaps
because of the strong wind which was breaking up the
bomber stream. We found out about that afterwards. We
had to wait a long time; I found out later that some crews
had given up and gone home.

   Many other night fighters were taking similar action. The
Mosquito raid at Kiel was ineffective. Only eleven Mosquitoes were allocated to this diversion and these were also
suffering dispersal by the wind. At least three Mosquitoes
never found Kiel at all and bombed Hamburg instead,
being joined there by several bombers of the main bombing
force who were now in deep navigational trouble.
   The plot made up after the war of aircraft lost on this
raid was one of those deposited in the Public Record Office,
so that we have an exact picture of the locations where
bombers were shot down (see Map 19 on page 280).[1] The

1 The missing aircraft plot is in Public Record Office AIR 14/3221.

German fighters were not, at first, very successful. One German fighter shot down a Halifax of 425 Squadron burning into the sea near Heligoland. No bombers were lost over Denmark, but two were shot down south of the German border. They were probably shot down by Flak, and their positions seventy miles south of the intended route shows how far the wind was pushing these aircraft. The bombers turned south-east over the Baltic for the next leg of their route. The German fighters now appeared in strength, and six more bombers were shot down between the Baltic and Berlin, most of them in a straight line fifty miles south-west of the intended route, again showing how the main group of bombers were well off track. Sergeant Eric Meikle, of 115 Squadron, was the New Zealand bomb aimer in the first of those six shot-down aircraft.

After crossing the German coast to the east of Lübeck, we were attacked by a Ju 88 night fighter from below. (This was told me by an interviewing officer at Dulag Luft at Frankfurt.) He managed to knock out two engines and set the bomb bay on fire. I immediately pushed across the jettison bars and dropped the lot. I remember the blazing load cartwheeling through the sky. We altered course north, in an attempt to get across the Baltic to Sweden, but the damage to the aircraft was such that height was lost pretty rapidly and, at 1,000 feet, the skipper called out, 'Stand by for ditching.' As the wind would be causing a very heavy sea to be running, I said that I was going to bale out in preference to ditching – they were both equally hopeless cases. I left the aircraft at 900 feet and landed shortly afterwards in a field (near a village called Kröpelin in Mecklenburg). The wind was so strong that I was dragged a long way by my parachute, bouncing from frozen furrow to furrow as it was a recently ploughed field. I was the only survivor.

The head of the bomber stream should have flown in over the north-eastern suburbs of Berlin just after 23.15.

But, because of the wind problem, there was no 'stream', only a great gaggle of more than 700 aircraft spread over a frontage of at least seventy miles, with any centre there might have been well to the west of Berlin. The staff at Bomber Command Headquarters had advanced the Zero Hour by five minutes. This information had been broadcast to all crews, but the true strength of the north wind was still not appreciated in England, and aircraft arrived in the target area in all manner of ways. Some appeared up to ten minutes early over Berlin. The Berlin Flak and searchlight defences remained quiet, and the early arrivals often flew on further south, unaware that they had flown past the target. When the raid did open, such crews were amazed to see all the action behind them. Other crews realized from the H2S sets that they had reached Berlin and these were now flying wide orbits, waiting for the raid to commence. Crews in the later waves were equally surprised to see Flak fire, Pathfinder markers and bombing well to the left instead of ahead. Finally, there were the crews whose navigators had detected the true strength of the wind; their aircraft had throttled back and were making wide, time-wasting zigzags to the north of Berlin. In short, the bomber force was in considerable disarray.

The Pathfinder marking plan to be employed was entirely different to any used during the eighteen previous raids on Berlin. The Aiming Point was at the eastern end of the Tiergarten gardens, and the intention was to destroy the area north and east of the centre, which had so far escaped serious damage. The marking method to be used was 'Newhaven with Emergency Skymarking'. There is no need to describe the detailed visual Newhaven plan and timetable, for two reasons: the Pathfinders were scattered by the wind, though not as badly as the Main Force, and there were patches of low cloud scudding across the target area, so conditions were not suitable for a visual identification of the Aiming Point. The Pathfinders did the best they could under most difficult conditions, but there was no concentration of marking, only a mixture of Target Indicators and Skymarkers being blown rapidly across the target.

The Main Force bombing can be split into three groups of experience. Those crews still north of Berlin when the raid opened had the least trouble. They came in, bombed a marker, and were delighted to be swept through the Flak and searchlight area so fast by the wind. A cruel dilemma faced those crews who had been blown past Berlin before the raid opened. An unknown proportion bombed some town found on H2S or simply dumped their bombs and set off home. But many crews conscientiously decided to turn back and attempt to bomb the markers. There are several accounts from men who partook of this dangerous activity. Pilot Officer Frank Leatherdale was a navigator in 115 Squadron.

As Zero Hour approached, our gunners reported considerable Flak and searchlights astern and we decided to turn around to get back over the target, to bomb the markers on the correct heading. It took us twenty minutes to fly across Berlin – twenty very worrying minutes, as we had to contend with the enemy defences and the risk of meeting over-friendly aircraft head on. From this crawl northwards over Berlin, I estimated that the wind was something like 100 knots – a speed we had not heard of in those days. Our slow ground speed was proof of this.

We eventually bombed the target some twenty to twenty-five minutes late. This was very worrying in a Lanc II; our Hercules engines gobbled fuel at height and we dug deep into our reserves.

The decision to turn back cost some their lives. Flight Lieutenant Bill Jackson was a Canadian pilot in 166 Squadron.

I decided to go around again and make another bombing run – a mistake. We were shot down east of Berlin by what we believed to be a night fighter which manoeuvred beneath us and strafed us from a top-mounted gun, along the whole length of our Lancaster. The plane caught fire and I ordered the crew to abandon the aircraft. After determining that five of the crew had been killed in the attack, my engineer and I baled out. The plane appeared to blow up about one and a half minutes after this. Because of the high winds, we landed about thirty miles south of Berlin.

It was not the best of nights for the reintroduction of the Master Bomber technique. Wing Commander Lane (call sign *Redskin*) and his deputy, Wing Commander Anderson (call sign *Pommy*) turned up on time. Wing Commander Lane orbited the target and attempted to control the raid. Several men remember his broadcast comments. Understandably, he was able to give little positive direction to the crews but he gave much general encouragement in a distinctively Canadian and often excitable series of remarks. One such was, 'Those bastards wanted a war; now show them what war is like.' Other quotations reported are not printable. Other men remember the calm and cultivated English voice of the Deputy Master Bomber occasionally contributing a remark.

The bombers flew away from Berlin, their crews often thinking that it had been a successful raid because so many bright lights were seen on the ground. The reason for this is an interesting and unusual one that I do not think has been recorded before. The reader will remember Hajo Herrmann, the innovative former German bomber pilot who had introduced the Wild Boar fighter action over targets and who formed the single-engined night-fighter unit which had first used that tactic. He was last seen in this book as the commander of the 30th Fighter Division, made up of three *Geschwader* of those single-engined fighters. But this organization had been proved unwieldy because the Wild Boar units were more usefully operated when attached to the established fighter divisions in whose areas they were located. So the 30th Fighter Division was disbanded early in 1944. But Hajo Herrmann was still well favoured by Goering and he had been transferred to the command of the 1st Fighter Division, which contained all of the fighter units in a large area of Central Germany, with its headquarters in Berlin, in the headquarters building of the famous pre-war fighter unit, Geschwader Richthofen. Herrmann was thus, in some ways, responsible for the air defence of the Berlin area; Goering had jokingly said, 'I need you here to defend my home at Karinhalle.'

Herrmann was now able to put yet another product of his fertile mind into practice.

I wanted to ignite a mass of phosphorus when the raid opened, to increase the amount of illumination available to the Wild Boar pilots. It took me some time to gather together a sufficient quantity of phosphorus but it was ready for this night. It was to be lit by the Flak and searchlight units. I even asked Goebbels to relax the blackout of Berlin, to produce even more light from under the cloud, but he said it would be too much work to remove all the blackout covers from the street lights. So then I asked him to tell the population to turn on their lights and draw their curtains. He said that he would not have been able to persuade the people to do that.

When the raid came, the weather conditions were variable. There was thin, low cloud, with many gaps. Because of the wind conditions and because of the gaps in the cloud, I thought that the glare of the phosphorus might work against our pilots. I waited until the last minute. I stood on the top of my headquarters, watching, but I could not make up my mind. Reports about the cloud were coming in from the staff downstairs; some areas of the city had eight-eighths, others were clear. The whole area involved was over a hundred kilometres in diameter.

The raid started. My Flak liaison officer was with me –

Oberst Werner, a famous First World War pilot with the
Pour le Mérite, a nice man. He ordered some searchlights
to be illuminated in various parts of the city, so that I
could see what the cloud conditions were like overall. I let
the Pathfinders come in. But, when the first of the main
bomber force arrived, I ordered the phosphorus to be lit
and all the searchlights to be turned on, the searchlights
to aim not through the gaps but at the cloud, to produce
diffused light so that the fighters would have the
maximum diffused light, but no direct glare.

I was amazed. It was so bright that I could have read a
newspaper. You could see all the surrounding houses and
trees and there were fantastic shadows. Even the birds
started singing. Then the action became too hot. The
falling splinters came down with a noise like celestial
music, so I took shelter down below.

Hajo Herrmann's activities are probably responsible for the
comment in one Bomber Command report: 'Berlin . . .
Numerous ineffective searchlights.'[1]

But this novel action brought only mixed success for the
German fighters. Only six bombers were shot down inside
that hundred-kilometre area around Berlin, a Pathfinder on
the northern edge of the city and five more bombers on the
southern exits. Greater success eluded Herrmann for two
reaons. The incomplete cloud cover was an obvious hin-
drance, but a more significant reason was that the heyday of
Wild Boar was over. The single-engined fighters were still
obliged to come in over a target city, but the twin-engined
fighters equipped with SN-2 radar were not. They could follow the bomber stream to a target but then preferred to loop
round to the other side and wait for the bombers to emerge.
But at least nineteen more bombers came down on the first
part of the return route, and Hajo Herrmann remembers
arguing that some of these should be credited to his phosphorus illumination plan, because the initial contact

1 Public Record Office, AIR 14/3455.

between some of the successful German fighters and their
victims must have been his illuminated area. The strong
wind, he argued, then carried the actual combat and the subsequent descent of the falling bombers further away from
the target than on a normal night. These were valid points,
and the following account by one of the successful German
pilots is a good example of what happened as bombers left
the Berlin area. Junkers 88 pilot Emil Nonnenmacher again:

We flew off to the south of Berlin, not directly over the
city. There we saw a Halifax silhouetted against the cloud
below. I tried to get behind him, but not too low because
he was outward bound from the target and, if I had
attacked from below, he would have seen me against the
light on the ground. As we flew further south, it was
getting darker and darker so I knew that I had to be
quick. I had him well in the gun sight; his shape was
about three times bigger than the ring and I aimed at the
left inner engine. I pulled the trigger and he caught fire
at once. It was the brightest burning bomber I ever saw.
The left wing broke off in no more than four or five
seconds. The entire wing actually broke upwards. Then
the rest of the aircraft started spinning. That was all. We
watched it go all the way down; it was in two or three
parts when it hit the ground.

Let us, for the last time in this book, turn from the action in
the air to look at what happened on the ground. Nearly
2,500 tons of bombs fell somewhere. On this occasion we will
work from the outside towards the centre. A total of 126
communities outside Berlin reported bombs, mostly in fields
or woods, but 86 buildings were destroyed and 1,483 were
damaged in those places, and 30 people were killed and 141
injured. Perhaps half of the bombs fell in Berlin itself; it is
impossible to be more precise. Every part of Berlin along the
bombers' route in from the north was hit, from the very
northern suburbs to the extreme south twenty miles away.

There were two partial concentrations, the first in the Horst Wessel district in the north and the second in a large area south and south-west of the centre. This area had been bombed many times before. The quantity of housing destroyed and damaged was never calculated (or if it was, it was not retained in the Berlin records). The number of casualties is given as 47 people dead, 156 injured and 190 missing – very low figures considering the scale of the raid – and an estimated 24,000 people were forced to leave their homes because of varying degrees of damage. There are long lists of industrial, cultural, commercial and public buildings hit; here are a few items taken at random from that list: the Swedish Embassy, the Steglitz Town Hall, a theatre, the Mercedes Cinema, five hospitals, a church, a butter warehouse, a grain silo, the Kreuzberg Gasworks where there was a large fire in a gasometer, the offices of the National Milk and Fat Industry, three breweries, a Gestapo building, Himmler's bunker, three military establishments and one naval establishment. The names of nine important war-industry factories are also in the list. It can be classed as a raid of medium effect, the partial success being due to the large number of aircraft dispatched on the raid.

Once again, let us not forget the human side. Brigitta Kirschstein was a six-year-old girl who had the misfortune to live not far from the bombers' Aiming Point. Her father had been a professional pianist before the war but he had disappeared while serving as an infantryman in Russia in 1942. Brigitta and her mother were two of those people recorded as 'bombed out' that night. Their experience can illustrate the sufferings of so many civilians in Hitler's wartime Germany and also the condition of their city at the end of the Battle of Berlin.

I wanted to take all sorts of things down to the shelter – dolls and suchlike – but my mother said we would soon be back and I only took the teddy bear. We went down to the basement. Most of the other people in our block of flats were also there; the cellar was absolutely full –

mainly women and children, lots of children – only a few
old men. There were always a few people who stayed at
the front of the shelter, looking out, and they were saying
that it was a very stormy night. I think the bombing
started quickly; we were late getting into the shelter. I
remember hearing the first planes – a sort of whooshing
noise, as if you have a whole swarm of mosquitoes coming
together, an enormous noise, very frightening.

Then the bombs came, quite near, but not in our block
of flats yet. Then someone said that the front of the block
was on fire but I didn't see any of this; I think I was
probably playing with some other children's toys. We
weren't frightened as long as someone else was there; it
was only later when I saw the looks on the people's faces
who had been forced out of their cellar next door that I
got frightened; they looked ashen and the children were
all crying. Then, a bit later, those who were on the front
called my mother out. There was a fire now in our own
flat. I went just to the steps of the cellar with Mother and
could see it not far away. It was the kind of fire which,
later in your life, you dreaded to see because of the
memory of that night – nice orange fire, with black
streaks shooting out from the windows and the roof, and
the noise of glass tinkling – a very strange noise, just like
a musical triangle being played; on and on it went. Also,
enormous heat; I was quite hot. We were only twenty
metres or so across the courtyard from the flat. I
remember the extraordinary wind and the flames roaring
as though they wanted to go right up to the sky.

Someone said, 'Frau Kirschstein. Shall we try to get
your piano out? It's not too late.' She said, 'No. No one is
going into a burning building because of that piano.' I
think they took her point. They were all elderly people
and I think they were relieved. We could hear the actual
notes of the piano as debris fell on to it. Then we were
blown over. I don't know what happened. That was a
very frightening moment. I couldn't find my mother; I
had lost my security. Someone picked me up and I was

soon back with Mother, but I was crying now. I found out afterwards that a bomb had fallen in the courtyard and left a crater, but it must have been only a small bomb.

It was well into the next day when we came out of the shelter. All of us from the cellar kept together. Our homes were gone – and I left my teddy bear behind in the cellar. I got it back about a year later but I think the rats had got at it by then. Someone must have taken the lead but it was a drudging kind of walk with us, just carrying a small bag and the obligatory blanket which we always took down to the cellar to keep us warm and to dip in water and put over our heads in case we had to escape through fire. We were cold and wet and hungry. Most of the fires were out but there was a lot of smouldering.

We set off across the ruins. The most terrifying thing was that pieces of hot, glowing charcoal and timbers and stones were falling down from the buildings we passed. We stumbled on, over the ruins, until we reached the Am Spittelmarkt Station. There were no trains and people were sitting or lying on the lines and the platforms. I fell asleep. The next night we had to move on, still walking out of the ruined area until we reached a large building – possibly a bank or a collection place where the bombed-out families were staying. I played with my friend Elizabeth and, with the rest and the warmth and some food, our spirits soon returned. But poor Mother was very tired. Her skin had gone dark and grey in those last two days and her mouth was serious and very sad. She talked of Father with a hopeless expression on her face. He was missing in Russia.

Everything was very difficult for Mother. Berlin had been so heavily bombed in recent months that it was difficult to find which official buildings were still operating and making decisions. We were eventually evacuated to a small town in the east. But Mother never recovered from the bombing that night and from losing my father. She had only been married a few years and it took her a long time to overcome all our problems. She

never regained her self-confidence and bounciness. Right
up to her death in the 1970s, she looked back on that
time as being very vivid and unhappy. Some people talk
of the good old days but there were very few good old
days for that generation. It was much easier for us
younger ones to remodel our lives.

Despite all the problems, the bomber force had still not
suffered heavy casualties, but that other tragic aspect of the
bombing war – the slaughter of young men in aircraft – was
now about to be highlighted.

The intended route home for the bombers was a relatively direct one. After leaving the target area, the route
was mostly due west, with just a modest 'dog leg' to the
north to keep clear of the Ruhr defences before taking a
familiar route over Holland and out across the North Sea.
The track distance from the edge of Berlin's Flak area to
the coast was 370 miles, with a planned flying time of 112
minutes. The Germans were to exact a toll of exactly one
bomber for every two minutes of that route.

There were two reasons for this heavy loss. The first was
the degree of efficiency shown by the Germans in the Tame
Boar operation, and the second was the effect of the wind,
which helped the Germans. Because of the scattered arrival
and bombing at Berlin, the bombers started their return
flights from many different points. The fighters did not
have to find a compact, narrow stream of aircraft five miles
wide and seventy miles long – a small target in the vast night
sky – but found the bombers spread out by the wind in a
great scattered mass on a frontage of more than fifty miles
and with a length of up to 150 miles. The width of what
was supposed to be the bomber stream would continue to
grow until the survivors flew out all over the Dutch coast
spread over a frontage of 130 miles. The main concentration of aircraft remained to the south of the intended
route throughout that flight.

The German fighters found these conditions most suitable, and the carnage began. A smaller bomber force would probably have been more elusive, but about 740 bombers emerged from the target area and streamed their way to the west, with no abrupt changes of course and with no diversions to distract the night fighters' attention. The entire strength of the night-fighter force was up, the majority of it waiting south of Berlin to catch the bombers as they emerged from the target area. Nineteen bombers were shot down on the first sixty miles of the return route. Some fighters had to break off then, because of fuel shortage, but there were still enough to carry on the air battle. The German controllers had cleverly kept the units of NJG 1, mostly based in Holland, on the ground during the earlier part of the night; these units were now ordered up, and the bombers flew straight into their home territory. There was no part of that route from Berlin to the coast where fighter attacks were not taking place.

I have accounts from three German crews operating on that deadly route. They illustrate two factors: how flexible the German night-fighter defences had become and how relatively easy it was for competent German crews to find bomber victims. Unteroffizier Erich Handke was the radar operator in the Messerschmitt 110 of Major Martin Drewes, the *Gruppenkommandeur* of III/NJG 1. This unit had been detached to Northern France for the recent series of raids on Southern Germany. Major Drewes had taken off from St Dizier earlier in the night but had quickly realized that the bombers' inward flight was too far to the north. He landed at Twenthe in Holland and was thus perfectly positioned to take off again for the return flight of the bombers. This is Handke's account.

We made for radio beacon *Philip* at Paderborn. The weather was perfect – a new moon, no cloud and perfect visibility. As for the running commentary, there was some jamming but I could hear it. From this, I realized that the bombers were flying on a broad front between Bielefeld and Kassel. A smaller group seemed to be flying round

south of the Ruhr but the main group was more to the
north.

When I thought we must be nearly there, I switched on
my *SN-2* and immediately had a contact passing in front
of us. I guided Drewes in behind it; it was about two and
a half kilometres away. I could see three other contacts,
all flying the same course. I guided him to within 400
metres, as usual from behind and below. At about 300
metres, Drewes spotted it above us.

We moved up on it and climbed to get about fifty
metres directly underneath the rear turret. It was a
Lancaster, at a height of 6,000 metres and flying straight
and level. We were not spotted. When we were in the
firing position, Drewes fired with the *schräge Musik* and
hit the right inner engine – at first, too far behind, but
quickly correcting the aim and firing ahead. The engine
started to burn beautifully and we pulled away. The
Lancaster flew on for two minutes, still burning; we could
see the big bulge of the radar scanner under the fuselage
quite clearly.

When we had observed the crash, I plotted the exact
position with the help of the radio beacon and wrote
down the exact time.

Soon afterwards, we found ourselves among another
group of contacts. We closed on one; this one was doing a
banking search. The visual contact came suddenly; we
had actually passed underneath it before we saw it. We
set the right inner engine on fire again but this time it
flew on for fifteen minutes, right through a Flak area. We
didn't follow it. We saw it held in searchlights for a long
time. Drewes waited till it had left the Flak area and
attacked it again, from directly behind, and it went down.
We saw three men parachuting. We made several more
attempts but things became difficult. The targets seemed
to be flying faster and the *SN-2* was giving trouble. We
kept circling back and trying again. We finally gained a
firm contact, another Lancaster at 6,000 metres. It was
climbing, so our final closing was a slow affair. We

opened fire but then had to get out of the way fast because the bomber burst into flames in both inner wing tanks and fell violently. We only just got out of the way in time. It went straight down and crashed.

There were no more after that.

The three shot-down bombers were probably aircraft of 57, 433 and 625 Squadrons; there were survivors – five men only of the 433 Squadron aircraft.

The three victims of Major Drewes were all standard Tame Boar contacts, all found for the pilot by Unteroffizier Handke's operation of the *SN-2* radar. The second German contribution is from another radar operator, Unteroffizier Hans-Georg Schierholz, whose pilot was Feldwebel Rudolf Frank of I/NJG 3. Their Messerschmitt 110 had no success on an earlier flight in the night and landed back at its home airfield of Vechta, quickly refuelled and took off again. But, instead of going on a Tame Boar search, this resourceful crew decided to operate in one of the local night-fighter boxes, the organization of which still existed eight months after Window had destroyed much of its usefulness. On this night, however, the wide spread of the bomber force was rendering the effects of Window almost useless, and the ground radars of Box *Leghorn* were able to give this crew a succession of good controlled contacts. Schierholz says:

It was a good box-fighting situation. There was good guidance from the ground. They gave us three perfect contacts and we shot all three of them down with *schräge Musik*. Not one of them saw us; I think they felt they were already safe on their way home. I recorded the positions in my log book; they were all Lancasters.

The three bombers were from 460, 630 and 635 Squadrons; there were only two survivors among the twenty-one crew members. The 635 Squadron aircraft was the first loss of this newly formed Pathfinder squadron.

It is significant that the losses of the six bombers described above were all due to the upward firing *schräge Musik* cannons now fitted in many German night fighters. Their use had become almost standard for those senior German pilots able to claim one of the latest aircraft fitted with the weapon. Hauptmann Paul Zorner took off from St Trond and flew eastwards to meet the returning bombers.

We became very hopeful when my radar operator obtained an *SN-2* contact at 6,700 metres. I spotted it two minutes later and made my first attack with *schräge Musik*, but without any result. I aimed again, at the left wing, firing two more bursts, but saw the rounds exploding well behind and above the bomber, which flew on unharmed. It seemed that the *schräge Musik* was not adjusted properly, so I made my next attack from the rear, using my forward firing cannons. I gave it two bursts in the left wing and it began to burn fiercely. It went down steeply and we saw it crash. We noted the place on a bearing of 150 degrees from light beacon *Xantippe*.

Zorner's victim was a Lancaster of 12 Squadron; three of the crew died.

Night fighters were not the only danger. Some bombers strayed into Flak-defended areas. The local searchlights and guns usually remained quiet while a bomber was tracked by radar; there was not enough Window from a single aircraft to confuse the gun-laying radars. When the bombers were well within range, the searchlights would then be lit, and the gun batteries opened up. There are many stories of crews suddenly being caught in this way at such places as Magdeburg, Osnabrück and Münster. Most of these aircarft were able to twist and dive their way through those hazards and survived to reach England, though often in damaged condition. But at least two and possibly three bombers fell to Flak at these places. Surprisingly, with the host of bombers being shot down by fighters, the only account I have from a bomber shot down returning from Berlin is from Warrant Officer Stan Boustead, the wireless operator in a 429 Squadron Halifax. It was this crew's second operation.

The navigator and bomb aimer were exchanging comments on the heading of the aircraft. We were pointing directly towards heavy Flak and searchlights, obviously Magdeburg. The navigator said that, owing to the heavy winds, we would have to track south of Magdeburg to keep clear of those defences.

Almost immediately, we were hit by Flak – CRUMP! CRUMP! CRUMP! – accompanied by the sound of tearing metal. I knew that the aircraft was mortally wounded and I switched back to intercom. Stan Wick, the pilot, said, 'This is it, chaps. Bale out.' I was conscious of a strong smell of raw aviation fuel and, when I drew the curtain of my wireless cubicle to don my 'chute, flames were licking down the inside of the fuselage like the inside of the furnace of an oil-fired boiler. We had a 600-gallon overload tank in the bomb bay that night.

I quickly followed the navigator out of the front hatch and the bomb aimer was donning his 'chute. He helped me out with his foot and I expected him to follow me but he never made it. The pilot and one of the gunners also died.

There were many more problems with Flak for those crews who were flying so far south of track that they came up against the formidable Ruhr defended area which was about sixty miles long and nearly as wide. Many of the crews whose navigators had been faithfully following the wind forecasts being broadcast from England found themselves faced with this barrier. Flight Lieutenant Ron Munday of 57 Squadron, on the last-but-one trip of his tour, describes the problems of such crews.

What to do next was one of the most critical command decisions I had to make during the tour. Having got that far south, any attempt to regain the original track would have resulted in us running out of fuel over the North Sea, so I took the decision to carry on.

The Ruhr was like a triangle, with the broadest defences at the top, in the Essen–Dortmund area. We hit just south of that, where the defences were a bit narrower. We could see Flak and searchlights, but no sign of fighters. A number of other aircraft were coned and being heavily fired on by Flak; we saw several go down – I recollect one exploding.

If you are having to battle through an area like this, it was a cynical method to hope that two aircraft would be coned and you could slip through but, unfortunately, it was we who were coned and provided the way through for the others. There was something called a 'Flak corkscrew' on which we had been instructed; we had only practised it infrequently, though I had it very much in my mind. We used it and lost that cone of searchlights fairly quickly.

About five minutes later, we were coned again and this time they were much more reluctant to release us. The recommended corkscrew manner was a maximum speed of 260 m.p.h. and a 3,000 feet height change; but that didn't work and I chose to modify it by increasing the speed up to 300 m.p.h. in the dive and making the altitude changes 10,000 feet each. That eventually threw them off about ten minutes later and without us being seriously hit because they simply couldn't set the fusing rings on the shells fast enough for such rapid changes. I say 'fusing rings' because I've still got one that was found embedded in one of the port engines. It fell out when the cowling was removed after the trip.

The crew were very good all the way through; there was so much at stake. When we reached the North Sea and had our coffee, the flasks in the bomb aimer's compartment were all mixed up because of that evasive action over the Ruhr. The bomb aimer mistakenly took my old Thermos which I used for urine. This rather Calvinistic Welshman felt that it was part of a deep-rooted English plot to humiliate the Welsh.

Flight Lieutenant Munday's crew were lucky. Nine bombers were lost over the Ruhr; the crew lists reveal that these were by no means all novices; some of the most experienced crews lost that night were shot down in this area.

Fifty-six bombers were lost on that return flight from Berlin to the Dutch coast. One more came down in the sea. This was a Pathfinder Lancaster of 97 Squadron which was damaged by Flak over the Ruhr. Instead of tackling the long North Sea crossing, Flying Officer P. H. Todd and his crew probably made for the shortest sea crossing between Calais and Dover. A distress signal was heard from them, but when the Lancaster ditched, it was nearer to the French coast than the English; six men were picked up by the Germans, but the flight engineer died.

Another aircraft was lost in a most unusual way. Earlier in the night, a Halifax of 158 Squadron had been forced to return early with engine trouble. It also sent out a distress signal and had to ditch in the sea just off the Norfolk coast. There was a huge explosion as it did so; the Halifax had come down in a coastal minefield. Australian Pilot Officer K. S. Simpson and his crew were all killed. When the main force of bombers returned, crippled aircraft and those short of fuel were putting down at strange airfields all over Eastern England. A 78 Squadron Halifax trying to land on one engine crashed at Cranfield, killing all of its crew, and a damaged Lancaster, with a dead tail gunner on board, crashed into a Flying Fortress at Dunsfold, but without further loss of life.

It had been a disastrous operation for Bomber Command. Seventy-two bombers were missing – forty-four Lancasters and twenty-eight Halifaxes. The loss rate for the heavies was 9.1 per cent. As usual the Halifaxes had suffered more severely at 13 per cent, compared to 7.6 per cent for the Lancasters. The losses can be further subdivided:

On the outward route – 9
In the Berlin area – 6
On the return route – 57

In addition, at least two aircraft had been wrecked in crashes in England and a third destroyed when it came down in the coastal minefield. The total number of aircrew casualties was 529, made up of 392 men killed, 133 prisoners of war and four men evading capture. These figures include two men killed in combat but whose aircraft returned, and four men who baled out over Germany also from aircraft which returned. To all of these losses should be added that of another Bomber Command aircraft, a Serrate Mosquito of 239 Squadron, whose crew were taken prisoner. The heaviest losing squadrons were 78 Squadron at Breighton, with five Halifaxes missing and one crashed, and 12 Squadron (Wickenby), 166 Squadron (Kirmington) and 115 Squadron (Witchford), each with four aircraft missing. The heaviest losing stations were Leeming, where 427 and 429 (Canadian) Squadrons each lost three aircraft, and Wickenby, where six aircraft were lost, including that of the commander of 626 Squadron, Wing Commander Quentin Ross, who died with all of his crew when shot down on the way back from Berlin.

It was not quite the heaviest loss of the war so far, being six less than the number lost attacking Leipzig just over a month earlier, but it was both the heaviest overall loss and the heaviest percentage loss in the nineteen raids on Berlin during this period. It is ironic that the previous heaviest loss on Berlin had been on the first raid of the series seven months earlier, on the night of 23/24 August 1943.

The Luftwaffe performance had been impressive. By using what evidence is available from Germany and from returned prisoners at the end of the war, a possible allocation of the causes of loss of the missing aircraft might be sixty to the night fighters and twelve to Flak. Individual night-fighter units submitted the following claims:

Unit	Claims
NJG 1	13
NJG 2	19
NJG 3	14
NJG 5	14
NJG 6	1
JG 300	7
JG 301	2
JG 302	7
TOTAL	77

Obviously some of these claims were not justified; in particular, those of the Wild Boar units – JGs 300, 301 and 302 – seem excessive considering the nature of the action. The performance of NJG 2 is worthy of note. This unit hardly existed at the opening of the Battle of Berlin, being composed then of the survivors of a *Geschwader* nearly wiped out in the Mediterranean. It had since been rebuilt, and its success on this night can be attributed to the performance of its Junkers 88s, so suitable for long Tame Boar operations, and to the fact that the unit's aircrews had never used the old box-fighting conditions and were thus much more responsive to the challenge of the free-lance fighting of a Tame Boar operation. German losses were fourteen fighters. Bomber crews who returned to England and Serrate and Intruder Mosquitoes claimed only six of these; it seems that the gunners in some of the shot-down bombers must have given a good account of themselves, because there was no bad weather at the German airfields to cause many crashes.

There is one vitally important aspect of all these statistics. When Bomber Command's Operational Research Section compiled its assessment of the night's operations, it was known that the bomber stream had been badly scattered by wind and it was also known, from the reports of returning crews, roughly where the bomber casualties had occurred. But many of those reports were of bombers shot down by the still unsuspected *schräge Musik*; no tracer had been seen, only the bursting into flames of stricken bombers. The Operational Research Section put together the scattering of the stream and the reports of losses and assumed that the exceptionally heavy casualties were due to individual bombers straying over German towns and being shot down by Flak. This was the Operational Research Section's conclusion: 'Not less than 45 aircraft are estimated to have been lost to Flak . . . Fighters achieved comparatively little success, because the strong wind that scattered the bomber stream proved unfavourable to consistent interception by fighters.'[1] That report was not completed until several weeks later, but the same assessment was certainly made at Bomber Command Headquarters as soon as the early reports were received. It was a tragic mistake. The Luftwaffe had mounted an excellent Tame Boar operation, and there was no reason why the Luftwaffe could not repeat such a success whenever Bomber Command ventured deep into German-defended air space.

Harris did not allow his squadrons long to lick their wounds. On the next night he sent 192 aircraft to attack a railway marshalling yard in France, as part of the pre-invasion communications campaign. Then, on the following night, 26/27 March, 705 aircraft were dispatched to Essen, where a successful Oboe marked raid took place. This relatively short incursion into Germany cost only nine bombers. After two nights of rest, major operations were again planned for the night of 29/30 March, even though the moon was growing in size; but the main raid of the night, to Brunswick, was cancelled.

Then came Thursday 30 March. The bomber crews believed that the current period of major raids had now ended, because of the moon, and were surprised when a maximum-effort raid was ordered. The target was Nurem-

1 Night Raid Report No. 562, Public Record Office AIR 14/261.

berg, a city deep in Southern Germany and as far into German-defended air space as Berlin. The reasons why Sir Arthur Harris chose such a target on such a night will never be known. He did not refer to this operation in his memoirs, even omitted to mark Nuremberg on the map of city targets attacked by Bomber Command, and consistently evaded questions over his selection of such a distant target on a moonlight night. We are left with surmise.

Harris knew that, after 1 April, the operations of Bomber Command would be strictly subordinated to the needs of the coming invasion. The last monthly period of complete freedom for him was thus coming to an end. He had achieved considerable successes in 1943 – the Ruhr, Hamburg, Peenemünde, Kassel – but the past winter had been one of considerable disappointment. Berlin had not been destroyed; bomber losses had been heavy. The initial weather forecast given to him for that night showed that Nuremberg might be clear of cloud. It is a reasonable assumption that he wanted a last success to end the current phase of operations. He ordered a visual marking raid. The morale benefits from a major blow on a city with such strong Nazi connections would be immense and would help compensate for the disappointments of the past months. And the German defences? All of Bomber Command's recent setbacks had been in raids to the north – Brunswick, Magdeburg, Leipzig, Berlin. The heavy losses on Berlin six nights earlier were being blamed on Flak and the strong winds which scattered the bomber stream. Nuremberg, even in moonlight, must have seemed worth the gamble.

But it all went wrong. A weather reconnaissance Mosquito sent out during the day brought back a report which showed that Nuremberg was likely to be covered by cloud and that the route to the target was clear, with no cloud there to give the bombers protection on the long flight to the target. *The Nuremberg Raid* was my first Bomber Command book; in it I quoted this comment by Sir Robert Saundby, Harris's deputy, about the revised weather report:

I can say that, in view of the met. report and other conditions, everyone, including myself, expected the C.-in-C. to cancel the raid. We were most surprised when he did not. I thought perhaps there was some top-secret political reason for the raid – something too top-secret for even me to know, but now I do not think that this was so.

Harris allowed the raid to go ahead. The Germans carried out a near perfect Tame Boar operation. The diversions were all ignored. Virtually the whole German night-fighter force was deployed at radio beacons ahead of the bomber stream. A long, 'straight-in' route allowed an easy interception. The bombers flew on in moonlight, leaving vapour trails. Fifty-nine bombers were shot down in just an hour on the main long leg of the approach route. Nuremberg was covered by thick cloud, and few bombs hit the city. When the force landed at the end of the raid, ninety-five Lancasters and Halifaxes were missing, 12.1 per cent of the force. It is estimated that seventy-nine of the lost bombers were shot down by night fighters. The miscalculations of the cause of loss on the previous raid to Berlin had concealed the true level of effectiveness now wielded by the Luftwaffe. It was Bomber Command's biggest loss of the war; more aircrew died – 545 men – than were lost by Fighter Command in the whole of the Battle of Britain.

For Bomber Command it was a sad end to that monthly bombing period, to the winter-long period known as the Battle of Berlin and to the much longer period which Sir Arthur Harris later called his 'Main Offensive'. The main efforts of Bomber Command were now required to prepare for the invasion of Normandy. The hope that Germany might be crushed by bombing alone – the 'bomber dream' – was gone.

12 THE RECKONING

No other Second World War bombing campaign against a single target was pressed so hard, for so long and at such cost as the attempt to destroy Berlin. Was that campaign a success for Bomber Command or a failure?

The Battle of Berlin consisted of six monthly periods of non-moon dark-night bombing in two parts, the first part being from 20 August to 9 September 1943, followed by the main part of the battle from 16 November 1943 to the end of March 1944. The figures below give a résumé of all Bomber Command's major raids to targets in Germany during those six bombing periods.

	Major raids	*Sorties*	*Losses (% of sorties)*
To Berlin	19	10,813	625 (5·8)
To other targets	22	14,045	678 (4·8)
TOTAL	41	24,858	1,303 (5·2)

(All heavy bomber sorties to Germany have been included. Mosquito sorties have been included only if they were to Berlin when a major raid was taking place. Appendix 3 analyses in more detail the casualties by aircraft type and at group and squadron levels in the raids to Berlin.)

Of the 10,813 bombers which took off to attack Berlin,

approximately 9,560 reached the target area and dropped 33,390 tons of bombs – 17,214 tons of high explosive and 16,176 tons of incendiaries. The high-explosive loads contained 6,811 of the 4,000-pound 'Blockbuster' blast bombs and 53 of the even larger 8,000-pounders. The incendiary loads contained an incredible number of Bomber Command's other main weapons, the 4-pound stick incendiary – at least 5 million of these were dropped in the Berlin area. But, as an illustration of just how great was Bomber Command's total effort during the war, the bomb tonnage dropped on Berlin in the battle just ended represents only 3·5 per cent of its 1939–45 bomb tonnage. The number of aircraft lost on the Berlin raids, however, was 7 per cent of the command's wartime losses.

And the human cost to Bomber Command? A total of 2,690 bomber crew members died over Berlin or on the routes to and from the target or were killed when their aircraft crashed in England. A further 987 men would languish in prison camps until the end of the war in Europe. Thirty-four men were shot down but evaded capture to make their slow way home, and eighteen went to Sweden from where they were more quickly returned.

Earlier in this book, I gave my opinion that the outcome of the Battle of Berlin would depend upon the answers to two questions: Would the Luftwaffe be able to recover from the setback to its long established defensive system caused by the introduction of Window, and would the Bomber Command Pathfinders be able to overcome the problems of blind marking over Berlin? In other words, it was the old formula of war: the balancing of the costs of a campaign against the success gained.

The answers to both questions have been provided in the main chapters of the book, but it would be useful to summarize the position. The night fighter, not the Flak battery, was the greatest cause of Bomber Command's losses all through the middle years of the war. Window, introduced in late July 1943, rendered virtually useless the German box system of night fighting. The ground radars which directed a night fighter into proximity with a bomber passing through a box, and the radar set in the fighter required for the final interception, were both swamped by the mass of false returns from the fluttering clouds of Window. The only unaffected form of night fighting was the makeshift Wild Boar method recently introduced, in which single-engined fighters were sent into action over the target cities using the various types of illumination available there. The Wild Boar method was forced upon the whole night-fighter force until a technical response to Window was found. The fifty-eight bombers lost on the first raid of the Battle of Berlin were a testimony of the good effect with which the night fighters made use of Wild Boar and were able to deal such a heavy blow on Bomber Command only five weeks after Window was first used.

Thereafter, the effectiveness of Wild Boar gradually diminished, but this was more than compensated for by the introduction of the virtually Window-proof *SN-2* radar which enabled the new Tame Boar method of fighting on the routes to be introduced at the turn of the year. The following list shows the loss rates of Bomber Command aircraft carrying out major raids against German targets during four different periods.

24 April to 23 July 1943, the last three months of mainly box night fighting – 4·9 per cent bomber casualties.

24 July to 16 August 1943, the introduction of Window and the initial period of German confusion – 2·9 per cent bomber casualties.

17 August to 31 December 1943, from the first widespread use of Wild Boar (on the Peenemünde raid) to the end of the year – 4·6 per cent bomber casualties.

1 January to 31 March 1944, the first three months of widespread Tame Boar use – 5·5 per cent bomber casualties.

These figures show how the use of Wild Boar as a standard method of night fighting brought back the losses inflicted on the bombers almost to the level experienced before Window, and how the Tame Boar method inflicted a greater casualty rate than before Window. There are still former German night-fighter men who say that the changes forced upon the Luftwaffe by the British introduction of Window produced in the long term greater benefit for the Germans than for the British, because the entire German night-fighter force could be effectively employed and not just the experienced crews who had claimed priority in the old box-system engagements.

In the Battle of Berlin, the Luftwaffe forced Harris to remove first his Stirlings from the front line and then the older types of Halifax. Even then, the new Halifaxes took a hiding every time they were committed to action, and Harris was forced to use them only intermittently. Then Harris was forced to break off operations to Northern Germany almost completely after the heavy loss of the Leipzig raid on the night of 19 February. Finally, with the Nuremberg raid at the end of March, the Luftwaffe showed that it had answered the question. It had recovered from Window. It could now defend any part of Germany.

What about that second question? How had the Pathfinders coped with the problems of the blind marking method used on all but one of the nineteen Berlin raids?

It had not worked. The confusion of woods, lakes and small towns outside Berlin after a long approach flight over inland Germany and then the great, sprawling mass of the city itself had defied the best efforts of the Pathfinders. The eighteen blind marking attempts can be analysed. There were two excellent results on the consecutive evenings of 22 and 23 November 1943, when all went well and the Main Force bombing wrought great destruction. There were two raids almost as good at the end of January 1944 – on the nights of the 28th and 30th – when the marking was sufficiently concentrated for serious damage to be caused. There were six other raids when the marking was at least confined to the limits of the city and most of the Main Force bombing hit Berlin, but no degree of concentration was possible. Finally, in eight of those eighteen raids, the marking was so scattered that many of the Main Force aircraft did not even hit Berlin. In at least three of those failed raids, strong winds and high cloud made the Pathfinders' task almost impossible, but the remaining disappointments were due to the general inability to overcome the problems of blind marking.

There were two main reasons why consistent blind marking was unattainable. First, the existing H2S sets with which most of the Pathfinder aircraft were equipped did not show enough definition of the ground for the average Pathfinder set operator to be sure of his exact position over Berlin. The H2S Mark III saga has been described in earlier chapters. Too few of these sets were available and they were rushed into service too quickly; H2S Mark III had little effect upon the Battle of Berlin. A second factor is worthy of more discussion. There were a number of first-class radar set operators in the Pathfinders who could have made something useful even of the old sets and even over Berlin, but there were not enough such men. Their shortage was part of the greater problem of the low level of experience in Pathfinder crews through the Battle of Berlin. The reader will remember Air Vice-Marshal Bennett's plea to Harris to secure all second-tour crews returning to operations in Bomber Command.[1] At the time of that appeal, 25 September 1943, Bennett pointed out that the average Pathfinder captain had only twenty operational sorties to his credit, compared to a level of thirty-two sorties when a survey had been made seven months earlier. Harris had not felt able to accede to that request, and the normal method of Pathfinder recruitment had continued. Two-thirds of new crews came from Main Force squadrons,

1 Public Record Office AIR 14/3546.

usually crews with about ten sorties to their credit, and one-third were 'direct entry' crews selected at training units, often without having any previous operational experience. In that same letter to Harris in September 1943, Bennett had complained that 'the direct entry crews are a tremendous burden for training in squadrons and it is a very long period before any such crew is raised to "above average" standards for marking'.

Since that time, the Pathfinders had suffered severe operational losses. In the six monthly periods of the Battle of Berlin, 198 crews were lost on operations, at least fourteen more in crashes, accidents, injury to crew members and other forms of wastage, and perhaps another sixty or seventy crews completed their tours and were released from operations. There was a horrifying six-week period between 16 December 1943 and the end of January 1944 when eighty-seven Pathfinder crews became casualties in missing or crashed aircraft. It is significant that the two heaviest losing squadrons in Bomber Command in the Battle of Berlin – 7 and 156 Squadrons – were both from the Pathfinders. The Pathfinders thus had to recruit and retrain to marking standards nearly fifty new crews each month during the Battle of Berlin. There was never a shortage of crews; the numbers required for operations were always provided. But the average level of experience continued to fall.

The standard first tour of operations in the Pathfinders was forty-five operations, including any operations flown earlier in the Main Force. A crew could then be rested before being called for a second tour of twenty operations. But, if a first-tour crew so wished, they could carry on after forty-five operations as far as sixty, this counting as a double tour and relieving them of the obligation to return for a further tour. Such crews were the most effective in the Pathfinders, with a great amount of recent operational experience behind them; they were the very stuff of the good blind-marker crews required to tackle a target like Berlin. But, when casualties were heavy, very few crews volunteered to carry on in this way; a flight commander in one of the Pathfinder squadrons during the Battle of Berlin says, 'I don't remember any; everyone breathed a sigh of relief when they reached the end of a standard tour and got away as quickly as possible.'

The results of all this were that the Pathfinders, on Bennett's own admission, started the Battle of Berlin with a low level of crew experience, suffered heavy casualties throughout the battle and could never during that winter find enough crews sufficiently experienced and qualified to make those H2S sets work properly over Berlin. No criticism whatsoever is intended by these comments. The Pathfinder crews tried and tried again. Their early return rates were the lowest in Bomber Command; their casualties were among the highest.

There was another factor: the composition and performance of the Main Force. However well the Pathfinders marked the target, no raid was successful if a Main Force carrying enough bombs did not come in and bomb the markers accurately. Let us look at the bomb loads first. The weight of an attack was not measured in the number of aircraft dispatched but in the tonnage of bombs carried. The early raids of the Battle of Berlin did not carry large tonnages because of the proportion of Stirlings and Halifaxes in the Main Force. But an early peak of over 2,500 tons was achieved on the night of 22 November 1943, when the increased numbers of Lancasters together with the use of the shortest possible route enabled this tonnage to be carried. The bombing results on that night were the most successful in the Battle of Berlin. But bomber casualties forced the removal of the Stirlings and the older Halifaxes from the Main Force, and on other nights even the Halifax IIIs were left out of the battle. At the same time, the improving Luftwaffe tactics forced the use of longer and longer routes. The figure of 2,500 tons of bombs was not achieved again until mid-February; less than half that tonnage was dropped on some of the midwinter raids. But by

February the battle was almost over; the Luftwaffe was forcing Bomber Command to abandon the task.

How many of the bombs loaded reached Berlin and were properly aimed at the markers? Surviving bomber crew members will confirm that the worst part of any flight was the bomb run. The temptation for a bomb aimer to release his bombs just a second or two early, to get rid of that lethal weight and allow his pilot to dive, increase speed and get out of the target area was almost irresistible. The same urge was present among the Pathfinders. The tendency for both marking and bombing to creep back was present on every raid but it was even more likely to be present when defences were fierce. The Bomber Command staff knew all this, and bombing tactics were planned accordingly. The Aiming Point for the Pathfinders was always placed beyond the centre of the area intended for destruction. A tail wind was used in planning the route through the target if possible. Pathfinder Backers-Up were ordered to overshoot existing markers by two or three seconds. Above all, at every Main Force squadron briefing, the crews were urged to press right on up *to the centre of the markers* before releasing their bombs, not to bomb the first markers they saw.

Some of the raids on Berlin were successful because these rules were observed. But there were too many other nights when they were not. An interesting correspondence took place in November 1944 between Air Vice-Marshal Bennett, commander of the Pathfinders, and Bomber Command Headquarters over what had gone wrong in the Battle of Berlin. The British Official History quotes Bennett's views:

'There can be no doubt', he said, 'that a very large number of crews failed to carry out their attacks during the Battle of Berlin in their customary determined manner.' He referred to 'enormous numbers' of reports each night about bombs being jettisoned in the North Sea or over Denmark and he said that the reports of Pathfinder crews 'consistently showed that the amount of bombing on the markers which they dropped was negligible.

I feel quite sure in my own mind', Bennett concluded, 'that many bombs were wasted *en route* in an effort to increase aircraft performance and that, unfortunately, the Command suffered from many "fringe merchants".'[1]

Undoubtedly Bennett was trying to deflect criticism of the Pathfinder performance over Berlin, but there is some truth in what he wrote. Morale among aircrews held up remarkably well during that winter, but there was a gradual loss of heart and determination as the winter drew on. The rate of early returns, always a measure of morale, increased, even the Lancasters being affected when the other aircraft types were not flying in the lower height bands to absorb the first attentions of the night fighters. Other aircraft jettisoned part of their bomb load in the North Sea. Then, at the target, there were what Bennett called the 'fringe merchants'. The presence of cloud and the scattering of Skymarkers by the wind on so many of the Berlin raids gave crews the opportunity to avoid the centre of the target and bomb on the edge of it, bringing back a 'cloud photograph' which did not reveal where they had bombed, or a photograph showing just a single Skymarker. But the earlier chapters in this book have shown how, on those nights when the Pathfinders were able to produce concentrated and accurate marking, the Main Force responded well, and Berlin suffered accordingly. It was no one's fault; the task of destroying Berlin was beyond Bomber Command's capabilities at that time.

What is amazing is the fortitude of the bomber crews in sticking to such a fearful task as well as they did. I asked more than three hundred ex-Battle of Berlin men about the state of morale on their squadrons. The Pathfinders, feeling themselves a selected élite, held well. The small number of Australian squadrons – three out of the four were flying Lancasters – were also steady. The Canadians of 6 Group had been expanded too rapidly, sometimes suffered from poor leadership and were mostly flying the Hal-

1 British Official History, Vol. II, p. 196.

ifax, which nearly always suffered heavier casualties than the Lancaster when committed to action. Their morale and that of most of 4 Group, which was completely Halifax-equipped, was not so high, although it varied from squadron to squadron. The picture in the Main Force Lancaster squadrons which bore the brunt of the Battle of Berlin was more one of enormous strain, mostly faced and endured, morale being much sustained by the crews' faith in the aircraft they flew.

These are a selection of individual views. Pilot Officer Joe Sheriff was a Canadian wireless operator on 57 Squadron at East Kirkby.

The Battle of Berlin did cause morale to sag. Crews were weary and angry, strained and more fearful of their next trip than usual, cursing 'Butch' Harris for his unrelenting demands and his apparently uncaring attitude towards his own men. The results didn't appear to come anywhere near justifying the losses and the hardship.

I knew three crews during the Battle of Berlin who obviously were in bad shape because of fatigue and should have been rested. Two didn't survive. One of the crews had several close calls and the pilot was a nervous wreck. On one trip they were hit by Flak and the navigator and wireless operator were injured. On another trip they were sprayed by shells from a night fighter. One shell came through the windshield right in front of the pilot – the shoulder of his jacket was sliced through. He was not injured but his journey home was a nightmare because of the blast of air through the hole in the windscreen and manhandling a Lancaster which had some of its controls damaged. It was obvious that this crew had had its nine lives and was so shattered by fatigue and tension that there was little chance of them surviving if they continued to operate. They were not rested and they perished.

In attacking Berlin, we paid dearly for a morsel.

Flight Sergeant Dennis Cooper was a wireless operator on 630 Squadron, which also flew Lancasters from East Kirkby.

'Lack of Moral Fibre' was a label which frightened everyone because, if you stopped flying, you were stripped of rank and posted out as an A.C.2 to some other station. There was a case of a gunner who twice damaged his turret so that the aircraft had to turn back; no aircraft could continue unless fully serviceable. Station Medical Officers had instructions to keep aircrew off the sick list. I broke out in boils under the crotch and on the buttocks after Berlin on the 15 February raid and the S.M.O. still passed me fit for flying. As a result, on my next op, I sat on the metal of my parachute harness and crushed the boils. With the pain and the cold, I was very uncomfortable until landing. After debriefing, I went to Sick Quarters where a very hard medical officer told me to drop my trousers and, using a scalpel, cut them. In spite of the fact that I fainted, I was on ops the next night. Bomber Command was terrified of too many people going sick and reducing the available force and that other crews might catch the 'don't want to fly' bug.

Crews were beginning to look untidy in dress and manner, and even the ground sergeants, who had previously thought nothing of us because we got our stripes too quickly, began to have pity on us as they could see what we were going through. Many of us could see no hope of completing a tour the way losses were showing. We drank and smoked too much when we were not flying and things were generally depressed.

Flying Officer Eric Tansley was a Halifax bomb aimer on 158 Squadron at Lissett.

We joined our squadron at a time when morale was extremely low. Losses had been heavy and it seemed to us that there were very few experienced crews left; certainly none were completing tours. Our flight engineer was evidently shattered by the mortality rate at the squadron because, almost overnight, he departed from our ranks, branded L.M.F.

I was assigned a room which I shared with another young officer; he seemed a very pleasant person. Less than a week later, I was in charge of a funeral party for the funeral of the pleasant young man and his crew. They had crashed and blown up returning from a raid.

We lived under great strain. I remember one occupation was looking for signs of 'twitch' in other aircrew and hoping all the time that oneself was still sane.

Sergeant Ken Scott was a twenty-year-old navigator on 101 Squadron at Ludford Magna who flew to Berlin fourteen times.

A strange symptom developed which I have not mentioned to anyone until now. At night, after getting to sleep, I would suddenly feel awakened by a buzzing sensation in my mouth. My face would then distort with the feeling that the flesh was being drawn back; I would then feel myself half-rising from the bed, with all the muscles and sinews of my torso and arms straining and stretching to breaking point. This sensation would reach a climax and then I felt myself falling back on the bed, exhausted. I would then awake to the reality that I hadn't moved at all in bed and it had been some kind of dream. This was all very exhausting and it happened perhaps two or three times a week. In time, I learnt not to resist, sort of lay back and let it all happen; this way, although it always ran the gamut, I felt less drained. After I finished my tour, I was never troubled with it again. I put it down, rightly or wrongly, as a symptom of stress.

Flying Officer Bob Lloyd was a Canadian pilot, flying Lancaster IIs of 408 Squadron from Linton-on-Ouse.

My navigator lost his mind during our 26 November trip to Berlin. My mid-upper gunner got hit in the ankle with a 20-mm shell on the same trip; he never flew again. My bomb aimer went absolutely wild over the target area on a later raid, to such a degree that we couldn't let him wear an intercom; the navigator had to drop the bombs. Then I finally got hurt, smashing my left femur, and the bomb aimer had to fly out the rest of his tour with another crew; he 'bought it' the first night out. They were as frightened as hell, but their morale was good. They flew until they couldn't fly any more. They could have begged off L.M.F. had they wanted to.

But there are less gloomy views. Pilot Officer David Oliver was a Lancaster pilot on 12 Squadron and then 626 Squadron.

Morale was high throughout the period that I was at Wickenby. An efficiently run station and intelligent leadership, including inspiration from a few whose exploits were legendary, helped a lot. Some other factors predisposed to high morale. The average age of aircrew was twenty or twenty-one and very few had the close attachments and responsibilities of wife and children. We were just as well educated academically as the young men of today but we were less socially and politically aware. We had not experienced the clamorous debate in the media on every conceivable subject, nor the continuous dissection of authority that goes on today. In the event, we were united in our belief in the cause and in giving unquestioning support to those in authority.

We were intensely preoccupied with our own crew and very strongly motivated not to let it down. Apart from our commanders and three or four other crews that were close contemporaries, we knew few other aircrew on the station as more than passing acquaintances. The effect on morale is less severe if casualties are not known to one personally. By far the highest casualty rate occurred amongst the very inexperienced crews, whom established crews were unlikely to know personally.

And youth is ever resilient. Sergeant Tommy Marchant was a flight engineer on 101 Squadron at Ludford Magna and then with the Pathfinders of 7 Squadron at Oakington. He obviously took in his stride his crew's seventeen raids to Berlin, probably a record for any crew in Bomber Command.

Being a mere lad of nineteen, with little emotional or imaginative maturity, I probably did not notice the signs of people cracking up. So far as I recall, none of our crew exhibited any signs of the stress etc. so beloved of dramatic film makers. I did sometimes wonder if I would survive but it certainly wasn't a recurring or dominant thought. I was more concerned as to whether the local pub would run out of beer and if a certain Waaf would be there.

I am sure that morale was quite high on the squadrons with which I served. I personally look back on those days as a happy and exciting adventure – the old 'Biggles' books of my youth come true for me – and a feeling that you really were contributing to the war effort. But then I didn't get shot down or injured.

Young Tommy Marchant's seventeen operations to Berlin lead into another story. At the end of the Battle of Berlin, Señor Adalbert Fastlich of Panama gave some money for the purchase of gold watches which were presented to those Bomber Command pilots who had flown most Berlin raids. It is believed that his brother had been killed in London by German bombing earlier in the war. (There may have been another contributor to this fund – Mr Harold Lindo of Jamaica, whose son, Squadron Leader Harold Lindo, a navigator on 103 Squadron, was killed on one of the Berlin raids.) The crew of which Sergeant Marchant was a member was found to have flown more

Berlin raids than any other, so was allowed to have two watches. One was for the pilot, Flight Lieutenant Bob Sexton from Queensland; the remainder of the crew drew lots for the second watch, and Marchant, the young flight engineer, was successful.

Let us turn now to the German side and try to assess what the efforts of the bomber crews achieved. The great disadvantage in any judgement of the outcome of the Battle of Berlin is that no comprehensive survey was ever made on the effects of the bombing that winter. The Berlin authorities produced excellent factual reports on the damage and casualties in individual raids, and this book has made much of those reports; but no overall assessment was made. The United States Strategic Bombing Survey, which studied the effects of bombing in many German cities, hardly mentions Berlin. A British Bombing Survey Unit was established, but the new Labour Government of 1945 refused to allocate funds for detailed surveys, and little work on Bomber Command's huge wartime effort was ever carried out by the British. Sir Arthur Harris's post-war dispatch[1] claimed that 6,427 acres or 33 per cent of Berlin's built-up area was destroyed by bombing during the whole war. (The 'built-up area' of a city was defined as that part of it which was more than 40 per cent occupied by buildings.) Of those 6,427 acres, an estimated 480 acres had been destroyed by bombing before the Battle of Berlin started, and a further 750 were credited to American bombing after the Battle of Berlin. A further unknown acreage should be credited to the numerous Mosquito raids made in the last year of the war, but this might be balanced by the damage caused in the non-built-up suburbs during the Battle of Berlin. This leaves approximately 5,200 acres, nearly 27 per cent of Berlin's built-up area, to be credited to Bomber Command in the Battle of Berlin. These figures tend to be confirmed

1 Public Record Office AIR 14/1962.

by Berlin's own records, which show that 556,500 or 37 per cent of the city's pre-war flats were destroyed during the war by all forms of bombing and by the street fighting with the Russians in 1945. The reasons why the huge bomb tonnage dropped on Berlin did not produce better results have all been described earlier in the book. The difficulty of concentrating both marking and bombing on those sectors selected for attack led to western parts of the city being hit too often and the eastern parts not often enough. There was a similar inability to concentrate both marking and bombing sufficiently for complete destruction to be achieved anywhere. Squadron Leader Arthur Fawssett, an Intelligence Officer at Bomber Command Headquarters at that time, writes:

What I think was not sufficiently appreciated at the time was that nothing less than another Hamburg in the space of two or three days, something quite unbearable, was needed, and that a long period of attrition was unlikely to achieve the aim and could be self-defeating, in that the more piecemeal the damage became, the more difficult it was to create a self-destructive holocaust.

Finally, there was the sound construction of Berlin's buildings and the width of the streets of this modern city, factors which reduced the spread of fire. Much destruction was undoubtedly caused, but sufficient of Berlin's housing remained, supplemented by quickly erected wooden accommodation, for all essential workers to be housed.

Turning now to the human casualties in Berlin during the battle, it can be estimated from the civilian records that 10,305 people died in the nineteen raids, made up as follows:

German civilians in Berlin	9,390
Foreigners (mostly forced workers)	637
Service personnel	187
Country areas outside Berlin	91

And what of civilian morale, that primary target? There is no need to spend long on this subject. The Germans' innate patriotism, the particularly tough character of the Berliners and the strict discipline of the Nazi Party combined to hold the spirit of Berlin sufficiently intact to weather the storm. There was fear and, at times, terror. There was apathy. There were temporary breakdowns in the supply of power and water, and of some administration, but restoration of all these was swiftly achieved. Berlin was never over-whelmed. There was never the mass, panic-stricken flight of people from the bombed city as was sometimes seen in other places. The Japanese Embassy in Berlin was sending regular telegrams to Tokyo on the state of the city. In January 1944: 'Internal collapse will certainly not be brought about by means of air raids.' Morale in Berlin was noted as falling to its lowest in January and February, but 'because the Government used its enormous power and influence well, the fighting spirit of the people has been intensified to the pitch of seeing no course but to fight to the finish'.[1] This assessment was made just when Harris was forced by the Luftwaffe to break off the Berlin raids.

Prominent among the means by which the authorities bolstered the population were the threat of what would happen to Germany if the war was lost and the massive retaliation promised by Hitler against Britain by the new 'Revenge Weapons'. Hitler retained the confidence of most people although he never came to see the bombed cities of Germany but remained away at his headquarters, loftily directing every aspect of Germany's war effort. Not for him the visiting of people in bombed streets as Churchill and the King and Queen did when London was 'blitzed' in 1940 and 1941. That work he left to his Gauleiters. Joseph Goeb-bels, either Reichstag Member or Gauleiter for Berlin con-tinuously since 1929, respected by the ordinary people, often out on foot in the bombed areas without a large

1 The signals were decoded by the British and are quoted in F. H. Hinsley *et al.*, *British Intelligence in the Second World War*, Vol, III, pp. 304–7.

escort, looked after Berlin, and much credit for the stead-fastness and performance of the city should go to him.

The effect of the bombing upon industrial production in Berlin is difficult to measure. The factories were never direct targets, although they were often hit. The fire at the Alkett tank factory on the night of 26 November 1943 is described in Speer's memoirs and is thus often quoted else-where as being an example of serious damage to the war factories.[1] Nearly every major factory in Berlin was hit at some time or another, but often only by a few bombs, and none of the large factories was destroyed. Fire-fighting and then reconstruction work at the factories had the highest priority. It is probable that a much greater direct effect upon Berlin's war production was achieved that winter by the area bombing of the semi-residential areas. Here were situated a mass of small workshop industries supplying components to the larger factories. These were often wiped out by a single bomb or large fire. Much dislocation of both raw materials and finished goods was also caused by bomb damage to railways and canal traffic in Berlin.

It is time to come to a conclusion. Should the results of Bomber Command's vast effort and heavy losses in the Battle of Berlin be classed as success or failure? How have others answered the question? Some views are so bland as to be of little use. Air Marshal Saundby, Harris's deputy, was a much respected man but he obviously did not wish to be controversial when summing up the Battle of Berlin in his book: 'There could be no doubt that the target marking by the Pathfinder Force had been carried out with great skill and that the operations of the night bombers had been highly successful.'[2] Harris was much more restrained:

Judged by the standards of our attacks on Hamburg, the Battle of Berlin did not appear to be an overwhelming success. . . . The

1 *Inside the Third Reich*, p. 289.
2 *Air Bombardment*, pp. 163–4.

Battle of Berlin cost us 300 aircraft missing, which was a loss rate of 6·4 per cent. This could not be considered excessive for a prolonged assault on this distant, most difficult, and most heavily defended target.[1]

The British official historians were more blunt: 'The expectations of the Commander-in-Chief had not been fulfilled and by that standard the Battle of Berlin had been a failure. . . . Moreover, in the operational sense, the Battle of Berlin was more than a failure. It was a defeat.'[2]

Harris's authorized biographer, Dudley Saward, who had been an officer on Harris's staff, disputes this view.

The Official History of the bomber offensive states in emphatic terms that the Berlin campaign was a failure, and that losses were at a level that made it impossible to continue the campaign. This is incorrect. The reasons for the cessation were twofold: by the end of March the nights were becoming too short for operations against such distant targets as Berlin and, secondly, the requirement for the preparation for the invasion of France. . . . The suggestion that the Berlin campaign was a failure is not supported by the facts. An examination of the results reveals not failure but success, but as Harris himself admits, judged by the standards of the attacks on Hamburg, the Battle of Berlin was not an overwhelming success. However, for Germany it was an unprecedented disaster.[3]

'*Unprecedented* disaster'? What about Hamburg?

And my views? The Battle of Berlin obviously reduced Germany's war effort and made a contribution to victory. Every anti-aircraft gun or fighter aircraft kept back to defend Berlin was one less which might otherwise be serv-

1 *Bomber Offensive*, pp. 187 and 188. Harris has his aircraft casualty figures all wrong. The total losses of missing heavy bombers were 624 aircraft in the whole battle and 499 in the main November 1943 to March 1944 period to which he may have been referring. The percentage rates were 5·8 for the whole period and 5·5 for the November to March period.

2 British Official History, Vol, II, p. 193.

3 *Bomber Harris*, p. 221.

ing at the fighting fronts. Berlin was itself a front. Every pane of glass broken in Berlin was a tiny drain on Germany's economy; every bomb which hit a small workshop or large armaments factory was a direct blow against the war effort; and every workman killed or prevented from coming to work because his family had been bombed out was one less man producing war material. But the extent of the achievements at Berlin was not sufficient either to satisfy the aims set for the battle – breakdown of civil morale and destruction so great that the normal life of Berlin would cease – or to justify the bomber casualties. The cost was too high in relation to results. Bomber Command lost the equivalent of its entire front-line strength in attempting to destroy Berlin, and a similar loss was incurred in raiding other targets in Germany during the same period.

The two questions posed earlier in the book, on the ability of Bomber Command to hit Berlin and of the Luftwaffe to defend it, now come together. The Luftwaffe hurt Bomber Command more than Bomber Command hurt Berlin.

13 THE AFTERMATH

They did not know it, but the Lancaster and Halifax men of Bomber Command would not return to Berlin during the remaining months of the war. There were three occasions, however, when R.A.F. commanders and planners thought about ordering major raids to the city. The first of these was in September 1944. A combined plan was produced for a massive joint daylight raid by Bomber Command and by American heavy bombers. The fighter escort for the more distant parts of the route could be provided only by the long range American P-38s and P-51s (Lightnings and Mustangs). Preparations reached a late stage, but the raid was cancelled because it was judged that there were not enough long-range fighter escorts to protect both bomber forces.

The second occasion when the R.A.F. heavies might have returned to Berlin was later in the autumn. An exchange of letters early in November 1944, between the headquarters of Bomber Command and the Pathfinders, shows that a resumption of heavy raids was being considered.[1] But nothing happened. The plans made at that time, however, were probably retained and examined again early in 1945 for a proposed operation called *Thunderclap*. This was a series of heavy raids by the then much more powerful

[1] See British Official History, Vol. 11, p. 196.

Bomber Command on four German cities which were important communications and supply centres to the Eastern Front where the Russians were now on Germany's border. The four cities chosen for attack were Berlin, Chemnitz, Dresden and Leipzig. It was hoped that massive destruction in these places would cause simultaneous collapse of Germany's ability to hold the Russians on the Eastern Front and of its internal system. The orders were issued to Bomber Command on 27 January. The Russians were informed of the plan a week later, at the Yalta Conference, and gave enthusiastic encouragement. The first raid took place on the night of 13 February; it fell not on Berlin but on Dresden, which experienced the second major firestorm of the war. Chemnitz was attacked twice, but Operation *Thunderclap* was never completed, and Berlin and Leipzig were spared these massive blows.

But Berlin did not escape completely from bombing in the last year of the war. A strong force of Mosquito bombers was built up in 8 Group; it was named the Light Night Striking Force and it carried out harassing raids on an increasing scale, independently of the heavy bomber force. The solitary 139 Squadron, which had supported the heavies all through the Battle of Berlin, was joined by eight more squadrons, and eventually up to a hundred aircraft could be dispatched on these operations. Some of the Mosquitoes were modified so that they could carry a 4,000-pound Blockbuster. So fast were the Mosquitoes that, during the final winter of the war, some aircraft flew to Berlin early in the night, bombed, returned, changed crews and rearmed, and then carried out a second raid later in the same night. So fast and high did the Mosquitoes fly that casualties were minimal. Berlin was their main target, and they concluded the war with raids against the city on thirty-six successive nights in February and March 1945. Gauleiter Goebbels noted in his wartime diaries the effects of these raids: 'These Mosquito raids have now become so heavy that they are almost comparable to a raid by a small force of heavy bombers . . . The millions of people in the

Reich capital are steadily becoming nervous and hysteri-
cal . . . It is a torture which overstrains the nerves in the
long run."[1]

The Mosquito raids ended on 21 April 1945 because the
Russians were about to enter the city, and what might justi-
fiably be called the Second Battle of Berlin was about to
begin. In the most vicious of street fighting, the Russians
worked their way steadily through from east to west, finishing off in the eastern districts the destruction which
Bomber Command had not been able to achieve there.
Hitler, earlier driven out of his headquarters in East Prussia
by the Russian advance, was at least present with the people
of Berlin during their final torment, although he rarely
ventured out of his underground bunker. He committed
suicide. The war ended.

Berlin was divided by the victors into four military sectors
and faced the task of clearing the rubble before the city
could be rebuilt. There were not many young German men
left, and most of the clearance was carried out by women,
the famous *Trümmerfrauen* – rubble women – of Berlin.
They hand-cleaned any bricks which could be re-used, and
the remainder of the bomb and battle debris was carried
away by lorry and piled into miniature hills. There were
neither sufficient lorries nor petrol to spare to haul the
material outside the city, so these hills were all inside Berlin,
in parks or other open spaces. So the *Trümmerberge* became
a permanent feature of Berlin's skyline and are now used
for such things as the siting of radio and television transmitters, radar receivers and artificial ski slopes and for the
flying of model aeroplanes. It was later estimated that 55
million cubic metres of wreckage were cleared. Someone
produced the interesting statistic that the average family
flat destroyed in the war produced 12.7 cubic metres of
rubble.

1 *The Goebbels Diaries: The Last Days*, pp. 138 and 146.

The three great Flak towers survived the war intact; they had been almost impregnable fortresses during the fighting with the Russians. After the war the occupying powers decided to remove them. The Americans were lucky; they did not have one in their sector. The Russians and the British gradually demolished their two towers in the Friedrichshain Park and the Tiergarten and, with much labour, removed the remains; the site of the old Tiergarten tower is now the rebuilt Berlin Zoo. The French made several unsuccessful attempts to blow up their tower in the Humboldthain Park but had to turn the area into a disposal site for the bomb rubble, covering all except the top gun platform; it is now a tree-covered hill, and on that top platform stands a sculptured symbol of 'Divided Germany'.

There is one part of Berlin where the British bomber crews will always remain. An area of woodland, part of the Grunewald Forest in the district of Charlottenburg, was designated as a British War Cemetery. From 1914–18 until the Falklands War of 1982 the British had a 'no repatriation' policy for their war dead, the bodies of whom had to remain within the country in which they died, although they could be moved for assembly purposes within that country. So the bodies of the R.A.F. men, both from Berlin and from a large surrounding area, were gathered together in that peaceful spot. More than four out of every five of the 3,576 graves are of R.A.F. men, a high proportion of them being men killed in the Battle of Berlin. A visitor entering through the gateway is immediately faced with a long, unusually narrow plot of gravestones, each row containing just seven graves. These are the communal graves of bomber crews. The first row contains the bodies of Flight Lieutenant John Bracewell, D.F.C., and his crew who died on their twenty-fourth operation in a Lancaster of 12 Squadron, shot down by a night fighter after bombing Berlin on the night of 24/25 March 1944, the last raid of the Battle of Berlin. It was a typical Bomber Command crew: five men from English counties, a Scot from Edinburgh, an Australian married to a Yorkshire girl. The ages of only four of the seven are recorded; the oldest was twenty-three.

What do the young R.A.F. men who fought in the Battle of Berlin and survived think about it all now?

Flight Sergeant E. O. Charlton, 97 Squadron:

Of course the Big City scared us all but there was a tremendous satisfaction in doing a trip there. It frightened me fartless but I still enjoyed it, as I did all my ops. I know this must sound mad but it is the truth. I am proud and glad that I had a crack at the Hun in the middle of his evil capital. My only regret, and it is still a very bitter one, is that I was shot down and did not last longer to do more sorties.

Pilot Officer J. Chatterton, 44 Squadron:

The Battle of Berlin that winter was my tour. My mind is full of night take-offs, climbing through cloud, icing, Berlin Flak – the sheer length and breadth of it – not of night fighters; we never saw one of those in our trips. I see photographs of crews sitting outside their briefing rooms on summer evenings, waiting for take-off – that wasn't my war, no sitting on the grass or playing cricket with the ground crew for us. We waited in the dark and cold and rain – that was our tour.

Pilot Officer W. N. McInnis, 426 Squadron:

After forty years or more, the Battle of Berlin is a 'dream'. I sometimes wonder if it really happened, although I know it did. On clear nights, the fires seemed endless and it took no imagination to realize the tremendous destruction being wrought on a beautiful city. I can still close my eyes today and see it all. Nothing can ever wipe out those scenes that now seem so stupidly wrong, yet seemingly necessary then.

Flight Lieutenant D. T. Conway, 467 Squadron:

My main impression of the Battle of Berlin was that it was
bloody dark, bloody cold and bloody dangerous, but
highlighted by sights of unbelievable beauty. A target well
lit up with Flak and searchlights, plus flares and bombs
exploding, was a spectacular sight, with planes flying
through as in a gigantic fish-bowl.

Flying Officer E. J. Densley, 101 Squadron:

Having done more than half of the big raids on Berlin,
we felt that there was a glamour which did not attach
itself to other targets. While one reason was undoubtedly
the difficulty of Berlin as a target, I really do think that it
was felt that we really were striking a blow against the
Nazis that would be devastating, and I always felt
surprised and disappointed that the war lasted for over a
year after I finished my tour.

Squadron Leader H. W. Trilsbach, 405 Squadron:

The Battle of Berlin was the worst part of my operational
flying. It involved the worst weather, the most Flak, most
searchlights and by far the greatest fighter opposition at
any time on my 'ops' career. Frankly, I don't want to see
the bloody place again from any angle. I just hope that
perhaps it proved to the Germans that war does not pay.
Oh, but what a terrible price the young Bomber
Command crews had to pay.

Pilot Officer G. J. A. Smith, 100 Squadron:

My main reaction is one of anger that some people today
write about the raids as being 'militarily and morally
wrong'. Germany had been preparing the attack on
England by the so-called V-weapons for a very long time
and, had they had the means and the opportunity, the
Nazis would have wiped out a large proportion of the
population of this country without a qualm. We felt that
we were doing our job. The cry that went up in those

days was, 'Good old R.A.F. Give them one for us!' Today, the tune seems to have changed.

Flight Sergeant R. E. C. Buck, 207 and 97 Squadrons:

Not a day goes by that I don't relive mentally my operational experiences. Even after all this time, my heart still bleeds for the boys I knew who were killed, especially my pilot. So many of them died unnecessarily, especially over Berlin. They were the cream of the nation. We paid far too high a price in the battle for Berlin and I think victory went to the Germans.

Pilot Officer C. J. Gray, 61 Squadron:

I sensed, both then and now, that our masters were disappointed in us. Berlin was the crucial battleground for Bomber Command, against which all the others pale into utter insignificance. Bomber Command failed to achieve what the air marshals had set their hearts on and promised to deliver – the total destruction of the capital city and with it the will of the German nation to continue the war. It was a double failure. The city was not destroyed, nor the German will. Far from it. It was the weapon itself, our Bomber Command, that was blunted and brought close to destruction.

Pilot Officer T. R. Lister, 158 Squadron:

I always think that we never quite sorted Berlin out. Perhaps it was too far; bomb loads were smaller, defences were very considerable, but we did paste it. Perhaps we could call it a draw.

Flight Sergeant J. Brown, 50 Squadron:

I still think the Battle of Berlin was the turning of the tide that brought us victory in 1945. But, when I look back in retrospect, and reflect that I was one of the first to tour Berlin immediately after the war and witnessed the horrific damage we had done to that city and inhaled the disgusting smell of death up one's nostrils which I still have to this day, I wonder, was it really necessary?

Sergeant H. Hudson, 106 Squadron:

It was a battle, no question. My own impression was that we were engaged in a tremendous effort to smash Germany and nothing else mattered.

EXPERIENCES

Several particularly interesting accounts of individual experiences during the Battle of Berlin could not be included in the relevant chapters because their length would have unbalanced those chapters. Twelve such accounts are presented here.

'Maximum Effort', by Sergeant K. F. Scott, navigator, 101 Squadron, describing the first raid of the battle, on the night of 23/24 August 1943.

We were listed on Battle Orders as the reserve crew. Being new to the squadron, we did not realize that we should have attended the briefing, so we were absent when details of the operation were given to the rest of the crews. Unfortunately, a F/Lt Rowland's crew was taken off ops after briefing, due to sickness. We were rounded up from various parts of the camp and rushed out to the aircraft. F/Lt Rowland's navigator's flight plan and chart were thrust into my hand and, before we knew it, we were airborne on our way to the 'Big City', on our second operation, with no meal, no briefing, just a flight plan, just twenty-four hours after being blooded on our first trip over Germany, which had been to an easy target.

Fortunately for us, the raid was timed to last forty

minutes over the target area and we were put in the last phase, otherwise we shouldn't have made it in time. Eventually we reached the target and were appalled at the task which confronted us. All we could see was what appeared to be a solid wall of smoke puffs from the spent Flak and the flashes from new explosions coming up. As we drew nearer and over the city, we realized that it wasn't so dense as we thought; we had been viewing ten miles or so of action in one scan.

'Ditched', by Sergeant J. Burland, flight engineer in 90 Squadron Stirling BK 779. On the night of 23/24 August 1943, the Stirling had been forced to take violent evasive action when coned in searchlights and attacked by a fighter over Berlin, and the aircraft may have been overstrained. Later, after the German coast had been crossed and the Stirling was over the sea in the German Bight, there was an explosion in the wing.

The starboard inner stopped at once. It started windmilling and wouldn't feather. Frank Mulvey and I were trying to sort that out when the starboard outer engine fell off. We didn't see it fall; it just disappeared. The wing was on fire underneath and we decided, by general consent, to bale out. We went back – the gunners and I – to the rear door and I suggested that we ditched instead; we shouldn't be jumping over the sea. So we took up ditching positions. The pilot asked the wireless operator to send out a distress signal and I think that is how he died, thrown against his set when we hit the sea later. The pilot said he didn't think we would ever get down. We had to come down from 15,000 feet and the big fear was that the wing would come off. The theory of ditching was to put the tail down first, then the nose. But there were only two engines working in the port wing and it was as black as hell. The starboard wing tip must have touched first; a level-flight indicator is no good five feet above the sea. We swung hard to starboard and were all thrown violently the other way. That was how the mid-upper gunner was lost; he was thrown through the door of the wooden bulkhead and right up the fuselage. I don't know what happened to the navigator but the pilot told me later that he was lost. The bomb aimer was stood behind the pilot's seat, trying to help, but he died as well.

The aircraft was going down quickly. The tail gunner was the only one to get out of the aircraft dry. I followed him out of the roof hatch and started to slide down the top of the fuselage but my dinghy pack, which was attached to my backside, caught under the rim of the hatch and I was stuck. I had horrible thoughts of drowning but, when the water reached me, I just floated off. The rear gunner was already in the dinghy. I can't swim but I felt a man alongside me, helping me. It turned out to be the pilot, still with his helmet and oxygen mask on. The aircraft had disappeared so fast you wouldn't credit it. Frank had actually got out while the cockpit was well under water and had come up from below. He had somehow got out of the hatch in the cockpit roof but he was concussed, probably bashing his head when we ditched. He wasn't much use for several days. We got him into the dinghy – a big hulking fellow – and that was that. There were only three of us. The aircraft had gone down like a steamroller.

The pilot thought that we were ninety miles from Denmark and sixty miles from Germany. We lost all the rations in the dinghy; I think we saw them floating away. We only had two very small 'seat-pack' dinghy tins of food – hardly anything. It rained after five days and we got our first drink. The weather was stormy and we were always being drenched; the waves were actually breaking on the tops of the rollers. We got toppled over once but we were lucky; we all held on to the rope and that big Canadian, Frank Mulvey, who had recovered from his concussion, turned it over again by brute strength. All our clothes were caked with salt and we became semi-delirious. I thought that we were in the boating lake at Hope Bank in Huddersfield.

We reached an area where there was much flotsam on the surface of the sea. Among it was a body; I think from the type of harness that it was that of an R.A.F. pilot. A seagull stood on the floating body. We had a cork ring on the end of a hundred foot line for swimming out to help others. I am sorry that I did not try to get to the body and remove the dog tags so that I could inform the family.

It was not until the evening of the eighth day that we were spotted by some Junker 52s which had degaussing rings on them; they were out clearing mines. A boat picked us up soon afterwards; I don't know what type of boat, we were in a poor condition by then. We were taken to Cuxhaven. I didn't tell the Germans who were guarding us that we had been to Hamburg four times a month before; I think some of the German sailors were from Hamburg. They treated us reasonably well and we recovered fast on a copious provision of lemon barley water.

'The Crashed Bomber', by Arno Abendroth, a fourteen-year-old Berlin schoolboy. He describes his activities on the morning of 24 August 1943.

No bombs had fallen near us but, as soon as it was light, I went out looking for Flak splinters. Then, after breakfast, my mother sent me off on my bike to see if my relatives were safe. I went to Auntie Herma's first; everything was okay there. Next I went to my grandparents. The way was barred by police but they allowed me through because I had my Hitler Jugend uniform on and the H.J. pass. They told me not to stay long.

I went to my grandparents' home. Grandma was jittery. The windows were all cracked; I looked through them and saw two blocks of flats across the park still burning. The fire brigade was there. Grandma told me that a four-engined bomber had crashed among the bushes and small trees in the park in between. I was astonished and looked out again. There was an aircraft engine just two metres away, stuck into the earth. Not only that, but the tip of a propeller, about a foot long, had come through the window and was stuck in the kitchen cupboard.

My grandmother had heard a droning noise, stopping and starting, getting lower and lower. My grandfather, an old First World War man, told her to take cover. Then there was a great crash. My grandfather thought it was a dud bomb. He went out with a torch and saw the two houses burning. He told grandmother to stay put while he went to help the people at the burning houses but they couldn't put the fire out. It turned out that the bomber's fuel tanks had fallen on the houses and set them alight; but no one was hurt.

Then she told me there were some dead airmen. I just had to see them. Grandma tried to stop me. 'Poor boys,' she said; 'they look so terrible.' But I had to see them. The bomber must have broken up in the air but not too high up; most of the pieces were close together. The police and Flak soldiers guarding the wreckage tried to keep me away but I hung around and eventually saw the row of four bodies, only partly covered with canvas. The men told me they had taken three bodies out of the forward part of the bomber and the fourth had been fetched out of a big pine tree. They told me they had identified the bodies as Canadians. They weren't badly mangled but I do remember their deathly pale faces, chalk white. These were the first dead men of the war I had seen, but I must say that I had a deep satisfaction at the sight of those dead *Terrorflieger*. They were our enemies.

Then a policeman made me go home. I was very cross and didn't do that, but went back to my grandmother's, hoping to get back to the bomber to get some souvenirs, but I never managed it. I was back home by midday and told my mother all about it.

'Return to Base', by Sergeant F. Gration, navigator of a 428 Squadron Halifax which force-landed in Norfolk after returning from the 23/24 August 1943 raid. The crew had a long train journey to their airfield at Middleton St George in County Durham.

We travelled on a small line until we hit the main line to the north. In those days, you ran from one train to the other and this was no exception. We all piled into a coach and then started to head into another coach where we could get seats. To our surprise, both end doors of our coach were locked.

Every compartment of our coach was full except one which had two officers in it. I headed in and the one at the door said, 'You can't come in here', and the other echoed him. That really got me somewhat disgruntled, so I gave them both a blast saying, 'I don't want to boast but last night we damn near got killed over Berlin fighting for you bastards. We are tired and we want to sit down.' They both insisted we couldn't go in, so I said a few choice words and went out, slamming the door. My pilot said. 'Do you know who the guy in the corner is?' and, when I replied in the negative, he said, 'It's King Haakon of Norway.'

'Shot down', by Sergeant T. Nelson, navigator in a 51 Squadron Halifax shot down just after leaving Berlin on 31 August/1 September 1943.

There came a tremendous jolt and then silence. Almost immediately, the flight engineer jumped into the navigation section and yelled, 'Escape hatch! Jump! Jump!' The curtain behind him was now open and I saw the entire port wing in flames. I pushed up my seat and clipped on my parachute pack. Together, we opened the escape hatch and Jack put his legs into the aperture. At that moment, the aircraft went into a nosedive. I do not know what happened to Jack but he must have fallen back into the plane and past me. The escape hatch was now above my head. I tried to raise my arm to grab the sill but the G-force was so great I could not raise it above my head. My arm fell back and I knew I was going to die.

At that moment an absolute sense of peace and well-being came over me. I have never known such tranquillity. If this is what happens at the moment of death, then no one should ever be afraid of it. And then I was out in the cold night air. I was falling feet first. My parachute pack had pulled off the shoulder straps and was floating about five feet in front of me. Quite casually, I pulled the straps towards me and tugged the D-ring. Seconds later I hit the ground.

It was pitch dark. I was in a field near some woods. All around me there were tremendous flashes but I could hear nothing. I was stone deaf. I bundled up my parachute, stowed it under a bush and ran into the darkness away from the explosions. Curly and Robbie later told me that they were captured almost immediately at the scene of the crash. They were made to remove the four bodies from the aircraft and my parachute was discovered close by. I have no recollection of seeing them or the plane but they told me that the three of us and the aircraft all landed within one hundred yards of each other. Their parachutes, too, were only open for a few seconds. We can only assume that an explosion took place after the plane had nosedived. This explosion blew off the nose of the aircraft, allowing the three of us in that area to fall free. Certainly none of us jumped to safety of our own accord.

As soon as it became light enough to recognize something, I was driven by a strange compulsion. In many briefings we had been told that the first thing that should be done after being shot down was to try to look as much like a native as possible. If you removed your badges of rank and cut the tops off your flying boots, you would appear to be dressed in a nondescript blue uniform and wearing shoes. To follow those instructions seemed to be the most important thing in my life. The boots had been specially made with a removable legging part. In the top of the boot was a tiny knife. I cut off my sergeant's stripes, my navigator's wing and the tops of my boots. What a mistake! When I floundered into a ditch my boots and trousers had become soaking wet. After removing the leggings, I found that the water had softened the leather and the kapok lining of the back of the 'shoes', and at every fifteen or twenty paces they came off like carpet slippers. I cursed the inventor of those boots for the next week.

As dawn approached, I took stock. I had a cut about three inches long on the right side of my head which was still bleeding. I was wet through. My boots kept falling off. I was alone, seven hundred miles from home. I saw what appeared to be an old mill standing alone. I crawled in and crept into some hay. Two or three times during the day I looked through a window and was amazed by the sight. R.A.F. Window was everywhere – on the ground, hanging in the trees, everywhere. I got the foolish notion that just like Hansel and Gretel's breadcrumbs, I might be able to follow it all the way home. Then I realized I would have to walk at night and hide up during the day. It had now started to rain. I was glad to be inside rather than outside. I fell into an exhausted sleep.

When I awoke, I was in even worse pain. The blood on the side of my head had now congealed but the parachute strap must have jerked my groin because it was now very painful to walk and, in fact, I could only really manage to hobble. I ate my chocolate ration. As soon as it became dark, I started walking once more but could only manage a few miles during the entire night. At dawn I went to sleep at the edge of a wood. Quite surprisingly, two deer, completely unaware of my presence, came within thirty feet of me. Somehow this gave me a little confidence. If they couldn't find me, neither could the Germans. But I was wrong. I was awakened about an hour later by loud voices. Three farmworkers were standing over me. One of them had a large fork about three inches from my throat. They forced me to my feet and led me with the fork at my back into a village about a mile away.

They took me to a large farmhouse, presumably where they worked, and all sorts of excited unintelligible chattering took place with the occupants. The entire family came out into the yard. Father, mother and teenage daughter. I must have looked a pretty sorry sight and they behaved very kindly towards me. I indicated I would like to clean up, so they brought me a large zinc tub of warm water. I stripped down to the waist in the yard, had a good wash and felt a lot better. They took me into the house and gave me a big meal of eggs, bacon and coffee. The coffee was *ersatz* and awful, but the eggs and bacon were delicious. In my mind I was contrasting this with England where food was so very strictly rationed. However, this was a farm and perhaps they had a few extras.

I was taken to Berlin, to Spandau prison. Later, I was taken into a room. Seated at a table was a kindly looking man in his sixties with white hair and glasses. He explained that he was from the Swiss Red Cross and needed to obtain our personal details so our families in England could be notified. He asked for my name, rank and number. Then he asked if I was wounded. I pointed to the scar on my head and the congealed blood around it. He asked if I had any complaints and I replied that I had received no food at all for the last twenty-four hours. He said that would soon be rectified. He then asked for my mother's name and address so that she could be notified of my capture and I gave it to him.

Then he casually remarked, 'You know, more than four hundred planes took part on your raid and the B.B.C. says that forty-five were shot down. Why do you face such tremendous odds night after night?' I replied that I had no knowledge of anything like that and consequently had no opinion. He just said, 'That will be all, then', and pointed to a door leading into the next room.

The room contained four or five R.A.F. boys who had

presumably been interviewed before me. A German *Feldwebel* with a rifle in his hand said, 'How do you like broadcasting home?' He took me to a window and pointed downwards. An army truck was parked in the yard outside with cables leading into it. Two turntables were rotating and obviously recording everything that had been said. It became painfully obvious that the kindly Swiss Red Cross representative was an unkindly German and I had committed a major error. Past security briefings drifted before me. 'If captured, give only your name, rank and serial number.' In moments of despondency in prison camps during the next twenty months, I would think about this exchange and wonder what would happen to me when I got back to England. In the event, I was never ever questioned about it and it at least served one good cause. Two days later, a lorry pulled up outside my mother's home in London. The driver told her that Lord Haw-Haw had given my name and address in the previous night's broadcast to England. So my mother knew I had been captured within a week of being shot down.

'Shot Down by Own Side', by Leutnant Rudolf Thun, a Messerschmitt 110 pilot of II/NJG 5, shot down over Berlin on 31 August/1 September 1943.

I was about to start a three-week leave together with my fiancée, but changed my mind when that evening we got the report of another bomber attack on Berlin. I sent my fiancée, dog and luggage ahead to my parents, who lived in the vicinity of Berlin, and decided to fly one last sortie before going on leave.

We arrived perhaps twenty minutes ahead of the British bombers over Berlin, but the Flak opened up immediately with all they had. Fortunately, it was a relatively bright night and it was thus easy to take evasive action when the row of little puffy grey clouds of Flak bursts came too close. Then I was caught in a couple of searchlights, and finally five had me in their beams. I probably could have easily outdived them but I did not want to give up altitude and – going by the book – had my radio operator shoot the starshell combination of the day, identifying myself as a German plane. Well, the searchlight beams kept right on me and, after a few seconds, I was hit from behind by a Wild Boar fighter who must have taken my 110, with underwing tanks outboard of the engines, for a four-engined plane – naturally, a British bomber. Some of those Wild Boar pilots had little or no experience as combat pilots. I got 20-mm hits in my instrument panel, my left engine and the left wing. The left aileron was about gone.

The Me 110 was difficult to fly on one engine, even without damage, but with the damaged left wing and without instruments I could not hold the plane either straight or level and gave the order to bale out. When I was ready to go, I saw that my radio operator was holding on for dear life and was afraid to jump, so I kicked him free while I was leaving.

Since it was night, I came down pretty hard but, as fate would have it, close to the Flak unit which had so kindly illuminated me. Even though I wore only a leather jacket, without rank insignia, and could as well have been British, a *Feldwebel* explained to me beaming that they had just downed a plane by blinding it with their searchlights. I exposed him somewhat unkindly to the facts of life and, shortly thereafter, expressed myself on the telephone equally frankly to the officer who commanded the Flak unit. He was quite apologetic and sent a car. After a search, I found my radio operator and then went to Döberitz to report to Major Radusch. He was very gracious, received me with champagne and next morning lent me his private liaison aircraft for a round trip to my airfield at Greifswald to change my clothes and get my holiday gear. By late afternoon, I was with family, fiancée and dog, not necessarily in that order.

'The Zoo Flak Tower', by Horst Kesner, a sixteen-year-old *Flakhilfer*, describing the night of 22/23 November 1943.

There was a so-called *Hilfszug Bayern*, a column of lorries which brought food to the Bunker when a big raid was expected. It was named after the organization which had supplied the Nuremberg rallies and the May Day rallies of the Hitler Youth each year, hence the name, *Hilfszug Bayern* (Bavarian Relief Column). We soldiers had to unload the food; because it was so much better than our own rations, we naturally organized some of it for ourselves. The food was wonderful but, because so many people were so well fed, the toilet problem became terrible.

There was an *Oberfähnrich* who was in charge of keeping the passageways open to the toilets. He got a decoration for this, and for his other work of course, which included sorting people out with a megaphone when they were crowding in before a raid. But it was good for the people in the bunker; the good food satisfied them and the walls were so thick that they could not hear the bombs outside, only our guns on top, firing away.

The people were crammed in every room and in every section, right up to the fourth floor where the military section began. They crowded into the passages so that we had to step over them as they slept on the floor. I think we had up to 20,000 people on the worst night. In the morning, when the raid was over, it took hours to get everyone out.

'The Berlin Zoo', by Ursula Gebel, a twenty-three-year-old secretary.

My family were shareholders in the Zoo which meant that we had free entrance at any time. In the afternoon of 22 November, being very fond of animals, I went there. I remember staying for a long time at the elephant cage, watching them performing tricks and stunts with the keeper. There were six females and one baby elephant.

Just before closing time, the baby elephant turned the handle of a barrel organ and played a goodbye melody.

Next day I went back to the Zoo because I had heard that it had been heavily bombed. It was closed but I managed to get inside through a damaged entrance. I was amazed. There were water-filled bomb craters everywhere and all the buildings were destroyed and burnt out. All the big animal houses were gone. The six female elephants and the baby were nothing but blackened carcasses, roasted to death by phosphorus bombs. A terrible smell lingered above the total destruction of my beloved Zoo. There were blasted and dead animals everywhere. The only living thing, in his big pond, was a big bull hippopotamus called Knautschke, still swimming while above him his shelter burned down.

I knew a lot of the keepers. With tears in their eyes, they told me about the horrible night. All the brown bears, the polar bears, the camels, the zebras, the antelopes, the ostriches and all the beasts of prey – lions, tigers, panthers, leopards, hyenas – were dead; the keepers had been forced to shoot many of the burning and crazed animals. All the wild birds were gone. Of the apes, only one orang-utan – a female called Cleo – managed to escape into the nearby park. She had been found sitting in a big tree with her baby but she died from a heart attack and her body was hanging in the tree. Flak soldiers brought the baby, Muschi, down the next day and sent it to the Zoo at Copenhagen.

In the big aquarium, all the glass cases were broken and the water had poured out, sweeping alligators and crocodiles, as well as all the fish and snakes, out into the open where they perished in the November cold of this night.

'Prisoner of War', by Sergeant O. Roberts, mid-upper gunner in a 49 Squadron Lancaster shot down over Berlin on the night of 2/3 December 1943.

I jumped out into the middle of the Flak, immediately over the centre of Berlin. I looked down and saw the fires and searchlights. One searchlight suddenly focused on me and held me in its beam for some time. Having heard tales of machine-guns firing up the beams, I quickly manoeuvred myself out of it. I descended away from the target area and landed in a tree which was about forty feet high. I had no wish for the Germans to find me in such a spot as I had heard tales of *Terrorflieger* being hung by lampposts and my predicament seemed too inviting, so I released my harness and fell to the ground, dislocating my shoulder and injuring my leg so that I was unable to walk.

I lay there all night in the freezing cold. Fortunately I had my flying kit on but I still caught pneumonia. The first person I saw when day broke was a man on a bike. I blew my whistle and he came over to see me. He said he had been a prisoner of war in 1914–18 in England. He was reasonably friendly and went for the Army. The Army duly arrived on horses, searched me and then handed me over to the Luftwaffe, who took me to a nearby searchlight post, the one that had me in its beam on the way down. The *Feldwebel* in charge was quite offended that I had got out of the beam. 'We were showing you the way down,' he said.

I spent the day at this post, being shown off to their girlfriends whilst they smoked my fags and ate my chocolate. I was transferred that evening to what appeared to be a private nursing home in Berlin. The lady in charge gave me two apples to eat and sent for a doctor. The doctor arrived, wearing a black swastika armband. He took a look at me and walked out, saying, '*Terrorflieger!*' This was the first German who had showed any animosity to me.

The next day I was transferred to another hospital which was staffed by British P.O.W.s. After a couple of days at this hospital, it was decided that my pneumonia was getting worse and so I was transferred to the

Hermann Goering Luftwaffe Hospital on the Unter den Linden. Here I was treated very well but I was caught up in the German propaganda machine. At the time of my capture, I was a very young looking nineteen-year-old and the German press was publishing reports that Winston Churchill was sending children in the bombers as the Luftwaffe had shot down so many crews. My photograph was published in the *Völkischer Beobachter* as one of 'CHURCHILL'S BABES'.

I stayed in this hospital for a further two weeks, and was there on the night of 16 December when Bomber Command paid another visit to Berlin. The sirens sounded and I was taken to the air-raid shelter with the other patients. I was sitting on a bunk bed in the shelter when a 'Cookie' dropped outside. It didn't whistle; it rattled on the way down and shook all the building when it exploded. An old German *Oberfeldwebel* sitting next to me said, 'Da boot is on der oder foot, ja?' to which I said, 'You ain't kidding, mate.' Needless to say, I was just as pleased as my hosts to hear the sound of departing aircraft.

During all the time I was in Berlin, the Germans treated me very kindly, with respect, and undoubtedly saved my life.

'Strained Nerves', by Sergeant F. Collis, 207 Squadron.

My first operation was as a second pilot with a crew which had an American pilot and navigator. It was to Berlin on 29 December 1943. The two Americans flew in a manner which would have raised a few eyebrows in the R.A.F. After take-off, they argued about everything that should have been mutually accepted, such as which course to take, at what height, and this was the pattern throughout the flight.

We had an adventurous trip, which I thought was the norm, because it was my first op. And I thought it would be my last. We were coned in searchlights and the pilot appeared not to have had much instruction over evasive action, because he heaved the plane all over the sky without any method of getting away from the vicinity of the searchlights. The plane was hit by Flak but nobody was injured, although some spent Flak hit the navigator on the bottom of his foot. In spite of the fact that I am a Canadian, I didn't realize that the American language could be so descriptive. It was a most perilous trip and was made all the more frightening because I could see what was going on and knew what I would do, but I had no power to control the movements of the plane. By the grace of God, we got back. [The two Americans and all of their crew were killed when shot down on the next raid to Berlin.]

We operated as a complete crew for the first time on a raid to Berlin on 1 January 1944 – an eventful trip. But, when we were scheduled to operate again the next night, my Australian mid-upper gunner came to me and said that under no circumstances would he go on an operational trip. He didn't care if everybody called him 'yellow', but that was final. I always considered that he was courageous to admit that he was frightened to death.

'Press on Regardless', by Sergeant K. Apps, mid-upper gunner in a Lancaster of 12 Squadron which was lost on the night of 1/2 January 1944.

We taxied out; our target, as usual, was Berlin. Before we reached the runway, the Skipper called up to say that we had an engine overheated and, after a quick vote, the crew decided to cross fingers and get the old lady off the ground as quickly as possible. This we did, only to find as we climbed over the aerodrome that the guns started firing on their own and there were tracers flying everywhere; this was due to a short in the electrics. The rear gunner and myself quickly dismantled the Brownings, therefore leaving the plane with no armament at all – and still, the young, motley crew decided to press on towards the target.

When we came up to the Dutch coast, we heard from

the navigator that the Gee box had gone U/S, so we had no homing device. Still, this didn't deter us. With all that expensive load in the belly, it was on to Berlin or bust. We didn't believe in dumping in the sea.

We reached the target and released our bombs. It made us a total of twenty-four sorties, so we thought – home now to a tot of rum, eggs and bacon, and a nice long sleep, but it was not to be. Turning south, leaving the target, we felt both lucky and on top of the world but, suddenly, the engineer called to say that our petrol was disappearing at a staggering rate. Thank goodness we had our reserve to get us to the North Sea. WRONG! When he switched over, this went just as quickly. Those four Merlins just went silent and, at 20,000 feet if you haven't any power, the old lady decides to put her nose down and find terra firma pretty quickly.

The order came to bale out, so on with the emergency oxygen bottle and into the fuselage to get the parachute, only to find the rear gunner out of his turret, staggering around with no oxygen. I dragged him up to the side hatch, put the rip-cord in his fist, doubled him up and pushed him out. He got down safely. I then jumped myself. I was on my own at four o'clock in the morning. It was a long and silent journey down, so many things to think about. What was going to happen to me?

'Evader', by Pilot Officer G. G. A. Whitehead, the pilot of a 76 Squadron Halifax which was badly hit by Flak in the nose of the aircraft over Berlin on the night of 20/21 January 1944. The bomb aimer was killed, the wireless operator wounded and the navigator lost all his charts; the compasses became unserviceable, and one of the engines failed. The aircraft gradually lost height.

When we got clear of the Flak area, we sorted ourselves out. The first thing I did was to spot Polaris out of the starboard window and I kept it in sight, directly to my right – rather basic navigating. We had a second pilot with us

that night and I sent him and the flight engineer to get the
wireless operator to the rest position. They all behaved
very well. Then the navigator went back to make sure the
bomb aimer was dead. He soon confirmed it. Nobody said
much. I just wanted to get the rest of them home.

I consulted with the navigator and asked him what a
course due west would do for us. He had no maps at all,
although he may have looked at the small pilot's map
which I had. We decided that due west was a good route
– the shortest way to England, just clear of the Ruhr, and
with a narrower section of the North Sea to cross. We
kept losing height and at one stage we got down to below
10,000 feet. I ordered that we jettison as much stuff as we
could. I deliberately didn't discuss our chances. I just said
we would press on for as long as possible and try to get
home. We kept aiming west. There was complete cloud
cover below and we saw nothing of the ground.

We went on for some time, still desperately looking for
a break in the cloud, which seemed to be getting less
dense. Then the flight engineer told us we wouldn't have
more than a few minutes on the starboard engines
because the linkages from the fuel cocks had apparently
been damaged and we couldn't use much of the fuel
which was left in the starboard wing tanks. Until then,
lack of fuel was not deemed to be one of our problems.

I told everybody to make sure their parachutes were
handy and to be prepared for an emergency of some
sort. I didn't know whether we were over the land or the
sea. Then, within a minute or two, the cloud became
broken and we could see the ground. We were down to
about 4,000 feet by that time. What I did next may have
been stupid – I don't know – but I called up 'Darkie', the
emergency request for any English airfield to put their
lights on and tell us to come in. There was no reply.

So I ordered the bale-out and we went in an orderly
manner. We were getting a bit talkative but we felt rather
proud that we did everything according to the correct
drill, starting with me saying, 'Quiet everyone. Parachute.

Parachute. Prepare to bale out.' The mid-upper gunner attached the wounded wireless operator to a static line and he went out and survived. Then the rest of the crew went and finally, after what seemed an age, I went out of the forward hatch.

I was very surprised to find myself in France. I found out later that a strong wind change had taken us well south. I came down near Lens, in a mining area. I was given a little help at a Polish miner's home and then set off to walk south. While walking across a plain I looked up and saw the large Canadian memorial on Vimy Ridge. I walked through Arras, right past the German headquarters near the station, with a large swastika flag hanging at the front. I found out later that these were the pre-war offices of the Imperial War Graves Commission. Then I walked further south down the road to Bapaume, round Peronne and on to Ham. I was passing through the First World War battlefield areas and saw many cemeteries.

When I got to Ham I used the advice given on escape procedures. I looked for a large house which appeared to be inhabited by one of the professional classes; these were unlikely to be collaborators. You were then to observe the house for some time and, in the evening, knock on the door and say, 'Je suis anglais, R.A.F.' You had two chances then. This is exactly what I did but an old lady slammed the door and I shot off fast. I went to the other side of the town and found a house with a brass plate showing that a veterinary surgeon lived there. I knocked on the back door and everything was okay. The lady who helped me was Madame Semelagne. I visited them several times after the war and they came to my home until she died in the 1970s. I eventually got into the escape line and came home via Paris, Pau, the Pyrenees, Madrid and Gibraltar, reaching England in the first week in May. The navigator and the rear gunner also evaded; they stayed in the north and were liberated by Canadian forces after the invasion.

APPENDIX 1

R.A.F. Bomber Command Order of Battle and Operational Performances in the Battle of Berlin.

Notes

(1) All Lancaster squadrons were equipped with mixed Mark Is and IIIs unless otherwise stated.
(2) Aircraft which were ditched some distance out to sea are classed as 'missing', but those which came down within a few miles of the coast or were pointed out to sea after being abandoned by their crews in bad weather are classed as 'crashed'.
(3) Men who died of wounds as prisoners of war are counted as 'killed'.

No. 1 Group

Dispatched 2,598 Lancaster sorties on nineteen Berlin raids. Aircraft casualties: 143 Lancasters missing (5·5 per cent), 29 crashed and 1 wrecked by explosion just before take-off. Personnel casualties: 899 men killed, 231 prisoners of war, 10 evaders and 2 interned. Point of interest: suffered the heaviest overall casualties of any group in the Battle of Berlin.

12 Squadron, Wickenby

Dispatched 272 Lancasters on nineteen Berlin raids. Casualties: 17 aircraft missing (6·25 per cent) and 4 crashed or wrecked in ground accident; 78 men killed, 44 prisoners of war and 5 evaders. Suffered the heaviest missing rate in those 1 Group squadrons which went right through the Battle of Berlin.

100 Squadron, Grimsby

Dispatched 308 Lancasters on nineteen Berlin raids. Casualties: 16 aircraft missing (5·2 per cent) and 4 crashed; 115 men killed, 19 prisoners of war and 1 evader.

101 Squadron, Ludford Magna

Dispatched 363 Lancasters on nineteen Berlin raids. Casualties: 22 aircraft missing (6·1 per cent) and 3 crashed; 133 men killed and 42 prisoners of war. Operated A.B.C. Lancasters from 7 October 1943. Dispatched the second highest number of sorties in Bomber Command in the Battle of Berlin.

103 Squadron, Elsham Wolds

Dispatched 319 Lancasters on nineteen Berlin raids. Casualties: 15 aircraft missing (4·7 per cent), 4 crashed and 1 wrecked by explosion before take-off; 107 men killed and 13 prisoners of war. Lowest missing rate in those 1 Group squadrons which went right through the battle. Dispatched more aircraft on one night – 30 Lancasters on 26/27 November 1943 – than any other squadron in Bomber Command.

166 Squadron, Kirmington

Operating Wellingtons until 18 September 1943, Lancasters from 23 September. Dispatched 270 Lancasters on sixteen Berlin raids. Casualties: 17 Lancasters missing (6·3 per cent) and 2 crashed; 109 men killed and 24 prisoners of war. Suffered the highest missing rate in 1 Group, though missed three of the Berlin raids (see 12 Squadron).

460 (Australian) Squadron, Binbrook

Dispatched 385 Lancasters on nineteen Berlin raids. Casualties: 23 aircraft missing (6·0 per cent) and 5 crashed; 135 men killed, 41 prisoners of war, 2 interned and 1 evader. Dispatched more aircraft to Berlin than any other squadron in Bomber Command. Suffered the highest missing aircraft casualties in 1 Group and the second highest in Bomber Command.

550 Squadron, Grimsby and North Killingholme

Formed on 25 November 1943. Dispatched 163 Lancasters on thirteen Berlin raids. Casualties: 6 aircraft missing (3·7 per cent) and 3 crashed; 50 men killed and 16 prisoners of war.

576 Squadron, Elsham Wolds

Formed on 25 November 1943. Dispatched 121 Lancasters on twelve Berlin raids. Casualties: 9 aircraft missing (7·4 per cent) and 2 crashed; 57 men killed and 13 prisoners of war.

625 Squadron, Kelstern

Formed on 10 October 1943. Dispatched 211 Lancasters on sixteen Berlin raids. Casualties: 10 aircraft missing (4·7 per cent) and 1 crashed; 59 men killed, 10 prisoners of war and 3 evaders.

626 Squadron, Wickenby

Formed on 7 November 1943. Dispatched 186 Lancasters on sixteen Berlin raids. Casualties: 8 aircraft missing (4·3 per cent) and 1 crashed; 56 men killed and 9 prisoners of war.

300 (Polish) Squadron, based at Ingham and Faldingworth, was equipped with Wellingtons and took no part in the Battle of Berlin.

No. 3. Group

Dispatched 598 Lancaster sorties on nineteen Berlin raids and 280 Stirling sorties on three raids. Aircraft casualties: 39 Lancasters missing (6·5 per cent) and 37 Stirlings (13·2 per cent). Personnel casualties: 411 men killed, 124 prisoners of war and 1 evader. Point of interest: the combined Lancaster and Stirling casualty rate of 8·7 per cent was the highest in Bomber Command groups in the Battle of Berlin.

15 Squadron, Mildenhall

Dispatched 25 Stirlings and 71 Lancasters on nine Berlin raids. Casualties: 2 Stirlings and 5 Lancasters missing (7·3 per cent); 45 men killed and 5 prisoners of war.

75 (New Zealand) Squadron, Mepal

Dispatched 46 Stirlings on three Berlin raids. Casualties: 9 aircraft missing (19·6 per cent); 56 men killed and 12 prisoners of war. Suffered the highest missing rate in Bomber Command, though took part in only three of the Berlin raids.

90 Squadron, Wratting Common and Tuddenham

Dispatched 38 Stirlings on two Berlin raids. Casualties: 3 aircraft missing (7·9 per cent); 16 men killed and 5 prisoners of war.

115 Squadron, Little Snoring and Witchford

Dispatched 259 Lancasters IIs on nineteen Berlin raids. Casualties: 21 aircraft missing (8·1 per cent); 116 men killed, 30 prisoners of war and 1 evader. Flew more sorties to Berlin and suffered more losses than any other squadron in 3 Group. Suffered a higher missing rate than any other Lancaster squadron in Bomber Command.

149 Squadron, Lakenheath

Dispatched 30 Stirlings on three Berlin raids. Casualties: 3 aircraft missing (10·0 per cent); 14 men killed and 7 prisoners of war.

196 Squadron, Witchford

Dispatched 6 Stirlings on one Berlin raid. Casualties: 1 aircraft missing; 3 men killed and 4 prisoners of war. Transferred to transport duties after 25 November 1943.

199 Squadron, Lakenheath

Dispatched 25 Stirlings on three Berlin raids. Casualties: 3 aircraft missing (12·0 per cent); 15 men killed and 6 prisoners of war.

214 Squadron, Chedburgh

Dispatched 32 Stirlings on three Berlin raids. Casualties: 5 aircraft missing (15·6 per cent); 12 men killed and 18 prisoners of war (5 men from one of the lost aircraft were rescued from the sea). Transferred to 100 Group for R.C.M. duties after 23 January 1944.

218 Squadron, Downham Market

Dispatched 30 Stirlings on three Berlin raids. Casualties: 3 aircraft missing (10·0 per cent); 19 men killed and 2 prisoners of war.

514 Squadron, Foulsham and Waterbeach

Formed on 1 September 1943. Dispatched 208 Lancaster IIs on fifteen Berlin raids. Casualties: 7 aircraft missing (3·4 per cent); 32 men killed and 14 prisoners of war (one crew was rescued from the sea). Suffered the lowest missing rate in 3 Group squadrons on Berlin raids but suffered heavier losses on non-Berlin raids.

620 Squadron, Chedburgh

Dispatched 12 Stirlings on two Berlin raids. Casualties: 2 aircraft missing (16·7 per cent); 10 men killed and 5 prisoners of war. Transferred to transport duties after 19 November 1943.

622 Squadron, Mildenhall

Dispatched 23 Stirlings and 60 Lancasters on nine Berlin raids. Casualties: 4 Stirlings and 6 Lancasters missing (12·0 per cent); 58 men killed and 16 prisoners of war.

623 Squadron, Downham Market

Dispatched 13 Stirlings on three Berlin raids. Casualties: 2 aircraft missing (15·4 per cent); 15 men killed. Disbanded on 4 December 1943.

No. 4 Group

Dispatched 1,183 Halifax sorties on nine Berlin raids. Aircraft casualties: 92 Halifaxes missing (7·8 per cent), 14 crashed. Personnel casualties: 487 men killed, 226 prisoners of war and 4 evaders. Point of interest: suffered the second highest percentage casualty rate (after 3 Group) in Bomber Command in the Battle of Berlin.

10 Squadron, Melbourn

Dispatched 133 Halifax IIs and IIIs on eight Berlin raids. Casualties: 10 aircraft missing (7·5 per cent); 58 men killed and 12 prisoners of war.

51 Squadron, Snaith

Dispatched 150 Halifax IIs and IIIs on nine Berlin raids. Casualties: 9 aircraft missing (6·0 per cent); 33 men killed and 30 prisoners of war. Flew most Berlin raids and most sorties to Berlin in 4 Group squadrons.

76 Squadron, Holme-on-Spalding Moor

Dispatched 146 Halifax Vs and IIIs on eight Berlin raids. Casualties: 5 aircraft missing (3·4 per cent) and 1 crashed; 19 men killed, 15 prisoners and 4 evaders. Suffered the lowest casualty rate in those 4 Group squadrons operating thoughout the Battle of Berlin.

77 Squadron, Elvington

Dispatched 134 Halifax IIs and Vs on seven Berlin raids. Casualties: 15 aircraft missing (11·2 per cent) and 1 crashed; 96 men killed and 21 prisoners of war. Suffered the highest percentage losses, the most personnel casualties and, with 158 Squadron, the highest overall aircraft losses in 4 Group on Berlin raids.

78 Squadron, Breighton

Dispatched 144 Halifax IIs and IIIs on seven Berlin raids. Casualties: 12 aircraft missing (8·3 per cent) and 4 crashed; 74 men killed, 30 prisoners of war.

102 Squadron, Pocklington

Dispatched 122 Halifax IIs and Vs on seven Berlin raids. Casualties: 13 aircraft missing (10·7 per cent) and 3 crashed; 56 men killed and 45 prisoners of war.

158 Squadron, Lissett

Dispatched 136 Halifax IIs and IIIs on eight Berlin raids. Casualties: 15 aircraft missing (11·0 per cent) and 1 crashed; 71 men killed and 44 prisoners of war. Suffered most missing aircraft (with 77 Squadron) on Berlin raids.

466 (Australian) Squadron, Leconfield

Dispatched 93 Halifax IIIs on six Berlin raids. Casualties: 7 aircraft missing (7·5 per cent); 31 men killed and 21 prisoners of war.

578 Squadron, Burn

Formed 14 January 1944. Dispatched 59 Halifax IIIs on five Berlin raids. Casualties: 4 aircraft missing (6·8 per cent); 22 men killed and 7 prisoners of war. A squadron member, Pilot Officer C. J. Barton, won the only Victoria Cross awarded in Bomber Command during the Battle of Berlin period, posthumously, on the Nuremberg raid of 30/31 March 1944.

640 Squadron, Leconfield

Formed 7 January 1944. Dispatched 66 Halifax IIIs on five Berlin raids. Casualties: 2 aircraft missing and 3 crashed; 27 men killed and 1 prisoner of war.

No. 5 Group

Dispatched 3,002 Lancaster sorties on twenty Berlin raids (nineteen main raids and the all-Lancaster diversion on 21/22 January 1944, when Magdeburg was the main target). Aircraft casualties: 128 Lancasters missing (4.3 per cent) and 13 crashed. Personnel casualties: 802 men killed and 141 prisoners of war. Points of interest: flew the most raids and the most sorties to Berlin but suffered the lowest percentage casualty rate in Bomber Command, both in the Berlin raids and in raids to other targets in this period.

9 Squadron, Bardney

Dispatched 254 Lancasters on twenty Berlin raids. Casualties: 7 aircraft missing (2.8 per cent) and 3 crashed; 53 men killed and 9 prisoners of war.

44 (Rhodesia) Squadron, Dunholme Lodge

Dispatched 246 Lancasters on twenty Berlin raids. Casualties: 16 aircraft missing (6·5 per cent); 103 men killed and 11 prisoners of war. Suffered the highest percentage casualty rate, most personnel casualties and, with 57 Squadron, the highest overall aircraft casualties in those 5 Group squadrons which went right through the Battle of Berlin.

49 Squadron, Fiskerton

Dispatched 273 Lancasters on twenty Berlin raids. Casualties: 7 aircraft missing (2·6 per cent) and 2 crashes; 40 men killed and 18 prisoners of war. Suffered the lowest percentage missing rate of all Bomber Command squadrons in the Battle of Berlin.

50 Squadron, Skellingthorpe

Dispatched 281 Lancasters on twenty Berlin raids. Casualties: 8 aircraft missing (2·8 per cent) and 1 crashed; 48 men killed and 14 prisoners of war.

57 Squadron, Scampton and East Kirkby

Dispatched 282 Lancasters on twenty Berlin raids. Casualties: 16 aircraft missing (5·7 per cent); 87 men killed and 25 prisoners of war. Flew the most sorties to Berlin in 5 Group and, with 44 Squadron, suffered the most losses.

61 Squadron, Syerston, Skellingthorpe and Coningsby

Dispatched 267 Lancasters on twenty Berlin raids. Casualties: 11 aircraft missing (4·1 per cent); 71 men killed and only 2 men prisoners of war.

106 Squadron, Syerston and Metheringham

Dispatched 281 Lancasters on twenty Berlin raids. Casualties: 8 aircraft missing (2·8 per cent) and 2 crashed; 56 men killed and 4 prisoners of war.

207 Squadron, Langar and Spilsby

Dispatched 242 Lancasters on twenty Berlin raids. Casualties: 15 aircraft missing (6·2 per cent); 84 men killed and 19 prisoners of war.

463 (Australian) Squadron, Waddington

Formed 25 November 1943. Dispatched 147 Lancasters on fourteen Berlin raids. Casualties: 10 aircraft missing (6·8 per cent); 65 men killed and 5 prisoners of war.

467 (Australian) Squadron, Waddington

Dispatched 270 Lancasters on twenty Berlin raids. Casualties: 9 aircraft missing (3·3 per cent); 64 men killed and only 1 prisoner of war.

619 Squadron, Woodhall Spa and Coningsby

Dispatched 258 Lancasters on nineteen Berlin raids. Casualties: 10 aircraft missing (3·9 per cent) and 5 crashed; 72 men killed and 12 prisoners of war.

630 Squadron, East Kirkby

Formed 15 November 1943. Dispatched 201 Lancasters on seventeen Berlin raids. Casualties: 11 aircraft missing (5·5 per cent) and 1 crashed; 62 men killed and 18 prisoners of war.

617 Squadron, the specialist bombing unit in 5 Group, took no part in the Battle of Berlin.

No. 6 (Canadian) Group

Dispatched 688 Halifax sorties on nine Berlin raids and 532 Lancaster II sorties on eighteen raids. Aircraft casualties: 55 Halifaxes missing (8·0 per cent) and 25 Lancasters missing (4·7 per cent); 6 Halifaxes and 5 Lancasters were destroyed in crashes. Personnel casualties: 437 men killed, 127 prisoners of war, 9 evaders and 9 interned.

408 Squadron, Linton-on-Ouse

Dispatched 205 Lancaster IIs on fifteen Berlin raids. Casualties: 8 aircraft missing (3·9 per cent) and 1 crashed; 57 men killed and 5 prisoners of war. Suffered the lowest missing aircraft rate, with 432 Squadron, in 6 Group.

419 Squadron, Middleton St George

Dispatched 112 Halifax IIs on seven Berlin raids. Casualties: 9 aircraft missing (8·0 per cent); 34 men killed and 30 prisoners of war.

420 Squadron, Tholthorpe

Returned from Middle East, converted to Halifaxes and recommenced operations on 15 February 1944. Dispatched 24 Halifax IIIs on two Berlin raids. Casualties: 1 aircraft missing and 1 crashed; 2 men killed and 7 prisoners of war.

424 Squadron, Skipton-on-Swale

Returned from Middle East, converted to Halifaxes and recommenced operations on 15 February 1944. Dispatched 20 Halifax IIIs on two Berlin raids. Casualties: 2 aircraft missing; 14 men killed and 1 prisoner of war.

425 Squadron, Tholthorpe

Returned from Middle East, converted to Halifaxes and recommended operations on 19 February 1944. Dispatched 14 Halifax IIIs on one Berlin raid. Casualties: 2 aircraft missing; 14 men killed.

426 Squadron, Linton-on-Ouse

Dispatched 210 Lancaster IIs on eighteen Berlin raids. Casualties: 13 aircraft missing (6·2 per cent) and 3 crashed; 88 men killed, 9 prisoners of war, 7 interned and 2 evaders. Dispatched more aircraft to Berlin and took part in more Berlin raids than any other squadron in 6 Group but also suffered the heaviest overall casualties.

427 Squadron, Leeming

Dispatched 111 Halifax Vs on eight Berlin raids. Casualties: 7 aircraft missing (6·3 per cent) and 1 crashed; 44 men killed and 10 prisoners of war.

428 Squadron, Middleton St George

Dispatched 106 Halifax IIs and Vs on seven Berlin raids. Casualties: 5 aircraft missing (4·7 per cent); 18 men killed, 15 prisoners of war and 2 interned.

429 Squadron, Leeming

Dispatched 87 Halifax IIs and IIIs on six Berlin raids. Casualties: 7 aircraft missing (8·0 per cent); 34 men killed and 16 prisoners of war.

431 Squadron, Tholthorpe and Croft

Dispatched 70 Halifax IIs and IIIs on five Berlin raids. Casualties: 5 aircraft missing (7·1 per cent); 26 men killed and 5 prisoners of war (4 men from one of the lost aircraft were rescued from the sea).

432 Squadron, Skipton-on-Swale and East Moor

This squadron operated Wellingtons until the end of October 1943, then Lancaster IIs until the end of January 1944, then Halifax IIIs. Dispatched 117 Lancasters and 10 Halifaxes on eleven Berlin raids. Casualties: 4 Lancasters and 1 Halifax missing (3·9 per cent) and 1 Lancaster crashed; 29 men killed and 8 prisoners of war. Suffered the lowest missing aircraft rate, with 408 Squadron, in 6 Group.

433 Squadron, Skipton-on-Swale

Formed on 25 September 1943 but did not fly on operations until 20 January 1944. Dispatched 57 Halifax IIIs on five Berlin raids. Casualties: 4 aircraft missing (7.0 per cent) and 2 crashed; 18 men killed and 6 prisoners of war (all of the crew from one of the lost aircraft were rescued from the sea).

434 Squadron, Tholthorpe and Croft

Dispatched 77 Halifax Vs on seven Berlin raids. Casualties: 12 aircraft missing (15.6 per cent) and 2 crashed; 59 men killed, 21 prisoners of war and 1 evader. Suffered the highest missing rate in 6 Group and in all Bomber Command Halifax squadrons on Berlin raids.

No. 8 (Pathfinder Force) Group

Part One – Heavy Bomber Squadrons

Dispatched 1,561 Lancaster sorties and 197 Halifax sorties on 19 Berlin raids. Aircraft casualties: 93 Lancasters missing (6.0 per cent) and 12 Halifaxes missing (6.1 per cent); 13 Lancasters crashed, 1 exploded on the ground, and 1 was shot down by a German Intruder. Personnel casualties: 650 men killed, 134 prisoners of war, 8 evaders and 7 interned.

7 Squadron, Oakington

Dispatched 353 Lancasters on nineteen Berlin raids. Casualties: 26 aircraft missing (7.4 per cent); 146 men killed and 39 prisoners of war. Suffered more aircraft missing and more aircrew casualties on the Berlin raids than any other squadron in Bomber Command and a greater percentage loss than any other squadron in 8 Group.

35 Squadron, Graveley

Dispatched 182 Halifaxes (mostly IIs and IIIs, possibly some Vs) and 14 Lancasters on thirteen Berlin raids. Casualties: 9 Halifaxes and 1 Lancaster missing (5.1 per cent); 36 men killed, 31 prisoners of war and 4 evaders.

83 Squadron, Wyton

Dispatched 253 Lancasters on nineteen Berlin raids. Casualties: 16 aircraft missing (6.3 per cent), 1 crashed and 1 destroyed by explosion on ground before take-off; 104 men killed and 10 prisoners of war.

97 Squadron, Bourn (with a short transfer to Gransden Lodge at the end of August 1943)

Dispatched 342 Lancasters on nineteen Berlin raids. Casualties: 17 aircraft lost (5.0 per cent), 7 crashed and 1 shot down by Intruder; 120 men killed, 26 prisoners of war and 4 evaders.

156 Squadron, Warboys and Upwood

Dispatched 362 Lancasters on nineteen Berlin raids. Casualties: 24 aircraft missing (6.6 per cent) and 2 crashed; 168 men killed and 11 prisoners of war. Dispatched more aircraft to Berlin than any other squadron in 8 Group. Suffered more men killed in Berlin raids than any other squadron in Bomber Command.

405 (Canadian) Squadron, Gransden Lodge

Dispatched 15 Halifax IIs and 221 Lancasters on nineteen Berlin raids. Casualties: 3 Halifaxes and 8 Lancasters missing (4.7 per cent) and 3 Lancasters crashed; 69 men killed, 17 prisoners of war and 7 interned. Despite high initial casualties on Halifaxes, the squadron's missing rate on Berlin raids was the lowest in 8 Group.

635 Squadron, Downham Market

Formed on 20 March 1944. Dispatched 13 Lancasters on one Berlin raid. Casualties: 1 aircraft missing; 7 men killed.

Part Two – Mosquito Units

139 Squadron, Wyton and Upwood

Dispatched 167 aircraft in various supporting roles on eighteen Berlin raids. The squadron suffered no casualties on these raids, nor on any other raids during the Battle of Berlin period.

627 Squadron, Oakington

Formed on 12 November 1943. Dispatched 58 aircraft in support of nine Berlin raids. One Mosquito was lost; the crew evaded capture.

692 Squadron, Graveley

Formed on 1 January 1944. Dispatched 9 aircraft in support of two Berlin raids without loss.

105 and 109 Squadrons, Marham

These Oboe-equipped squadrons did not fly to Berlin because of the limited range of Oboe but they sometimes supported the Berlin raids by route marking and bombing night-fighter airfields in Holland and France; some of their other operations were also timed to have a diversionary effect in support of the Berlin raids. No casualties were incurred in any of these supporting operations.

1409 (Meteorological) Flight, Oakington

Carried out weather reconnaissance flights prior to most of the Berlin raids and provided a Mosquito for a Master Bomber on the last Berlin raid. No casualties.

100 (Bomber Support) Group

The group was not formed until November 1943. The first Radio Counter-Measures operations were flown on 2 December, and the first Serrate operations on 16 December. 68 R.C.M. sorties were flown on eleven nights when Berlin was raided, but many of these sorties were not directly linked to the Berlin raids; no R.C.M. aircraft were lost on these nights. 63 Serrate sorties were flown in direct support of eleven Berlin raids, with 3 Mosquitoes and 1 Beaufighter being lost; at least 8 German night fighters were claimed as destroyed.

141 Squadron, West Raynham

The squadron pioneered the use of Serrate under Fighter Command control while based at Wittering. After transfer to 100 Group on 4 December 1943, flew 9 Beaufighter and 27 Mosquito Serrate patrols on ten 'Berlin' nights. 1 Beaufighter lost; 2 men killed.

169 Squadron, Little Snoring

Transferred from Fighter Command in December 1943. Flew 14 Mosquito Serrate patrols on five 'Berlin' nights. 1 Mosquito lost; 1 man killed and 1 prisoner of war.

192 Squadron, Feltwell and Foulsham

Operated Wellingtons in 3 Group until 25 November 1943, through taking no part in the Battle of Berlin. After trans-

fer to 100 Group, flew 68 R.C.M. sorties, mostly in Halifaxes but some Mosquitoes and possibly some Wellingtons,
on eleven 'Berlin' nights. No casualties.

239 Squadron, West Raynham

Transferred from Fighter Command on 9 December 1943.
Flew 11 Mosquito Serrate patrols on four 'Berlin' nights.
Lost 2 Mosquitoes on these nights; 1 man killed and 3 pris-
oners of war.

515 Squadron, Little Snoring

Joined 100 Group just before the end of the Battle of Berlin
but took no part in any of the Berlin raids.

(In addition to Bomber Command's effort in the Battle of
Berlin, two long-range Mosquito Intruder squadrons of
Fighter Command – called Air Defence of Great Britain for
part of this period – regularly operated in support of bomber
raids. These were 418 (Canadian) and 605 Squadrons.
These squadrons' operations and casualties during the
Battle of Berlin have not been researched, but they should be
given credit for harassing German night fighters on nights
when major bombing raids were taking place. Other Mosquito night-fighter squadrons from the home defence force
also sent a few crews on Intruder operations but these were
not as effective as 418 and 605 Squadrons.)

APPENDIX 2

Luftwaffe Night-Fighter Order of Battle in the Battle of Berlin

Nachtjagdgeschwader 1

This was a long established and successful unit, based mainly in Holland. The standard aircraft was the Messerschmitt 110, although I Gruppe operated a few Heinkel 219s and II Gruppe held a few old Dornier 217s at the beginning of the period.

Stab (Headquarters Flight) – based at Deelen.

I/NJG 1 – based at Venlo.

II/NJG 1 – based at St Trond, and then St Dizier from early March 1944.

III/NJG 1 – based at Twenthe, with a large detachment to Wittmundhafen from mid-February 1944, then the whole unit moved to Laon/Athies in March 1944.

IV/NJG 1 – based at Leeuwarden until mid-March 1944, then St Trond.

Nachtjagdgeschwader 2

This unit returned from the Mediterranean in the late summer of 1943 and was rebuilt to become a very effective part of the home defence. A few Messerschmitt 110s were initially used, but then the Junkers 88 became standard equipment.

Stab – based at Gilze Rijen.

I/NJG 2 – based at Gilze Rijen, with 2nd Staffel at Parchim, then the whole unit to Bad Langensalza.

II/NJG 2 – based at Parchim, then Quakenbrück.

III/NJG 2 – refitted at Stuttgart/Nellingen then, when ready for operations, moved in turn to Schiphol, Neuruppin, Venlo, Gilze Rijen and Twenthe.

Nachtjagdgeschwader 3

This was the second of the regular home defence units to be formed; its main role before the Battle of Berlin had been the defence of the German Bight and the major German ports. The standard aircraft was the Messerschmitt 110, but a few Dornier 217s were still in use at the start of the Battle of Berlin; Junkers 88s, originally used in small numbers for the long-range interception of R.A.F. mine layers and courier aircraft flying to Sweden, appeared in greater quantity during the winter.

Stab – based at Stade.

I/NJG 3 – in August 1943 was split between Vechta (1st Staffel), Wittmundhafen (2nd Staffel) and Kastrup (3rd Staffel), but the whole unit was concentrated at Vechta by March 1944.

II/NJG 3 – based at Schleswig/Jagel, with 4th Staffel at Westerland until 21 January 1944; most of the unit moved to Langendiebach and Vechta in March 1944.

III/NJG 3 – in August 1943 split between Lüneburg (7th Staffel), Nordholz and later Lüneburg (8th Staffel) and Stade (9th Staffel), but the whole unit later concentrated at Stade.

IV/NJG 3 – 10th and 12th Staffeln were based at Grove, 11th at Aalborg (where pilots were promised a Knight's Cross if they could shoot down one of the fast British courier aircraft flying to Sweden); 11th Staffel moved to Westerland during the Battle of Berlin.

Nachtjagdgeschwader 4

This unit's bases were mainly in Belgium and Northern France, covering the bomber approaches to Southern Germany, but some *Gruppen* were moved to Germany during the Battle of Berlin. The main aircraft used were Messerschmitt 110s, though a few Dornier 217s were still in use at the start of the Battle of Berlin.

Stab – based at Metz, then Chenay.

I/NJG 4 – based at Florennes and Laon/Athies in August 1943, was moved to Brandis in December but was all back at Florennes by March 1944.

II/NJG 4 – based at St Dizier, then Coulommiers.

III/NJG 4 – based at Juvincourt, then Mainz/Finthen.

Nachtjagdgeschwader 5

This was a new unit, with bases around Berlin and in Northern Germany, still being formed when the Battle of Berlin started. Aircraft used were all Messerschmitt 110s.

Stab – based at Döberitz.

I/NJG 5 based at Stendal with 3rd Staffel at Völkenrode, but later all at Stendal.

II/NJG 5 – based at Parchim with 4th Staffel at Greifswald, but later all at Parchim.

III/NJG 5 – the *Staffeln* of this unit served at many bases: Neuruppin, Greifswald, Kolberg, Werneuchen, Königsberg/Neumark, Parchim and Mainz/Finthen, but at the end of March 1944 most of the unit was at Brandis.

IV/NJG 5 – not formed until September 1943; its main base was Brandis, but some *Staffeln* served at Erfurt and Vechta.

Nachtjagdgeschwader 6

This *Geschwader*, based in Southern Germany, was not fully operational in August 1943, being used as a training and refitting unit. It took an increasing part in operations when Bomber Command started attacking targets in its area at the end of the period. The aircraft used were Messerschmitt 110s.

Stab – based at Schleissheim.

I/NJG 6 – formerly IV/NJG 4, transferred from France; based at Mainz/Finthen.

II/NJG 6 – based at Neuburg/Donau, then Stuttgart/Echterdingen.

(III/NJG 6 was serving in Southern Europe, and IV/NJG 6 in Romania.)

Nachtjagdgruppe 10 was a development unit based at Werneuchen, but its aircraft and crews were used on operations.

Jagdgeschwader 300 was the original Wild Boar unit based at Bonn/Hangelar (*Stab* and I Gruppe), Rheine (II Gruppe) and Oldenburg (III Gruppe); later bases used were Deelen (Stab) and Wiesbaden/Erbenheim (III Gruppe). Its aircraft were Messerschmitt 109s and Focke-Wulf 190s.

Jagdgeschwader 301 was formed in September/October 1943 and was mostly based in Southern Germany, at Schleissheim and Neuburg/Donau, though III Gruppe was at Oldenburg. Its aircraft were Messerschmitt 109s and Focke-Wulf 190s.

Jagdgeschwader 302 was formed in September/October 1943 with bases at Döberitz (*Stab*), Jüterbog (I Gruppe), Ludwigslust (II Gruppe) and Zerbst (III Gruppe). Its aircraft were all Messerschmitt 109s.

APPENDIX 3
BOMBER COMMAND STATISTICS

The purpose of this appendix is to give more detail on and some analysis of the bare figures given at the opening of Chapter 12 for Bomber Command's operations in the Battle of Berlin. The large number of sorties flown allows some interesting comparisons and conclusions to be made.

Unless otherwise stated, the contents of the appendix are all based upon the nineteen major raids of the Battle of Berlin and the diversionary raid to Berlin by twenty-three Lancasters on the night of 21/22 January 1944, when Magdeburg was the main target.

Aircraft Types
The following table shows the statistical part played by different types of aircraft in the raids to Berlin.

	Dispatched	Abortive (% of dispatched)	Missing (% of dispatched)	(Missing as % of 'pressed on')
Lancaster	8,291	601 (7.2)	428 (5.2)	(5.6)
Halifax	2,068	285 (13.8)	159 (7.7)	(8.9)
Stirling	280	46 (16.4)	37 (13.2)	(15.8)
Mosquito	174	13 (7.5)	1 (0.6)	(0.6)
TOTALS	10,813	945 (8·7)	625 (5·8)	(6·3)

The table shows how the Lancasters bore the brunt of the Battle of Berlin, dispatching more than three-quarters of all sorties. It can be estimated that, with their heavier bomb loads per aircraft, the Lancasters carried 91 per cent of the bombs dropped at Berlin, compared to only 8 per cent by the Halifaxes and only 1 per cent by the Stirlings. The heavier rates of early returns (abortives) and the heavier casualty rates for Halifaxes and Stirlings are also clearly seen. The missing aircraft have been expressed as a percentage of those which 'pressed on' after the early returns had turned back to show how the real casualty rates of Halifaxes and Stirlings over German-defended territory were even higher than might be apparent if only the simple percentages of those dispatched were shown.

Survival Rates in Shot-Down Aircraft

The knowledge of which crew members in shot-down bombers were killed allows the survival rates in the different aircraft types to be calculated, and the numbers involved are a large enough sample for valid comparisons to be made between the different types. Aircraft which crashed in England or made controlled ditchings in the sea and those aircraft flying to Sweden have not been included; the solitary Mosquito lost is also excluded.

	Aircraft lost	Men killed (%)	Men survived (%)
Lancasters	421	2,461 (81·8)	548 (19·2)
Halifaxes	151	703 (65·0)	379 (35·0)
Stirlings	35	183 (73·8)	65 (26·2)
TOTALS	607	3,347 (77·1)	992 (22.9)

The following points emerge from these figures:

(1) The chances were always heavily against survival when a bomber was shot down.

(2) The chances were much worse in a Lancaster, with its

high-explosive bomb load and badly situated escape-hatches. The number of men surviving from the average seven-man crew in a Lancaster was 1·3, compared with 1·8 in a Stirling and 2·45 in a Halifax.

(3) The Halifax crews had the best chance of survival. It was a well designed aircraft with good escape-hatches. The presence of the wireless operator and navigator in the nose of the aircraft, close to the forward escape-hatch, instead of in the mid-section of the fuselage as in the Lancaster and Stirling, gave these men in particular a better chance of survival.

Squadrons

Sorties

The most sorties in the Battle of Berlin were flown by those Lancaster squadrons which contained three flights of aircraft; these were mainly in 1 and 8 Groups. This is a list of the ten squadrons dispatching the most sorties to Berlin. (The group in which each squadron served is shown in brackets.)

460 Squadron (1)	385 sorties
101 Squadron (1)	363 ,,
156 Squadron (8)	362 ,,
7 Squadron (8)	353 ,,
97 Squadron (8)	342 ,,
103 Squadron (1)	319 ,,
100 Squadron (1)	308 ,,
57 Squadron (5)	282 ,,
50 Squadron (5)	281 ,,
106 Squadron (5)	281 ,,

Squadrons with the most sorties in other groups were:

3 Group, 115 Squadron: 259 sorties
4 Group, 51 Squadron: 150 sorties
6 Group, 426 Squadron: 210 sorties

Overall Casualties

The squadrons suffering the most casualties were also all equipped with Lancasters. ('Aircraft lost' includes aircraft missing, crashed or, in one case, shot down by an Intruder; 'Prisoners, etc.' includes men interned in Sweden or evading capture after being shot down.)

	Aircraft lost	Men killed	Prisoners, etc.
460 Squadron (1)	28	135	44
7 Squadron (8)		146	39
156 Squadron (8)	26	168	11
97 Squadron (8)		120	30
101 Squadron (1)	25	133	42
115 Squadron (3)	21	116	31
12 Squadron (1)		78	49
100 Squadron(1)	20	115	20
103 Squadron (1)		107	13
166 Squadron (1)	19	109	24

The heaviest losing squadrons in other groups — 77, 78, 102 and 158 in 4 Group, 44 and 57 in 5 Group and 426 in 6 Group — each lost sixteen aircraft.

Percentage Casualties

The casualty picture changes completely when attention is turned to the percentage casualties suffered by squadrons rather than overall casualties, with the Halifaxes and Stirlings featuring prominently. These are the ten squadrons suffering the greatest percentage loss of their aircraft dispatched on the Berlin raids.

75 Squadron (3), Stirlings	19·6 per cent
434 Squadron (6), Halifaxes	18·2 ,, ,,
620 Squadron (3), Stirlings	16·7 ,, ,,
214 Squadron (3), Stirlings	15·6 ,, ,,
623 Squadrons (3), Stirlings	15·4 ,, ,,
102 Squadron (4), Halifaxes	13·1 ,, ,,
622 Squadron (3), Stirlings	12·0 ,, ,,
199 Squadron (3), Stirlings	12·0 ,, ,,
77 Squadron (4), Halifaxes	11·9 ,, ,,
158 Squadron (4), Halifaxes	11·8 ,, ,,

It should be pointed out, however, that none of the Stirling squadrons flew more than three Berlin raids. The nearest Lancaster units were 576 and 115 Squadrons, with 9·1 and 8·1 per cent casualties respectively.

The squadrons with the lowest loss rates were:

50 Squadron (5), Lancasters	3·2 per cent
49 Squadron (5), Lancasters 467 Squadron (5), Lancasters	3·3 ,, ,,
514 Squadron (3), Lancaster IIs	3·4 ,, ,,
106 Squadron (5), Lancasters	3·6 ,, ,,
9 Squadron (5), Lancasters	3·9 ,, ,,
61 Squadron (5), Lancasters 76 Squadron (4), Halifaxes	4·1 ,, ,,
408 Squadron (6), Lancaster IIs	4·4 ,, ,,
428 Squadron (6), Halifaxes	4·7 ,, ,,

The number of aircraft missing (though not crashed) from squadrons is also available for raids on targets other than Berlin for the whole of the period under survey. If these are added to the aircraft missing on the Berlin raids, it is possible to identify the squadrons suffering the most overall losses and the heaviest percentage losses for all forty-one nights when major operations were flown to Germany during the Battle of Berlin period. The highest *overall* casualties were in these squadrons:

156 Squadron (8), Lancasters	48 aircraft missing
7 Squadron (8), Lancasters	44 ,, ,,
78 Squadron (4), Halifaxes	38 ,, ,,
77 Squadron (4), Halifaxes ⎫	
101 Squadron (1), Lancasters ⎪	
166 Squadron (1), Lancasters ⎬	34 ,, ,,
460 Squadron (1), Lancasters ⎭	

And the heaviest *percentage* casualties:

434 Squadron (6), Halifaxes	12·9 per cent
77 Squadron (4), Halifaxes	10·6 ,, ,,
431 Squadron (6), Halifaxes	9·8 ,, ,,
102 Squadron (4), Halifaxes	8·3 ,, ,,
78 Squadron (4), Halifaxes	7·8 ,, ,,
429 Squadron (6), Halifaxes	7·7 ,, ,,
427 Squadron (6), Halifaxes	7·2 ,, ,,

(A minimum number of ten raids has been used before squadrons were included in these tables; this excludes the Stirling squadrons, which were not operating on raids to Germany for three-quarters of the period.)

Comparison of 1 and 5 Groups' operations

A study of the tables of squadrons with the lowest casualty rates in the Berlin raids (see page 380) shows that six of the ten squadrons were from 5 Group and none were from 1 Group. One of the surprising aspects of the Battle of Berlin casualty statistics is that 5 Group's losses were consistently lower than 1 Group's throughout this period. These are the relevant figures for the Berlin raids:

	Dispatched	*Missing (%)*
1 Group	2,598	143 (5·5)
5 Group	3,002	128 (4·3)

Because both groups took part in every raid to Berlin under seemingly identical conditions, the large difference in casualty rates is significant. If 1 Group could have reduced its casualty rate to 5 Group's level, the 1 Group squadrons would have been spared the loss of thirty-one Lancasters and crews. The difference is repeated, though not to such a marked extent, in the eighteen major raids to other targets in which the two groups were involved in the same period. These are the figures for those other raids:

	Dispatched	Missing (%)
1 Group	2,645	106 (4·0)
5 Group	3,074	110 (3·6)

The saving to 1 Group over the whole period would have been more than forty-three aircraft and crews.

Why was there such a large difference between two groups which were operating the same types of aircraft (Lancasters I and III), drew their crews from the same sources, were carrying out identical bombing tasks in the Main Force and had airfields situated similar distances from Germany? The only difference in background was that 5 Group had been equipped with the Lancasters for a longer period, since early 1942, compared to 1 Group's first receiving Lancasters at the end of 1942. 5 Group started the Battle of Berlin in a more settled condition, with ten squadrons which had been operating Lancasters for up to fifteen months. 1 Group started the battle with only five Lancaster squadrons with up to nine months' experience of the aircraft type. During the battle, 5 Group expanded to add only two new squadrons; 1 Group added four more Lancaster squadrons and saw another squadron convert from Wellingtons. This background may have given 5 Group's servicing elements an advantage by being more accustomed to the Lancaster. But that difference should not have produced such a large imbalance in casualties. There was another reason.

It was the declared policy of 1 Group's commander (Air Vice-Marshal E. A. B. Rice) that the way to win the bombing war was to deliver the greatest possible bomb tonnage to Germany. He ordered loading trials for a Lancaster, progressively adding more weight to find what was the maximum load that could be carried and at what point the limit would be reached. That point was reached when the Lancaster's wheel struts started to buckle as it moved out to take off. Squadron records show that 1 Group's aircraft were consistently loaded with greater bomb loads than were 5 Group's. (There is no other group with which to compare at this time; 8 Group's Pathfinder aircraft had completely different loads, and the few Lancasters operated by 3 and 6 Groups were mainly Mark IIs.) A sample search of aircraft in the records of 103 Squadron in 1 Group and 57 Squadron in 5 Group on six raids in the Battle of Berlin shows average bomb loads of 9,317 pounds and 8,986 pounds respectively. The effect of this, of course, was that the 1 Group Lancasters could not achieve the same height as the 5 Group aircraft, were less manoeuvrable – 'wallowing' is the word often used – and consumed more petrol.

So the 1 Group Lancasters set off for Berlin with greater bomb loads, but the study of the operational statistics available shows that few of the extra bombs reached the target. First, there were the early returns. These are the figures for the nineteen Berlin raids:

	Dispatched	*Returned (%)*
1 Group	2,583	207 (8·0)
5 Group	3,002	166 (5·5)

In other words, if the 1 Group return rate could have been reduced to the 5 Group level, sixty-two extra Lancasters and their loads would have pressed on to Berlin. (These figures do not include fifteen aircraft of 1 Group which returned from one raid after misinterpreting a recall signal intended for Wellingtons.)

There was a further loss of bomb tonnage when crews jettisoned part of their bomb loads in the North Sea to improve performance. Obviously no figures are available, but observations along the route followed by 1 Group suggested that their crews were regular offenders, so much so that the operational orders for Bomber Command for a raid just before the Battle of Berlin began stated: '*Maintenance of Height*. Lancaster aircraft of 1 Group are not to jettison in order to gain extra height.'[1]

When the bombers were met by the Luftwaffe, the decisive effect of those heavy bomb loads was apparent. It has been obvious throughout the 'operational' chapters of this book that the bombers flying in the lower height bands of the bomber stream received the first attentions of the night fighters. A large sign hung in the crew room at Binbrook, home of an Australian squadron in 1 Group: 'H-E-I-G-H-T spells S-A-F-E-T-Y'. But 1 Group's policy meant that its more heavily laden Lancasters were thus intercepted more often than the 5 Group aircraft. Finally, when under attack, the lack of manoeuvrability resulted in a reduced chance of evasion. Those different casualty rates for the two groups were the result.

There was even a significant difference in the survival rates among the crew members in the shot-down bombers in the two groups, with many more men surviving from the 1 Group aircraft. The figures are:

	Men killed (%)	*Surviving (%)*
1 Group	780 (76·3)	242 (23·7)
5 Group	750 (84·2)	141 (15·8)

1 Bomber Command Operation Order, 2 August 1943, Public Record Office, AIR 14/391.

I do not wish to press this, but the only cause I can think of for this large difference is that 1 Group crews abandoned their aircraft when under attack more quickly than those in 5 Group. If this was the case, 101 men in 1 Group saved their lives through this.

Conclusion

It is possible to calculate what proportion of the greater bomb tonnage loaded at the airfields of 1 Group actually reached the target. Let it be assumed that each group sent 1,000 Lancasters to Berlin under the conditions of that period, using figures for bomb tonnages and abortive and loss rates already established. The only element of estimation is that half of the aircraft shot down were lost before bombing the centre of the target; that estimate has been used throughout this book. No figures can be included for bombs jettisoned on the way to the target.

	1 Group	*5 Group*
1,000 Lancasters take off, carrying these bombs:	4,159 tons	4,012 tons
These turn back, reducing the tonnage by:	80 aircraft 332·8 tons	55 aircraft 220·7 tons
These are shot down, half of them before bombing, reducing the tonnage by:	55 aircraft 27·5 aircraft 114·4 tons	43 aircraft 21·5 aircraft 86·2 tons
The remaining aircraft, dropped at the target:	292·5 aircraft 3,711·8 tons	923·5 aircraft 3,705·1 tons

So 1 Group's policy resulted in only a small extra tonnage of bombs reaching the target (6·7 tons) but at a cost of fourteen extra Lancasters and about 100 aircrew lost.

There is one more point. The consistently higher casualties in 1 Group squadrons must have reduced the general level of experience in those squadrons. This in turn must have had an effect upon the level of experience of those crews which went from 1 and 5 Groups to those Pathfinder squadrons to which they were responsible for providing two-thirds of the new Pathfinder crews. 1 Group sent crews to 156 Squadron, 5 Group to 83 and 97 Squadrons. It is interesting to see that the relative casualty rates in the 1 and 5 Group Main Force squadrons were mirrored in their respective Pathfinder squadrons. The missing rate for 156 Squadron's aircraft in all major raids in the Battle of Berlin period was 6·6 per cent; the average for 83 and 97 Squadrons was 4·5 per cent. These are significant differences.

APPENDIX 4
156 SQUADRON
LANCASTER

This is the report on the examination of the wreckage from Lancaster JB 640 of 156 Squadron, lost on the night of 2/3 January 1944 near Berlin.

Report on Aircraft Wreckage at R.A.F. Gatow

1. Report by H1601722 WO W. S. SPARKES of R.A.F. Laarbruch (Halifax and Lancaster Flight Engineer 431 R.C.A.F. Sqn, November 1943–July 1944). Total hours Lancasters 250 including 70 hours Waddington Lancaster 1968–1970.

2. Wreckage was inspected at R.A.F. Gatow on 26 August 1976 in company with WO Bennett R.A.F. Laarbruch. Majority of wreckage was contained in five crates which, for detailed inspection, would have required unpacking and laying out. Readily identifiable items were:

    a. 3 Packard built Rolls-Royce Merlin engines.
    b. 1 Hamilton propeller.
    c. 2 Lancaster main undercarriage legs and main wheel hubs.
    d. Lancaster centre section of main spar.
    e. Section of aircraft floor with frame of pilot's seat attached.
    f. Elevator and rudder transverse control tubes from under aircraft floor beneath pilot's seat.
    g. Auto-pilot clutches – in 'Clutches OUT' position – and auto-pilot gyro unit.
    h. H2S indicator.

    j. Browning .303 machine-gun breech cover and feed mechanism marked in white paint 'JB 640'.

    k. 1 empty bomb carrier.

3. Following items of crew equipment were identified:
    a. 4 parachute canopies.
    b. 2 pairs of parachute attachment hooks from an observer type harness.
    c. 2 oxygen masks.
    d. Remains of 1 pair suede type flying boots (very large size) and bottom part of leather escape type flying boot.
    e. 2 Mae West inner stoles.
    f. 1 aircrew whistle, 1 escape map, remains of French banknote, part of Dalton computer.
    g. The securing portion of pilot's Sutton harness with all four straps in position and locked by locking pin.

4. The 3 Packard Merlins, whilst extensively impact damaged, were in good condition with very little corrosion. Indications were that they had not been in service for any length of time – no servicing marks on nuts, etc. and manufacturer's seals still intact on contact-breaker covers. The engine data plates were missing from all 3 engines. The propeller had a circular hole ½ inch diameter in one blade, 2 feet from tip in the mid-chord area. Two .303 Brownings from wreckage were examined at the Station Armoury; they were complete except for the flash eliminators.

5. Nothing identifiable was found of that section of the aircraft, rear of the main spar, in fact the wreckage consisted of the fuselage forward of the main spar and its attached wing stub. The remaining part of fuselage is either still at crash site or more likely was detached at time of crash and recovered at that time.

Conclusion

Lancaster III JB 640 was one of 550 Lancaster IIIs delivered to the service from June to December 1943, JB 640 being delivered ex 32 MU to 156 (PFF) Squadron, R.A.F. Warboys, on 25 November 1943, from where it was posted missing from a raid on Berlin 3 Jan. 1944.

    The wreckage was of a Lancaster III whose engines were of

'low mileage', it was fitted with H2S, standard on Pathfinder aircraft, whereas only 25 per cent of Main Force were so equipped.

The hole in propeller's blade is consistent with 13-mm calibre damage; this could point to the aircraft being attacked by a fighter. If this was in the target area, it would almost certainly have been a single-engined 'Wild Boar' fighter, whose secondary armament was 13-mm calibre.

As it was not normal practice to swop guns between aircraft, it is probable that the guns recovered were from the front turret of JB 640 and it is this aircraft which was recovered from the crash site.

ACKNOWLEDGEMENTS

Participants

The following men and women were involved in the Battle of Berlin. I am extremely grateful to all of them; this book could not have been written without their help.

Bomber Command Aircrew

(Ranks are those held between August 1943 and March 1944. The names of some men may appear in more than one squadron.)

7 Squadron: F/Lt R. Edwards, F/Sgt A. Frewin, Sgt D. Ingram, Sgt H. E. Jacobs, Sqn Ldr C. J. Lofthouse, Sgt T. C. Marchant, W/Cdr P. K. Patrick, F/Lt R. J. Sexton, F/Lt G. J. South, P/O A. R. Speirs, WO I. Taylor, Sgt C. A. Thomson, WO T. Tilley, P/O G. R. Woodward, Sgt G. W. Wright. *9 Squadron*: Sgt A. Cordon, Sgt K. R. Goldspink (now Golde), Sgt H. Hannah, WO R. Smith, Sgt P. A. S. Twinn. *10 Squadron*: F/Sgt D. A. Blackford, F/Sgt P. J. Byrne, P/O A. L. Fuller, F/O D. E. Girardau, Sgt P. Jenkinson, WO J. S. Manson, P/O D. F. Shipley, P/O F. R. Stuart. *12 Squadron*: Sgt K. Apps, Sgt E. Brooks, Sgt L. J. Collins, P/O P. G. R. Grealy, F/Sgt H. H. Hoey, F/Sgt S. R. Holding, F/Lt R. B. Leigh, P/O D. R.

Oliver, F/Sgt G. Rose, F/Lt V. Wood, Sqn Ldr J. G. Woollatt. *15 Squadron*: F/Lt O. V. Brooks, F/O H. N. Burrows, F/O R. A. Horner, Sgt J. E. Paine, F/Sgt H. Sutcliffe. *35 Squadron*: F/Lt J. Annetts, F/Lt A. R. Ball, Major J. K. Christie, P/O J. M. Colledge, Sqn Ldr E. K. Creswell, W/Cdr D. F. E. C. Deane, F/Sgt K. J. Ewell, F/Sgt C. A. Hill, P/O N. J. Matich, P/O H. Matthews, F/Lt H. A. Millar, Capt K. Stenwig, Sgt W. E. Sutton. *44 Squadron*: F/O G. Baxter, P/O J. Chatterton, F/O C. E. Haynes (died 1985), F/Sgt H. E. Palmer, P/O H. Rogers, F/Sgt M. M. Scott, WO A. G. Strickland, Sgt J. R. Sutton, Sgt R. W. Tucher. *49 Squadron*: Sgt G. K. Chapman, F/O F. A. Harpham, F/O J. D. Harris, Sgt A. Morgan, Sgt N. D. Panter, Sgt O. Roberts, F/Lt T. D. Taylor, Sgt D. C. Tritton, P/O Tudor Jones, WO E. M. Webb. *50 Squadron*: P/O A. L. Bartlett, F/Lt M. J. Beetham, F/Sgt F. R. Brand, Sgt C. H. Brown, F/Sgt H. Brown, F/Sgt J. Brown, Sgt R. J. Dunn, F/Sgt J. P. Flynn, Sgt D. C. Lynch, Sgt R. A. McCullough, F/Lt K. Odgers, Sgt R. Payne, P/O H. F. Roberts, P/O W. C. B. Smith. *51 Squadron*: F/Sgt W. A. Clarke, P/O M. C. Foster, Sgt T. Nelson, Sgt D. W. Thompson. *57 Squadron*: F/O S. Bradley, F./Sgt A. G. Buckley, F/Lt H. H. Chadwick, F/Lt A. W. Fearn, Sgt R. A. Hammersley, F/Lt E. T. Hodgkinson, F/Sgt H. J. Knights, F/O H. B. Mackinnon, F/Lt R. V. Munday, P/O H. F. Roberts, P/O J. Sheriff, WO D. R. Waddell, P/O H. Welland. *61 Squadron*: Sgt J. D. Barnes-Moss, WO D. C. Davies, F/O J. H. Dyer, P/O C. J. Gray, F/Lt H. N. Scott, F/Sgt A. E. Wilson. *75 Squadron*: P/O W. G. Lake, Sgt L. P. Parsons, F/Sgt R. W. Rogerson, P/O A. R. Speirs. *76 Squadron*: Sgt L. I. Brown, F/Lt H. D. Coverley, Sgt A. W. Davis, Sgt W. G. Day, P/O F. P. G. Hall, F/O R. G. McCadden, Sgt F. Newton (died 1985), Sgt M. Ransome, F/Lt E. A. Strange, P/O V. A. Thomson, P/O W. Wanless, P/O G. G. A. Whitehead, Sgt P. G. Wilmshurst. *77 Squadron*: F/Sgt J. Adamson, Sgt C. W. Brister, Sgt O. E. Burger, F/O J. Marvin, Sgt N. W. Parker, F/Sgt J. K. Pettigrew. *78 Squadron*: F/O E. H. Burgess, F/Lt B. S. Downs, F/Lt A. Forsdike, Sgt J. Greet, P/O J. C. Palmer, P/O V. A. Robins, Sgt H. D. Wood. *83 Squadron*: F/Lt G. Baxter, F/Sgt F. J. Chadwick, Sgt G. K. Chapman, F/O F. A. Harpham, F/Lt C. E. Haynes (died 1985), F/O B. Moorcroft, W/Cdr J. Northrop, F/Lt A. J. Saunders, Gp Capt. J. H. Searby (died 1986), WO J. W. Slaughter, WO A. G. Strickland. *90 Squadron*: Sgt E. W. Armstrong, F/O D. A. Beaton, Sgt J. Burland, Sgt A. R. Clarke, F/Lt W. S. Day, F/Sgt L. W. J. Durrant, Sgt P. Foolkes, Sgt R. A. James. *97 Squadron*: Sgt J.

Arthurson, F/Sgt J. L. R. Baker, F/Sgt R. E. C. Buck, W/Cdr K. H. Burns, F/Sgt E. O. Charlton, F/Lt C. S. Chatten, Gp Capt. N. H. Fresson (Station Commander, flew on a raid with the squadron), WO W. H. Layne, Sgt H. J. Lazenby, F/Sgt W. D. Ogilvie, Sqn Ldr E. E. Rodley, F/Sgt A. J. Tindall. *100 Squadron*: P/O J. Booth, Sgt E. J. Clark, P/O S. N. Cunnington, Sgt L. Y. Easby, WO R. G. Fenton, Sgt E. J. Gargini, F/Sgt K. W. Harris, F/Sgt W. Kondra, P/O G. J. A. Smith (now Crowley-Smith), Sgt H. Widdup. *101 Squadron*: Sgt J. H. G. Allison, Sgt D. Brinkhurst, W/Cdr G. A. Carey-Foster, P/O G. R. Fawcett, F/Lt L. E. Gibbons, F/O J. Gillmore, Sgt R. Herscovitch (now Hurst), P/O A. McCartney, F/Lt D. M. Macdonald, Sgt T. C. Marchant, P/O C. K. Maun, Sgt F. H. Quick, F/O C. R. S. Ricketts, Sgt K. F. Scott, F/Lt R. J. Sexton, F/Sgt K. G. Thompson, WO T. Tilley, Sgt G. W. Wright. *102 Squadron*: F/O G. A. Griffiths, F/Lt N. McPhail, F/Sgt N. Pearce, F/O W. J. C. Seeley, Sgt K. Symes, F/Lt J. W. Ward. *103 Squadron*: WO C. W. Annis, P/O J. T. Birbeck, Sgt G. T. Bishop, Sgt J. E. Brown, F/O J. A. Day, F/O E. J. Densley, F/Sgt K. W. Harris, Sgt J. McFarlane, F/Lt A. Muggridge, W/Cdr E. D. Nelson, F/Lt N. Olsberg, Sgt J. Spark, Sgt T. D. G. Teare. *106 Squadron*: F/Lt C. J. Ginder, Sgt H. W. Hudson, F/Lt G. S. Milne, F/O D. A. Pagliero, F/O W. Seymour. *115 Squadron*: Sgt J. W. Carter, F/Sgt D. W. N. Franklin, F/Lt A. Howell, P/O F. R. Leatherdale, Sgt E. A. Meikle, F/O P. H. Paddon, Sgt J. G. Swan. *139 Squadron*: F/O D. Carter, F/Lt G. F. Hodder, F/Sgt J. Marshallsay, F/Sgt E. R. Perry. *141 Squadron*: F/Sgt J. A. Carter, Sqn Ldr F. F. Lambert. *149 Squadron*: Sgt P. Bates, Sgt A. G. Clarke, Sgt E. J. Webb. *156 Squadron*: F/Lt P. A. Colham, Sgt L. J. Collins, F/Lt J. A. Day, F/O A. S. Drew, Sgt D. H. Evans, F/Sgt H. C. Geddes, F/O J. Gillmore, F/O C. R. Johnson, F/Lt R. B. Leigh, F/Lt A. Muggeridge, Sgt G. S. Richardson, F/Lt Baron L. A. Terlinden, F/Sgt G. Thorneycroft, F/Lt H. J. Wright. *158 Squadron*: WO G. S. Almond, P/O A. E. Bryett, P/O A. M. Glendinning, F/O J. D. Koch, F/O W. A. Lennard, P/O T. R. Lister, F/O A. R. McGillivray, Sgt D. E. Slack, Sgt E. A. Tansley, F/O T. C. Walker. *166 Squadron*: F/Sgt H. C. Geddes, F/Lt W. R. Jackson, Sgt H. F. Jamieson, Sgt J. Robinson, F/Sgt L. Wayte. *199 Squadron*: Sgt A. E. Nixon, Sgt R. Taylor. *207 Squadron*: P/O W. H. Baker, F/Sgt R. E. C. Buck, Sgt S. Carter, P/O F. Collis, Sgt T. H. Gladders, F/Sgt D. G. J. Griffiths, Sgt A. Hepworth, F/Sgt L. W. Mitchell, F/Sgt L. Sutherland, Sgt A. T. C. White. *214 Squadron*: F/Sgt A.

Boyd, F/Lt W. S. Day, Sgt R. W. G. Elliott, F/O K. E. W. Evans, F/O
G. H. Hart, W/Cdr D. J. McGlinn. *218 Squadron*: Sgt R. Davey, Sgt
D. Ingram. *405 Squadron*: Sgt C. O. Beardman, F/O C. L. Davies,
P/O H. Gowan, Sgt J. G. McLaughlan, Sqn Ldr P. G. Powell, F/Lt
W. D. Renton, Sqn Ldr H. W. Trilsbach. *408 Squadron*: F/O R.
W. Butcher, F/Sgt W. Cooke, WO M. J. Harrison, P/O E. D. Har-
vey, 2nd Lt M. R. Humphrey, F/Sgt P. E. Liwiski (now Lewis),
P/O R. T. Lloyd. *419 Squadron*: Sgt J. G. McLaughlan, F/O S. G.
Philp, F/O W. R. Touchie, F/Sgt K. P. White. *420 Squadron*: F/Sgt
P. A. Dubois, Sgt H. J. Gibbs, F/O I. A. Macdonald. *425 Squadron*:
F/Sgt H. C. Mooney. *426 Squadron*: F/O C. L. Davies, WO E. J.
Houston, F/O R. E. Luke, P/O W. N. McInnis. *427 Squadron*: Sgt
R. F. Dean, F/Sgt P. A. Dubois, Sgt J. L. Fontaine, Sgt H. J. Gibbs,
F/Sgt H. G. McLean, F/O J. Moffat, P/O G. S. Schellenberg, WO
G. C. Southcott. *428 Squadron*: Sgt S. A. Baldwin, WO G. S.
Brown, F/O F. E. Churchill, Sgt R. S. Dutka, Sgt F. Gration, Sgt
N. Lee, F/Sgt M. A. McAulay, F/Sgt E. Scott Jones. *429 Squadron*:
WO S. Boustead, F/O D. Finlay, Sgt R. L. Kift, WO C. E. Whit-
more, P/O J. L. Widdis. *431 Squadron*: F/Sgt P. Bauset, P/O A. E.
Freeman, F/O H. Krantz, W/Cdr W. F. M. Newson, Sgt W.
Sparkes. *432 Squadron*: P/O J. A. Banks, P/O D. A. McCoy, F/O
R. D. Plommer. *433 Squadron*: Sgt R. F. Dean, WO J. G. McLaugh-
lan, F/O K. P. White. *434 Squadron*: P/O J. F. Acquier, F/Sgt J. D.
Campbell, F/O H. Kranz, Sgt J. E. Nicholls, P/O J. E. Pollard. *460
Squadron*: Sgt G. Cairns, P/O S. A. Moorhouse, P/O T. E. Osborn,
F/Lt J. E. C. Radcliffe, F/O I. R. Richardson, WO M. Stafford,
F/Sgt J. Venning. *463 Squadron*: F/Sgt J. H. Frith, Sgt M. Holmes,
P/O A. J. Saunders. *466 Squadron*: F/Sgt P. Balderston, Sgt J. Ellis,
F/Lt W. L. Harrison (Intelligence Officer, flew on a raid to Berlin
with the squadron), F/O J. H. Rollins. *467 Squadron*: F/O H. J. C.
Bentley, Sgt S. Bethell, F/Sgt C. A. Campbell, F/Lt D. T. Conway,
P/O D. L. Gibbs, F/Lt W. H. Goldstraw, Sgt M. Holmes, P/O F. G.
Miller, Sgt G. Niblett, F/Lt A. J. Saunders, F/Sgt H. E. Twitchett,
F/O A. T. Youdan. *514 Squadron*: Sgt A. W. Birse, F/O H. G.
Darby, F/O R. Davey, F/Lt M. S. Emery (died 1985), F/O L. Green-
burgh, F/O P. J. K. Hood, P/O P. A. S. Twinn. *576 Squadron*: P/O
A. C. Blackie. *578 Squadron*: Sgt H. D. Wood. *619 Squadron*: F/Sgt
F. H. Baynton, Sgt D. J. Coomber, Sgt E. Davis, F/Sgt G. E.
Hexter, 1st Lt H. N. Knilans, WO R. Smith. *620 Squadron*: F/Sgt
J. L. Elliott, Sgt A. T. Gamble, WO L. F. Johns, F/O J. D. Sutton,
F/O E. Walker. *622 Squadron*: F/O H. N. Burrows, P/O R. Curling,

F/Sgt G. B. Dawkins, Sgt H. Harris, Sgt R. S. Kerslake, F/Sgt G. G. Marsh. *625 Squadron*: P/O J. E. Goldsmith, F/Sgt K. W. Harris, F/Sgt J. Marks, P/O R. W. Price, Sgt G. S. Richardson. *626 Squadron*: P/O W. B. Baker, P/O S. N. Cunnington, F/Sgt A. J. P. Lee (died 1987), WO R. J. Meek, P/O D. R. Oliver, F/Sgt G. Thorneycroft, F/Lt V. Wood. *627 Squadron*: F/Sgt J. Marshallsay. *630 Squadron*: F/Sgt D. Cooper, F/O A. J. Kuzma, F/Sgt L. N. Rackley. *635 Squadron*: F/Sgt W. D. Ogilvie, F/Lt Baron L. A. Terlinden. *640 Squadron*: Sgt K. Grantham. *1409 (Meteorological) Flight*: F/O N. W. F. Green, F/Sgt E. R. Perry.

Ground Staffs

Air Ministry: Air Cdre S. O. Bufton. *Bomber Command HQ*: Sqn Ldr F. A. B. Fawssett (died 1985), W/Cdr W. I. C. Inness (died 1986). *5 Group H.Q.*: Sqn Ldr J. Beach. *8 Group HQ*: Wg Cdr E. L. T. Barton, Air Cdre C. D. C. Boyce (died 1987), Gp Capt. H. Mahaddie. *R.A.F. Bourn*: ACW. Joan Huckle. *R.A.F. Graveley*: F/Lt P. M. S. Hedgeland.

The People of Berlin

Civilians: Arno Abendroth, Melieta Anklam (now Jüttner), Willi Dietrich, Ilse Förstellung (now Franke), Gerda Ganschow (now Stoewer), Ursula Gebel, Gerhard Hansa, Dr Horst Hartwich, Käthe Hauch, Anneliese Jung (now Hadland), Ursula Kath (now Dr Besser), Norbert Kelling, Brigitta Kirchstein (now Ansdell-Evans), Herta Loewcke (now Smith), Erika Machon, Ingeborg Minter (now Traumann-Minter), Reinhold Neumann, Renate Nigmann, Hildegard Petermann, Ursula Reimann (now Lindemuth), Wilma Rodzyn (now Rodzyn-Hauck), Cecilia Schellhase (now Götz), Heinz Schittenhelm, Werner Schlecking, Ellen Slottgo (now Ellis), Ingeborg Spie (now Paetzke), Manfred Spielberg, Robert Stoebe, Herbert Strobach, Ingeborg Tafel, Alice Wawrzyniak (now Fischer), Else Wolter. *Servicemen*: Hermann Bock, Hans-Joachim Hamann, Walter Nedoma, Heinz von der Hayde. *Flakhilfers*: Ulrich Bley, Gerhard Eichel, Joachim Härtel, Horst Jorek, Horst Kesner, Günther Lincke, Heinrich Möller, Theodor Pamin. *Foreigners*: Léon Butticaz (French), Karl de Haas (Dutch).

Luftwaffe

Oberst Hajo Herrmann, commander in turn of JG 300, 30th and 1st Fighter Divisions. *I/NJG 1*: Feld. Fritz Habitch, Uffz. Hermann Vollert. *III/NJG 1*: Uffz. Erich Handke, Oblt Fritz Lau. *IV/NJG 1*: Hptm. Adolf Breves, Oblt Georg-Hermann Greiner, Lt Fritz Rumpelhardt. *I/NJG 2*: Oblt Heinz Rökker. *III/NJG 2*: Emil Nonnenmacher. *I/NJG 3*: Uffz. Benno Gramlich (also in NJG 10), Uffz. Hans-Georg Schierholz, Hptm. Paul Zorner (also in III Gruppe). *II/NJG 3*: Uffz. Josef Krinner, Uffz. Otto Kutzner, Uffz. Bruno Rupp. *IV/NJG 3*: Uffz. Walter Heidenreich. *I/NJG 4*: Lt Wilhelm Seuss (also in IV/NJG 5). *II/NJG 5*: Lt Peter Spoden. *III/NJG 5*: Lt Günther Wolf. *I/NJG 6*: Oblt Hans Engels.

Personal Acknowledgements

Pride of place here must go to two people who have carried out a vast amount of archival research on my behalf – Chris Everitt of Eton Wick, for his work at the Public Record Office, and Arno Abendroth, for similar help in the archives of his native city of Berlin and for his interpreting work during a ten-day visit to Berlin which a combination of his arthritis and the stairs of many blocks of flats without lifts made particularly arduous for him. I cannot praise too highly their diligence and skill and am most grateful to them for their help and for their friendship.

I also wish to single out for thanks my typist, Janet Mountain, who has, with the minimum of fuss and the maximum of efficiency, typed the correspondence and two drafts of the manuscript for the tenth consecutive book for me. Also deserving of special thanks is my wife, Mary, for loyal support, coping with unexpected visitors, drawing maps and a multitude of other tasks.

I wish to thank these many other people who are not so closely connected with me and whose help was therefore given through sheer goodwill and not for any obligation. Presentation of names by country or in alphabetical order does not imply any order of merit; I am equally grateful to all. *England*: Susan and Paul Hobson and Alan Taylor of Boston; Jim MacDonald of Hanworth, Middlesex; Peter Richard of London; Peter Sanderson of Ruskington, Lincolnshire; Jock Whitehouse of Hundon, Suffolk. *Overseas*:

Johan Breugelmans of Aarschot, Belgium; Robert E. Docherty of Taunton, Massachusetts; Birger Hansen of Copenhagen; Joyce and Roy Inkster of Toronto; Leo Johnson of Winnipeg: Norbert Krüger and family of Essen; Professor James Tent and family of Berlin and Alabama; Harold Thiele of Neu Ulm; Doctor W. H. Tiemens of Arnhem; Allan J. Vial of Broadbeach, Queensland; Rolph Wegmann and Bo Widfeldt of Linköping, Sweden.

I am also grateful to the staffs of the following organizations and official bodies who have been so helpful: The Air Historical Branch (particularly Eric Munday, Evelyn Boyd and Phyllis Fuller), AR8b and the Personnel Management Centre, all of the Ministry of Defence; the Imperial War Museum (particularly Mike Willis); the Swedish Embassy in London (Group Captain Jan Westberg); the Landesarchiv and the Landesbildstelle (Norbert Kelling) in Berlin; the Gemeinschaft der Jagdflieger e.V. (Horst Amberg); 75 (New Zealand) Squadron Museum (Peter Strugnell and Pilot Officer P. R. Turvey).

Quotations from Crown Copyright documents in the Public Record Office are by permission of the Controller of H.M. Stationery Office.

I would like to thank the editors of the following publications for printing my appeals for participants in the Battle of Berlin. United Kingdom: *Air Mail, Air Pictorial, Birmingham Post, Eastern Daily Press, Grimsby Evening Telegraph, Lincolnshire Echo, Lincolnshire Standard, The* (London) *Standard, Manchester Evening News,* (Newcastle) *Evening Chronicle,* (Nottingham) *Evening News, Western Morning News.* Canada: *Hamilton Spectator, London Free Press, Manitoba Senior's Journal,* (Moncton) *Times Transcript, Toronto Sun, Vancouver Sun, Victoria Times Colonist, Winnipeg Free Press.* Berlin: *Berliner Morgenpost, Die Welt am Sonntag* (particularly Jürgen Uhrig). The newsletters or magazines of the following organizations: Aircrew Association, 7 Squadron Association, Mildenhall Register, N.W. Branch of the R.A.F. Ex-P.O.W. Association, Pathfinder Assocation, Stalag IVB Association, Wickenby Register, Air Gunners' Association of Canada, R.C.A.F. P.O.W. Association, Royal Canadian Legion R.A.A.F Association, New Zealand R.S.A. Aircrew Association.

BIBLIOGRAPHY

BEKKER, CAJUS, *The Luftwaffe War Diaries* (London: Macdonald), 1966.

CHORLEY, W. R., *To See the Dawn Breaking – A History of 76 Squadron* (Ottery St Mary: Chorley), 1981.

CHORLEY, W. R., and BENWELL, R. N., *In Brave Company – A History of 158 Squadron* (Ottery St Mary: Chorley & Benwell), 1977.

COOPER, ALAN W., *Bombers over Berlin* (London: Kimber), 1985.

FREEMAN, ROGER A., *Mighty Eighth War Diary* (London: Jane's), 1981.

The Goebbels Diaries: The Last Days (London: Secker & Warburg), 1978.

GOMERSALL, BRYCE, *The Stirling File* (Tonbridge: Air Britain and Aviation Archaeologists), 1979.

HARRIS, MARSHAL OF THE R.A.F. SIR ARTHUR, *Bomber Offensive* (London: Collins), 1947.

HARVEY, J. DOUGLAS, *Boys, Bombs and Brussels Sprouts* (Halifax, Canada: Goodread Biographies), 1986.

HINSLEY, F. H., THOMAS, E. E., RANSOM, C. F. G., and KNIGHT, R. C., *British Intelligence in the Second World War*, Vol. III, Part 1 (London: H.M.S.O.), 1984.

JANSEN, A. A., *Wespennest Leeuwarden* (Holland: Baarn), 1976–7.

MIDDLEBROOK, MARTIN, *The Nuremberg Raid* (London: Allen Lane), 1973, 1980.

MIDDLEBROOK, M., *The Battle of Hamburg* (London: Allen Lane), 1980.

MIDDLEBROOK, M., *The Peenemünde Raid* (London: Allen Lane), 1982.

MIDDLEBROOK, M., and EVERITT, CHRIS, *The Bomber Command War Diaries* (London: Viking), 1985.

MUSGROVE, GORDON, *Pathfinder Force* (London: Macdonald & Jane's), 1976.

OBERMEIER, ERNST, *Die Ritterkreuzträger der Luftwaffe, Jagdflieger 1939–1945* (Mainz: Hoffmann), 1966.

PRICE, ALFRED, *Instruments of Darkness* (London: Macdonald & Jane's), 1977.

RUMPF, HANS, *The Bombing of Germany* (London: Muller), 1963.

SAUNDBY, AIR MARSHAL SIR ROBERT, *Air Bombardment* (London: Chatto & Windus), 1961.

SAWARD, DUDLEY, *The Bomber's Eye* (London: Cassell), 1959.

SAWARD, D., *Bernard Lovell* (London: Hale), 1984.

SAWARD, D., *Bomber Harris* (London: Cassell), 1984.

SPEER, ALBERT, *Inside the Third Reich* (London: Weidenfeld & Nicolson), 1970.

THOMPSON, WALTER R., *Lancaster to Berlin* (St Albans: Goodall), 1985.

WEBSTER, SIR CHARLES, and FRANKLAND, NOBLE, *The Strategic Air Offensive against Germany, 1939–1945* (London: H.M.S.O.), 1961.

Index

The city of Berlin and the Battle of Berlin are not indexed except for the chapter describing wartime Berlin, but the districts of Berlin are indexed under 'Berlin'. Other German cities are only indexed when they were the subject of bombing raids. Passing references to aircraft types and technical devices are not indexed.

AEG factories, 22, 87
Aachen, 237
Abercromby, W/Cdr W., 204–5
Airborne Cigar (A.B.C.), 100,
    179, 203, 354
Air Ministry, 93–4, 136, 173–4
Allcroft, F/O F. C., 215
Alkett factory, 22, 147, 323
Ammann, Uffz. F., 73
Anderson, W/Cdr E. W., 278,
    286
Annetts, F/Lt J. W., 43
Apps, Sgt K., 349
Arguswerke, 22, 146
Arthurson, Sgt J. W., 187
Augsburg, 274
Austin, F/O J., 74

B-17 (Flying Fortress), 9, 174
BMW factory, 22, 146, 148
Baake, Lt W., 40
Bailey, Sgt J. C., 61
Baker, P/O W. H., 110–11
Balderstone, F/Sgt P., 244
Baldwin, F/Lt W. G., 199n.
Ball, F/Lt A. R., 55–6
Barnes-Moss, Sgt J. D., 198
Bartlett, F/Sgt A. L., 125
Barton, P/O C. J., 360
Battle of Hamburg, 2, 8–10, 12,
    23–5, 101, 150
Battle of the Ruhr, 2, 9–11, 150

Baxter, F/Lt G., 128
Beaufighters, 33, 180
Beetham, F/O M. J., 125n.
Bell, Sgt H., 89
Bennett, AVM D. C. T., 12, 32,
    94, 96–7, 205, 278, 310–14
Bennett, Lowell, 137
Bentley, F/O H. C. J., 205–6
Berlin, description of, 21–27
    districts:
    Borsigwalde, 147
    Charlottenburg, 87, 141, 145,
        257, 329
    Friedenau, 257
    Friedrichshain, 26
    Gesundbrunnen, 27
    Grunewald, 116–17, 207, 257,
        329
    Havel See, 28
    Horst Wessel (Weissensee),
        227, 256, 290
    Humboldthain, 26, 163, 329
    Köpenick, 71, 207
    Kreuzberg, 257, 290
    Lankwitz, 69, 71
    Lichtenberg, 228, 256
    Lichterfelde, 71
    Mariendorf, 71
    Marienfelde, 71, 108
    Mitte, 45, 71, 141, 145
    Moabit, 83, 87, 143, 146, 258

Neukölln, 142, 149, 192, 208, 228
Reinickendorf, 108, 147
Schöneberg, 67–8, 257, 259
Siemensstadt, 22, 87
Spandau, 22, 116
Steglitz, 71, 290
Tegel, 116, 147, 148
Tegeler See, 27, 129
Tempelhof, 66, 71, 192
Tiergarten, 87, 141, 145, 149, 329
Wannsee, 208
Wedding, 83, 87
Wilmersdorf, 257
Zehlendorf, 256
Zoo, 26, 67–8, 142, 260, 344
Berlin War Cemetery (British), 59, 216n., 249, 329
Blakeman, F/O A. W., 215
Borsigwerke, 22
Boustead, WO S., 298
Boyce, Air Cdre C. D. C., 12, 64
Bracewell, F/Lt J. H., 329
Brister Sgt C. W., 41
Britton, P/O D. B., 106
Brooks, F/Lt O. V., 281
Brown, F/Sgt J., 236, 332
Brunswick, 223–4, 248, 261
Bryett, P/O A. E., 58
Buck, F/Sgt R. E. C., 186, 332
Bufton, Air Cdre S. O., 7–9
Burland, Sgt J., 335
Burns, W/Cdr K. H., 32, 77, 81, 95
Butticaz, L., 108–9, 155

Carey-Foster, W/Cdr G. A. 106n., 120
Carter, Sgt S. W., 248
Casablanca directive, 6
Cayford, F/Lt D., 54–5
Chadwick, Sgt H., 38
Chadwick, F/O H. H., 193
Chalklin, Sgt S. K., 248–9
Charlton, F/Sgt E. O., 330
Chatterton, P/O J., 107, 212, 330
Chatton, Sgt C. S., 74–5

Chemnitz, 327
Churchill, Winston, 2, 7–9, 93–4, 174
Cochrane, AVM Hon. R., 205
Coldham, F/Lt P. A., 224
Collis, Sgt F., 348
Cologne, 16, 105, 145
Conway, F/Lt D. T., 331
Cooper, F/Sgt D., 316
Corona, 100
Crofts, Sgt R., 43
Cromarty, P/O J. D. R., 216n.
Crombie, F/Sgt D. C. C., 184–5

DIW factory, 22
DWM factory, 22, 148
Daggett, P/O S., 246
Daimler-Benz factory, 22, 27, 137
Dams raid, 32
Darby, F/O H. G., 184
Davies, P/O A. C., 183
Day, F/O J. A., 87
Day, F/Lt W. S., 60
Dear, F/O, 180
Densley, F/O E. J., 331
Dornier 217s, 14
Dornier factory, 22, 148
Drane, F/O P., 186
Dresden, 327
Drewes, Maj. M., 294–6
Dubois, F/Sgt P. A., 242

Eden, Anthony, 90
Eichel, G., 258
Elliott, Sgt R. W. G., 57
Essen, 303
Evill, AM Sir D., 8

Fastlich, Sr A., 319
Fauquier, W/Cdr J. E., 32, 64, 77
Fawcett, P/O G. R., 185, 218
Fawssett, Sqn Ldr F. A. B., 321
Fenton, F/Sgt R. G., 253
Fidge, WO, 193
Flakhilfers, 28, 153–4, 208, 258, 344
Frank, Feld. R., 49, 296

Frankfurt, 105, 124, 189, 247, 274
Frankfurt-on-Oder, 263–4, 269
Fraser, WO H. S., 111
Fresson, Gp Capt N. H., 35
Freya radar, 14
Friedrichshafen, 32

Galland, Gen. A., 102
Ganschow, G., 163
Gebel, U., 345
Gee device, 279
Geiger, Hptm. A., 40
Goebbels, Josef, 24, 71, 287, 322, 327
Goering, Hermann, 9, 101, 287
Gowan, P/O H. A., 80
Grace, W/Cdr E. J., 270
Gramlich, Uffz. B., 267–8
Gration, Sgt F., 338
Gray, P/O C. J., 332
Greenburgh, F/O L., 200
Greet, Sgt J., 74
Greig, Capt N., 137

H2S, 11–13, 28, 100, 103, 178, 264
H2S Mark III, 94, 99, 103, 106–7, 112, 114–16, 122, 127, 134, 138, 147, 174–5, 182, 191, 207, 215, 221, 247, 251, 310
Haas, K. de, 158
Hager, Lt J., 40
Halifaxes, 11, 33, 99, 173, 220, 272–3, 275, 377–8
Hall, Sgt F. P. G., 81
Hallenbruch, Ofw., 250
Hamburg, 202–3, *see also* Battle of Hamburg
Handke, Uffz. E., 41, 294–6
Hands, Sgt R. L., 196
Hannah, Sgt H., 135
Hanover, 98, 225, 227, 239, 241
Hansa, G., 17
Harris, ACM Sir A.,
    plans for Battle of Berlin and

requests for support, 1–3, 8–9, 174–5
and directives, 7
his early operations, 23
decisions to mount raids, 29–31, 85, 91, 102–4, 112, 119, 176, 189, 202, 210, 224, 230, 262, 270, 275–6
suspends Berlin raids, 93, 273
rejects Bennett's requests for second tour crews, 96–7, 310
removes Stirlings from German raids, 118
his post-war book 151n.
attitude to Halifaxes, 173, 220, 232, 272
and Nuremberg raid, 304–5
estimates of damage to Berlin, 320, 324
Harrison, F/Lt W. L., 199
Hartwell, P/O R. C., 57
Hartwich, H., 166
Harvey, Sgt J. D., 213
Hauch, K., 67
Hauck, W., 165
Haynes, F/O C. E., 128, 148
Heinkel 219s, 14, 232
Heligoland, 232–3
Hellier, P/O R. A., 116, 126
Henderson, P/O R., 117
Henley, F/Sgt D., 83–4
Henschel factories, 22, 137
Herbert, F/O D. W., 196
Herrmann, Oberst H., 16, 47, 80, 101, 286–8
Hilton, W/Cdr R., 123
Hitler, Adolf, 9, 142, 259–60
Holford, W/Cdr D. W., 185–6
Homewood, F/Sgt J. W., 231
Hornibrook, F/Lt H. K., 58–9
Hudson, Sgt H., 333
Hughes, P/O R. H., 196

I.G. Farben factories, 29, 103

Jackson, F/Lt W. R., 285
Jeschonnek, Gen. H., 9
Junkers 88s, 14, 204, 222

Kassel, 98, 145
Kesner, H., 344
Kiel, 225, 227, 277, 282
Kilsby, F/Lt N. W., 245–6
Kirchstein, B., 290
Knight's Cross (*Ritterkreuz*),
    20–1, 40, 198, 231–2, 373
Korfu device, 222
Kutzner, Uffz. O., 252

Lahey, P/O L. E. N., 43
Lambert, Sqn Ldr F. F., 180
Lancasters, 3, 8, 11, 33–4, 99,
    175, 220, 377–8
Lane, W/Cdr R. J., 278, 286
Leatherdale, P/O F. R., 285
Lees, P/O F. J., 110
Leigh, F/Lt R. B., 26
Leipzig, 137–8, 189, 198,
    270–72, 301, 309, 327
Leverkusen, 29–30, 112
Lewis, F/Sgt V. C., 62
Lichtenstein radar, 15, 221, 234
Lincke, G., 154
Lindo, Harold, 319
Lindo, Sqn Ldr H. L., 319
Lister, F/Sgt T. R., 279n, 332
Little, W/Cdr E. J., 84
Lloyd, F/O R. T., 317
Lofthouse, Sqn Ldr C. J., 53–5
Ludwigshafen, 91, 93, 103–7,
    111
Luftwaffe
  Units
  Oberbefehlshaber Mitte, 126,
    217
  XIV Korps, 102
  1st Fighter Division, 287
  1st Flak Division, 67, 152
  8th Flak Division, 43
  30th Fighter Division, 101,
    286–7
  5th Flak Regiment, 152
  NJG 1, 14–15, 19, 38–40, 125,
    194, 294, 302, 371
  I/NJG 1, 121, 232, 250, 371
  II/NJG 1, 17n, 81, 371
  III/NJG 1, 294, 371
  IV/NJG 1, 78, 371

NJG2, 14, 204, 302, 372
I/NJG 2, 48, 372
II/NJG 2, 372
III/NJG 2, 282, 372
NJG 3, 14–15, 39, 106, 281,
    302, 372–3
I/NJG 3, 49, 194–5, 296, 372
II/NJG 3, 234, 372
III/NJG 3, 373
IV/NJG 3, 373
NJG 4, 14, 39, 373
I/NJG 4, 373
II/NJG 4, 373
III/NJG 4, 373
IV/NJG 4, 374
NJG 5, 14, 39, 126, 302,
    373–4
I/NJG 5, 373
II/NJG 5, 19, 51, 343, 374
III/NJG 5, 19, 51, 86, 178,
    374
IV/NJG 5, 121, 237, 374
NJG 6, 230, 302, 374
I-IV/NJG 6, 374
JG 300, 16, 39, 101, 302, 374
JG 301, 101–2, 302, 374
JG 302, 101, 302, 375
NJ Gruppe, 10, 267, 374
III/KG 3, 101n., 215
I/KG 7, 80, 101n.
Airfields
Aalborg, 373
Bad Langensalza, 372
Bonn/Hangelar, 47, 374
Brandis, 374
Coulommiers, 373
Deelen, 371, 374
Erfurt, 121, 239, 374
Florennes, 373
Gilze Rijen, 48, 282, 372
Greifswald, 51, 80, 374
Grove, 373
Gütersloh, 195
Jüterbog, 375
Juvincourt, 373
Kastrup, 372
Kolberg, 374
Königsberg/Neumark, 178,
    374

Langendiebach, 372
Laon/Athies, 371, 373
Leeuwarden, 41, 178, 371
Ludwigslust, 375
Lüneburg, 194–5, 265, 373
Mainz/Finthen, 373–4
Neuburg/Donau, 374–5
Neuruppin, 372, 374
Nordholz, 373
Oldenburg, 73, 374–5
Parchim, 51, 372, 374
Quackenbrück, 372
Rechlin, 49
Rheine, 374
St Dizier, 294, 371, 373
St Trond, 17n., 297, 371
Schiphol, 372
Schleissheim, 375
Schleswig/Jagel, 234, 250, 372
Stade, 372–3
Stendal, 373
Stuttgart/Echterdingen, 374
Stuttgart/Nellingen, 372
Twenthe, 294, 371–2
Vechta, 296, 372, 374
Venlo, 232, 250, 371–2
Völkenrode, 373
Werneuchen, 267, 374
Westerland, 372–3
Wiesbaden/Eibenheim, 374
Wittmundhafen, 49, 371–2
Zerbst, 375
Luke, F/O R. E., 25

MacDonald, Sgt G. W., 56–7
McFarlane, Sgt, J. M., 35
McGlinn, W/Cdr D. J., 37
McInnis, P/O W. N., 330
McKenna, Gp Capt A. F., 89
Magdeburg, 198, 224, 230–32,
    261
Mair, W/Cdr A. C., 130
Mannheim, 35n., 91, 93, 107,
    126, 189, 217n.
Marchant, Sgt T. C., 319–20
Marsh, F/Sgt G. G., 60
Marshallsay, F/Sgt J., 240
Massie, P/O A., 41

Master Bombers, 29, 32, 64–5,
    77, 95–6, 109, 278, 286
Meikle, Sgt E. A., 283
Messerschmitt 110s, 14, 19, 237
Meurer, Hptm. M., 232
Milch, Feldmarschall E., 221
Minter, I., 192
Mitchinson, F/Sgt C. A., 60
Möller, H., 153
Mönchengladbach, 78, 93
Moorcroft, F/O B., 115, 127
Morris, F/Sgt A. C. N., 239
Mosquitos, 11, 33
Moulton-Barrett, P/O G. E., 193
Muggeridge, F/Lt A., 231
Müller, Hptm. F. K., 47
Munday, F/Lt R. V., 88, 252,
    298
Munich, 91, 93, 274
Munro, F/Lt R., 35
Murrow, Ed, 137

Naxos device, 73, 222
Nelson, W/Cdr E. D. M., 135
Nelson, Sgt T., 339
Neumann, R., 69
Newhaven marking, 30, 284
Newton, Sgt F., 66
Nigmann, R. 161
Nixon, Sgt A. E., 57–8
Nonnenmacher, E., 282, 289
Normandy invasion, 118, 261
Nuremberg, 77, 95, 303–5, 309

Oboe device, 11–12, 30, 38–9,
    240–1, 263, 277, 303
Oliver, P/O D. R., 318

Parramatta marking, 30
Pathfinders, *see* Royal Air Force,
    8 Group
Patrick, W/Cdr P. K., 211
Peenemünde, 9, 16–17, 29, 32,
    93, 95, 101, 109
Peirse, AM Sir R., 23
Philipsen, Sqn Ldr A. P., 57
Portal, ACM Sir C., 2, 7–8, 174
Powell, Sqn Ldr P. G., 65
Preston, WO F., 38

Public Record Office, 8, 96, 282

Quapp, F., 208

Randall, F/O F. A., 89
Ransom, Sgt M., 242
Read, F/Sgt H. A., 72
Reimann, U., 168
Regensburg, 8–9, 93
Renton, F/Lt W. D., 212
Rheydt, 78, 93
Rice, F/Lt C. J., 251
Rice, AVM E. A. B., 383
Richardson, F/O I. R., 129
Roberts, Sgt O., 346
Robinson, Gp Capt B. V., 35, 62
Rogerson, F/O J. G., 251
Rökker, Lt H., 48
Rollings, F/O C. R. G., 42
Rollinson, W/Cdr J. D., 247
Ross, W/Cdr Q. W. A., 301
Royal Air Force
    Bomber Command, 10–13,
        75, 91–4, 96, 99–100, 275,
        302–25 *passim*
    Coastal Command, 94
    Fighter Command, 33, 305,
        370
    Transport Command, 118
    1 Group, 10, 33, 37, 66, 100,
        103, 120, 136, 188, 212–13,
        230, 236, 239, 353–6, 381–6
    3 Group, 10, 57, 66, 75, 79,
        118, 220, 356
    4 Group, 10, 66, 79, 173, 220,
        230, 242, 265, 272, 315,
        359–60
    5 Group, 10, 33, 66, 75, 79, 89,
        96, 100, 120, 204–5, 230,
        236, 263, 278, 361–3, 381–6
    6 (R.C.A.F.) Group, 10, 66,
        130, 220, 230, 239, 272,
        314, 363–6
    8 (P.F.F) Group, 3–4, 10–13,
        94–9, 103–4, 188, 213, 230,
        235, 255, 309–13, 366–9
    100 Group, 94–5, 100, 180,
        221, 369–70

Light Night Striking Force,
    327
'Y' Service, 39
7 Squadron, 53, 179, 209–11,
    241, 243, 269, 311, 319,
    366, 378–9, 381
9 Squadron, 108, 110, 135–6,
    361, 380
10 Squadron, 34, 245, 247,
    272, 359
12 Squadron, 103, 190, 197,
    209, 297, 301, 318, 329,
    349, 354, 379
15 Squadron, 220, 281, 356
35 Squadron, 55, 75, 80, 173,
    367
44 Squadron, 196, 212, 330,
    361, 379
49 Squadron, 35, 111, 179,
    346, 361, 380
50 Squadron, 117, 125, 196,
    200, 236, 332, 362, 378,
    380
51 Squadron, 33, 38, 117,
    339, 359, 379
57 Squadron, 88, 131, 193,
    296, 298, 315, 362, 378–9,
    383
61 Squadron, 198, 238, 332,
    362, 380
75 Squadron, 61, 83, 356, 380
76 Squadron, 66, 81, 241–2,
    350, 359, 380
77 Squadron, 41, 247, 359,
    379–81
78 Squadron, 33, 74–5, 269,
    300–301, 360, 379, 381
83 Squadron, 46, 99, 117,
    124, 147, 204, 367, 386
90 Squadron, 60, 73, 335, 357
97 Squadron, 32, 74, 77,
    186–9, 300, 330, 332, 367,
    378–9, 386
100 Squadron, 38, 75, 185,
    255, 331, 354, 378–9, 381
101 Squadron, 100, 106n.,
    120, 135, 179, 185, 216,
    218, 229, 253, 279n., 317,
    319, 331, 334, 354, 378–9

102 Squadron, 36, 230, 360, 379–81
103 Squadron, 35, 82, 87, 119, 135, 319, 354, 378–9, 383
105 Squadron, 11, 33, 368
106 Squadron, 333, 362, 379–80
109 Squadron, 11, 33, 368
115 Squadron, 134, 238, 283, 285, 301, 357, 379–80
139 Squadron, 33, 88, 98, 126, 327, 368
141 Squadron, 180, 251, 369
149 Squadron, 40, 357
156 Squadron, 26, 108–9, 117, 210, 216, 224, 231, 271n., 311, 367, 378–9, 381, 386–8
158 Squadron, 33, 58, 75, 279n., 300, 316, 332, 360, 379–81
166 Squadron, 285, 301, 355, 379
169 Squadron, 270, 369
192 Squadron, 370
196 Squadron, 357
199 Squadron, 57, 357, 380
207 Squadron, 40, 89, 110, 193, 248, 255, 332, 348, 362
214 Squadron, 34, 37, 357, 380
218 Squadron, 71n., 358
239 Squadron, 301, 370
405 Squadron, 32, 72, 80, 104, 130, 255, 278, 331, 367
408 Squadron, 130–31, 213, 317, 363, 380
418 Squadron, 370
419 Squadron, 364
420 Squadron, 242, 263, 364
424 Squadron, 263, 364
425 Squadron, 263, 283, 364
426 Squadron, 25, 183, 330, 364, 379
427 Squadron, 301, 364, 381

428 Squadron, 72, 338, 365, 380
429 Squadron, 298, 301, 365, 381
431 Squadron, 365, 381
432 Squadron, 179, 365
433 Squadron, 220, 247, 255, 296, 365
434 Squadron, 366, 380–81
460 Squadron, 89, 103, 108, 129, 136–7, 183, 212, 296, 355, 378–9, 381
463 Squadron, 255, 362
466 Squadron, 173, 199, 244, 360
467 Squadron, 110, 205, 331, 363, 380
514 Squadron, 119, 184, 193, 200, 358, 380
515 Squadron, 370
540 Squadron, 76
550 Squadron, 190, 212, 355
576 Squadron, 196, 355, 380
578 Squadron, 220, 360
605 Squadron, 370
617 Squadron, 112, 363
619 Squadron, 204, 363
620 Squadron, 34, 358, 380
622 Squadron, 60, 220, 358
623 Squadron, 84, 358, 380
625 Squadron, 296, 355
626 Squadron, 301, 318, 356
627 Squadron, 133, 136, 240, 368
630 Squadron, 231, 247, 296, 316, 363
635 Squadron, 296, 368
640 Squadron, 220, 255, 360
692 Squadron, 368
1409 (Met.) Flight, 30, 278, 369

Airfields
Bardney, 361
Binbrook, 238, 355, 384
Bourn, 35, 177, 367
Breighton, 33, 74, 301, 360
Bradwell Bay, 136
Burn, 360
Catfoss, 255

Chedburgh, 34, 56–7, 357–8
Coningsby, 362–3
Cranfield, 300
Croft, 247, 365–6
Downham Market, 358, 368
Dunholme Lodge, 361
Dunsfold, 300
East Kirkby, 315–16, 362–3
East Moor, 365
Elsham Wolds, 35, 119, 178, 354–5
Elvington, 359
Feltwell, 370
Fiskerton, 361
Foulsham, 119, 370
Gransden Lodge, 367
Graveley, 35, 62, 203, 367–8
Grimsby, 185, 190, 255, 354–5
Holme-on-Spalding Moor, 241, 359
Kelstern, 355
Kirmington, 301, 355
Lakenheath, 357
Langar, 89, 362
Leconfield, 74, 185, 360
Leeming, 301, 364–5
Linton-on-Ouse, 177, 317, 363–4
Lissett, 33, 316, 360
Little Snoring, 357, 369–70
Ludford Magna, 100, 119, 185, 203, 317, 319, 354
Marham, 38, 368
Melbourn, 359
Mepal, 356
Metheringham, 362
Middleton St George, 225, 339, 364–5
Mildhenhall, 356, 358
North Killingholme, 355
Oakington, 30, 35, 62, 211, 241, 269, 319, 366, 368–9
Pocklington, 131, 240, 360
Scampton, 362
Skellingthorpe, 362
Skipton-on-Swale, 364–5
Snaith, 359
Spilsby, 362

Stradishall, 131
Syerston, 362
Taddenham, 357
Tholthorpe, 364–6
Upwood, 367
Waddington, 362–3
Warboys, 210, 216, 367
Waterbeach, 184, 358
West Raynham, 180, 369–70
Wickenby, 190, 301, 354, 356
Witchford, 301, 357
Woodhall Spa, 363
Wratting Common, 357
Wyton, 99, 124, 205, 367–8
Rumpelhardt, Uffz. F., 178
Rupp, Uffz. B., 234
Ruhr, *see* Battle of the Ruhr

SN-2 radar, 176, 178, 195, 204, 221–3, 235–5, 288, 295–7
Sambridge, F/Lt A. H. J., 254
Saundby, AM Sir R., 93, 304, 323
Saward, W/Cdr D., 94, 324
Sayn-Wittgenstein, Maj. H. Prinz zu, 204, 231
Schellhase, C., 259
Schierholz, Uffz. H. G., 49, 193, 296
Schlecking, W., 258
Schnaufer, Oblt. H. W., 40–41, 178–9, 198
Schräge Musik weapons, 179, 204, 222–3, 235, 266, 295, 297, 303
Schweinfurt, 9, 93, 174, 274
Scott, Sgt K. F., 216, 317, 334
Searby, Gp Capt J. H., 95, 205
Serrate device, 95, 180, 221, 239, 251, 263, 270, 277, 301–302, 369–70
Seuss, Lt W., 121, 237, 266
Sexton, F/Lt R. J., 320
Shard, F/Lt R. N., 269
Sheriff P/O J., 315
Shimield, Sgt E. H., 110
Shipley, P/O D. F., 245
Shipway, F/Lt A. C., 115–16, 127

Siemens factories, 22, 87, 146, 148
Simpson, P/O K. S., 300
Slade, F/Lt I. C. B., 62
Slottgo, E., 156
Smith, P/O G. J. A., 331
Sparkes, WO W. S., 216n., 387
Speer, Albert, 27, 141, 147, 192 323
Spie, I., 169
Spielberg, M., 146
Spoden, Lt P., 19, 51–3
Stafford WO M., 183–4
Stanley, Sgt P. F., 58
Stettin 217
Stirlings, 12, 33, 99, 118, 275, 377–8
Stockton, Norman, 137
Streib, Maj. W., 41, 43
Stuart, F/Sgt F. R., 34
Stuttgart, 123–6, 131–2, 274
Sutton, F/O J. D., 56

Tame Boar tactics, 41, 221–4, 226–7, 229–30, 264–6, 270–71, 281, 293, 296, 302, 305, 308–9
Tansley F/O E. A., 316
Taylor, F/Sgt I. T., 243
Teare, Sgt T. D. G., 82
Telefunken factory, 22
Telge, Hptm., 81
Thompson, F/Sgt K. G. 135, 229, 279n
Thomson, F/Lt T. R., 231
Thun, Lt R., 343
Todd, F/O P. H., 300
Todt Organisation, 27, 228
Trilsbach, Sqn Ldr H. W., 331
Triplow, F/Sgt H., 38
Twinn, Sgt P. A. C., 119

U-Bahn stations, 24, 27, 257–8, 260
United States Army Air Force (and 8th Air Force), 2, 6, 174

V.K.F. factory, 22
Victoria Cross, 62, 360
Vollert, Uffz. H., 121, 250
Van der Hayde, Lt H., 152
Von Lossberg, Oberst V., 221

Wanganui marking, 30
War correspondents, 137
Watson, WO W. A., 179
Wawrzyniak, A., 162
Weinrich, Maj. H., 102
Wellingtons, 11, 22, 33
Wheeler, Sgt H. S., 36
White, W/Cdr J. H., 109
White, F/Sgt O. H., 61
Whitehead, P/O G. G. A., 350
Wick, P/O S. A., 298
Widdup, Sgt H., 255
Wild Boar (*Wilde Sau*) tactics, 15–18, 38, 40, 47–53, 62, 77, 92, 215, 221, 228, 302, 308–309
Willetts, Gp Capt A. H., 35, 54, 62
Williams, F/Sgt W. S., 71n.
Wilson, F/Lt G. H., 116
Window device, 13, 15–16, 18, 38, 176, 195, 221, 296–7, 307–8
Wolf, Lt G., 19, 51
Wolter, E., 159
Woollatt, Sqn Ldr. J. G., 197n.
Wright, W/Cdr C. L. Y., 117
Wright, F/Lt H. J., 271n.
Wulff, Oblt U., 178
Wuppertal/Barmen, 145
Würzburg, 14, 155

Y-Gerät device, 222
Yalta conference, 327

Zahme Sau, see Tame Boar
Zeiss factory, 22
Zorner, Hptm. P., 194–6, 265–6, 269, 297